AMERICAN HORTICULTURAL SOCIETY

AMERICAN HORTICULTURAL SOCIETY

Southeast

SMARTGARDEN™ REGIONAL GUIDE

DK

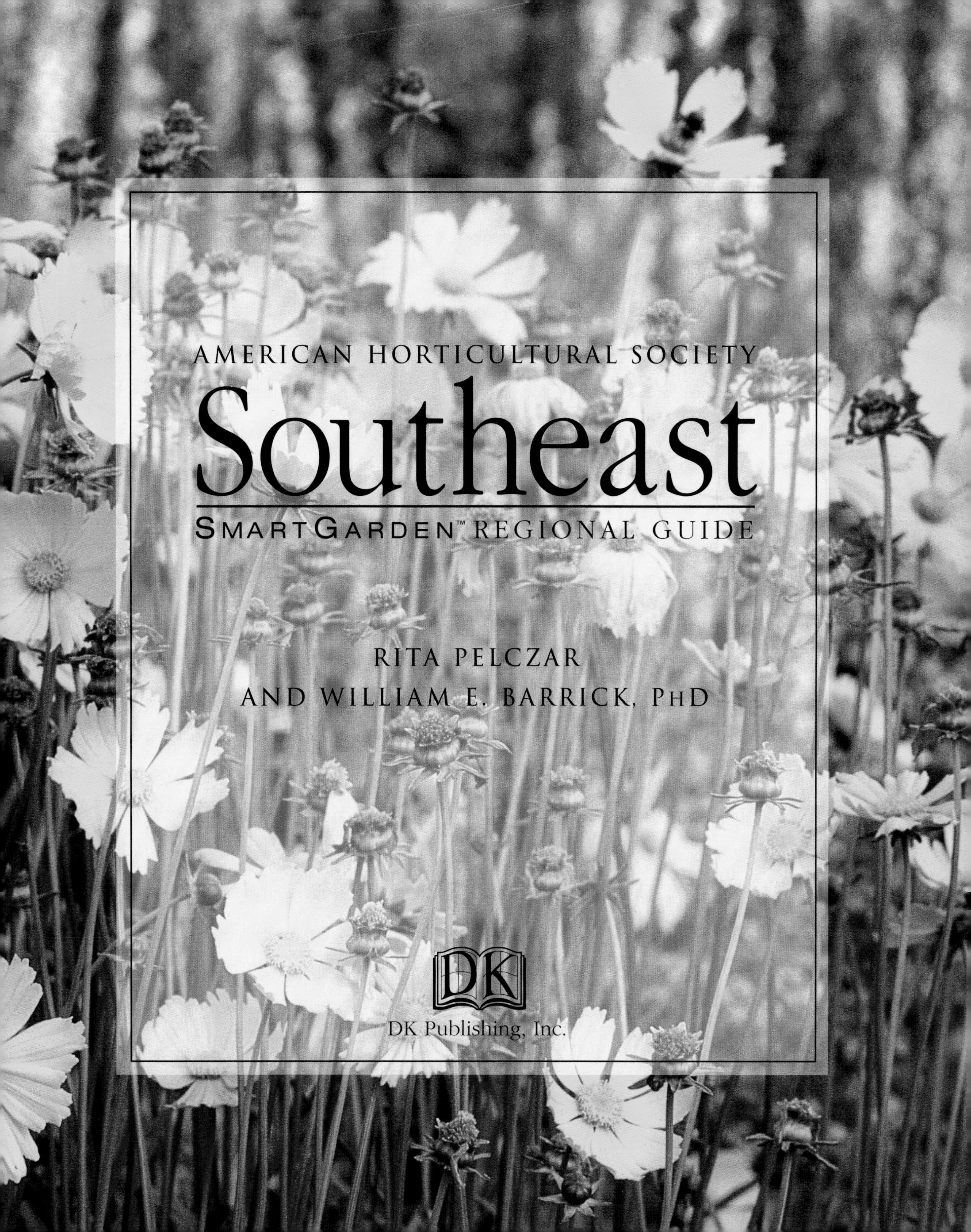

AMERICAN HORTICULTURAL SOCIETY

Southeast

SMARTGARDEN™ REGIONAL GUIDE

RITA PELCZAR
AND WILLIAM E. BARRICK, PHD

DK Publishing, Inc.

LONDON, NEW YORK, MUNICH,
MELBOURNE, AND DELHI

Senior Editors Jill Hamilton, Anja Schmidt
Senior Art Editor Susan St. Louis
Designers Melissa Chung, Miesha Tate
Creative Director Tina Vaughan
Project Director Sharon Lucas
Production Manager Chris Avgherinos
DTP Co-ordinator Milos Orlovic
Picture Research Chrissy McIntyre
Publisher Chuck Lang

Horticultural editor Trevor Cole
Horticultural consultant William E. Barrick, PhD

Contributing writers Felder Rushing
Editorial assistance Rip Noyes, John Searcy
DK Photo Access Library Neale Chamberlain, Richard Dabb

First American Edition, 2004
00 01 02 03 04 05 10 9 8 7 6 5 4 3 2 1

Published in the United States by
DK Publishing, Inc.
375 Hudson Street
New York, New York 10014

DK Publishing, Inc. offers special discounts for bulk purchases for sales promotions or premiums. Specific, large-quantity needs can be met with special editions, including personalized covers, excerpts of existing guides, and corporate imprints.
For more information, contact Special Markets Department, DK Publishing, Inc., 375 Hudson Street, New York, NY 10014
Fax: 800-600-9098.

A catalog record for this book is available fromthe Library of Congress

Reproduced by Colourscan, Singapore
Printed and bound in Spain by Artes Graficas Toledo, S.A.U.

See our complete product line at
www.dk.com

CONTENTS

PART I

THE TEN SMARTGARDEN™ TENETS

PART II

PLANT CATALOG

PART III

GARDENING TECHNIQUES

APPENDICES

FOREWORD

My two families with forty aunts and uncles were eighth-generation settlers from Scotland. When they arrived in North Carolina there were no garden centers to visit or arboreta and botanic gardens to tour. Plants were propagated by division or by cuttings rooted under glass canning jars. Seeds were ordered from Mr. Burpee in Pennsylvania or Mr. Hastings in Georgia. Only after World War II did the plant palette begin to change and sound scientific gardening information become more accessible to the average gardener.

Now, as it was then, successful gardening is based on coordinating factors such as light, temperature, water, and nutrients, and coping with the elements, critters, and the gardener's age. Advances in technology are making plant selection easier; recently the USDA Plant Hardiness Zone Map was updated using current information from weather stations around the country. The development of the AHS Plant Heat Zone Map in 1997 completed the circle of information available to determine the total range of temperature tolerance for each cultivated plant. In time, all of the coded plants listed in this book and others will be available online, accessible by zip code.

The passage of time has brought many wonderful innovations to gardening in the Southeast, yet over the course of my career, I have increasingly become aware of the mistakes that people live with in their gardens day after day that reduce the pleasures of gardening. Too many gardeners put up with plants that have outgrown their space, or are barely surviving.

This leaves the gardener with crucial questions to answer. How can I replace and replant with the most desired effects and create a SMARTGARDEN™? What tasks can I attempt and what should I have a professional do? And how do I accomplish this while being a good steward of the earth? The SMARTGARDEN™ program described in this book answers all these questions and many more. Using these ideas and techniques, you can create a garden that is successful, environmentally responsible, easy to maintain, and—most important—fun!

I know you will enjoy the process of re-evaluating your garden and your gardening practices from this new perspective!

H. Marc Cathey, PhD
President Emeritus,
American Horticultural Society

PART I

THE TEN SMARTGARDEN™ TENETS

These tenets offer the key to a scientifically sound, environmentally responsible approach to gardening. An assessment of your site and lifestyle directs your gardening choices with maximum efficiency. Integration of new technologies with proven practices and the effective use of available resources provide guidance for selection and maintenance of your garden plants. Most importantly, each practice is considered with respect to its environmental impact, to help you make the most responsible gardening choices.

KNOW YOURSELF

A lot of thought should go into gardening before you even pick up a trowel. Since you are going to determine the garden's dimensions, style, and makeup – and you will be primarily responsible for its maintenance – the best place to begin is to take a reading of your personal likes and dislikes and your abilities and limitations. In subsequent tenets we will consider the characteristics of the site, appropriate criteria for selecting plants, and ways to ensure that your gardening efforts reap successful results by using an environmentally responsible approach. But before you can begin to put that important information to good use, it is critical to examine your preferences, priorities, and point of view.

What you want
The owners of this property made careful decisions about how they wanted to use their space. Another owner might well have decided to plant the area entirely in grass and shrubs, and a third could have created a playground.

Be realistic

As much as you would enjoy spending many hours in your garden, you have other commitments that limit your availability, and you may be sharing your outdoor space with others who prefer nongardening activities. Physical constraints might also inhibit your gardening pursuits, and your budget may not accommodate your elaborate gardening visions. However, with some thoughtful planning and a bit of compromise, your SMARTGARDEN™ can oblige your varied outdoor requirements, limitations in time and physical ability, and, yes, even a budget that lacks a certain desired heft.

In a nutshell: think about your time, your physical condition, and your budget, and take on a garden only of the size and complexity you can handle.

The space-time continuum

Once you know where a garden best fits within the overall landscape, the next step is to determine its size and shape. While the shape is largely a design consideration, the size depends a great deal on the plants you want and the time you have to tend them.

Some gardens will require little of your time once they are established. A bed of flowering shrubs underplanted with a groundcover needs only occasional attention. An extensive flower bed or large vegetable patch, on the other hand, needs regular tending throughout the growing season. Of course, the bigger the garden, the more time it requires to plant, weed, harvest, deadhead, edge, and prune. The best plan is to start small, then expand if you find you have the space, time, resources, and energy.

Planning the site

When you are deciding where you should place your garden and what size to make it, you need to consider not only the conditions that make it suitable for growing plants, but also how the garden will be integrated into the landscape as a whole. For example, if you have children who need space for a swingset or to play basketball or frisbee, siting your garden at the other end of the yard might be wise – at least until they outgrow these activities. Obviously, you need a plan.

Fully integrated
A carefully considered mixture of plants and hardscaping – the nonplant elements – results in a garden that beautifully blends with and complements the house. Container-grown plants generally require more care than those that are grown in the open ground.

Garden plans

Whether your garden aspirations are complex and ornate or you are planning on a somewhat more modest scale, you should map out your garden on paper before you pick up your trowel or buy your first plant. Although these garden plans may vary in complexity from a rough sketch to an exquisitely executed artwork, there are just a couple of basic types of sketches that you need to use at this stage. The first one is used to map out existing features and microclimates, information that you need to determine which plants will thrive and where. A more detailed garden sketch, which should be done on graph paper to scale, shows your entire property – both physical features and garden areas.

Unless you are starting with an empty lot, you will need to sketch the existing features of your landscape, such as the house, walkways, and driveway. The more accurate your sketch, the more useful it will be for planning. Don't forget to note sunny and shady areas, hedges and fences that block the wind, unusually wet or dry spots, neighboring buildings, attractive or unattractive views, and other positive and negative features.

You may find that you want to make adjustments: remove a tree, repair or improve a walkway, relocate the doghouse. Some of these changes will be easy; those that are more complex can be completed over time. Make corresponding notes on your plan to track the direction in which you are heading.

Next make a list of the activities that you enjoy doing in the yard. Of course, you also need to consider anyone who may spend a significant amount of time in the yard, whether it be your spouse or partner, children, or anyone else. The landscape use checklist (opposite) will help you identify the various uses and activities that fit your space and budget.

Once you have a prioritized list of gardening and nongardening activities for your yard, you can begin designating areas for each. Some areas will overlap, so make sure that the activities are compatible for use of the same space – playing football in the herb garden just won't work. On the other hand, patios and decks are perfect locations for container gardens and adjacent raised beds. Keep in mind that different kinds of plants (for example, perennials, vegetables, and shrubs) can often be combined in the same garden area as long as they have similar cultural requirements.

Making a Plan

This exercise is useful for those who have just acquired a new property as well as for those who are considering a major (or even minor) relandscaping project. Documenting existing conditions will point you in the right direction when the time comes to choose specific elements.

FEATURES TO CONSIDER FOR THE SKETCH

When drawing a sketch of your property, include all features that are permanent or at least long-term. Once your sketch is completed, you may want to make several copies. That way you can try out different designs for arranging beds and hardscaping features on paper before you actually get to work.

Don't forget to include any of the following features that are applicable. There may well be more features in your yard that you should include.

- Perimeter of the yard
- House
- Driveway
- Walkways and paths
- Garage, shed, or other service outbuildings
- Gazebo, patio, deck
- Hammock
- Swingset/sandbox
- Pool
- Doghouse, kennel, run
- Existing trees
- Existing beds or gardens
- Hedges, fences, walls
- Water faucets
- Areas of sun and shade
- Wet or dry areas
- Views to highlight
- Views to hide

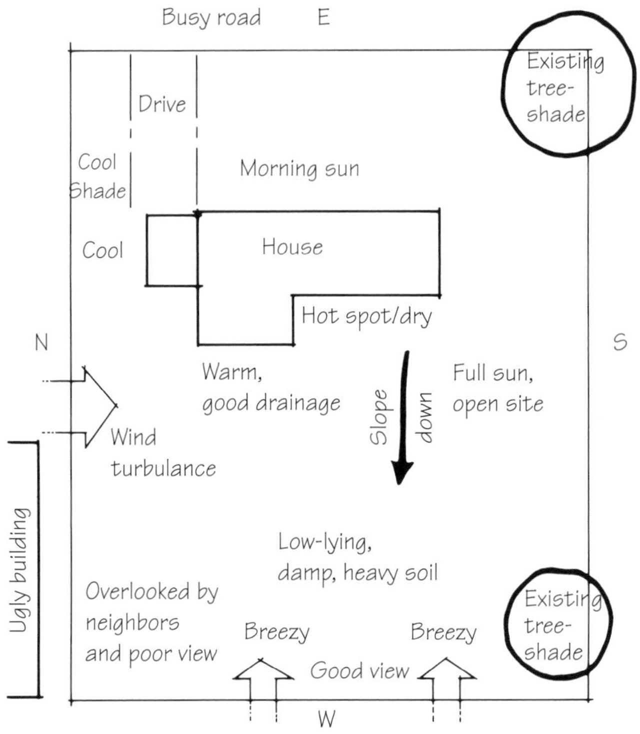

Putting it down on paper
All of the important cultural and design elements of the property have been included in this sketch. Note that there are no specific plant features indicated except for the trees, which are being considered more as producers of shade than as living plants. Consideration of individual plants comes later.

KEEP YOUR PLANS FLEXIBLE

Don't fret if there isn't room in your landscape to accommodate all of the activities you have in mind. Long-range planning can extend your choices, and spreading the implementation of your plan over the course of several years also reduces the shock to your bank account.

As you and the others who use your yard mature, priorities for landscape use will change. The area designated for a sandbox for youngsters might be transformed into a patio after a few years. Once the old swing set in the backyard has lost its appeal, it can be replaced with a mixed border or small vegetable garden.

Like children, plants grow up, and their increasing size alters the landscape. Perennials that once filled in between young evergreen shrubs may need to be moved as the shrubs reach their mature size. Aggressive perennials may be overrunning your borders. Choices must be made; something will need to go. As your trees expand in height and spread over the years, the area beneath them becomes shadier. If the grass growing in the trees' shadow becomes thin and weak, it may be time to replace it with a shade-loving groundcover or a simple mulch, or perhaps you will choose to thin or raise the crown of the tree (*see p. 29*) to allow more light to reach the grass.

Remember: plants don't live forever. The demise of a plant often opens up opportunities for including new and perhaps more interesting plants in its place.

Adapting to physical challenges

If you or members of your household have physical limitations, these need to be considered in your planning. Raised beds and containers can be built and placed with accessibility in mind. Paved walkways can put outlying beds within easy reach of those who might otherwise be able to enjoy them only from a distance, and stepping-stones or paths within planting areas afford easier and safer movement through the garden for maintenance.

Careful selection and placement of plants within the landscape is important for physically challenged gardeners. Once established, many trees, shrubs, and groundcovers will require a minimum of care. These can be placed at the periphery of the yard. More labor-intensive gardens should be placed where they are most easily accessed and where tools and water

LANDSCAPE USE CHECKLIST

Planning space to accommodate your outdoor pastimes will help you determine the best placement and size of your plantings, and prioritizing these areas will help you develop a working plan.

Nongarden areas/activities:

- Relaxing (including deck and/or patio)
- Outdoor cooking/eating
- Swimming
- Sports and active play
- Sandbox, tree house, playhouse, swing set
- Utility areas: trash cans, air conditioning/heating units, compost pile
- Work and storage spaces: garden shed, cold frame, firewood storage
- Pet areas
- Paths and walkways
- Driveway/parking
- Lawn
- Other, including walls and fences and overhead structures

Garden areas:

- Vegetable/fruit
- Herbs
- Flowerbeds
- Woodland garden
- Shade trees
- Wildflower meadow or naturalized area
- Foundation planting
- Pond
- Containers
- Raised beds
- Cut flowers
- Hedges
- Speciman trees and shrubs

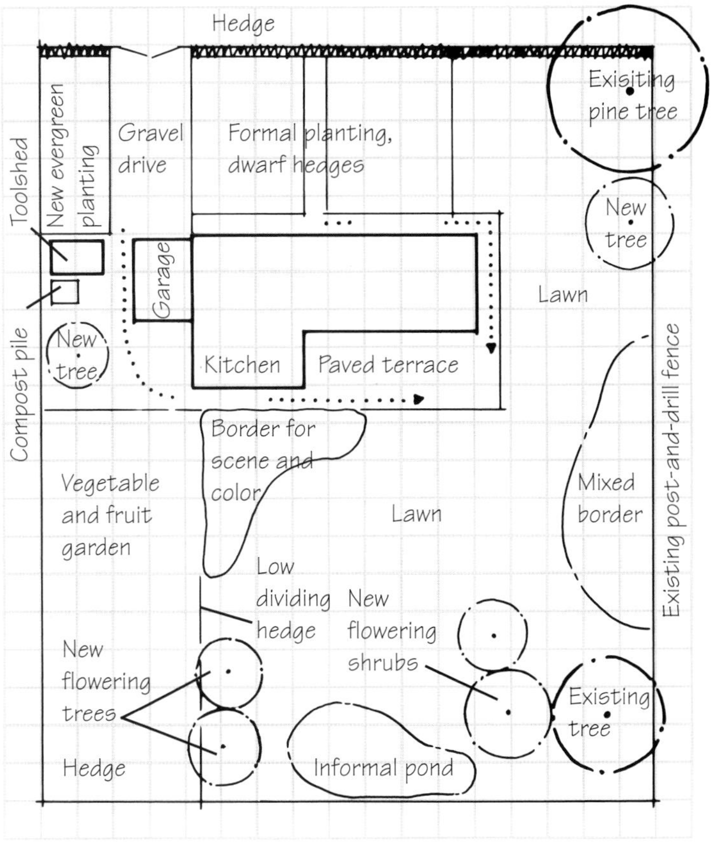

One step closer

The first sketch shown to the left is now fleshed out with desired planted areas (beds, borders, hedges, and the like) and hardscape features (driveway, terrace, and pond). The template is now ready to be made into a reality.

Easier access
If gardening is difficult for you, growing plants in a raised bed such as this one will bring them up to your level. Even if you are not an active gardener, the plants will be closer to your eyes and nose.

are located nearby. Also remember the potential danger posed by thorny trees and shrubs, low branches, and surface roots. Of course, these points apply to any sensibly designed garden, but they are of more obvious and immediate importance to the physically challenged.

A number of ergonomically designed gardening tools make gardening easier if physical ability is limited. Despite our best efforts to remain fit, chances are that eventually we will all lose some mobility or strength. Your SmartGarden™ should become easier to maintain as plants mature, but no garden is maintenance-free. Fortunately, physical limitations needn't eliminate gardening activities, especially if they are considered in your garden plan.

Lawns and turf alternatives

The majority of homeowners consider a lawn an essential part of the garden, although it is the most labor-intensive and the most demanding in terms of resources and money. A well-maintained lawn, fertilized in spring, mown regularly, and watered during periods of drought, forms a solid green sward that stands up to traffic. Given little maintenance and no supplemental water, however, lawns go brown and dormant during drought, and they quickly become infested with perennial weeds that smother the grass.

One repetitive chore that consumes a great deal of gardening time is mowing the lawn, and maintaining a healthy lawn can be a genuine challenge in many parts of the country. Irrigation systems may be necessary in areas that experience extended periods of dry weather during the growing season. Weeds, insect pests, and diseases may necessitate the use of pesticides or biological controls that can be costly and time-consuming to apply. This doesn't mean that

LAWNS AND ALTERNATIVES

A healthy lawn ties the garden together and creates space.

It is important to choose the best grass for your conditions: few grasses, for example, will thrive in the shade. In the upper South, rye, fescue, and bluegrass – either singly, or in blends – will do well over the fall, winter, and spring, but tend to brown out in the heat and humidity of summer. In the middle South, Bermuda, zoysia, and to some extent St. Augustine do well, with some winter damage some years. Lower South and Gulf Coast gardens can use them all, plus centipede, which has a yellow-green color cast but needs less maintenance.

The most important factor for success of any lawn is the cutting height; Bermuda is the only turfgrass that grows thickly when mowed close; others need higher settings to get full leaf- and root-growth, which are important to the survival of the lawn and pest and weed control.

Most lawn grasses are easily started from plugs or seed, with the exceptions of St. Augustine and hybrid Bermuda grasses, for which seed is not available. It is important to water newly installed lawns two or three times a week for a few weeks to get them established, but over-watering (even in hot, humid Gulf Coast areas) causes root and disease problems. It is far better to water the lawn deeply and infrequently, as needed, than to sprinkle lightly two or more times a week. Fertilizing the Southern lawn is tricky as well, it may cause winter injury and aggravated weed and disease problems. In spring, wait for the lawn to "green up" and mow a couple of times first. In fall, give the final feeding at least two months before the first frost.

Designing a garden with a smaller lawn area, neatly edged and carefully tended, can create dramatic opportunities for groundcovers, mulched shrub and flower beds, and patio or deck areas, while still retaining the important "unifying" open-air effect.

Groundcovers for sun and for shade are found elsewhere in this book, and can help reduce the amount of lawn – and its maintenance.

Both a conventional lawn and a graveled area fill the roles of unifier and provider of spaciousness.

you should exclude all turf from your landscape, but be aware that it is an area that requires a significant investment in time and money. To reduce the expense, reduce the size of the lawn. A small area of grass is much easier to maintain than a large expanse.

If you decide to reduce the lawn area of your yard, you have a number of options. Consider a wildflower meadow or a large bed of groundcovers, which will require some seasonal care – perhaps two or three times a year – but not nearly the time and effort involved in trying to maintain a perfect lawn.

Another alternative to lawns are the various soil coverings, such as paving, gravel, or mulch. These can serve as walkways or seating areas. Individual planting beds and trees can be extended by removing the turf between them and connecting the areas with mulch. Use broad curves for the outline of the mulched area to facilitate mowing, because mowing around a large area that contains several trees takes much less time than mowing around individual trees. Although the initial cost and labor output of creating these areas may be greater, the reduction in maintenance time and expense over the long run may be significant.

Low-maintenance plantings

Every garden – even the simplest container garden – requires some maintenance, but there are definitely some plants that require less attention than others. Consult your nursery, extension service, and other local experts (*see* Appendix, *pp. 386–389*) to identify such plants for your immediate area. Also, there are certain strategies that minimize the effort you must put into a planting for it to look good.

Many of these strategies are simply a matter of working with nature rather than against it: select plants that are adapted to the specific conditions present in your yard; water plants deeply rather than frequently so that roots grow downward and are capable of retrieving water over a greater area; remove weeds before they set seed and spread; and use mulch to conserve water and suppress weeds. Building raised beds and containers and filling them with soil may seem like a lot of work initially, but once constructed, they can provide a planting area that is within easy reach for maintenance.

A SMARTGARDEN™, when carefully analyzed, designed, implemented, and maintained, can reward any gardener for years.

Stay off the grass
Not a single blade of grass figures into this part of the property. Designed for low maintenance, it provides a pleasant sitting and socializing area while incorporating easy-care plants in both gravel and a raised bed. The solitary but exuberant container provides some color and serves as a focal point.

ASSESS YOUR SITE

The best place to begin your journey toward a SmartGarden™, as with any project that involves major change, is first to determine where you stand. Take a look around your property. Observe the existing vegetation, the lay of the land, the soil, the degree of light and shade, and determine both your average temperature range and your first and last expected frost dates.

Evaluating strengths & limitations

If your yard is shady, plants that thrive in low light levels will be the most successful. If part of your yard is shaded and another area receives full sun, your options increase; however, siting a plant in the area that satisfies its particular light requirement is essential. If your region receives limited precipitation during the growing season, consider xeriphytic plants (those with low water requirements); if you have wet areas, a bog garden might be your best choice. Although these factors limit gardening options, each can be viewed as a strength if the appropriate plants and garden style are chosen.

Examine the existing plants carefully. Are there trees or shrubs that are struggling to survive or that require excessive maintenance? Plants that outgrow their space or suffer from chronic disease or pest problems may be the wrong ones for your site, and it may be best to remove them entirely.

Evaluating the existing nonplant features in your landscape is an important part of your site analysis. Are there problem areas – a steep slope or an awkward swale? Are your walkways functional? Have you set aside areas for relaxation? Does everyone have space to pursue outdoor interests?

Your observations will point you toward those improvements that need to be made to maximize your gardening success and satisfaction with the least amount of strain on you, your resources, and the environment. Your site analysis will also provide clues for selecting plants (or other nonplant features) that will fit in with your conditions.

It helps to know something about basic plant requirements with respect to the environment, including aspects of soil; how temperature, shade, and exposure define your selection of garden plants; and how microclimates present options for savvy gardeners. After you examine your existing growing conditions, you may decide to make some changes or improvements. In Tenet 3, methods for modifying your site will be outlined. But first let's take a look at what you have to work with.

Get to know your soil

Becoming familiar with the character of your soil is key to your gardening success. Important aspects include texture, structure, drainage and water-holding capacity, pH (acidity or alkalinity), and fertility.

One way to get to know your soil is to have it professionally analyzed. A soil test reveals details about your soil's chemistry that cannot be observed with the naked eye. Soil test kits for home use are available in a wide range of prices and sophistication. You can also send a soil sample to a local soil-testing lab. Public soil-testing labs are relatively inexpensive, but they may be slow during peak seasons. Private soil-testing labs may be a bit more costly, but they are often faster and some offer more extensive tests than those available through the extension labs.

Metamorphosis
Combining careful planning with smart horticultural practices will transform this neglected yard into a beautifully integrated area (opposite) that will easily accommodate a wide variety of gardening and leisure activities.

SOIL TEST REPORT

A soil test report provides basic information about the fertility of your soil. It is very useful when you are determining the amounts of fertilizer to add (or to hold off on adding) to your soil.

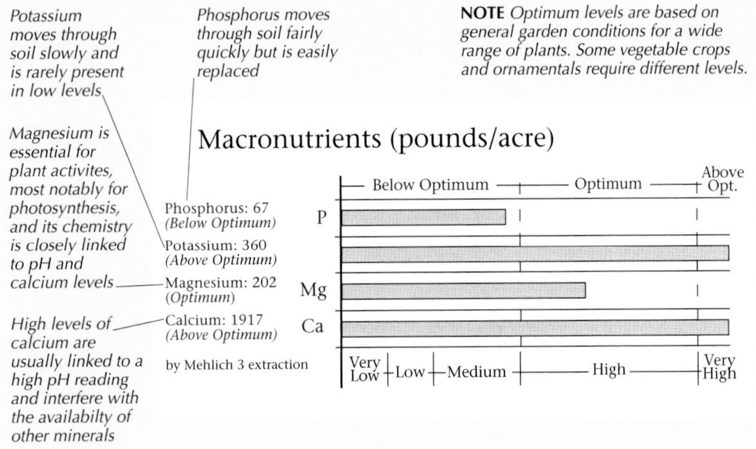
Potassium moves through soil slowly and is rarely present in low levels
Phosphorus moves through soil fairly quickly but is easily replaced
NOTE Optimum levels are based on general garden conditions for a wide range of plants. Some vegetable crops and ornamentals require different levels.
Magnesium is essential for plant activites, most notably for photosynthesis, and its chemistry is closely linked to pH and calcium levels
High levels of calcium are usually linked to a high pH reading and interfere with the availabilty of other minerals
Macronutrients (pounds/acre)
Below Optimum
Optimum
Above Opt.
Phosphorus: 67 (Below Optimum)
P
Potassium: 360 (Above Optimum)
Magnesium: 202 (Optimum)
Mg
Calcium: 1917 (Above Optimum)
Ca
by Mehlich 3 extraction
Very Low
Low
Medium
High
Very High

Soil texture

All soils are made up of solid material and spaces between the solids – in roughly equal proportions by volume. About 90 percent of the solid portion of most soil is weathered rocks and minerals. These particles are classified according to size, and are, from smallest to largest, clay, silt, and sand. Most soils are a combination of particle sizes, often with one or another predominating. The relative amounts of each type of particle determines the soil texture. Loam is a soil that contains roughly equal amounts of all three soil particle types and is usually well suited for growing a very wide range of garden plants.

A soil's texture has a major influence on such soil characteristics as water retention and nutrient movement. For example, a sandy soil drains faster than a clay soil, and a clay soil retains nutrients better than a sandy one; therefore, watering and fertilizing schedules should be adjusted accordingly.

Soil texture will also influence your selection of plants. Some plants – those that generally have low water requirements – thrive in a sharply drained, sandy soil. Others benefit from a more constant supply of moisture and nutrients; these usually grow better in a loam or clay loam, which hold on to water longer and release it more slowly than sandy soil. You can get an idea of the texture by rubbing some dry soil between your fingers. Sandy soil has a gritty feel to it; silt is much smoother; and clay, when dry, forms dense, hard clumps that are not easily broken apart. When wet, clay can be formed into balls or ropes.

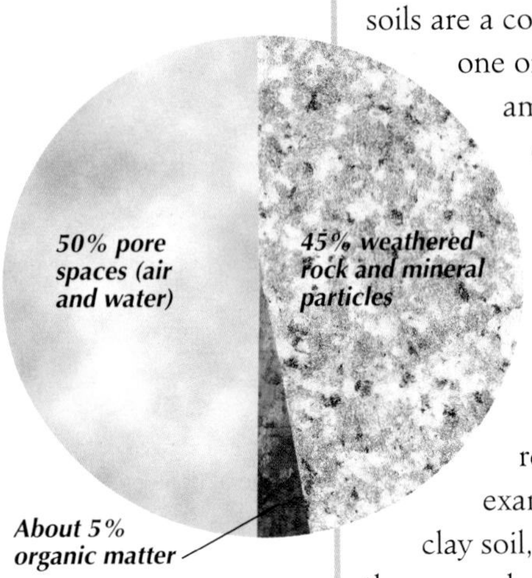
50% pore spaces (air and water)
45% weathered rock and mineral particles
About 5% organic matter

The space between
Healthy, productive soil contains the same amount of space (taken up by air and water) as it does actual particles. Smart gardening practices strive to preserve this balance.

Soil structure

The structure of a soil is determined by how the various solid portions of the soil are arranged – particles can be separate, as in the case of pure sand, or bind together to form clusters, or aggregates (tiny clusters of particles). The arrangement has significant impact on the movement and retention of water, nutrients, and air in the soil.

The remaining solid part of the soil is organic matter, which makes soil more conducive to plant growth by enabling the formation of soil aggregates. Aggregates form when soil organisms break down organic matter into humus, an amorphous, gummy material that binds particles together (*see* The nature of humus, *p. 31*). Pore spaces between the aggregates are relatively large, and yet smaller spaces between soil particles occur within the aggregates. This combination provides a balance between the movement of water and air and the retention of moisture and nutrients, and makes it easier for plant roots to grow down through the soil.

To improve soil structure, spread organic matter on the soil surface and incorporate it into the upper six to eight inches (15–20cm) of soil every year in areas that are cultivated on an annual basis. For more permanent areas, work organic matter into the soil at planting time. After that, organic mulches can be applied around plants each year; the activities of soil organisms and other natural processes will incorporate much of the organic matter into the soil.

Drainage/water-holding capacity

Plant roots require both air and water for healthy growth. The pore spaces in soil accommodate both, but during rain or irrigation, water forces air out of the pores. Drainage refers to the movement of water through the soil; water-holding capacity is the ability of a soil to retain water after rainfall or irrigation. During dry periods, air-filled pores predominate. Coarse-textured (sandy) soils tend to drain quickly, retaining little water. They also warm up faster in the spring and are generally easy to work. Fine-textured (clay) soils retain both water and nutrients longer than a sandy soil and may become waterlogged. The same material – organic matter – that improves the drainage of a heavy clay soil can increase the capacity of a light sandy soil to retain water.

Different areas of your property may drain very differently. After a heavy rain, one area may stay wet much longer than others. If you plan to garden in a wet spot, you should choose plants that are well adapted to such conditions.

SOIL DRAINAGE TEST

To assess your soil's drainage, perform the following test. Wait at least a few days after the last rain until your soil has dried a bit, then dig a hole 4 inches (10cm) deep, large enough to accommodate a 46-ounce (1.4kg) can. Remove the top and bottom of the can and place it in the hole, firming the soil around the outside. Fill the can to the top with water, then observe how long it takes to drain. Ideally, the water level will drop about 2 inches (5cm) in an hour. This indicates that your soil drains well but also will retain the moisture necessary for the healthy growth of a wide variety of garden plants.

If the water level drops less than an inch (2.5cm) after an hour, your soil does not display sufficient drainage to accommodate many plants. Either limit your choice of plants to those that like constant moisture, or take measures to improve the drainage. If the water level drops 4 inches (10cm) in an hour, your soil drains too fast, and unless you plan to grow only plants that tolerate very dry soils, you will need to add organic matter to help retain soil moisture (and will also need to water as necessary).

Remember that different areas of your landscape may display marked differences in drainage and this test should be done in each one.

Soil pH

The acidity or alkalinity of your soil is critical to plant health. The measurement of the degree of acidity or alkalinity, the pH scale, rates solutions from most acidic (0) to most alkaline (14), with 7 being neutral.

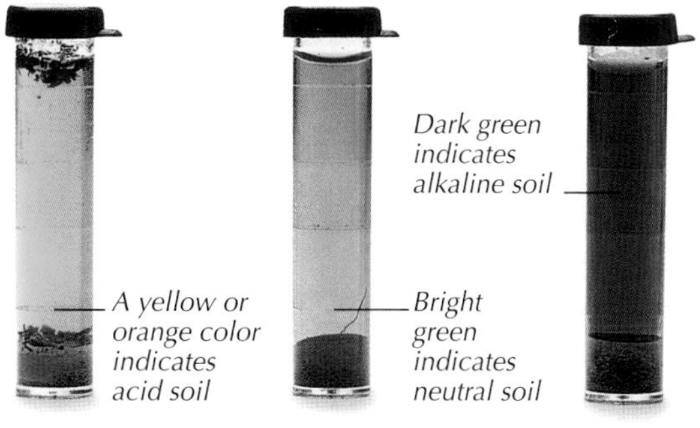

Determining pH
Kits are available for testing the acidity, neutrality, or alkalinity of your soil at home. They give a good general indication of pH.

The pH of your soil is determined by many factors, such as the type of rock from which the soil originated, the amount of precipitation, and the type of vegetation growing on it.

The optimal soil pH for most plants is between 6.0 and 7.0. Deficiencies of essential nutrients often occur outside of this range, damaging plants and sometimes making them more susceptible to diseases and pests. Furthermore, acidic soils inhibit the survival of certain beneficial organisms, including earthworms, mycorrhizal fungi, and many bacteria. These organisms are responsible for the decay of organic matter and thereby help plants obtain nutrients.

Soil pH can be modified (to change soil pH, *see* p. 30), but to determine which materials and how much you will need to add to your soil, you will first need to perform a soil test (see the opposite page).

The acid test
Some plants, including azaleas (left) and rhododendrons and their relatives, thrive only in acidic soils. They will fail if not provided the conditions that maintain acidity.

Not all are alike
The availability of nutrients in the soil depends on the pH level. Note how many of them are less available in acidic soils.

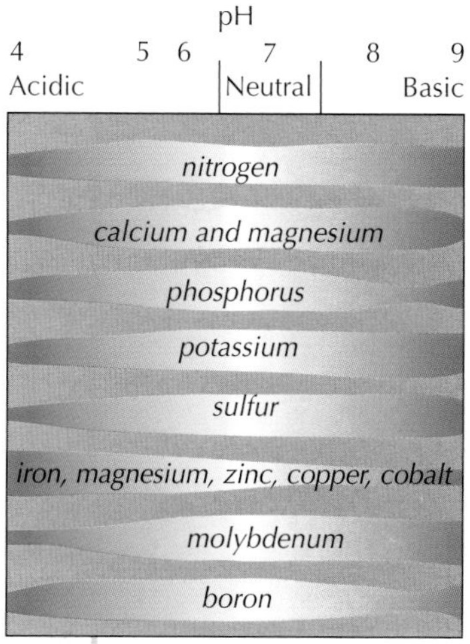

Soil fertility

There are 16 essential nutrients necessary for plant growth. Carbon, hydrogen, and oxygen are derived from air and water, and the remaining nutrients are supplied from the soil. The macronutrients – nitrogen (N), phosphorus (P), and potassium (K) – are needed by plants in large quantities; the secondary nutrients – calcium (Ca), magnesium (Mg), and sulfur (S) – are needed in moderate quantities; and the trace elements – boron (B), chlorine (Cl), copper (Cu), iron (Fe), manganese (Mn), molybdenum (Mo), and zinc (Zn) – are essential but needed only in very minute quantities. Determining the existing nutrient levels in your soil can help identify the kind and amount of fertilizers needed.

Avoiding chlorosis
Yellow leaves with dark green veins on citrus, azalea, and some other plants is a sign of chlorosis, a mineral deficiency often caused by soggy or alkaline soils. To control, improve drainage, add organic matter, and/or treat the ground with chelated iron.

Types of fertilizers

There are many different kinds of fertilizers available that can supply essential nutrients to your plants. Derived from a variety of sources, both natural and synthetic, they are available in a range of formulations that have been developed for different uses, from fast-acting foliar sprays to timed-release pellets. Some contain a single nutrient, and others multiple nutrients.

The three mineral nutrients used in the greatest quantity by plants are nitrogen (N), phosphorus (P), and potassium (K). A fertilizer that contains all three macronutrients is called a complete fertilizer. The three numbers on a bag of a complete fertilizer – the analysis – refer to the percentages by weight of nitrogen (N), phosphorus (phosphate, expressed as P_2O_5), and potassium (potash, expressed as K_2O), in that order.

Many complete fertilizers contain other nutrients that are also essential for healthy plants but are used in smaller quantities (secondary and micronutrients). These are usually listed on the label.

Organic fertilizer is derived from an organic – or once-living – source. Cow, horse, poultry, and sheep manures, fish emulsion, alfalfa and soybean meals, wood ashes, and compost are examples of organic fertilizers. Since most are somewhat lower and more variable in nutrient content than chemical fertilizers, you will need to use more of the material to obtain the nutrition your plants require. Because organic fertilizers are typically slow to break down in the soil, they have several advantages over chemical fertilizers: they remain available to plants over a longer period of time, they don't leach out of the soil as quickly, and they don't usually "burn" (dehydrate) roots. One of the most significant qualities of organic fertilizers is that they improve the structure and ecological balance of soil, which promotes healthy plant growth.

Apply it correctly
Spread the appropriate amount of fertilizer in a ring around a plant at and beyond its dripline – the outermost reach of its branches – then work it into the soil or cover it with mulch.

NUTRIENT CONTENT OF FERTILIZERS
(ALL VALUES ARE APPROXIMATE)

	% Nitrogen (N)	% Phosphorus (P_2O_5)	% Potassium (K_2O)
Organic			
Animal manure	0.6	0.1	0.5
Compost	0.5	0.3	0.8
Bone meal	2	14	-
Sewage	7	10	-
Seaweed meal	2.8	0.2	2.5
Blood meal	12	-	-
Mushroom compost	0.7	0.3	0.3
Rock phosphate	-	26	12
Wood ash	0.1	0.3	1
Cocoa shells	3	1	3.2
Inorganic			
Balanced fertilizers		available in various proportions	
Ammonium nitrate	35	-	-
Superphosphate	-	20	-
Muriate of potash	-	-	60
Potassium sulfate	-	-	49

FERTILIZER FORMULATIONS

Fertilizer comes in many forms. Many synthetic fertilizers are available in a dry, granulated form, which is easy to spread, and the nutrients are usually readily available. Some granulated fertilizers are coated with sulfur or plastic so that their nutrients are slowly released over time.

Some synthetic fertilizers are sold as concentrated liquids or powders that require diluting. These are applied as liquids to the soil around plants or as a foliar spray. Foliar fertilizing using a water soluble solution can provide quick relief for plants that are suffering from a nutrient deficiency.

Fertilizer spikes are compressed, dry fertilizer that has been formed into a stakelike solid. Commonly used for trees and shrubs, they are inserted into holes drilled into the soil around the root zone.

Manure can be fresh or dried, resulting in a considerable difference in weight and nutrient content, not to mention smell.

Urban soils

Soils in urban environments often suffer from detrimental effects of construction and high-density populations. Compaction, contamination, poor drainage, nutrient imbalances, and excess temperatures are common. When the force of foot and vehicular traffic is exerted on the soil, it compresses and compacts the soil and breaks up soil aggregates. Compacted soil is a major cause of tree decline in urban environments.

Soil contamination occurs when building materials are spilled or dumped. Some contaminants are toxic to plants, while others cause more indirect damage, such as altering the soil pH. Gardening on badly contaminated sites may be limited to growing in raised beds and containers filled with imported soil.

In addition to suffering nutrient imbalances, many urban soils are infertile simply because topsoil and organic matter are often removed during construction, leaving an infertile subsoil that drains poorly and has very poor aeration. Taking the time to improve your soil is usually the best solution (*see* Building soil with organic matter, *p. 30*).

Heat absorbed by buildings, roads, sidewalks, and vehicles adds considerably to the air temperature of the urban environment, which in turn raises the soil temperature. This "heat-island effect" can significantly alter the chemical and biological characteristics of soil. One of the easiest and safest ways to counteract this effect is to apply an organic mulch to the soil surface (*see* The mulch advantage, *p. 47*).

Bring on the cold
Peonies, such as this plant 'Festiva Maxima', need a period of cold and do not grow well where winters are short and comparatively mild.

Temperature ranges

All plants have an optimal temperature range for growth. They also have temperature limits (both high and low), beyond which injury or death is likely to occur. These temperatures vary from one plant to another – some plants have a wide temperature range, others are far more limited – a major reason that locations with widely different climates support distinct plant species. Gardeners deal with this preference for temperatures on a daily basis.

Sheltered beauties (far left)
This hybrid banana (*Musa* 'Orinoco') needs a spot sheltered from cold and strong winds that could damage its large leaves. They require winter protection in much of this region.

Fleeting beauties
Tulips, like these 'Fringed Elegance', do not grow well in the heat of the Deep South. They will generally flower the first year but only produce foliage in subsequent years. Most gardeners treat them as annuals.

USDA Hardiness Zones

Winter hardiness is the ability of a plant to survive the winter conditions in a given location. Cold is an important feature of the winter environment, but several other factors influence hardiness, including soil moisture, relative humidity, and buffeting winds. For example, while a dianthus may tolerate frigid temperatures in a garden, it often fails to survive winters where soils stay wet, and although a number of broad-leaf evergreens thrive in cold temperatures, these evergreens may suffer severe desiccation if they are exposed to winter winds.

F°	Zones	C°
below -50°	1	below -46°
-50° to -40°	2	-46° to -40°
-40° to -30°	3	-40° to -34°
-30° to -20°	4	-34° to -29°
-20° to -10°	5	-29° to -23°
-10° to 0°	6	-23° to -18°
0° to 10°	7	-18° to -12°
10° to 20°	8	-12° to -7°
20° to 30°	9	-7° to -1°
30° to 40°	10	-1° to 4°
above 40°	11	above 4°

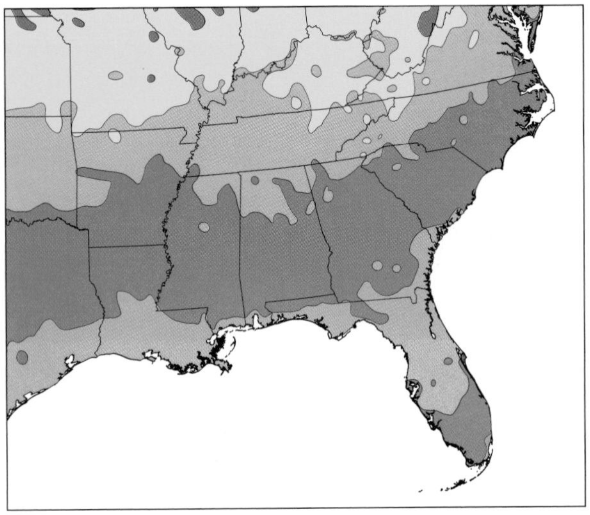

To assist gardeners with identifying plants that will survive the winter temperatures in their gardens, a system of mapping and coding was developed. The USDA Plant Hardiness Zone Map, which was revised and updated in 2003, identifies 15 hardiness zones in the United States according to the average minimum temperatures experienced.

Thousands of plants have been coded to the USDA Plant Hardiness Zone Map based on the lowest temperatures they will survive. Also considered in the rating is the plant's cold requirement: many plants require a certain amount of cold in order for their buds to break dormancy in the spring. Therefore, the hardiness rating is actually a range from the coldest zone in which the plant will survive to the warmest zone that satisfies its cold requirements.

The influence of cold temperatures on plant survival is more complicated than simply the lowest temperature experienced by the plant. Other factors such as the rate of temperature drop, the duration of the cold, the amount of temperature fluctuation, and the snow or mulch cover on the soil surrounding the plant affect its ability to survive winter conditions.

AHS Heat Zones

The amount of heat that plants are exposed to in summer is equally critical. The American Horticultural Society Plant Heat Zone Map was developed in 1997. AHS President Emeritus Dr. H. Marc Cathey supervised the development of the map, using data collected from the National Climatic Data Center and the National Weather Service. The map divides the US into 12 heat zones according to their average annual number of "heat days." A heat day is defined as a day in which temperatures reach or exceed 86° F (30° C). AHS Heat Zone 1 averages less than one heat day per year, while Zone 12 averages more than 210 heat days.

Average Number of Days per Year Above 86°F (30°C)	Zone
<1	1
1 to 7	2
>7 to 14	3
>14 to 30	4
>30 to 45	5
>45 to 60	6
>60 to 90	7
>90 to 120	8
>120 to 150	9
>150 to 180	10
>180 to 210	11
>210	12

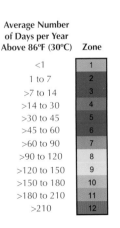

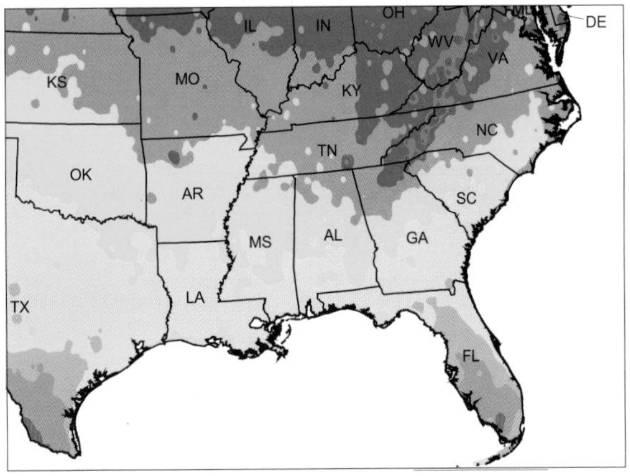

Like hardiness zones, the heat zones for a particular plant are given as a range. The first number indicates the hottest zone in which it will grow successfully; the second represents the zone with the minimum amount of summer heat necessary for it to complete its annual growth cycle.

As for cold hardiness, heat tolerance in plants involves more than just temperature. Summer rainfall – and the lack of it – limits the successful cultivation of many plants. High humidity rings the death knell for many plants that thrive in drier conditions with similar heat. Some plants are able to thrive in warmer zones if nights are cool. Qualities of the soil – its fertility, acidity or alkalinity, and drainage – also influence the summer survival equation. These factors should also be taken into account when selecting plants.

Although temperature is not the only determinant involved in a plant's ability to thrive in summer conditions, it is an important factor, and one that has been extensively assessed for the use of gardeners. For specific zones for many plants that grow in the Southeast, see the Plant Catalog.

Identify light and shade levels

As you stroll around your yard, observe which areas receive full sun and which areas are shaded by trees or surrounding structures. Because light levels change with the time of day, the season, and from one year to the next, this is an ongoing project. As the sun travels across the sky, a shady morning garden may be basking in full sun by early afternoon. In summer, when deciduous trees (those that shed their leaves each year) are in full leaf, a bed that received spring sun may be densely shaded. The angle of the sun as seasons change also alters the level of light in a garden. Furthermore, as trees mature, they cast increasingly broader shadows – beds that were planted in full sun several years ago may become cloaked in the shade of trees that grow nearby. As your garden matures, stay abreast of changing light levels and the impact on your plants.

To assess your garden's current level of light, examine the shade patterns during the course of a sunny day. Note areas that receive shade in the morning, midday, and early and late afternoon. By noting the position of surrounding trees (taking into consideration whether they are deciduous or evergreen) and the changing angle of the sun, you should be able to approximate the light levels in your garden for the entire year with reasonable accuracy.

Identifying your garden areas according to the light categories on this page will help you select plants with corresponding light requirements.

Full shade
Areas beneath trees with a dense canopy where no direct sunlight penetrates and reflected light is reduced, or that stand in the all-day shadow of tall buildings or evergreens, are considered to be in full shade. Careful selection of plants for such minimal light levels (and the reduced moisture levels that often occur in areas with low light) is necessary.

Full sun
Areas that receive at least six hours of direct sun during the day are considered in full sun and are desirable for vegetables, fruit, roses, and a wide range of flowering plants. Some plants that thrive in full sun in cooler northern climates, however, may require some afternoon shade in warmer areas of the Southeast.

Partial shade
Some gardens receive dappled shade throughout the day. If you stand in dappled shade, you should be able to glimpse portions of the sky through the leaves above. Other gardens are more densely shaded for a part of the day but receive bright sunlight for two to six hours. Both are considered partially shaded. A wide variety of plants are suited to this level of light.

Identify your microclimates

Areas within the same yard can present quite a variety of growing conditions, and it is important to recognize the garden limitations and possibilities of each. A microclimate – a portion of your yard where growing conditions differ from surrounding areas – can be a dry, shady spot or one that is constantly wet. It may be a narrow strip that is protected by a hedge, or an area warmed by its proximity to a building or stone wall.

To identify microclimates in your yard, note areas that seem slightly out of sync with the rest of the yard or other yards in the neighborhood – spots where spring flowers open earlier or later than others of the same kind, locations where blooms last longer, or areas that require more or less frequent watering than surrounding areas. These observations will suggest the need for plants that accommodate the nuances of your microclimate. They may also offer the opportunity to grow plants beyond the prevailing cultural limitations (particularly the overall hardiness and heat zone ratings) of your landscape.

EXISTING VEGETATION

Trees provide shade, and shady areas are typically several degrees cooler than adjacent areas in the sun. Shady spots also tend to stay wetter longer. Some plants that thrive in the sun where summers are cool can be grown in warmer climates if they are provided some shade. Dense vegetation can also block or reduce winds that cause a rapid loss of moisture by plants and soil. Planting a windbreak to provide protection from prevailing winds is one way you can help create a microclimate in your yard.

Microclimates are not static, however, especially those influenced by vegetation. As plants grow or are pruned or removed, conditions can be dramatically altered: a sunny garden may become shaded as the tree canopy expands; a wet area may become drier as groundcover plants grow and absorb more water; and a shade garden may be exposed to full sun if an old tree becomes damaged and needs to be removed. The gardener, as always, must be adaptable.

STRUCTURES AND HARDSCAPING

A house, garage, fence, or wall can also serve as a windbreak. These structures cast shade as well – the north side of a wall running east to west tends to be cooler and damper; the sunny south side will be notably warmer and drier. Such a wall creates two distinct microclimates that are separated by mere inches. Each side will support a culturally distinct set of plants. Although the difference in climate on either side of a wall that runs north to south is more subtle, the west side will tend to be warmer than the east side.

In temperate zones, a south-facing wall, particularly if it receives full sun, is a great place to grow sun-loving tropical or subtropical vines – such as *Bougainvillea* and black-eyed Susan vine (*Thunbergia alata*) – as annuals. The soil warms earlier in the spring, boosting early growth, and because the wall collects and holds heat,

Liquid asset
A wet, shady spot of your yard can support the growth of many attractive bog and woodland plants that would fail in sun.

Dry oasis
A shady dry spot has been transformed into a refuge with the masterful use of gravel, water, and adaptable plants.

moderating cooler night temperatures, growth will continue later into the autumn.

Because the area is cooler, plants growing on the north side of a building emerge from dormancy later than those on the south side. Air temperatures are influenced by the material and color of nearby structures: white or light colors reflect daytime light and heat back onto the plants; dark colors absorb heat.

SOIL SURFACES

The color of paved surfaces and mulch has a similar effect on nearby plants. Dark mulches absorb heat and can be used to warm the soil. Light-colored paving reflects light and heat back to surrounding areas. Heat-tolerant plants that thrive in sunny locations are usually the best choices near unshaded driveways and sidewalks.

WATER

Large bodies of water have a moderating effect on temperature, but even a backyard pond or pool can contribute a similar influence. Plants located at the edge of a pond not only have more water available in the soil, but they also benefit from a more humid environment created by evaporation from the pond.

COASTAL GARDENS

Gardens located near the seashore have special requirements. Plants must be able to tolerate salt spray, strong winds, and sandy soil. However, the moderate temperatures and higher humidity allow for growing a broader palette of plants, including marginally hardy ones. Soil can be improved by adding organic matter, and windbreaks can provide protection. Surprisingly, solid walls do not afford as much protection as salt-tolerant trees and shrubs, which act as filters to the salt spray as well as a buffer to the wind. Once a living barrier is established, less tolerant plants can be grown and benefit from the nurturing aspect of the ocean.

A nod to Monet
Open water provides limitless opportunities to create artistic compositions of plants, structures, and the reflected sky.

TOPOGRAPHY

Unless your yard is flat, its topography will influence your growing conditions. Marginally hardy plants and those that produce cold-sensitive, early spring flowers are more likely to be damaged by frosts if they are located in a frost pocket. Slopes also affect runoff: water can collect in a low area, making an ideal location for a bog garden. Steep slopes can be tamed and runoff reduced by using retaining walls to create level planting areas. Now let's explore ways to modify your existing garden conditions.

A little protection
Even a thinly constructed fence can provide enough wind protection to give shelter to delicate ferns and marginally hardy plants.

ADAPT WHEN NECESSARY

So you've assessed yourself and your lifestyle and have critically analyzed your site. Now it's time to make some decisions about your gardening conditions. Reconciling your personal interests, style, and budget with the physical limitations of your yard may require some compromises. But if any reasonable improvements to your site will enhance the long-term success of your garden, they should be considered. Drastic changes are not recommended for a SMARTGARDEN™, particularly those that will be difficult or time-consuming to maintain.

Fixed and variable factors

Certain aspects of a gardening site – temperature extremes, rainfall, elevation, proximity to city or the ocean – cannot be altered, and the plants you grow should be inherently compatible with those existing conditions. Radical attempts to change your microclimate are generally unfruitful and a frustrating waste of your time.

On the other hand, some modifications can alter the growing conditions significantly to the advantage of your gardens. Adding soil amendments such as organic matter (*see p. 30*) or limestone or iron sulfate to decrease or increase the acidity (*see* Adjusting soil pH, *p. 30*) is often necessary, particularly in areas where builders have removed topsoil. Regrading a backyard to improve drainage, or removing trees to allow more light into an area, may dramatically expand your gardening opportunities. The cost of such major modifications should be evaluated against the potential results. Sometimes compromises in garden size, placement, plant selection, and hardscaping options (nonplant features, such as patios) offer satisfying and less costly solutions.

Conditions vary, depending on the location of your garden within the landscape. Parts of your yard may be in full sun while others are shaded; some areas may be exposed to persistent winds from which other areas are protected; drainage patterns may result in a wet zone in one part of the yard and dry conditions in another. Identifying the distinct characteristics of each area provides the gardener with an opportunity to grow plants with varied requirements within a single landscape. Matching the requirements of the plants you want to grow as closely as possible to the conditions of a particular site will minimize adaptations that are necessary for healthy growth.

Staying dry
Make the best of a fast-draining area by creating a dry garden, using drought-tolerant plants set among stones, gravel, and sand.

Smart redirection
Instead of trying to grow grass in a wet spot, the owners of this property converted part of their land into a lush planting of woodland plants shaded by small trees.

Raise it up
Raised beds and supplemental irrigation enable this gardener to grow larger, better-quality vegetables.

The benefits of time

Keep in mind that time is an important dimension in gardening. An instant SMARTGARDEN™ is an oxymoron. Good things take time. Building a healthy soil doesn't happen overnight; it is an ongoing process. Likewise plants, particularly trees and shrubs, increase in size over the years, and they should be spaced with an eye toward their mature size. Although you may be tempted to purchase large plants in order to give your garden an established feeling from the start, this strategy has its drawbacks: larger plants are more expensive, and they often have more difficulty becoming established than smaller stock. By the time a large plant has settled in and has begun to produce significant growth, a specimen that was smaller at planting time might even have caught up with the larger one.

Time can be viewed as a wonderful dynamic – you can witness your garden's change with the passage of the seasons and the years as the design you envisioned becomes a reality. As plants and beds mature, they often require less maintenance because after their roots become well established, appropriately selected trees and shrubs will not require much attention, and, as groundcovers fill in, the need for weeding is reduced.

Worth the wait
Starting from scratch may seem daunting at first, but the satisfaction of watching a landscape grow over time is one of the major pleasures of gardening. Heavy work gives way to installing the structural "bones" of a garden area, followed by planting and then enjoying the rewards of all of your planning and hard work.

Raised beds for variety

Sometimes the plants you want to grow are at odds with your soil. Plants that require excellent drainage are poor choices for heavy, clay soils. On the other hand, a light, sandy soil will not sustain plants that require abundant moisture without reliable, abundant irrigation. If you want to include plants in your landscape with requirements that vary significantly from your native soil, consider growing them in raised beds or containers. Given the finite quantity of soil involved, its characteristics can be easily manipulated to suit the needs of desired plants.

Although limited in space, these gardens can be constructed or placed in sun or shade, protected or exposed locations, and watered frequently or minimally. They can also be built to accommodate easy access for gardeners who have difficulty bending or working in ground beds. The flexibility of raised beds gives the gardener an enormous selection of plants that might otherwise be ill suited for the conditions of the site (*see also p. 13*).

Culling the existing landscape

Before you begin adding plants to your landscape, it is important to review those that are already there. Some may have suffered damage or neglect and are now simply eyesores. Others may require a bit (or more) of maintenance. Certain plants in your yard may require significant time and energy to keep them healthy and attractive. This is particularly common with plants that were sited in inappropriate conditions in the first place. Transplanting to a different spot in the landscape or removing them altogether may be necessary.

Small trees and shrubs are often planted too close together. Although the short-term effect may be pleasing, after a number of years plants eventually become too crowded for their space. If such plants exist in your yard, determine if their value is worth the effort of constant pruning. Is transplanting them to another location a possibility, or should you simply remove them?

Most suburban lots can accommodate very few large trees. If the trees that were planted decades ago have overtaken the lot, you may want to consider removing one or two, or at least thinning their branches to allow more light to penetrate. Limbing up the tree – that is, removing the lower branches – can increase light penetration as well, and it opens the area beneath the tree for use.

Severe damage from disease, insects, winds, lightning, or other environmental stresses may have affected some trees and shrubs in your yard. Ask yourself if they are worth saving – it may be time to consider a replacement. Pruning or removing large trees may require a professional arborist.

WHEN TO CALL THE ARBORIST

Trees are a common and essential element of the southeastern landscape, providing shade to your home, garden, and leisure areas while lending a graceful aesthetic presence to your surroundings with views of foliage, fruit, bark, and habit throughout the year. To protect these valuable horticultural commodities, there are times when a certified arborist must be brought in to evaluate or treat declining, sick, or damaged trees.

Arborists, popularly known as tree surgeons, are professionals trained in tree care. They can diagnose problems, recommend treatments, fertilize, prune, spray, and remove trees safely.

Contact an arborist if large or out-of-reach limbs have broken, often a result of storm damage, or when large-scale pruning must be done. A proper cut, made either from the ground or in the tree's canopy through the use of ropes and harnesses, will enable the tree to heal quickly and eliminate entry points for insects or disease. Birches, cherries, and magnolias can be especially vulnerable to wounds that are not properly treated.

When insects or diseases become a problem for your trees, arborists can recommend and provide a number of helpful remedies. In cases where a specific pest besieges a species of tree, such as mistletoe infestations, oak galls, or fire blight of ornamental pears, an arborist can prescribe a number of remedies to control the problem and, in some cases, encourage regenerative growth. Arborists can also recommend and perform removal of dead or declining trees. Consult your state association of arborists for a list of certified professionals.

A job for the professional
Any time you have to get both feet off the ground, call a licensed, insured arborist.

Thinning and limbing up

When large trees limit the opportunities for growing other plants in a yard, either because they take up a great deal of space, or they cast dense shade, removal is not your only option.

Thinning a tree involves removing a percentage of its branches so that more air and light can penetrate through the remaining canopy without stimulating a great deal of vigorous, new growth. This is accomplished by cutting specific branches back to where they connect to a larger limb. This type of pruning is often beneficial to the tree: weak, unhealthy, and crowded branches can be removed, and air circulates better through the canopy. Plants that are growing beneath the tree will receive more light. If you want grass to grow under a tree with a dense canopy, thinning is critical.

Limbing up involves removing low limbs back to the main trunk in order to allow access to the area beneath the canopy; it effectively raises the crown. Ideally this process should begin early in the tree's training, but it can be done to large trees as well. When you are removing lower limbs from a young tree, do it gradually – this will cause less shock and promote a stronger trunk. As the tree gains height and girth, continue to remove the lowest branches. Generally, the best time to prune trees is when they are dormant, during the fall and winter.

Making this cut helped reduce wind resistance
This cut raised the crown

Thinning a tree
This is often done to reduce the overall size of a tree, to allow more light and air to penetrate through the crown, and to reduce wind resistance and stress from wide-spreading, heavy branches. Thinning requires more skill than limbing up.

Entire branch was removed
Part of this large branch was removed

Limbing up (crown lifting)
Removing some of a tree's lower branches creates more room for people or vehicles to pass more freely or to expose a street light that has become hidden in the branches. This is generally the easier of the two options presented here.

Adapting soil conditions

Whether refining an existing garden or working an area that is new to cultivation, a number of conditions can be fairly easily modified, such as adjusting pH and modifying drainange and structure.

Many of these changes – particularly those involving the soil – are most easily addressed prior to planting. Once a garden has been planted, your ability to incorporate soil amendments is restricted. Whenever you dig soil, take the opportunity to incorporate amendments. It takes much longer for fertilizer and limestone to reach plant roots when placed on the surface of the soil than it does when those materials are mixed throughout the root zone.

ADJUSTING SOIL PH

As mentioned in Tenet 2, a soil test provides important information about your soil. If your existing soil pH restricts your selection of plants, you can adjust it by mixing certain minerals into the soil. Limestone – usually ground or dolomitic – is applied to raise the pH (decrease the acidity). Wood ashes also tend to raise the pH of soil. Elemental sulfur or iron sulfate are the most commonly recommended supplements for lowering pH. Aluminum sulfate can also be used to decrease acidity, but it may cause aluminum toxicity in some plants.

Many sources of organic matter, including pine needles, oak leaves, unlimed compost, and green manure (cover crops that are plowed into the soil), will increase the soil acidity as they are broken down by microorganisms. Peat moss is also an acidifier, but its use should be avoided because it takes so long – centuries, in fact – for it to regenerate in its native bogs. The amounts of various materials needed to produce the desired pH level will vary depending on your soil texture and the amount of change needed. Modifying the soil pH takes time; it may require repeated applications.

An extreme case
You may not have ducks taking up permanent residence in your yard, but many properties have spots that are poorly drained. Either take measures to drain the area, or consider creating a bog garden or even a pond.

DEALING WITH DRAINAGE

If your soil drains too slowly, you have several options. You can limit your selection to plants that like wet soils, add material to the soil to improve drainage, or build raised beds and fill them with good, loamy soil before planting. To improve drainage of a compacted soil, add organic matter. If the subsoil is compacted, you may need to break up the hardpan or add subsurface drainage tiles to carry excess water away from planting areas.

For vegetable gardens with poor drainage, a hill-and-furrow planting method can be used: broad rows can be built up above the soil surface, with furrows running between the rows to divert excess water. Conversely, if your soil drains too quickly, use the furrows for planting. Rain or irrigation water will be channeled into the furrows where plants are growing.

For gardens where the soil drains too quickly, the addition of organic matter will improve water-holding capacity, and mulching will reduce evaporation loss. But supplemental irrigation may be necessary unless you choose plants that thrive in dry soils.

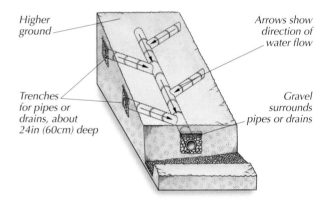

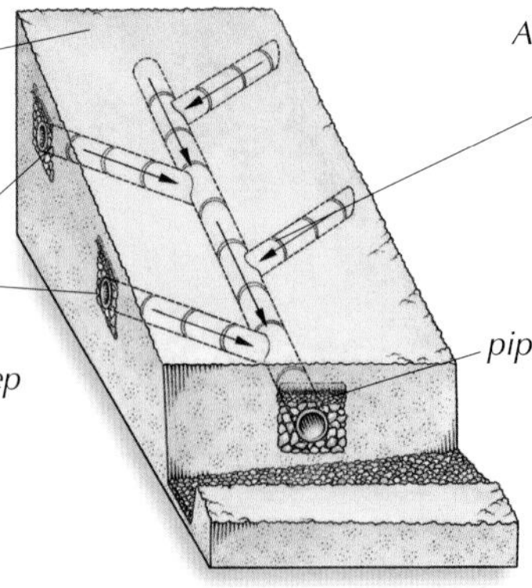

Improving drainage
Connect pipes or tiles together in a gravel-filled trench. On sloping ground, lay the pipes or tile drains to run parallel to the ground. On level ground, slope pipes away from ground level.

Building soil with organic matter

Organic matter – compost, leaf mold, grass clippings, rotted manure, or any material that was once alive – has a nearly miraculous power to improve almost any soil. Added to a clay soil, it facilitates drainage by creating soil aggregates with pore spaces between them; in a sandy soil, it bolsters water retention. The best way to provide continuous, well-balanced nutrition for plants is to build up the soil with organic matter.

As both microscopic (for example, bacteria) and macroscopic (such as earthworms and fungi) soil organisms digest organic matter, they release nutrients in a usable form for plants to absorb through their roots. Unlike quick-release chemical fertilizers that offer a glut of nutrients that may wash away with the next rain, decomposition of organic matter is a continuous process; nutrients are released slowly over a long period of time.

There are many good sources of organic matter, and many of them are free and readily available. Kitchen and yard wastes can be composted and within a few months yield a rich soil supplement (*see* Composting wastes, *p. 56*). Leaves raked during the fall become crumbly leaf mold, especially if they are chopped and mixed with a bit of soil to encourage their decomposition. Manure is often free for the hauling from a nearby farm or stable, or it can be purchased in bags from a home-supply or hardware store. Green manure is a cover crop that is sown, grown, and then turned back into the soil. A winter cover crop is an efficient method of adding nutrients and organic matter to a vegetable garden.

Mushroom compost *Peat* *Manure*

Brown gold

Here are just three of the many different kinds of organic matter that can be added to the soil in order to improve the structure and water retention.

A distinction is often made between leguminous and nonleguminous cover crops. Both add organic matter to the soil, but legumes, such as clover and vetch, contribute additional nitrogen as a result of their symbiotic relationship with nitrogen-fixing *Rhizobium* bacteria in the roots. As the legume roots decompose, nitrogen is released back into the soil. Of course, the amount of specific nutrients any given organic matter contains depends on the source and condition of the organic matter. For example, most compost contains 1.5 to 3.5 percent nitrogen, 0.5 to 1 percent phosphorus, and 1 to 2 percent potassium. Wood ashes – which tend to raise pH – contain little nitrogen, 1 to 2 percent phosphorus, and 3 to 7 percent potassium.

A soil that is well furnished with organic matter will sustain a healthy population of organisms, resulting in both improved soil structure and a good source of the raw materials needed by your garden plants. This is recycling at its best.

USING SOIL AMENDMENTS

Given the diverse nature of soil conditions throughout the Southeast, there are a number of varying conditions that warrant the use of amendments. The region's large number of urban sites often feature conditions where soils have become compacted and depleted of nutrients. While tilling can ease compaction issues, organic amendments such as leaf mold or composted manure can enrich soils and create a more suitable nutritional environment for all of your plants.

There is also a wide array of regionally available organic amendments in the Southeast. Examples include finely ground pine bark, compost, or manure. Such organic matter should also be used as amendments in areas where thin, lean, or sandy soils are common.

In areas where heavy soils predominate, such as those with a high component of clay where ample soil nutrition may be present, amendments such as organic matter can be introduced in order to improve drainage and air circulation. In troublesome areas where dense soils make amendment difficult, your best choice may be to create raised beds or berms with good quality topsoil that can support a variety of landscape plantings.

The nature of humus

After organic matter is thoroughly decomposed by soil microorganisms, it produces a material called humus, which exists as a very thin layer around soil particles. There is some misunderstanding about this term. The material commonly sold in bags that bear the label "humus" – usually compost or peat – would be more accurately labeled "humus-producing material," because microorganisms use it to make true humus, which is the end product of organic matter decomposition.

Humus contributes significantly to the soil environment by facilitating the aggregation of soil particles (which improves soil structure), holding nutrients against the force of leaching, increasing aeration, retaining water, and acting as a buffer to moderate a soil's acidity or alkalinity.

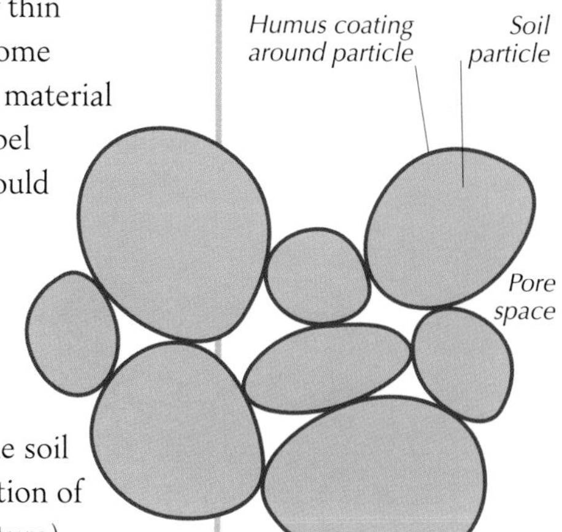

Up close

This diagram shows a much enlarged view of a few particles of soil. Each particle is coated with humus, the end product of microbial breakdown of organic matter. Humus aids in the retention of moisture and nutrients and promotes the formation of aggregates, which in turn leads to increased pore space: all very good things for soil.

The carbon:nitrogen ratio

One of the most critical characteristics of organic matter in terms of plant nutrition is the carbon to nitrogen ratio (C:N ratio). Fresh organic matter has a high carbon content compared to its nitrogen content. As the organic matter breaks down, the ratio changes as the relative amount of nitrogen increases. In most fully matured compost, the C:N ratio is between 30:1 and 10:1. When organic matter with a high C:N ratio (above 30:1), such as sawdust or grass clippings, is added to soil, microorganisms use nitrogen from the soil, and a temporary nitrogen deficiency can occur in plants. To avoid this deficiency, use composted organic matter. If mulching with a noncomposted organic material, apply a top-dressing of a nitrogen fertilizer prior to spreading the material.

PICK THE BEST PLANTS

One of the most important steps in establishing and maintaining a SmartGarden™ is selecting the right plants. Matching the cultural requirements of plants with your specific garden environment significantly increases the likelihood of successful cultivation and minimizes the maintenance effort. Preferences for water, light, soil type and acidity, tolerance of wind, humidity, salt spray, and air pollution, and resistance to diseases and pests are important factors in plant selection. Some conditions, such as soil pH, can be adjusted to accommodate the needs of desired plants. Others, such as salt spray near coastal regions or air pollution near industrial areas, are essentially fixed and limiting factors in the selection process.

Practical considerations

Identifying the USDA Plant Hardiness and AHS Heat Zones of your site is a logical first step in choosing plants you would like to grow. If a plant does not have the hardiness or heat tolerance for the zone in which you garden, you should choose another plant, unless you are willing to take extra measures to protect it. For example, tropical and subtropical plants can be grown in a container outdoors in temperate zones and brought indoors for winter (*see* Growing tropical plants in the Southeast, *p. 38*). Consult the Zone maps on p. 22 to determine your USDA Hardiness Zone and your AHS Heat Zone. Use those numbers as a starting point to select plants that will thrive in your garden's temperatures.

There may be areas of your yard that are unsuitable or impractical for growing plants of any kind. Consider a nonplant alternative such as a fence (in place of a hedge), a walkway, patio, or deck (in place of a lawn, bed, or similar planting), or a gazebo (in place of a large shade tree). These spaces are important elements of a landscape because they provide you with a minimum-maintenance area for moving through your gardens comfortably, or room for relaxing and enjoying your planted areas.

So you have an area in your yard and you want it to do something, but you need to consider the options: Provide shade? Simply look nice? Attract birds? Smell good? Block a view? Separate one area from another? Cover the ground? Provide a space for active play?

What are the site's physical factors, including sun, water, soil, wind, and microclimate? Will it support plants? If no, use the site for some other purpose, or think hard about what you would need to do to modify it. If yes, consider the specific plant features you'd like and require: leaves, flowers, fruit, form, bark, fragrance, size, shape, longevity, adaptabilty, productivity, hardiness, specific needs such as pruning, support, or deadheading to look its best, and susceptibility to pests and diseases.

Choose plants that meet the desired criteria and will grow well in the available microclimate, and determine how many will be needed.

The next consideration is your budget. If you can wait for a small plant to grow to its mature size, or let groundcovers and other similar plants multiply, you will spend less. You should also determine when to buy the plant, and put it in the ground.

Two solutions
Using plants is not always the solution to a given landscape problem: the conditions and the planning process may logically lead you to choose a hardscaping option over a garden.

Compromise
Instead of draining this area, the gardener chose to create a pond feature. Plants adapted to the conditions thrive, and the entire area is a place of delight instead of one of constant maintenance.

Plant categories

Plants are grouped according to their lifespan. The major categories are annuals, biennials, perennials, and woody plants.

ANNUAL

An annual completes its life cycle in a single season. It grows from seed, develops vegetatively, bears flowers, and produces seed for the next generation and then dies, all in less than a year.

BIENNIAL

A biennial requires two growing seasons to complete its life cycle. Most biennials produce vegetative growth their first season; they flower, produce seed, and die their second season.

It takes two
In spite of its specific name, *Lunaria annua* (honesty) grows most commonly as a biennial, requiring two years to complete its life cycle.

Follow the sun
Sunflowers are annuals that must have full sun to thrive.

PERENNIAL

A perennial is a plant that lives for more than two years, and a herbaceous perennial is a nonwoody perennial that survives from one growing season to the next because its roots or underground storage organs (such as a bulb, corm, or tuber) persist.

Sun-lover
Achillea species (yarrows) are mostly tough, adaptable perennials that grow well in dry, sunny spots.

Shade seeker
Green-and-gold (*Chrysogonum virginianum*) grows best with some shade, especially in the hottest part of the afternoon.

WOODY PLANT

A woody plant is also a type of perennial, but it possesses a more permanent structure that persists above ground from season to season. Woody plants may be deciduous or evergreen. Examples include shrubs, trees, and some climbers and groundcovers.

Always green
Daphne odora (near left) is a typical evergreen, always bearing leaves at any given time. However, evergreens normally shed some leaves periodically.

Leaf droppers
Hydrangea species and cultivars (far left) are all woody plants that are widely used in shrub borders and as specimens. Being deciduous, they shed their leaves for winter.

Perennials grown as annuals

Some plants are referred to as annuals, when they are actually perennial in their native habitat or in another Hardiness Zone. This has led to a bit of confusion among gardeners. True annuals – plants that grow, flower, produce seed, and die in a single growing season – have a Hardiness Zone of zero because they cannot tolerate cold winter temperatures, and so hardiness is not an issue.

Many plants that are grown as annuals in temperate climates, such as sweet basil, snapdragon, coleus, and moonflower, are perennial in warm climates; such plants are sometimes referred to as horticultural annuals, meaning that they can be grown as annuals in regions where they will not survive as perennials. They may also be referred to as tender perennials.

Delphinium 'Dark Magic'

Lupine (*Lupinus* 'Beryl, Viscountess Cowdray')

Foxglove (*Digitalis purpurea*)

Plant adaptations

Why do some plants flourish in full sun, while others languish or outright die unless they are provided with at least some shade during the hottest part of the day? Why do some plants thrive in bogs and open water, and others are perfectly at home in deserts or on cliffsides? Although most garden plants have roughly the same structure – roots, stems, leaves, flowers – nuances in their morphology equip them for a wide variety of conditions. This is fortunate, because this means there are plenty of plants, both naturally occcurring and selected, whose requirements and preferences match your conditions. Understanding the characteristics that make a plant suited to particular conditions will help you recognize those that are likely to do well in your garden environment.

Ornamental grasses
Varieties of many native grasses are now finding favor with gardeners because of their versatility and long period of ornamental value.

SHADE

Plants that grow best in the shade tend to have large, flat leaves with a fairly thin outer layer of cells. This allows maximum area and minimum resistance for absorbing light needed for photosynthesis and growth. In general, plants that grow in shady conditions produce fewer flowers and seeds than those grown in sun – this limited reproductive activity conserves a great deal of energy that can be directed toward vegetative growth. Thus, the ornamental display of many shade gardens relies more heavily on foliage color and texture than on flowers.

Shady situation
Savvy gardeners prize shade for the opportunities it provides to create garden pictures using foliage color and texture as well as overall plant habit.

HEAT AND DROUGHT

Xeriphytic plants have developed several strategies for reducing water loss and dealing with high temperatures. Many have smaller leaves with a thick, waxy layer, called the cuticle, on the leaf surface that protects it from drying out as well as providing some protection against insects. The reduction in both surface area and protective coating minimize moisture loss. Alpine plants that survive in areas where soil water is frozen for much of the year, and unavailable for absorption by plants, often exhibit similar traits.

Another adaptation that enables many plants to tolerate dry climates is pubescence – the presence of fine hairs – on leaves. These hairs help shade the leaf surface from the hot sun and trap moisture lost by the leaf through transpiration, thus maintaining a higher humidity level immediately around the leaf surface. The higher humidity reduces the transpiration pressure in the leaf, slowing the rate of moisture loss. Leaf arrangement and color also affect the absorption of heat. Leaves that point upward, arranged vertically toward the sun – such as *Yucca* and *Phormium* – absorb less heat than those with leaves oriented at right angles to the stem. Light-colored plants (typical of many heat-tolerant plants, including several species of *Euphorbia, Sedum,* and *Verbascum*) absorb less heat than dark plants.

Resistant roses
Rosa rugosa var *alba* and its many relatives thrive in hot, dry, cold, and windy sites.

COLD AND WIND

Some plants that grow well in cold, windy sites (such as along the coast, on open plains and prairies, or at the tops of mountains) have a prostrate growth habit, minimizing their exposure to drying winds. Trees and shrubs that survive in regions with cold winters are sensitive to environmental signals such as dropping temperatures and decreasing day length, initiating changes that induce dormancy to prepare them for winter, often indicated by leaf drop or a change in evergreen foliage color. As temperatures decrease, certain solutes – dissolved substances – accumulate in cells, reducing the likelihood of their freezing and rupturing. This is essentially making use of plant "antifreeze."

Site-specific challenges

Identifying the varied growing conditions of your site will help you select plants that will thrive with the least amount of assistance on your part. For example, an area of your yard that drains poorly and remains wet for long periods of the season is a likely site for a bog garden. The sunny strip alongside the street or driveway, subject to reflected heat and baking sun and far from the water faucet, lends itself to a xeriphytic planting of drought-tolerant plants. The shady north side of your house is a likely spot for shade-loving shrubs and groundcovers.

The conditions of some gardening sites are more challenging than others, and they may significantly restrict plant selection. If you live by the seashore,

Four combinations
You can create spectacular gardens in almost any given condition: sunny and dry (upper left), sunny and wet (upper right), shady and wet (lower left), and shady and dry (lower right). Only the most extreme conditions – such as the darkest, driest woodland or a sunny lake – will preclude you from achieving the garden you want.

you should select plants that tolerate salt spray and wind. If your soil is rich in limestone, plants that thrive in alkaline soil are a logical choice. Trees that have proven to adapt to the stresses of air pollution and compacted soil are the best options for planting alongside busy streets and in high-traffic urban areas. The lists in the Plant Catalog offer you a guide to regionally adapted plants to use in the variety of specific conditions that may be present in your garden.

Some areas may represent exceptions to the general conditions that are present in your yard and may offer possibilities for growing plants beyond those typically suited for your region or location (*see* Identify your microclimates, *p. 24*).

Plants for local conditions

For centuries, plant breeders have selected and developed varieties of plants with qualities that make them particularly well adapted to certain conditions, often extending the area in which that plant has traditionally been grown. Disease-resistant tomatoes are a notable example.

Many, if not most, of the cultivated plants that we grow have been selected because someone thought they were (for example) showier, bigger, smaller, healthier, or more fruitful than other plants like it. It may have been a planned cross that was part of a breeding program at a major seed company, or it may have been a serendipitous event – a gardener noticing a plant that was somehow different in some significant way than others. Sometimes seed of the selection observed and saved by a gardener is passed around to friends and handed down to children.

New varieties are continually being developed, grown, and compared at commercial seed companies and public institutions. Many regional plant breeding programs are associated with land grant colleges (*see* Appendix *p. 386*) or botanic gardens and arboreta (*see p. 387*).

Research has led to the breeding and selection of plants that better withstand environmental adversity. This means that certain varieties may extend the growing range or conditions where the plant can be successfully grown.

Discriminating variety selection can also reduce the impact of pests and diseases that frequently infest gardens in your locale. There may be varieties of the plants you want to grow that display an inherited resistance or tolerance to the problem. This preventive approach to pest and disease control is a simple way to reduce the need for applying pesticides. Local garden centers and Extension Services are often able to provide the names of disease- and pest-resistant varieties of fruits, vegetables, and ornamental plants for your area.

GROWING TROPICAL PLANTS IN THE SOUTHEAST

Many plants commonly grown as annuals are in fact tender tropical perennials. These include such well-known plants as aloes, clerodendrums, and bougainvilleas, and many species used in planters and hanging baskets, such as spike-dracaena, fan-flower, and bacopa. While these plants grow well during summer, they will not stand freezing and must be given protection over-winter if you wish to save them. Many are easy to replace, while others become overly large if kept indoors for the winter. Some are easy to store dormant until spring, but most need to be kept in a cool but well-lit location. Avid gardeners who have suitable locations often enjoy the challenge of bringing these plants through the winter and growing them on.

Dormant bulbs and corms, such as gladiolus, amaryllis, caladium, and tuberous begonias, should be lifted in fall after the first hard frost has blackened the stems. Turn them upside down to drain any water from hollow stems, and allow to air-dry in a frost-proof location for a day or so. Break off surplus soil but do not wash the roots clean, and store in barely moist peat moss or vermiculite in a cool but frost-free location. The ideal temperature is around 40°F (5°C). Inspect plants every few weeks, and water lightly if the storage material is very dry or if the roots shrivel.

Plants that don't become fully dormant should be dug and potted in fall before frost and kept in a sunny window, sun porch, or greenhouse where the temperature remains above 50°F (10°C). Bring plants indoors before night temperatures get close to freezing, or severe leaf-drop may occur. In spring, acclimatize overwintered plants to outdoor conditions gradually, since they may sunscald and desiccate badly if this process is hurried.

In addition to the commonly grown annual plants, many of the plants enjoyed as house plants, such as flowering maples, plumbago, lantana, and lemon trees, can benefit from a period outdoors during the summer. Be certain that they are hardened off properly in early summer and that they are brought back indoors well before first frost.

All plants that are being brought inside should be inspected closely for pests and diseases that can spread rapidly in the close conditions of a sunny window ledge. It is far easier to treat a problem outside than to try to spray once it is indoors.

Cannas (*Canna* species and cultivars) produce lush, bold foliage and brilliantly colored flowers.

Mature size and growth habit

Trying to achieve a mature appearance in your new garden is tempting, but it can lead to problems. If you space your plants too closely together, the result is almost always unsatisfactory. Plants soon become crowded, they may become more susceptible to disease, and they compete for water and light. Flower and fruit production may be reduced. Often, their growth habit is altered – instead of full, wide-spreading branches, plants may appear sparse and gangly as they stretch in search of light.

When deciding which plants to include in your yard and where you want to place them, be sure you have room to accommodate the mature size of each selection, no matter what its eventual size will be. Repeated pruning of a shrub during the growing season will be made unnecessary if your initial selection is based on the desired mature size. Many nurseries supply the mature dimensions on the plant tag or label. Consult the Plant Catalog to avoid making a major mistake.

If the growth habit of a plant is something worth featuring, be sure to provide adequate room. For example, a Harry Lauder's walking stick (*Corylus avellana* 'Contorta') is best placed in an open area where its unusual form can be appreciated. A low, spreading plant such as creeping juniper needs plenty of lateral room to develop; otherwise, it may overtake nearby plants or walkways.

Training plants from an early age to enhance their natural habit or to direct growth in a certain manner can be an effective way to manage plant size.

Variations on a theme
Plants are very adaptable and respond to pruning and training to produce an amazing variety of shapes, including the espalier and standard shown here.

Carefully pruned specimen plants can serve as focal points and accents, esepecially in a small garden. Some plants can be trained to grow against a wall, a technique known as espalier; this requires a minimum of garden space and is an effective use of a blank wall.

Another choice you will be confronted with when selecting your plants is which size to purchase. Although a larger plant may give you a fuller look than a smaller version of the same plant, you will need to weigh the additional expense against the immediate effect. In a few seasons, small plants often catch up to plants that were larger at the time of purchase (*see* The benefits of time, *p. 28*).

If you do start with young plants, it is still possible to achieve a mature look while waiting for them to grow. Maintain temporary herbaceous plantings in the space between young woody plants. Annuals survive for only a single season, and as your trees and shrubs spread in the coming years, perennials can be dug and transplanted to other areas.

Tree forms

Trees may be the biggest of all the voices in your garden choir, but they do show a remarkable range of differences. Use these differences to create a varied backdrop for the rest of your garden plants and structures. Remember, it may take several to many years for the tree to develop its fully mature form.

Half-standard *Fastigiate* *Multistemmed* *Weeping standard*

Growth habits

There are many shapes a plant can take, whether naturally or by manipulation though horticultural practices. It is often best to consider a plant's shape before thinking about its flowers – the shape will remain long after the flowers are gone. The Plant Catalog presents some options for selecting plants based on their habit.

Cushion- or mound-forming *Clump-forming* *Climbing and Scandet*

TAKE GOOD CARE OF THE EARTH

Every garden activity we undertake has a ripple effect on our plants, soil, water, and wildlife. We apply fertilizer to our lawns and, depending on the type and quantity, it can either bolster a healthy soil environment or leach through the soil and pollute local streams. By encouraging certain plants to grow and removing others, we influence whether and what wildlife inhabits our gardens. The material that we select to surface our paths and driveways also has an impact – positive or negative – on water runoff and soil erosion.

Choices and compromises

In our efforts to develop and maintain satisfying landscapes, we must try to achieve our goals without putting a strain on our environment. Simply by adjusting watering schedules, selecting the most effective mulch material, or timing the application of a pest control measure with precision, we can increase the efficiency of our gardening efforts and minimize the effect on the environment.

Some of the modifications we make in our gardens may require a balanced counteraction. For example, removing debris from a bed to keep it neat deprives soil of organic matter. Replacing the leaves with an organic mulch such as compost or shredded bark, however, supplies the organic matter while achieving the desired tidy appearance. Recognizing the impact of our activities, using resources efficiently and avoiding waste, must become second nature in the SMARTGARDEN™.

Whether planning a new bed, maintaining a lawn, or pruning a tree, gardening activities require choices. Consideration of environmental consequences should be an important part of the criteria you use for selecting one technique over another.

Basic decisions such as whether an area should be maintained as lawn or developed into a bed, whether to encourage wildlife (and if so, which kind), and whether a tree that casts dense shade should be removed all need to be weighed against their impact on the overall landscape. Sometimes a compromise in expectations, technique, or timing can be effective in achieving the desired change without causing significant environmental consequences.

Another example of compromise is reducing the amount of nitrogen fertilizer applied to plants that are subject to water stress – vegetative growth may be reduced, but so will the water needs of the plant.

Using every corner
Growing a wide range of plants makes efficient use of limited space and also attracts a diverse mix of wild creatures (many beneficial) into your garden.

Beneficial for all
Gardening in an age of shrinking habitats and resources should make every enlightened gardener consider both the plants and the wildlife that depend on them when making gardening decisions.

Serious disease or pest problems can be reduced by adjusting your planting schedule for several vegetable crops. Thinning a tree canopy that casts dense shade, rather than removing the tree, can accomplish the desired outcome of increasing light penetration without destroying a habitat and food source that supports a variety of wildlife.

Conserving water

Given the droughts and high average temperatures many parts of the country have been experiencing in recent years, not to mention the increase in population density, water consumption for gardening is a growing concern. There are a variety of conservation strategies you can use in your garden to reduce water consumption.

Someone's dinner table
Don't forget that lawns are still very popular with blue jays and other creatures that depend on them for food.

While all plants need water to thrive, some need less than others, and some plants are better equipped than others to obtain and retain water. For instance, succulent plants store water in their fleshy leaves or their stems and underground structures for use when needed. Leaves of lamb's-ears (*Stachys* spp.) and wormwood (*Artemisia* spp.) are covered with fine white hairs that shade the leaf surface and prevent moisture loss. Many ornamental grasses and prairie natives have deep roots that range far to seek water. Some leaves are oriented so that the minimum amount of sunlight falls on their surfaces, reducing leaf temperature. These and other characteristics of drought-tolerant plants minimize the need for supplemental watering (*see* Plant adaptations, *p. 36*).

You do not need to limit your plant selection to drought-tolerant species. Plants that require more frequent watering, however, should be grouped together, ideally close to a water source. By designing your garden according to the plants' water requirements, it is easier to develop efficient watering systems tailored to the needs of different sections of the garden.

REDUCING RUNOFF

A great deal of potentially beneficial garden moisture is lost to runoff. Grading your beds can help direct the flow of water to where it will be most useful. Studies suggest that significantly more water penetrates into the soil through a diverse planting of groundcovers than through turf, and reducing lawn area will increase water absorption.

A rain barrel that collects water from the roof saves water that would otherwise be lost as runoff. Several manufacturers produce plastic rain barrels with hardware to connect the downspout with the barrel, and a faucet so you can access the water. Rain barrels can be attached to drip irrigation systems or simply used to fill your watering can. An added benefit of collecting rainwater in areas with wells that supply hard water – water that contains a high level of soluble salts – is that since rainwater is soft, it will not cause mineral deposits that can clog up drip irrigation nozzles, and you can use the water on plants that need acidic soil conditions. Don't forget to cover barrels and other containers to control mosquitoes.

Solid-surface walkways and driveways prevent water from penetrating into the soil, and the water

Not thirsty
Drought-tolerant plants, such as junipers, lavender cotton, and sedums, grow well even with a limited water supply.

REDUCING RUNOFF AND RECYCLING NATURE

The Southeast region is filled with lakes, rivers, and wetlands that, along with underground aquifers, provide the water we take for granted when we turn on the tap. Many of these water sources are now in danger of contamination from chemicals and from over-consumption. Contamination comes from excess fertilizers and chemicals that leach into the soil from farming and gardening, from erosion of soil following snow melt in spring or after a summer storm, as well as from the runoff from roads, parking lots, and driveways. Contamination occurs when chemicals are carried into water sources, upsetting the balance of nature. The nitrogen in chemical fertilizers, for example, may leach through the soil and be carried into the groundwater following a heavy rainstorm. Using slow-release formulations of lawn fertilizers lessens the chance of this occurring, since the nitrogen is released over a period of time. Before manufacturers changed their formulas, phosphates in laundry detergents were responsible for the algae that clogged many lakes and rivers.

As gardeners, we can make a positive impact on our watersheds by following conservation practices in our garden. Apply fertilizers sparingly and at the proper time so they are absorbed by actively growing plants. Use compost whenever possible in preference to chemical fertilizers, because the nutrients need to be broken down by soil organisms and are not immediately soluble. Use garden chemicals only when needed, not "just in case," at the rate recommended by the manufacturer, and apply only enough to wet the foliage, not to the point where it is dripping on the soil. Watch the weather: applying garden chemicals just before rain is a waste of time and effort, and it adds to water contamination. Most garden chemicals degrade into nontoxic substances fairly quickly in contact with the soil, but this process is delayed if rain carries them through into the ground water.

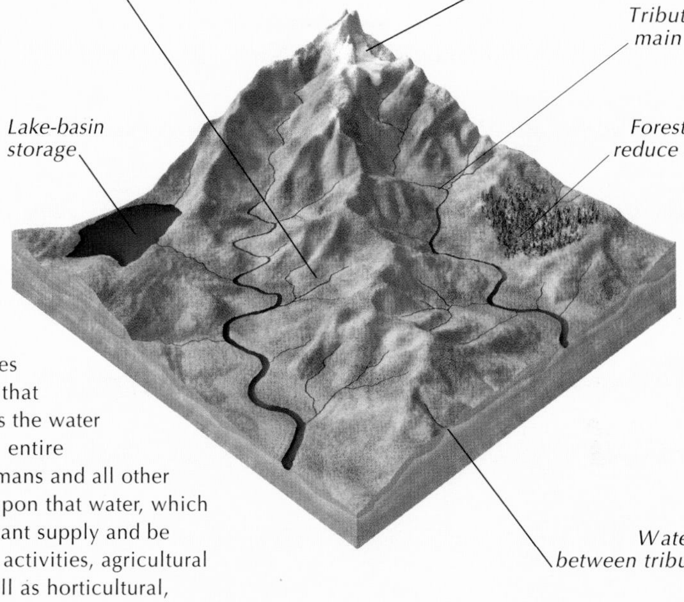

It's all connected
A river and its network of tributaries forms a vast system that collects and recycles the water that flows within an entire watershed area. Humans and all other life are dependent upon that water, which needs to be in constant supply and be relatively pure. Our activities, agricultural and industrial as well as horticultural, positively and negatively affect our water.

that runs off of these surfaces often leads to erosion or drainage problems. When installing a driveway or walkway, consider using a permeable surface through which rainwater can be absorbed. Driveways can be constructed of gravel, and beautiful walks and patios can be fashioned from unmortared stone set in sand.

Supplementing nature

Water requirements are affected not only by the type of plant and the density of the planting, but also by a number of environmental variables, such as temperature, wind, sunlight, and season.

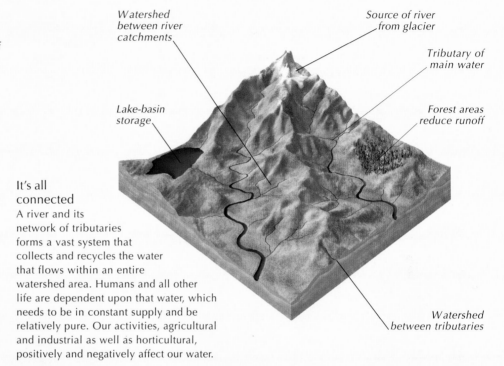

Dry quarters
Even some tiny plants can get by without much water: *Sedum spurium* 'Dragonsblood' is at home in a spot that provides little water; in fact, it may grow best in such a setting.

Soils also vary in their capacity to retain water. Thus there is no fixed rule for how often you will need to water: observing your plants and checking your soil offer the best clues.

Plants provide several clues when they are suffering from a lack of water. The observant gardener looks for these signs and waters thoroughly before the plant suffers long-term or irreversable damage. The following are common symptoms or clues to water stress. The symptoms you first notice will vary somewhat from one kind of plant to another:

- dullness or a subtle change in foliage color
- reduced growth
- reduction in flowers or fruit
- wilting or curling of leaves
- footprints remain when grass is walked upon
- lawn turns dull, then bluish, and eventually straw-colored or brown

All plants should be watered when they are first set out, and regular watering should continue until their roots are well established. It is important to water thoroughly (and at the base of the plants; you don't need to give plants a shower when you water them) to encourage deep root development. Plants with an extensive and deep root system can obtain more water from the soil and are less subject to injury from temperature fluctuations.

Early morning or evening (in other words, before or after the heat of the day), are the best times to water – less will be lost to evaporation. Avoid wetting plant foliage, because wet leaves are more prone to disease.

WHEN TO WATER

Hard and fast guidelines about how often to water simply don't exist. You need to take into account the individual microclimate of your garden, the nature of your soil, and the quantity and size of the plants you are growing. Then you need to factor in the weather. Temperature, humidity, and wind velocity all contribute to the loss of moisture from the soil, especially when coupled with plants that have a relatively large leaf surface to transpire water. This loss of water from the soil is known as the evapotranspiration rate and, coupled with the water-holding capacity of your soil, determines how frequently supplemental water will be required.

As you can see from the map below, the evapotranspiration rate is moderate to high throughout the Southeast, and you will need to keep a close watch on your plants for signs of stress (see symptoms above), and on weather forecasts for predicted rain, to judge whether or not to water. Remember, too, that new plants do not have an extensive root system and are more likely to suffer from dryness than well-established plants. Also plants with large, soft leaves are more prone to dryness than those with stiff leaves. It is often possible to conserve water by watering individual plants showing signs of stress to save them, rather than by applying water to an entire bed.

Your soil type also governs the frequency of watering. On light, sandy soils, shallow soils, or those with a high proportion of rock and gravel, water will be required more often, and your soil will benefit greatly from the addition of large amounts of organic matter (*see p. 30*). Where soils are poor and water is at a premium, consider planting xerophytic plants (those requiring little water) in preference to more commonly grown woody plants and perennials.

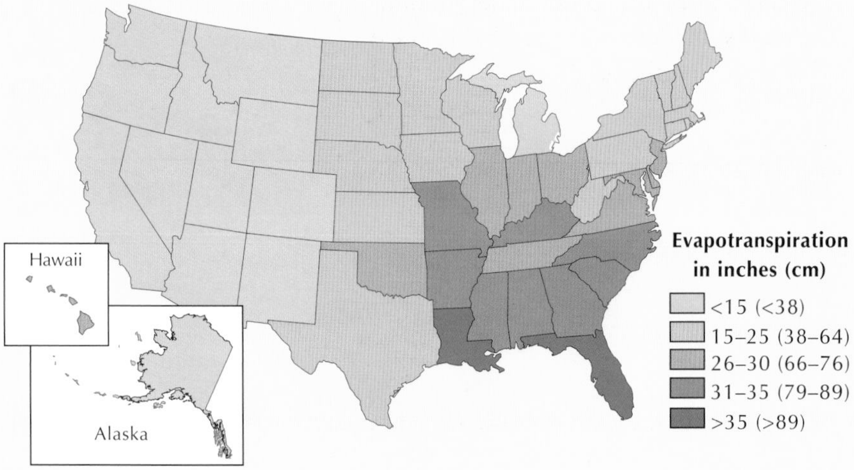

HAND WATERING

Using a watering can or hose with a water breaker to deliver a drink to your gardens allows you to get "up close and personal" with your plants on a regular basis. You are likely to detect disease and insect problems soon after they appear. However,

Where to water

Knowing where to water is as important as knowing when. Direct it to the base of the plant and to the soil, so that the water goes directly to the root zone.

this system requires a great deal of time and may be impractical for large gardens. It is, however, perfectly suited for special, individual plants, small beds, and for those plants growing in containers.

Wasting water
Sprinkler systems are a valuable method of applying water to lawns and gardens, but be sure to maintain the piping and hardware for maximum efficiency, and do your best to avoid waste by making sure the system is on only when water is needed.

TRICKLE IRRIGATION

One of the most efficient watering systems is drip or trickle irrigation. Although it takes some effort to set up initially, in the long run it saves time. Trickle systems can be designed to accommodate any garden size or style. Water is delivered directly to the root zone of desired plants or areas through emitters at the end of water tubes. Little water is lost to evaporation or wasted on areas between plants. The spacing of emitters and rate of flow can be adjusted as necessary. This system can also be used for container plants.

If your water is hard, however, you may find that the narrow tubes of a trickle irrigation system become clogged with minerals. If a tube is clogged or becomes displaced, plants can suffer before the problem is noticed and rectified.

SOAKER HOSE

Also called a seep hose, a soaker hose allows water to drip out slowly into the soil along the length of the hose. Soakers are similar to drip systems but are easier to move from place to place. They are particularly useful in vegetable gardens, where they can be stretched along the rows, and in densely planted flower beds where they can wind through the entire planting area.

SPRINKLERS

For permanent plantings, an underground, automated sprinkler system can be installed, preferably before the garden is planted. The hardware of these systems must be checked and maintained for efficiency, and plants near nozzles must be monitored; if they grow over the nozzles, they may block or divert the spray. These systems can be programmed to run on a timer.

Portable sprinkler systems are relatively inexpensive and versatile, but they rarely deliver

Soaking a raised bed
Because soil dries out faster in a raised bed than in the open ground, growing vegetables or other plants this way often requires supplemental irrigation. A soaker hose provides water directly to the soil with very little loss by evaporation.

Mulchberries
They're called strawberries for a good reason: gardeners long ago realized the value of mulching these plants, so much so that straw became part of their standard culture and of *Fragaria*'s common name.

a uniform spray. Hoses connect the water source with a variety of sprinkler attachments – fans, oscillators, pulsating heads. A significant amount of water from sprinklers is lost to evaporation, and use of overhead sprinklers may lead to an increase in foliar disease problems.

Mulching for moisture

Mulching around plants conserves moisture in a number of ways. By physically covering the soil, less moisture is lost to surface evaporation, and the daytime temperature in the root zone in mulched soil is less than for bare soil, especially in hot sun. Mulches inhibit the growth of weeds that compete with your plants for water, and mulches help prevent soil crusting, the dry surface layer that impedes water penetration into the soil, leading to runoff and erosion.

Summer mulches are particularly important for soil moisture retention as well as weed control. But wait until the soil has had a chance to warm up in the spring before applying it, or new growth may be delayed. The best time to mulch depends on the plants that you are growing. In the vegetable garden, cool-season vegetables such as peas and spinach can be mulched much earlier than heat-loving tomatoes and melons. Give perennials enough time to emerge from the soil before mulching your flower beds.

In a climate with cold winters and warm summers, mulching to provide winter protection is most effective when applied after the ground has become cold and plants have entered dormancy. Mulching too early can delay normal hardening of growth for winter. Many perennials will benefit from a winter mulch after their tops have died back. This helps moderate winter moisture and temperature levels in the soil, which are especially critical with new plantings.

There are some disadvantages to mulching that should be recognized; however, when and how much mulch you apply can minimize these. For example, some animals such as mice and rabbits may find an organic mulch to be a suitable spot to build their nests. These garden inhabitants can cause damage to shrubs and young trees in winter if they gnaw at the base of trunks or stems. Do not allow mulch to build up around the base of plants. This problem can be further minimized by waiting until after you have experienced several hard frosts before you apply the winter mulch. Mice and rabbits will likely have already found another location for their winter home by then. In spring, mulch needs to be pulled back from perennials to allow new growth to emerge and to prevent a buildup of excessive moisture around stems, which can lead to disease.

The mulch advantage

Mulching with the right material, applied at a proper depth and at the appropriate time, provides numerous advantages to garden plants in addition to retaining moisture and suppressing weeds. Mulch protects plant roots from extremes of heat and cold and creates a physical barrier between foliage and soil-splashing rain, which helps prevent the spread of disease. In vegetable gardens, mulch keeps fruit —such as tomatoes, squash, cucumbers, and melons—clean, preventing their direct contact with the soil, where fruit-rotting organisms very likely lurk. Also, mulching may reduce the need for fungicides.

Mulching does not warm or cool a soil; rather, it moderates the temperature changes. This influence is accomplished by shading the soil from the hot sun during the day and by the retention of moisture. Water changes temperature more slowly than air. So the more moisture contained in soil, the slower the rate of temperature change around a plant's roots. Often winter damage occurs to the roots of plants, not because of the low temperature to which they are subjected, but because of rapid changes in temperature of a dry soil. These rapid changes can cause perennials to heave out of the soil, exposing their roots to cold, dry air, killing the plant. Mulching helps minimize such losses.

Mulching defense
For woody plants, apply a mulch to cover the entire root zone. Leave a 4-6in (10-15cm) gap around the stem base; mounding mulch onto woody stems may cause rot.

HOW MUCH MULCH

How much mulch should you apply? Too much can impair plant growth by suffocating roots and preventing moisture from reaching the soil, but too thin a layer will not sufficiently suppress weed growth or retain moisture. In general, a 2–3in (5–8cm) layer of organic mulch is appropriate. Replace the mulch as it breaks down instead of mulching too thickly at the beginning of the season. Always keep mulch away from the crown or stems of plants to avoid the buildup of excessive moisture and increase the likelihood of disease. In vegetable gardens and annual beds, organic mulch can be incorporated into the soil at the end of the season; it will improve soil structure and fertility. Around permanent plantings, mulch breaks down gradually, releasing nutrients that are carried to the roots by rain. In both cases, an organic mulch promotes a healthy soil environment.

Recycling into mulch
All of the mulching materials above (from the top, they are bark, compost, and leaves) could come from the garden to which they are returned. Recycling all heathy plant debris makes good sense.

MULCHING MATERIALS

The material you select for a mulch depends on availability, personal taste, and the type of garden. Both organic and inorganic mulches are available, and each is suited to several different types of garden applications.

Straw works well in the vegetable garden, but can look messy and contribute unwanted weed seeds to a perennial border. More attractive organic mulches, such as shredded bark, pine straw, or cocoa hulls, are a better choice for flowerbeds, trees, and shrubs.

Weed barrier fabrics (landscape fabric or geotextiles) – material made out of polypropylene fibers – allow water and air to penetrate but prevent weed growth. They can enhance the efficiency of an organic mulch. They are usually placed directly on the soil surface and slits are cut through it for planting. An organic mulch, such as shredded bark or cocoa shells, is usually applied on top to hold it in place and provide a more attractive appearance.

Inorganic mulches include plastic, pebbles, and marble and stone chips. Black plastic is often used to mulch melons and cucumbers, since they benefit from the heat captured by the plastic in addition to a virtually total suppression of weeds. Rock gardens and beds of cacti and other succulents generally require drier conditions, and they may resent the moisture retained under a layer of shredded bark. Mulching with gravel or stone is probably the best solution for such gardens.

The color of the mulching material will affect its absorption or reflection of solar heat. Dark-colored mulches absorb more heat, warm the soil earlier in the spring, and maintain the heat later into autumn. Light-colored mulches absorb less heat, and they reflect heat and light upward toward the plants.

Plants themselves can serve as a mulch as they spread to cover the soil surface, crowding out weeds and shading the soil from the heat of the sun. Clematis benefit from such a mulch; many of them require a cool, shaded location for the roots along with plenty of sun for the above-ground portions of the plant. These requirements are met when the clematis is planted at the base of a coniferous shrub – the shrub provides a living mulch for the roots, as well as support for the clematis vine to grow upon.

Of course, plants require water, so although a mulch of living plants is an effective method of weed control and soil temperature moderation, it may actually increase the water requirement for the area.

In a woodland garden, trees and shrubs annually provide their own mulch of leaves and needles. Be sure that leaves and needles are raked off of desired groundcovers and herbaceous perennials growing beneath trees.

Managing without chemicals

Keeping your garden neat and preventing weeds from taking over doesn't require chemical warfare. Weeds can be pulled, cut, burned (where legal), smothered, and suppressed – the most effective method of control depends upon the types of weeds and the specific garden situation.

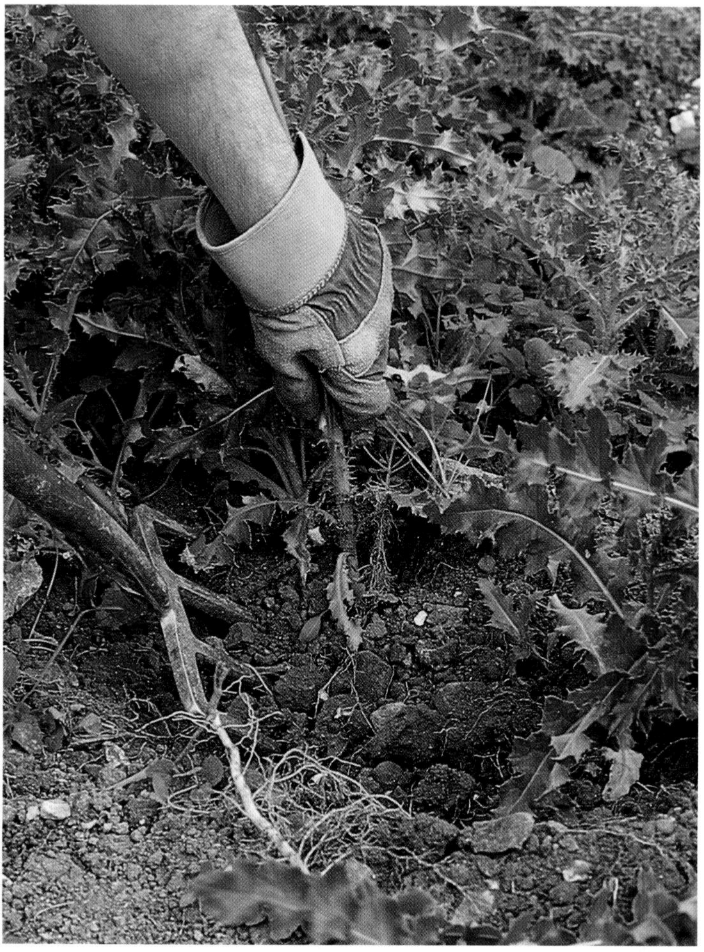

Don't wait

Don't let weeds progress this far before tackling them. Many methods can be used to keep them under control, including hand-weeding, if done on a regular basis.

In a new garden, weeding can require a good bit of effort. But as garden plants become established and spread to cover the open ground, your weeding efforts will lessen, particularly if you practice some routine weed-management tasks. Eliminate your weeds before they become established and reseed themselves. It is more productive to spend a little time weeding on a routine basis than to let the weeds get an upper hand, eventually requiring a major cleanup effort. Mulching after you weed will prevent many weeds from returning (*see* The mulch advantage, p. 47).

Solarization provides excellent initial weed control for a new planting. The area to be solarized should be mowed very low and watered well. Cover it with black plastic, secured at the edges, and leave it for at least six weeks – longer if possible. The temperature in the top several inches of soil rises significantly, baking the surface vegetation as well as most weed seeds, roots, and soil pathogens.

To suppress the germination of weed seeds, corn gluten can be applied to a soil surface. This material, which is a natural byproduct of milling corn, is a good source of nitrogen, and it inhibits seed germination. Applied to established lawns, it prevents the germination of crabgrass and other annual weeds. It can be applied in a vegetable garden after vegetable plants have emerged. It is also useful in establishing a groundcover bed: groundcover plants are set, corn gluten is applied and watered in, the bed is mulched, and weeds are suppressed.

Edging a bed with a solid barrier, such as brick, stone, or wood, helps prevent creeping weeds from gaining entry.

A flame thrower is an effective tool for weeding nonflammable surfaces such as gravel paths, paved patios, and driveways as well as for spot-treating persistent weeds. Never use a flame thrower close

Both useful and beautiful
A simple edging of wood or stone or similar material keeps creeping weeds such as Canada thistle and quackgrass at bay and will provide a very attractive addition to an otherwise very utilitarian part of your garden.

to desirable plants that may be scorched, or near a flammable mulch or other flammable surfaces.

Boiling water, while somewhat cumbersome, has a similar effect on weeds as direct flame. It is particularly useful for hard-to-weed spaces between pavers or bricks.

Useful and attractive
Plants of the aster family (Asteraceae), like these *Achillea* 'Summer Pastels', have many tiny flowers and will attract butterflies and other beneficial insects to feed on the nectar.

Encouraging desirable wildlife

Every year, more and more land is being cleared for homes and businesses, and wildlife habitats are being reduced or destroyed. Your SMARTGARDEN™ can be a haven for wildlife with a little planning. The three basic needs of wildlife – food, water, and shelter – can easily be met in a garden if you consider the type of wildlife you want to encourage and provide for them by including plants that produce nectar, flowers, seeds, and fruit, a source of water, and suitable habitats for nesting.

Adding feeders to your garden to supplement the plants will carry the banquet through the garden's lean times. Birdbaths or a small pond can provide sufficient water for your visitors, but remember to change the water frequently so it stays clean. If possible, leave some areas of the yard undisturbed for shelter. Dead trees and hollow logs provide homes for many wild creatures, as do unraked leaves (also see the Plant Catalog for plants to attract wildlife).

Maintaining a wildlife-friendly garden contributes to a well-balanced environment. Birds and bats feed on insects; butterflies, bees, and many other insects (and some bats) pollinate flowers; moles feed on grubs of root-eating beetles. Avoid using pesticides that will harm pollinating insects or birds, and be sure to read all pesticide labels carefully for warnings about potential dangers to wildlife.

Of course, not all forms of wildlife contribute to the health of your plants. Some wildlife may not be as welcome to your garden as others. There are some animals you would rather discourage from grazing in your azaleas, nibbling away at your bulbs, or feasting on your sweet corn. Like insect pests, take the approach of determining how much damage the critter is likely to inflict on your plantings, and if the level is unsatisfactory, take precautions to prevent the destruction.

Various techniques can be used to discourage deer, raccoons, voles, squirrels, and other potentially destructive forms of wildlife from damaging your plantings. Selecting plants that are unappetizing to the specific animal is a start – almost nothing eats daffodils! Other methods for discouraging foragers include fences or barriers, repellents, strategic placement of a scarecrow or an owl or snake lookalike, and a big dog.

Water magnet
Water attracts birds and others animals to your garden just as much as flowers and bird seed. They need to drink and bathe just like gardeners do, and some creatures, such as frogs, toads, and dragonfly larvae, will take up residence in a suitable water feature.

SOUTHEASTERN WILDLIFE

Ruby-throated hummingbird
A sure sign of the return of warm weather, hummingbirds are omnivorous feeders, eating small insects as well as visiting flowers and feeders for their nectar. Very territorial, you will probably only have one pair in your garden.

As more and more land is taken over for housing and business, the areas left for wildlife shrink. Some wild species are becoming accustomed to existing close to man and, by creating a wildlife-friendly garden, you can do much to encourage and protect them. Many birds, butterflies, and small mammals can survive alongside man, and by adding a pool you can attract frogs and dragonflies. Depending on the size of your property and the diversity of planting, you can provide suitable habitats for a wide range of birds, animals, and insects. Many of these will be beneficial and will aid you in keeping pests under control. Snakes, spiders, and toads may not be your favorite garden guests, but they play an important role in reducing plant problems. The following lists contain some of the more common wildlife you may find in your garden, or whose presence you'll want to encourage.

Ladybird beetle
This ladybug is looking for aphids and other pests to eat, as will its offspring.

Overwintering birds can help you by feeding on weed seeds and the egg masses of garden pests if you encourage them to stay around by putting out feeders. Those commonly found include: • black-capped chickadee • purple finch • house finch • American goldfinch • Eastern towhee • house sparrow • European starling • blue jay • hairy woodpecker • downy woodpecker • pileated woodpecker • white-breasted nuthatch • brown creeper • cedar waxwing • evening grosbeak • pine grosbeak • northern cardinal • gray partridge • mourning dove • American crow.

Spring brings an influx of birds either passing through or that will stay all summer. They all help by feeding on seeds and emerging insects. Some that you are likely to see are: • American robin (some may overwinter) • common grackle • brown-headed cowbird • red-winged blackbird • tree swallow • barn swallow • purple martin • scarlet tanager • Baltimore oriole • song sparrow • chipping sparrow • gray catbird • brown thrasher • northern mockingbird • common flicker • yellow-bellied sapsucker • Eastern bluebird • killdeer • whip-poorwill • house wren • Carolina wren • wild turkey • Acadian flycatcher • eastern kingbird • ruby-throated hummingbird • warblers (many species).

Eastern tiger swallowtail
The larvae of butterflies can eat garden plants, but few cause major damage.

Many small mammals will make their home in your garden and feed on seeds and insects, sometimes causing damage in the process. Some larger ones, such as skunks and raccoons, will also find their way in, but others, such as groundhogs and deer, are best excluded if possible. You may catch glimpses of some of these: • opossum • eastern mole • smoky shrew • short-tailed shrew • bats (several species) • armadillo • eastern chipmunk • red squirrel • gray squirrel • flying squirrel • deer mouse • meadow mouse • house mouse • meadow vole • prairie vole • cottontail rabbit • striped skunk • groundhog (woodchuck) • raccoon • red fox • white-tailed deer.

Although they frighten many people, reptiles and amphibians are gardener's friends, eating many of the pests that attack plants. Among those that should be encouraged are: • eastern garter snake • American toad • tree frog • leopard frog.

Eastern chipmunks
These rodents forage for seeds and nuts in mixed woods or brush.

Butterflies and moths add movement to a summer garden. They will be attracted by plants rich in nectar and by a patch of wet mud or a very shallow pool area. Some of the more common and striking are: • mourning cloak • monarch • black swallowtail • orange sulphur • great spangled fritillary • painted lady • luna moth • hawk moth • hummingbird moth.

Other garden invertebrates include: • crickets • dragonflies • honeybees • bumblebees • wasps • walking sticks • cicadas • spiders • millipedes • centipedes • sowbugs (pillbugs) • slugs and snails.

Red fox
Mammals also benefit from the conditions provided by gardens.

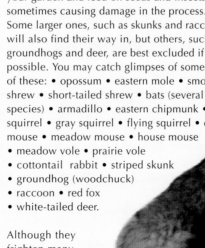

WORK WITH NATURE

Every aspect of gardening, from selecting your site and your plants to accommodating their spread and cleaning up debris, will be easier and more successful if you work with nature to achieve your goals. Although a garden alters a landscape to some extent, it should exist in harmony with its environment. The key is to follow nature's leads and to harness its forces to work on your behalf.

Learning from natural habitats

Plants with similar growth requirements should be grouped together in your garden, growing as they would in their natural habitat. Shrubs and perennials that thrive in low light can be planted beneath trees that furnish the necessary shade; those that require constant moisture can be grouped in a bog garden or at the edge of a pond; and those that thrive in full sun and dry soil can be combined in a sunny rock garden or xeriphytic planting.

In addition to grouping plants that share similar natural habitats, keep in mind any additional cultural requirements or special care that the plants might need when you are planning your garden. For example, vegetables and annual flowers generally require more fertilization and water than established perennials and woody plants. If the vegetable or annual flower beds are positioned within easy reach of a water faucet or rain barrel, their additional needs can be easily accommodated. Natural cycles of growth, reproduction, and decomposition can be put to work to your garden's advantage, and many problems can be avoided if you mimic natural patterns and solutions for reducing plant stress.

Just as the environment affects the growth of plants in your garden, everything you do in your garden has an impact on the environment. As environmentally responsible gardeners and stewards of the Earth, working in cooperation with nature rather than attempting to control it just makes good sense.

Seize the shade
Although it may be considered a drawback by some, a shady spot – or entire property – presents a vast number of exciting opportunities for creating beautiful garden compo-stions and restful havens.

Natives and non-natives

One way to increase the odds that your plants are well adapted to your conditions is to select plants native to your region. By incorporating indigenous species, your garden not only reflects its geography, but it will also help sustain native wildlife.

Be sure that the natural habitats of your plant choices are reflected in the conditions within your yard. If your yard is open and sunny, it may be ideal for meadow wildflowers or rock garden plants. If it is heavily shaded, woodland natives are more appropriate. Regional wildflower and native plant societies can assist you with identifying native species and finding responsible retail sources.

Never collect plants from the wild without permission. Rare plants – those that may be difficult to obtain, but are not necessarily endangered – are put at risk when collectors dig them and remove them from their natural habitat. Many plants can be obtained without exploiting natural populations. Many nurseries, native plant societies, and private growers propagate their own rare plants and offer plants or seed for sale or exchange. Also, permission is sometimes given to individual plant collectors or native plant societies to dig and remove native plants from construction sites before the area is graded or built upon. In this way, many stands of both rare and common natives have been saved from the bulldozer.

Worth copying
Many natural habitats are worth recreating in your garden, and some of the most popular are the wetlands: lakes, ponds, streams, bogs, wet prairies, and marshes. As with all habitats, it is important to know what constitutes a wetland and how it can be best and most easily maintained.

REGIONAL HABITATS WORTH EMULATING

Lady Bird Johnson Wildflower Trail, Callaway, Georgia
In addition to this wildflower trail, Callaway is noted for its collection of more than 700 azaleas, including many native species.

There are several habitats in the Southeast. The transition is usually quite gradual, but the range of plants growing in each one is distinctive. As population pressure consumes remaining natural areas, plant diversity is decreasing. With a little effort, gardeners can recreate elements of a particular region and help conserve the rarities.

Deciduous woodland
Once the major habitat of much of the Southeast, most areas have now been logged and many cleared as well. The remaining areas have a surprising range of plants, and any well-treed lot can easily be adapted to recreate this habitat.
Garden-friendly plants:

- Arrowwood Viburnum (*Viburnum dentatum*)
- Downy Serviceberry (*Amelanchier arborea*)
- Mountain Laurel (*Kalmia latifolia*)
- Silverbell (*Halesia carolina*)
- Summersweet (*Clethra alnifolia*)
- Bloodroot (*Sanguinaria canadensis*)
- Canadian Columbine (*Aquilegia canadensis*)
- False Solomon's Seal (*Smilacina racemosa*)
- Spring Beauty (*Claytonia virginica*)
- White Trillium (*Trillium grandiflorum*)
- Beautyberry (*Callicarpa americana*)
- Bottlebrush Buckeye (*Aesculus parviflora*)
- Oakleaf Hydrangea (*Hydrangea quercifolia*)
- Indian Pink (*Spigelia marilandica*)
- Blue Phlox (*Phlox divaricata*)

Examples of deciduous woodland found in:
Alabama – Birmingham Botanical Gardens
Virginia – Great Smoky Mountains National Park, Shenandoah National Park

Meadow
Where soils are hard or shallow, seasonally dry from little rainfall, or where trees and large shrubs have been removed by construction or forestry practices, the dominant habitat resembles that of the Midwestern prairies. Composed of grasses and perennial wildflowers, this is a popular garden subject, although not as labor-free as many think.
Garden-friendly plants:

- Little Bluestem Grass (*Schizachyrium scoparium*)
- Prairie Dropseed Grass (*Sporobolus heterolepis*)
- Switchgrass (*Panicum virgatum*)
- Black-eyed Susan (*Rudbeckia hirta*)
- Milkweed (*Asclepias syriaca*)
- New England Aster (*Aster novae-angliae*)
- New England Blazing Star (*Liatris borealis*)
- Purple Coneflower (*Echinacea purpurea*)
- Showy Goldenrod (*Solidago speciosa*)

Great Smoky Mountains National Park
Spanning the North Carolina–Tennessee border, this park is home to a wide variety of wildlife and plants. There are more than 800 miles of trails.

- Wild Bergamot (*Monarda fistulosa*)

Examples of meadow gardens found in:
Georgia – Callaway Gardens
North Carolina – North Carolina Botanical Garden

Wetland and Coastal
The many lakes, rivers, and bayous and the extensive coastline of the Southeast provide ample opportunity to discover this type of habitat. Given a wet soil, it is easier to grow moisture-loving plants than to install drainage.
Garden-friendly plants:

- Bald Cypress (*Taxodium distichum*)
- Black Gum (*Nyssa sylvatica*)
- Beach Plum (*Prunus maritima*)
- Buttonbush (*Cephalanthus occidentalis*)
- Virginia Sweetspire (*Itea virginica*)
- Winterberry (*Ilex verticillata*)
- Cardinal Flower (*Lobelia cardinalis*)
- Joe Pye Weed (*Eupatorium maculatum*)
- Swamp Milkweed (*Asclepias incarnata*)
- Sweet Bay (*Magnolia virginiana*)
- Dwarf Palmetto (*Sabal minor*)
- Sweet Shrub (*Calycanthus floridus*)
- Blue Flag (*Iris virginica*)

Examples of wetland and coastal gardens found in:
Louisiana – Briarwood
Mississippi – The Crosby Arboretum
South Carolina – Magnolia Plantation and Gardens

Magnolia Plantation and Gardens
The 500-acre site has a formal garden and large plant collections, especially azaleas and camellias, but is renowned for its use of mass sweeps of color.

Endangered and threatened plant species are those that the federal government has recognized as being in danger of extinction and are protected by law. The most common cause for this status is reduction or loss of the natural habitat of the species, but commercial collection of rare plants has also threatened their survival. Responsible propagation by native plant growers of species that are rare or at risk has increased considerably in recent years; this helps increase the population and the availability of these vanishing plants to consumers. You should always investigate commercial sources of rare plants to be sure they were nursery propagated and were not collected from the wild.

North American Native
Commonly called New York aster, *Aster novi-belgii* is native to much of eastern North America. Many attractive cultivars have been selected.

The term "native plant" is the source of some confusion. Plants have been introduced from one area to another throughout the history of mankind, and some plants have adapted so well to their new environments over such a long period of time that it is often hard to distinguish the natives from the introduced species. Some plant traffic between geographic areas predates human history, seeds having been conveyed by glacial movements, floods, prehistoric animals, or other means. The field of botanical archaeology has made interesting discoveries about prehistoric plant movement that continues to shed more light on natural plant history.

For the purpose of this book, a native species is one that, as far as can be determined historically, is indigenous – native – to the *state* or *region*. (More broadly, the issue is defining what is meant by the "region": is it a given continent, country, or state, or is it the area within 25 miles (40km) of your property?) An exotic species is one that has been introduced from outside the region. An invasive exotic is a species that has adapted so well to its new environment that it has escaped cultivation and is capable of overtaking the habitats of native plants, upsetting the balance of nature.

The nativity of species within a genus is often widespread. For example, the genus *Quercus* – the oaks – include species that are indigenous to various regions within North America, as well as Europe, the Middle East, Asia, and Northern Africa. Species of *Iris* hail from countries as widespread as China, Japan, Ukraine, Afghanistan, Turkey, Algeria, and the United States – from Alaska to the Mississippi Delta. Obviously, even though they are closely related, plants with such diverse native habitats have an equally wide range of cultural requirements. So although you can probably grow more than one species of oak or iris in your garden, there will be other members of those genera that require quite a different habitat.

Non-native plants from regions with similar climates and soils can add diversity to your landscape. To get ideas for plants that will grow well in your garden, observe plants that thrive in other nearby gardens, and ask your neighbors and staff at local public gardens as well. But take care to avoid those that are too well adapted. When these plants encroach upon your garden, diligent efforts are often necessary to limit their spread or eliminate them from your yard altogether.

Plants that are recognized as serious pests have been put on federal and state lists of noxious weeds. Legislation and regulation efforts to eradicate stands and control the spread of these pests is ongoing at federal, state, and local levels.

A large clan
Phlox divaricata is a favorite for inclusion in woodland gardens. All but one of the genus' 70 species hail from North America.

Truly superb
Lilium superbum, the American turkscap lily, graces wild and cultivated spots where there is moist, acidic soil in sun to part shade.

INVASIVE PLANTS

While the majority of the plants we grow are well behaved, a few can be thought of as garden thugs, willing and eager to choke out their neighbors and colonize large areas. Others have escaped from cultivation and are invading natural habitats and replacing the native flora, *Lythrum* (purple loosestrife) being a prime example of this. These are termed "invasive exotics," and their cultivation should be approached with caution. For example, the seeds of Mimosa (*Albizia julibrissen*) carry for a long distance. If you live in town, this tree is unlikely to spread into natural areas, but if your home is close to a woodland, consider growing something else that poses less of a threat to the natural balance of things.

Invasive exotic trees and shrubs include: *Albizia julibrissin* (Mimosa), *Sapium sebiferum* (Chinese tallow), *Ligustrum sinense* (Privet), *Lonicera* species (Bush honeysuckle), and, in Florida only, *Casuariana* species (Australian pine). **Climbers** of concern include: *Hedera helix* (English ivy), *Lonicera sempervirens* (Japanese honeysuckle), *Lygodium japonicum* (Climbing fern), *Pueraria lobata* (Kudzu), *Rosa multiflora* (Multiflora rose), and *Wisteria floribunda* and *W. sinensis* (Japanese and Chinese wisteria). **Perennials** of note include: *Colocasia esculenta* (Taro), *Fallopia cuspidatum* (Japanese knotweed), and *Phyllostachys* species (bamboo).

Multiplication and division

Many garden plants reseed themselves. This natural process can work to your benefit – providing new plants for next year's garden and for giving to or exhanging with other gardeners – or it can create unnecessary weeding. Before selecting a plant and placing it in a bed, determine whether and how prolifically it self-sows.

Some biennials – plants that complete their life cycle over the course of two growing seasons – can become permanent features in your garden through the process of self-sowing. The flowers of woodland forget-me-not (*Myosotis sylvatica*), honesty (*Lunaria annua*), and several foxgloves (*Digitalis* spp.) produce seed that germinates and grows vegetatively the first season and develops flowers the next. With such plants, it is important to recognize the nonflowering plant so that it can be left to grow – and not inadvertently weeded – to bloom the following year.

A number of annuals and perennials also self-sow. Some are such prolific seed producers that weeding the seedlings becomes a chore. If this is the case, deadheading the spent blooms before they have a chance to form and disperse their seed will reduce or eliminate the problem. If there is already a problem, diligent weeding should remedy this.

Quite a few of the garden flowers that are sold in nurseries or by seed companies are hybrids – varieties produced by controlled crosses of specific parent lines – so their seedlings often do not resemble the parent plant in some important aspects. Be aware that your seedlings may be shorter, taller, less disease resistant, or a different flower or leaf color (sometimes amazingly unattractively so) than their parent. Open-pollinated varieties, on the other hand, generally produce seed that is "true to type." Seed of such flowers or vegetables can be collected from these plants for growing the following year with some confidence about their inherited characteristics.

Herbaceous perennials that thrive in your garden may require dividing every few years. Take advantage of this natural increase to acquire more plants. For most perennials that bloom in spring, summer or fall division is recommended. Summer or fall bloomers are usually divided in spring.

Although the procedure varies somewhat with specific plants, division generally involves digging the entire clump, cutting it into smaller sections, discarding old, worn-out portions, replanting the vigorous divisions, and watering them thoroughly.

Composting wastes

One way you can work with nature to improve your soil is to build a compost pile or bin. Here, kitchen and garden wastes of many kinds can be converted into a nutrient-rich soil amendment. It takes several weeks to months for raw organic matter to become thoroughly decomposed and garden-ready in an active compost pile. There are a variety of factors that influence the rate of decomposition; the most important being the initial size of the organic matter, moisture in the pile or bin, temperature of both the surrounding air and the compost itself, air circulation

Composting bin
A simple cage constructed from lumber and chicken wire can hold garden refuse and other materials as it breaks down into compost.

within the pile, and the progressive status of the carbon:nitrogen ratio as the materials break down. Organic matter that has been shredded decomposes faster than if it has been left whole, because there is more surface area exposed. Decomposition rates are higher when conditions are warm and damp than when they are cold and dry. Air circulation increases the rate of composting, because the organisms responsible for decomposition need sufficient air to do their job. (For more on the carbon:nitrogen ratio, *see* p. 31.)

However, other than occasional turning, and a bit of added moisture when it's very dry, nature – in the form of industrious micro- and macroorganisms – does most of the work for you.

COMPOST BINS AND TOOLS

A number of useful products are available to help you produce your own compost. Compost bins can be constructed out of wood, heavy-gauge wire fencing, cinder blocks, or other common materials. They can also be purchased ready-made. Designs range from simple bins to more elaborate constructions that feature cone-shaped tubs, interlocking layered shelves, and twist-top ventilation systems. Some designs feature tumblers or drums that rotate to facilitate mixing. Mixing or stirring an open compost pile can be done with a garden fork or a compost aerator, a tool specifically designed for the purpose, composed of a shaft with handles or a bar at one end for holding, and short paddles on the other end that are inserted into the pile, then turned and lifted. Vermicomposting is a system using redworms, night crawlers, or earthworms in an enclosed container to break down organic matter such as grass clippings and kitchen wastes. The worm castings that are shed are a rich source of nutrients.

In an undisturbed woodland environment, the seasonal accumulation of leaves on the forest floor is part of a natural recycling process. As the leaves are decomposed by soil organisms, a steady supply of nutrients is released. In an effort to keep a garden neat, this cycle is often interrupted; leaves are raked and removed. The nutrients can be restored, however, and the neatness maintained, if the raked leaves are composted and the finished compost returned to the garden. Once the compost is ready, it can be incorporated into the soil or applied as a topdressing or mulch (*see* pp. 47–49). It is also a useful addition to a soil mix for raised beds and containers. In an active compost pile, most weed seeds are killed by the heat generated during the decomposition process, but a few may survive and are usually easily removed.

By composting your kitchen and garden wastes, you are working in tandem with nature to improve the growing conditions for your plants while simultaneously reducing your contribution of solid waste to local landfills.

Prettier and stronger
A more sturdily constructed compost bin (which is easy to build) is more attractive and holds up longer than a simple cage (opposite). It should last for several years.

The view inside
Removing the front panel reveals the correct method of layering different materials, alternating "soft" (grass clippings and weeds) with "hard" (twigs and dead leaves) to speed decomposition.

General household waste
Plant remains are OK, but avoid including meat scraps and bones, which attract vermin.

Old straw
Make sure your compost pile heats up to destroy seeds contained in straw.

Weeds
As with straw above, a properly constructed and managed hot pile kills most weed seeds.

Hedge clippings
The smaller, thinner, and softer the clippings, the faster they will break down.

Bring it on
Good compost is best made from a wide variety of materials. Included on this page are just a few possibilities, including the spent bedding plants at left.

Aiding natural selection

Cleaning up a garden at the end of a growing season will improve its appearance through winter and, more importantly, contribute to its health the next season. This often involves a bit of "editing" – removing plants, plant parts, or pests.

- Branches of trees and shrubs that are damaged beyond repair should be removed with clean cuts. Stems displaying disease symptoms such as cankers or sunken lesions are usually best removed in order to prevent the further spread of disease.
- Minimize next year's insect pests by removing and disposing of obvious signs of infestation such as the "bags" of bagworms and the nests of fall webworms.
- Remove weeds before they go to seed.
- Rake leaves to avoid matting that may suffocate lawn or groundcovers; compost both weeds and leaves (but remember: no pest- or disease-infested material onto the pile; this material is best discarded along with your household trash).
- After they have died naturally or succumbed to frost, cut annuals at ground level, leaving the roots to break down in the soil; this is a particularly good practice where erosion is a problem. Or remove the plants, roots and all, then compost everything.
- Clean structures and stakes you plan to reuse. Those that cannot withstand winter weather should be removed, cleaned, and stored until conditions are suitable again in spring.
- Perennial plants that die back in fall can be cut to the ground unless they contribute to your winter landscape or provide food or cover for desirable wildlife.

Eliminating flowered stalks
Removing flowered stalks of herbaceous plants improves their appearance and may also stimulate further flowering.

Reducing stress

Just like humans, garden plants look and perform better if their level of stress is reduced.

Transplanting can be traumatic for plants and may lead to a condition known as "transplant shock." To avoid this, allow seedlings grown indoors to acclimate to their new environment gradually (called "hardening off"). Place them in a protected spot outdoors for a few days before transplanting them. Transplant on a still, overcast day, and drench soil balls with a high-phosphorus liquid fertilizer to stimulate root growth.

During dry weather, wind can cause serious damage by increasing a plant's transpiration (moisture loss) rate. When moisture lost through leaves exceeds the rate at which it is replaced by roots, leaves appear scorched or may drop off. This can happen during cold weather as well, when soil water is frozen and little is available to plants. Siting a garden where plants are sheltered from prevailing winds can prevent such damage, or wind-tolerant plants can be grown as wind breaks to protect nearby plants.

Rapid fluctuations in soil temperature in winter can damage roots. This problem can be avoided by watering and mulching thoroughly in fall. The temperature fluctuates less rapidly in moist soil than in dry soil. In warm climates, mulching and watering provide similar protection, particularly during hot, dry periods when soil absorbs radiant heat during the day. Watering during dry periods and shading the soil with mulch reduce heat and moisture stress that lead to injury.

Safe haven
Hardening off under some sort of cover enables plants to make a safe transition from their early life indoors to growing in the open ground and in the face of the elements.

MANAGE PESTS FOR A HEALTHY GARDEN

Integrated pest management (IPM) is a sustainable and environmentally sensitive approach to garden disease and pest problems. IPM was initially developed for commercial growers as a means of merging all available information regarding a crop and its documented or potentially troublesome pests and diseases into a comprehensive plan of action to maximize production and quality and to minimize environmental risks. IPM has been adapted as a useful tool for home gardeners and is a perfect fit with the SMARTGARDEN™ philosophy: to follow nature's leads and to harness her forces to work on your behalf.

Keeping the proper perspective

IPM is a multistep process. It includes taking steps to prevent problems or to reduce their severity, identifying and monitoring problems that do arise (using physical and natural control measures first), and, if necessary, applying the least toxic pesticide at the proper rate and at the proper time. When dealing with garden diseases and pests, it is important to keep in mind that a certain amount of damage is tolerable. Trying to maintain every leaf and flower in perfect condition is impossible. Accepting a level of tolerable imperfection does not mean ignoring damage when it occurs. The SMARTGARDEN™ approach is to assess the damage, identify the cause, estimate the potential for further damage, and, depending on that assessment, continue to monitor the problem and adjust cultural practices to reduce its spread, or proceed with a specific control measure. The key is to strive for balance rather than perfection.

An ounce of prevention

One of the best methods for dealing with plant problems is to prevent them from occurring. Healthy, well-adapted plants are less likely to be seriously damaged by the diseases or pests that invade the garden. They can withstand an infection (from diseases) or infestation (from insects or other animals) better than a plant that is struggling from the stress of neglect or placement in an inappropriate site.

How much is too much?
Gardeners who practice IPM know when the level of damage from a pest's activities has reached an unacceptable level.

Allies
Ladybird beetles (also widely called ladybugs) and a host of other insects and creatures can be recruited in the battle against plant pests.

How many should be tolerated?
This colorful caterpillar is the larva of the beautiful black swallowtail butterfly. A few will not cause much damage, but large numbers would pose a threat. It's up to you whether to reduce or eliminate them or leave them alone.

RESISTANT VARIETIES

Most plant diseases and many pests are quite specific for the host plants that they infect or infest. A disease that infects your lawn most likely will do no damage to your trees or shrubs. An insect that bores into pine trees will probably leave your other woody and herbaceous plants alone.

Susceptibility to diseases and pests varies from one variety of plant to another. Breeders have used this phenomenon to impart disease- and pest-tolerance and resistance to an ever-increasing number of new varieties of our garden plants.

Select varieties that are resistant to the pests and diseases in your area. For example, some tomato varieties are resistant to several fungal wilts, viral diseases, and certain nematodes that can devastate a susceptible variety. By selecting varieties of hosta with thicker, more substantial leaves, slug damage is often avoided or at least lessened.

SANITATION

Removal and disposal of disease-infected or pest-infested plants and plant remains from the garden is an important cultural tool that should be incorporated into your gardening efforts throughout the growing season. It should also be a designated part of your annual cleanup activities. Remember: although the heat generated by a well-managed compost pile is sufficient to kill pests and most disease-causing organisms, seriously diseased plants are best kept out of the compost pile, just as a precaution.

Many pests and disease-causing organisms overwinter in or on the remains of their former host, and if left in the garden will be ready and waiting to cause problems come spring. When practical, remove the source before the pest or disease has a chance to spread. Also, before you introduce any new plant into your garden, inspect it for pests and the symptoms of disease.

OTHER PREVENTION TECHNIQUES

Other cultural methods for preventing pest and disease problems include mulching to create a physical barrier between soil-borne spores and potential hosts, using physical barriers such as netting or row covers to exclude egg-laying female insects, planting to ensure adequate air circulation between plants, planting early or late to avoid a pest or disease at a predictable time each year, and removal of garden plants or weeds that may serve as alternative hosts to disease organisms or pests.

Resistance or something else?
The hosta shown above is free of slug damage, while the one to the right has obviously been severely attacked. The difference between the two could be the result of thicker, tougher leaves than are common to many hostas, or it could be due to the the gardener's efforts.

PEST-RESISTANT PLANTS

Some plants show a natural resistance to pests or diseases. Remember that resistance does not mean that the plants will not be attacked, just that they are not as susceptible to damage as others.

Birch: 'Heritage' river birch.
Crabapples: 'Adams', 'Beauty', 'Centennial', 'Centurion', 'Harvest Gold', 'Molten Lava', 'Prairiefire', 'Professor Springer', 'Red Snow', 'Sea Foam', and 'Sugar Tyme'.
Dogwoods: Hybrids between the flowering and kousa dogwoods, such as 'Appalachian Spring'.
Elms: New hybrids such as 'Homestead', 'Jacan', and 'Pioneer'.
Honeysuckle: 'Freedom'.
London plane tree: 'Bloodgood', 'Columbia', and 'Liberty'.
Roses: Many shrub roses, especially Tea, China, and Polyantha cultivars (e.g., 'The Fairy' and 'Mutabilis').
Viburnums: Modern hybrids such as 'Mohawk' and 'Cayuga'.
Bee balm: 'Aquarius' and 'Squaw'.
Phlox: Cultivars of *Phlox maculata* are more mildew resistant than those of *P. paniculata* and look very similar.

CROP ROTATION

Rearranging (rotating) the placement of plants from one season to the next is a valuable means of outwitting pests and diseases in vegetable gardens and annual beds. Most diseases and many insects are rather specific in their selection of host plants, and many survive the winter as eggs or spores in the soil around the plant that was the pest's host during the previous growing season. Replanting the same crop in the same space increases the probability of reinfection. Make it more difficult for the pest or disease: move your beans to the other side of the garden, and plant marigolds where you had China asters last year. This simple avoidance technique can significantly reduce recurring problems.

ROTATION OF VEGETABLE CROPS
Vegetables are divided into four groups: legumes and pod crops; alliums; brassicas; and solanaceous, root, and tuberous crops. Sweet corn and summer and winter squash do not fit into the major groups, but they still should be rotated. If you are growing only a small amount of these, it may be possible to include them in one of the groups (such as alliums). Otherwise, treat them as a separate group and rotate everything on a five-year basis.

Diagnosing and assessing damage

If you are unfamiliar with the plant problem confronting you, take a Sherlock Holmes approach: use all available clues and resources to pin down the culprit. Numerous books and publications are available to assist your diagnosis. Furthermore, local Cooperative Extension offices, botanical gardens, nurseries, and plant societies maintain diagnostic clinics and horticultural hotlines. Many of these can be conveniently contacted on the Internet (*see* Appendix, *p. 387* for regional resources).

You may have an expert horticulturist to whom you can turn with any plant problems. But no matter whom you ask, the prognosis will be based on the information that you provide. The more detailed observations you make, the more accurate the advice you will receive. Whenever possible, you should provide one or more specimens of the plant that demonstrate progressive symptoms for the expert to examine. Each specimen should be more than just a single leaf; it is helpful and sometimes necessary to see more than one leaf attached to a bit of stem to identify the plant as well as the problem.

Once you identify the specific cause of your problem, the next step is to learn more about the disease or pest and determine how much damage is likely to occur and whether and what type of control measures are warranted.

NOTING DAMAGE

- When did you first notice the damage?
- What are the symptoms? Examine all parts of the plant and be as precise as possible.
- Are the symptoms on more than one plant or kind of plant?
- How rapidly do the symptoms progress?
- How long has the plant been growing in its current location?
- Which kinds of treatment (for example, fertilizer, insecticide, herbicide, mulching) have been applied to the plant or to surrounding areas recently?
- Have you ever noticed this problem before? If so, is it different this time?
- Has there been any change in soil grade in the area surrounding the plants?
- Has there been any other change in the area surrounding the plant?

Know your enemy

Familiarizing yourself with the most common pests and diseases of the plants you grow is a major step to outwitting them. By knowing their appearance, life cycle, feeding and overwintering habits, potential hosts, and natural predators, you can work with nature to tilt the balance in favor of your garden plants.

For example, fireblight is a bacterial disease that infests apples, pears, pyracantha, hawthorn, quince, and several other ornamental plants, typically causing sudden twig dieback. Serious damage can often be avoided by limiting the use of nitrogen fertilizer on susceptible plants, since succulent new growth, which is stimulated by nitrogen, is most prone to infection. If the disease does cause dieback, pruning out and destroying infected stems will generally stop (or at least slow down) the spread of the disease before it causes serious damage. Left untreated, the infection may move into older wood, where it forms cankers in which the bacteria overwinter. More extensive removal of branches displaying such cankers may be required at this point.

Knowledge of the life cycle of a pest or disease-causing organism enables the gardener to apply countermeasures at the time when they will be most effective. For instance, parasitic nematodes effectively control several

A ROGUE'S GALLERY

INSECTS

Aphids: Small and generally on the growing tips or underside of leaves. Attack a wide range of plants, sucking sap and covering foliage with a sticky deposit.

Caterpillars: The young stage of butterflies and moths (such as gypsy moths) feed on leaves and shoots.

Mites: Tiny, red or yellowish, and live mostly on the underside of leaves and spin fine webs between stems. They cause tiny pale spots.

Slugs and snails: Feed on foliage and small plants, mostly at night. Slime trails make their presence easy to detect.

Bugs and beetles: A varied group of hard-bodied insects that feed mostly by chewing holes in leaves and stems

Grubs: The larvae of several beetles (and other insects) that live in soil and eat roots or suck sap.

Miners: Small larvae that tunnel inside a leaf leaving opaque areas or mines.

DISEASES

Anthracnose: Fungi that attack a wide range of plants, targeting foliage and fruit.

Mildews: Occur on many plants and are especially destructive during hot, humid weather and on dry soil.

Leaf spots: Caused by many different fungi, they occur on a wide range of plants. They start as small pale areas and spread, often coalescing to cover almost the entire leaf.

Blights: Shoots or branches wilt, growth stops, and the affected part dies. In fruit, development ceases and the fruit gradually withers.

Catch it in time
Diseases such as rusts (above), if caught early in their development, may be controlled by nonchemical means. Severe cases, however, may need chemicals for total control.

lawn pests, including Japanese beetle grubs. But they must be applied when the target pest is active; the nematodes persist for only about two weeks. By knowing that the grubs become active as the soil warms in spring, the nematodes can be applied when the grubs begin to feed.

PHYSICAL CONTROLS

Many pests and diseases can be controlled by physical means. For example, handpicking the pest or pruning diseased stems or branches is sufficient in many cases to prevent further spread. Brute force is sometimes effective: a hard spray of water can knock down a population of aphids or mites to a tolerable level. Colorado potato beetles and tomato hornworms can often be eliminated by hand – the pests are simply picked off the host plant and destroyed. This method is effective, however, only when the gardener is vigilant (and prepared for gore!).

Barriers can also prevent pest damage: a cardboard collar around young vegetable seedlings checks their destruction by cutworms. Tree wraps – sticky bands of material that are placed around the trunk of a tree – prevent the larvae of gypsy moths and similar leaf-eating caterpillars from reaching the tree's susceptible foliage. Tubular plastic cages and wraps placed around young trees protect their bark from the gnawing of mice or rabbits. Floating row covers made of a thin, light, and water-permeable fabric can block many flying pests from infesting vegetable plants. Birds can be thwarted from eating your cherries or blueberries by covering the trees or shrubs with a protective net before the fruit ripens.

When pesticides are necessary

The goal when using a pesticide is to achieve control with the minimum impact on the rest of the environment. Applying the right material at the wrong time, to the wrong plant, or at the wrong dilution can negate its effect or, even worse, cause more damage than the pest itself. Whenever you decide to use a pesticide, it is critical to follow all label instructions for safety.

DIRECTIONS FOR HANDLING

- Eliminate or minimize human, pet, and nontarget plant exposure to the pesticide. This is particularly important when dealing with concentrated formulations.
- Wear protective clothing, and wash it after use, separately from other laundry.
- Wash equipment used for measuring, mixing, and applying the pesticide, and store in a secure, designated location.
- Wash down or flush any hardscaped or soil areas that were exposed to pesticides or where pesticides may have been inadvertently spilled.
- Store pesticides in a safe, secure (preferably locked) location – out of the reach of children and pets – in their original containers and according to the label instructions.
- Thoroughly wash your hands and face – or better, shower – after applying pesticides.
- Dispose of unused pesticides and empty pesticide containers according to the label instructions.
- Keep a record of the application; include date, material applied, and plants treated.

Population explosion
Whiteflies are a widespread insect pest of both indoor and outdoor plants. Their populations can build up to large numbers quickly, and their sugary secretions support the growth of black sooty molds. As with most plant problems, early detection and diligent inspection will help keep them at bay.

Many synthetic chemical pesticides formerly available have been banned for environmental and safety reasons. A variety of environmentally friendly, nonchemical pest control alternatives have been developed, many derived from plants or minerals. These pesticides generally break down quickly into safe byproducts and thus are good choices for the pests they control. Like any pesticide, they may be toxic to humans or other nontarget animals and should be applied with care according to the manufacturer's instructions.

Types of pesticides

Pesticides work by direct contact, ingestion, or making the plant distasteful to pests. Some pests and diseases are susceptible just during one phase of their life cycle. Therefore, timing may be critical to achieving an acceptable level of control.

Contact pesticides require direct contact with an external part of the pest for effective control. They must be applied where the pest is or will be present. If a pest feeds on the underside of leaves, the pesticide should be applied to the leaf undersides. If only the upper surface of the leaf is sprayed, the pesticide may have little or no effect.

Other pesticides work only after ingestion – they must be consumed by the pest. Leaf-eating caterpillars and beetles are often controlled by an ingested pesticide that is applied to the foliage of the host plant. Many biological controls such as Bt (bacteria that control specific leaf and root eating pests) must also be ingested by the pest to be effective (*see* Beneficial microbes, *p. 69*).

Systemic pesticides are absorbed and carried within a plant. Sprayed on the foliage or applied to the soil, they are taken in by the plant and kill the pest when it feeds on plant tissues.

Repellents do not kill the pest but instead prevent it from harming the host plant by making it less appealing. Hot pepper sprays and predator urine are examples of repellents designed to keep animals from devouring garden plants. These generally require frequent application.

THE WAY CHEMICALS WORK

Different problems require chemicals to be applied in different ways. A combination of application methods may be needed to achieve a satisfactory level of control.

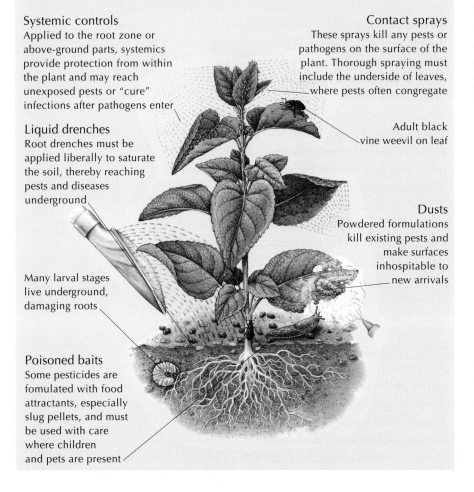

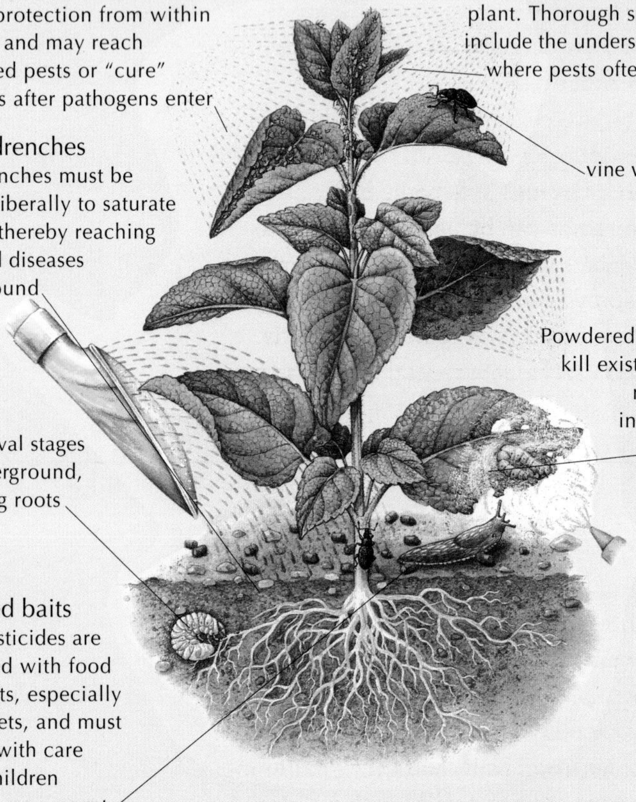

Systemic controls
Applied to the root zone or above-ground parts, systemics provide protection from within the plant and may reach unexposed pests or "cure" infections after pathogens enter
Contact sprays
These sprays kill any pests or pathogens on the surface of the plant. Thorough spraying must include the underside of leaves, where pests often congregate
Adult black vine weevil on leaf
Liquid drenches
Root drenches must be applied liberally to saturate the soil, thereby reaching pests and diseases underground
Dusts
Powdered formulations kill existing pests and make surfaces inhospitable to new arrivals
Many larval stages live underground, damaging roots
Poisoned baits
Some pesticides are fomulated with food attractants, especially slug pellets, and must be used with care where children and pets are present

Chemical pesticide formulations

Some pesticides can be applied directly, while others require diluting prior to application. Be sure always to dilute concentrated pesticides to the correct strength for the pest you are trying to control, and the host to which it is applied. Most pesticides are available in one or more of the formulations detailed below:

- Aerosols are ready-to-use sprays – usually contact poisons – that are under pressure. The pesticide is emitted as a fine mist.
- Dusts are finely ground pesticides combined with a fine inert powder that acts as a carrier. These are generally ready to apply from the bag.
- Granular formulations are similar to dusts, but the carrier is a larger particle, usually an inert clay. This formulation is most commonly used for pesticides that are applied to the soil.
- Wettable powders are water-soluble pesticides that are usually combined with a wetting agent to make mixing easier. They are mixed with water prior to application. They are usually applied as a spray but may be watered into soil when appropriate.
- Liquid concentrates are similar to wettable powders except that the concentrated pesticide is in liquid form.

Chemical pesticide alternatives

There are many alternatives to chemical pesticides that are available for combating garden pests and diseases, and many are just as effective as stronger chemical pesticides if they are used correctly.

BOTANICAL INSECTICIDES

Certain compounds extracted from plants are effective in controlling a variety of pests. Some of the more commonly available are:

- pyrethrum: an effective, broad-spectrum contact poison
- rotenone: commonly applied as a dust for short-term control of many leaf-eating caterpillars and beetles
- sabadilla: both a contact and stomach poison, effective against many true bugs, leaf-eating caterpillars, and thrips
- neem: repels some pests and interrupts the life cycle of many plant-eating caterpillars and beetles after ingestion.

Keep in mind that just because a pesticide is classed as a botanical, it may still be very toxic; rotenone in particular is very toxic to fish. Like any other pesticide, these must be used with extreme care, and always read the label.

INSECTICIDAL SOAPS

Derived from fatty acids and potassium salts, insecticidal soaps are applied as a dilute spray. They damage cell membranes of soft-bodied pests such as aphids, leafhoppers, whiteflies, and spider mites, and make them slip off the plant. In order to be effective, insecticidal soaps must come into direct contact with the pest. Some particularly sensitive plants can be damaged by insecticidal soaps; check the manufacturer's instructions and, if you are unsure, test the product on a small part of the plant first.

HORTICULTURAL OILS

These are refined petroleum products that are commonly used on dormant plants to smother overwintering insects and mites. Formulations called summer-weight oils can be applied to many plants during the growing season for controlling scales, whiteflies, and certain diseases. However, some plants are susceptible to damage by oils so, as with all pesticides, you should read all of the instructions carefully.

Vegetable oils, derived from agricultural crops, may also be used to control pests such as aphids, spider mites, whiteflies, thrips, and scales. They should not be used on begonias, fuchsias, or seedlings because they can damage the leaves.

Double protection
Rotenone (also called derris) has been applied to this plant to protect the leaves, and the square collar at the base protects the stem.

MINED MATERIALS

Another component of the arsenal of pest control weapons is material that is mined from the earth. Sprinkling diatomaceous earth – fossilized single-celled aquatic organisms – around plants provides a physical barrier against soft-bodied slugs and snails. Copper strips can be used as barriers to prevent damage by slugs and snails. Copper- and sulfur-based sprays and dusts can control fungal diseases such as powdery mildew and botrytis. These products can be detrimental to predatory mites, however, and should not be sprayed on young apples. Furthermore, the buildup of copper in the soil may be harmful to worms and, as it runs off into neighboring waterways, will affect fish.

Nature's pest control

Another method of thwarting garden pests is to enlist their natural enemies to work for you. Insects, nematodes, mites, microbes, and other organisms that feed upon or infect a plant pest are known as biological controls, and they are among the most effective ways of dealing with troublemakers in your garden. Beneficial organisms are fairly specific with respect to creatures they infect or consume, and they pose minimal danger to humans and other nontarget animals.

Some of the organisms that gardeners often lump together under the term "insects" are more correctly known simply as arthropods. Technically, true insects – such as ants, grasshoppers, butterflies, and beetles – are distinguished from other groups of common garden arthropods such as arachnids (spiders and mites) and crustaceans (pillbugs and sowbugs). Most of these creatures are neutral when it comes to their effect on garden plants; that is, they neither harm nor benefit them. They may, however, be a food source for birds, bats, or other wildlife, or they may help decompose organic matter. So in a sense, even though they do not directly help or harm plants, arthropods help maintain a well-balanced environment. Many arthropods benefit garden plants by hunting and eating other insects and mites that feed on plants. Others parasitize pests, often by laying their eggs inside the body of the pest, where they eventually hatch and consume their host; then the emerging female adults complete the cycle by laying eggs in new hosts. Predatory mites often consume plant-feeding spider mites. Many spiders build webs and feed on whatever prey wanders in and gets stuck. Others, such as wolf, jumping, and crab spiders, actively seek their prey on plants or on the ground. Among the pests they help control are aphids, leafhoppers, and numerous beetles and caterpillars. Avoid spraying pesticides when these garden-friendly creatures are present.

Sowbugs may occasionally be a problem, however, because they are sometimes attracted in large numbers to seedlings, feeding on them at ground level. If necessary, a colony of sowbugs can be destroyed by pouring boiling water on them.

COMMON PARASITES AND PREDATORS

Ground beetles: These black beetles are often seen running away from an overturned piece of wood. They feed on many pests that live in or near the soil surface, such as cutworms, root maggots, and slugs and snails. Some species climb and help control Colorado beetles and tent caterpillars.

Hover flies: Looking like tiny wasps, these dart about like hummingbirds and feed on aphids.

On patrol
A ground beetle actively searches for many kinds of garden pests to eat.

Lacewings: Seen mostly in early evening, these feed on aphids, small larvae, mites, thrips, and scale insects.

Ladybird beetles (ladybugs): Both the well-known adult and the larvae devour aphids and other plant feeders. They are fairly specific on food choice, so buying them and releasing them in your garden may not work. A recently introduced species from Asia should be viewed with mixed feelings: while it eats aphids, it also gives people a painful sting.

Parasitic wasps: Varying in size from very small to rather large, these wasps lay their eggs in the bodies of host insects. The larvae then feed on the host and kill it. They may look frightening, but they do not sting people.

Spined soldier bug: One of the stink bugs, with a wide, flat shape, this has pronounced horns on either side of the shell. It feeds on many harmful caterpillars, sawfly larvae, and Colorado beetle larvae.

Tachinid flies: Similar in looks to house flies, these lay their eggs on many pests, including cutworms, army worms, gypsy moth larvae, and tent caterpillars. The resulting larvae feed on the host and pupate on the corpse.

Centipedes: Not an insect but a good scavenger that feeds on a wide variety of soil-living pests, including millipedes and wireworms.

Lone hunter
A solitary wasp has captured an insect to take back to its nest for its young.

Attracting beneficial organisms

You can encourage predators and parasites of plant pests to inhabit your garden. Beneficial organisms can be purchased from distributors of natural pest controls. Make sure that when you release beneficial insects, there are pests for them to feed on; otherwise, they will seek another garden with a more tempting menu. Another potential problem is that some predaceous insects, such as the praying mantis, will feed on beneficial insects as well as your pests.

Either attracting or releasing beneficial insects into your garden will not give you instant results – your pests may be around for several days – but once the predators or parasites arrive, they will work to control the pest until the pest population is depleted. Do not apply any insecticides to your garden while your beneficials are doing their job or you may eliminate them.

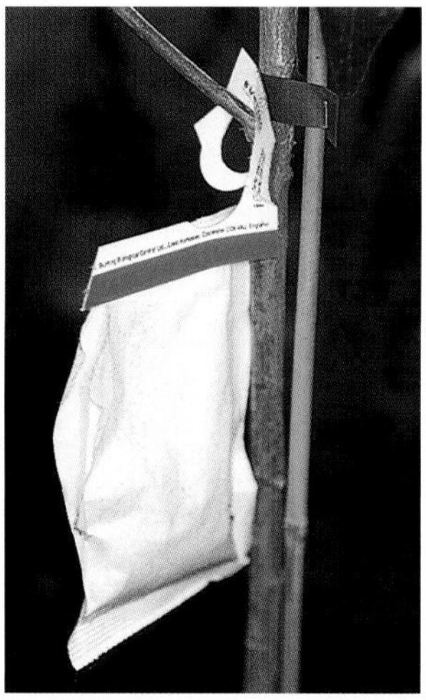

On target
Place containers of beneficial organisms on or near the plants you want to protect.

Beneficial nematodes

Some nematodes – microscopic, eel-like roundworms – are plant pests, but others are beneficial, residing in soils and infecting and reproducing in garden pests that spend part of their life cycle in the soil. Beneficial nematodes are effective for managing black vine weevil larvae, white grubs, and Japanese beetle grubs, among others. The nematodes penetrate a host insect through natural body openings, multiply within the host's body, and release bacteria that multiply and kill the pest.

Native populations of beneficial nematodes are generally too low to provide effective pest control. However, beneficial nematodes can be purchased and applied to your lawns and gardens. Timing of the application is critical, and as with all pest-control products, it is important that you follow all of the label directions carefully. When correctly applied, beneficial nematodes not only provide excellent control of the target pest but are extremely safe to humans and other nontarget animals because they can only inhabit particular hosts, for example, the vine weevil.

Beneficial microbes

Some microbial organisms can be recruited to control pests. *Bacillus thuringiensis* (Bt) is a bacterium available in several different varieties, each of which is effective against specific pests. The bacterium produces a protein that is toxic to a variety of insects, causing paralysis of their mouthparts or gut. Bt var. *kurstaki* (Btk) controls several destructive caterpillars, such as cabbage caterpillars, cabbage loopers, gypsy moth, tomato hornworm, and codling moths, as well as corn borers. Other strains, Btt and Bt var. san diego, provide control of leaf-eating beetles such as the Colorado potato beetle. It is important to select the appropriate variety of the bacterium for the pest at hand. Bt degrades in sunlight and, consequently, it must be reapplied in order to remain effective.

A related species, *B. popilliae*, controls Japanese beetles by infecting the grubs – the soil-borne larval stage – with a disease known as milky spore. The bacteria reproduce in the host and remain in the soil when the host dies, providing a long-term source for infection of other grubs.

Attracting predators
Even a small bit of wildflower meadow will attract large numbers of beneficial predatory and parasitic organisms into your garden.

8

KEEP A GARDEN JOURNAL

The more you know about your site, your plants, and potential problems you may encounter, the more success you will experience in gardening. Although numerous resources are available to guide your gardening endeavors, the most important is your own experience. Keeping records is among the most valuable gardening activities you can perform. Both your successes and failures provide lessons that will make you a better gardener.

A garden diary

Interrupting your planting or weeding efforts to jot down notes in a diary might seem like a nuisance at the time, but it will help you plan your garden efforts this season and for years to come. Record the names of those plants that have performed famously as well as those you'd rather forget – and be sure to indicate which is which! The moments you take to note your observations will save you time in the long run. When you repeat a mistake because you forgot a previous failure, not only is it a waste of time and effort, but it may result in the loss of an entire growing season or even longer.

A gardening diary is a simple way to keep track of what is happening in your yard. Some allow for multiple years' entries on the same page. Typically, one page is allotted to every week of the year, and it is divided to accommodate four or five years' worth of records. This allows you to look back to see what was going on in the garden at the same time in previous seasons. However, less elaborate systems can work just as well. A simple notebook or a calendar with enough room for your entries can accommodate any important details. The critical aspect of a garden diary is not what it looks like, but that you write in it. Regularly.

While garden notes needn't be lengthy, a few items are very important to include. Be sure to record the full name, including cultivar or variety, of any plant you acquire. Note the planting date and the plant's location in the yard. Then, when it's time to replant your strawberries and you want the same (or a different) variety than you planted half a dozen years ago (was it 'Surecrop' or 'Tristar'?), it is just a matter of checking your records. When you order vegetable and annual flower seeds, you can sit down with your notes, ordering those varieties you considered successful in the past and avoiding those that were disappointing. Having a record of where you purchased a given plant is sometimes helpful, especially for those hard-to-find varieties.

Diagrams of planting plans are also helpful. A sketch of your vegetable garden will assist planning future crop rotation schedules. A bed layout will remind you of the location of bulbs, ephemeral perennials (plants that complete their annual growth cycle in a very short time), or perennials that emerge late in the season, avoiding accidental damage when you are working in your garden before or after these plants are visible.

Making notes
Recording garden observations as you make them will produce a valuable record for the future. It can be as simple or as literary as you wish.

The four seasons
Many experienced gardeners strive to have something of interest in their gardens throughout the year. Noting when plants bloom or show other interesting features will be useful as you plan color combinations or theme gardens for a particular season. Clockwise from top left: *Narcissus* 'February Gold' in winter, *Crocosmia* 'Lucifer' in summer, *Baptisia australis* in spring, and *Acer rubrum* 'October Glory' in autumn.

The march of time
Photographs, especially if taken at regular intervals, document the progression of a garden (or even a single plant) from the time of its establishment to mature beauty.

Information to include

Your records should include as much of the following information as possible about your plants and their basic and specialized care:

• Source: where you obtained the plant (nursery, friend, local plant sale)
• Provenance: the plant's place of origin (where it was previously grown)
• Date acquired
• Size and condition
• Special characteristics that set the plant apart
• Exact planting location
• Dates of application of fertilizer and pesticides
• Notes on propagation where applicable
• Pruning schedule
• Additional care required

• Flowering and fruiting times. Observations about plant growth are helpful as you plan additions. Perhaps you want a shrub that blooms at the same time as those in an existing planting, or a raspberry that ripens after your blackberries. Keeping track of planting and harvesting dates in the vegetable garden helps you plan for an extended harvest.
• Diseases, pests, cultural problems. Many pests can be avoided by planting earlier or later than the pest's arrival to the garden (doing this is especially useful in vegetable gardening). This necessitates, however, knowing when to expect the unwanted visitor. Because these dates vary even within a region, the best source of this information is your own garden records. The onset of a disease or pest infestation is equally important to note on ornamental plants so that you can be prepared to minimize damage.

On screen
Suitable computer software can be an invaluable aid in keeping track of the comings and goings (and successes and failures) of your garden plants over the years.

Planting Record.XLS

	A	B	C	D	E	F	G	H	I	J
1	PLANT NAME	SOURCE	DATE PLANTED	PLANTING LOCATION(S)	NOTES					
2	Dalea greggii x 12	Desert Gardens	11/12/95	left of drive	little irrigation, good groundcover					
3	Leucophyllum 'Green Cloud' x6	Mesa Nursery	11/14/95	as screen near road	little irrigation, don't prune					
4	Ericameria laricifolia	Oasis Brothers	11/24/94	behind pool	prune dead out in winter					
5	Encelia farinose x 7	Hot Springs Selection	11/3/98	next to rockery	no water once established					
6	Baileya multiradiata x 12	Master Gardener Seminar	10/19/02	in flower border	irrigate every two weeks to keep bloom going					
7	Ceratonia siliqua	Best Desert Trees	10/18/91	behind pool	avoid overwatering					
8	Acacia greggii	Spooks Mountain Nursery	11/20/03	behind cactus mound	native shrub, or tree, if watered					
9	Pinus halpensis	Pines and Palms	9/10/94	near front spruce	a few deep waterings needed in summer					
10	Cupressus sempervirens x 9	Canyon Acres	10/12/90	windbreak on west	water deeply in summer					
11										
12										
13										

Sheet1 Sheet2 Sheet3

Ready Sum=0 ○ SCRL ○ CAPS ● NUM

Many gardeners have developed a personal computerized plant record system. Data can be added to files quickly, and multiple years of records can be conveniently stored. You can develop a long-range plan and keep track of your progress. Be sure to keep a backup of all your gardening files just in case something happens to the computer!

Some of the most fascinating garden records are photographs. A spectacular garden is all the more dramatic when you can compare the "before" and "after" shots. Growth of trees, combinations of perennials, and successful container plantings can be documented for future referral. Also, a photograph can be very helpful to someone trying to diagnose a plant problem or identify a plant.

Other items for the record

Always record major modifications you make to your soil, such as double digging and adding replacement soil. Keep your soil tests from year to year, and make note of the kind and quantity of organic and mineral amendments you incorporate. Records of your soil fertility and pH are most useful when changes can be observed over time. Be sure to identify areas that receive different treatments.

Routine maintenance such as mulching, watering, fertilizing, and pruning should be recorded. Knowing the quantities of mulch and fertilizer you use in a season helps estimate future purchases.

By studying the phenology of the plants in your landscape – their cycles of growth and development over the course of the year – you can time gardening activities to your specific conditions. The optimum time to plant particular seeds, to apply insecticides, to release beneficial insects, and other gardening activities can be determined by observing the growth cycle of your plants and relating their various stages to the environment as a whole. Because plants respond to environmental stimuli, such as day length and temperature, their growth cycles can be used to indicate other similarly stimulated events such as the arrival of an insect pest or the emergence of a weed. Applying preemergent crabgrass control to the lawn as the forsythia flowers fade is an example of a phenologically based practice. Similarly, when an insect infestation is first observed in your yard, look around and take note of what is blooming. If the insect reappears in following years when the same plant is in bloom, you can reasonably schedule your pest control methods to coincide with that particular plant's blooming time.

Timing is everything
One way to control crabgrass (left) is to apply a preemergent weedkiller to the soil as local forsythia flowers (below) begin to fade. This is well before you would notice even seedling crabgrass, so make a note in your diary.

CONSULT THE PROS

In today's media-rich environment, the challenge is not so much to find information about whatever topic you seek as it is to filter the available resources to make sure you locate those that are most reliable and valuable to you and your gardening efforts. The books, periodicals, websites, television and radio shows, and gardens that are most useful to you are largely determined by two factors: your gardening interests and your location.

Gathering information

If you are investigating the possibility of developing a rock garden, heirloom vegetable plot, or water feature, for example, you can find books, magazines, and websites devoted to the subject. To apply the information you gather to your backyard, you can look to more regional resources, such as a nearby botanical garden, a local chapter of a rock garden society, your state's cooperative extension service, and periodicals with a regional focus. Obtain the best resources available to you, then integrate the information into your garden plan.

The printed word

Certain resources become like trusted friends – you return to them time after time for advice. A stroll down the gardening aisle of a well-stocked bookstore reveals that there are titles for nearly every conceivable aspect of gardening. But all gardening references are not equal. Although some books, like this one, have a regional perspective, many are written from a more general point of view, and some will reflect conditions quite unlike those you confront. Take this into consideration when looking for advice from a nonregional reference.

Magazines and journals can inspire you with examples of what other gardeners are doing as well as keep you up to date on advances in the field. There are many periodicals to choose from, for every level of gardening and for just about any specialty. Some of these are national with a broad scope. Every region and many gardening subjects – from prairie gardens to tomato culture to water gardening – are represented on the periodical shelf at the bookstore. Many plant societies, botanical gardens, and nurseries publish a newsletter, and many of these are packed with useful information. If you are considering subscribing to a gardening magazine or newsletter, ask a gardener who shares your interests for a recommendation.

Local and regional newspapers are another source of timely gardening information. Many run gardening columns each week or biweekly that offer growing tips on a local level. Newspapers may cover gardens worth visiting in your area, as well as local gardening programs and events.

The printed word
Many reference books are available to buy from bookstores or to research at libraries. It's a good idea to consult more than one volume to get multiple (and often different!) insights on a given plant's characteristics and garden potential.

34 EARLY SPRING RED

CAMELLIA JAPONICA *'Coquettii'*

Evergreen shrub

In early to mid-spring the arching stems of this slow-growing shrub are covered with deep red, semi-double or double flowers. It makes an elegant addition to a border and will complement plantings in a woodland garden, but it can also be grown as a specimen in containers or in open ground. Choose a partially shaded site, out of the early morning sun, in moist, but well-drained, humus-rich acid soil. Use an ericaceous (lime-free) compost in containers.

↕ to 9m (28ft) ↔ to 8m (25ft)

CHAENOMELES X SUPERBA *'Crimson and Gold'*

Deciduous shrub

The deep crimson flowers with golden yellow anthers are produced by this Japanese quince from spring to early summer, and are often followed in the autumn by yellow-green fruit. Its wide, spreading habit makes it a useful shrub for ground cover, planting against walls or in a border, or it can be grown as an informal, low flowering hedge. Quinces trained against walls or used as hedges should be cut back after flowering.

↕ to 1m (3ft) ↔ to 2m (6ft)

RED

CORYDALIS SOLIDA *'George Baker'*

Perennial

This attractive tuberous perennial has deeply dissected greyish-green leaves. In spring, it produces bright red, with a hint of orange, tubular flowers. Plant it in a rock or gravel garden in full sun or partial shade, in well-drained fertile soil. 'George Baker' can be divided in the autumn if clumps become too large.

↕ to 25cm (10in) ↔ to 20cm (8in)

ERYSIMUM *'Blood Red'*

Perennial

Although perennial, wallflowers are often grown as biennial bedding plants, and planted in combination with tall-stemmed tulips. Left alone, they will live for several years, but can become woody and leggy with age. This variety has vivid, deep red flowers in spring, and is ideal for growing against a dry wall, or to brighten up the front of a sunny border or raised bed. Plant it in autumn in very well-drained, neutral to alkaline soil.

↕ ↔ to 30cm (12in)

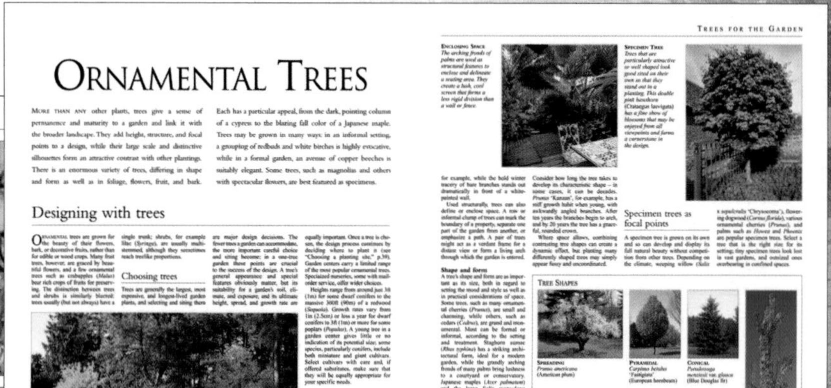
TREES FOR THE GARDEN

ORNAMENTAL TREES

Designing with trees

Choosing trees

Trees as design elements

Shape and form

Specimen trees as focal points

TREE SHAPES

Landscape painters
Employing a professional landscape designer or architect and contractor will not be inexpensive, but the results should be very rewarding.

The electronic approach

Websites on virtually every gardening specialty have cropped up over the last few years. A quick search on the Internet can reveal hundreds of articles about any gardening topic. You can spend many hours surfing the Net for specific information, or just enjoy exploring the breadth of subjects covered. Nearly every major garden club, plant society, and botanical garden, as well as many state cooperative extension services and university horticulture departments, have websites that you are welcome to peruse. In many cases, expert advice on almost any gardening subject is often only an e-mail away.

Many organizations may have regional chapters with individual websites. These can be a helpful source of local expert advice and can inform you of meetings, classes, and other events in your area. If you are looking for information on a specific plant, for example daffodils or roses, or a particular gardening topic such as rock gardens or bonsai, start with the appropriate national organization and go from there. Many organizations are listed on more general gardening websites, and the national organizations usually provide links to regional sites. *(For gardening websites see the appendix)*.

A gardening list serve – an electronic conversation among a group of gardeners – provides opportunities to ask, receive, and offer advice, and to share gardening experiences. Many organizations sponsor list serves. The accuracy of such advice, of course, depends upon the participants, but conversations are often lively and stimulating. If you are a member of the American Horticultural Society (AHS), you can learn about various list serves by visiting the society's website (www.ahs.org), then join one of many ongoing conversations on just about any gardening subject that interests you.

Many local radio and cable television stations are getting into the gardening act with shows that highlight local gardens, gardeners, and timely and regionally appropriate gardening information. Tune in and see what's new.

Being there

Although written and electronic references are invaluable aids to gardening, nothing is quite the same as a visit to a real garden for learning what you need to know and for inspiring you with ideas. Regional botanical gardens and arboreta afford visitors a chance to see plants they have read or heard about in a real growing situation, and experts are often available to answer your questions.

Some public gardens offer classes and workshops on a variety of subjects, and some provide training for Master Gardeners (see following page). Most offer volunteer opportunities – a great way to work with trained gardening staff, learning garden techniques first hand.

Mirror lake
Bellingrath Gardens, Alabama
This 950-acre estate has 56 acres of formal gardens and features displays of azaleas, camellias, roses, and many native plants.

Cypress Gardens, South Carolina
Although this garden is noted for its water shows, it has spectacular displays of azaleas and a large collection of flowering sub-tropical plants that can be seen on foot or from a flat-bottomed boat.

MASTER GARDENERS

The Master Gardeners program began in the early 1970s in Washington State as a way to train volunteers to help gardeners find reliable solutions to their gardening problems. Today there are master gardener programs in every state, coordinated by each state's Cooperative Extension Service.

Programs vary somewhat from one state to another, but in general, volunteers are selected and trained in basic horticultural practices. Training often includes plant identification, diagnosis of plant problems with appropriate recommendations for treatment, soil and fertilizer recommendations, lawn care, pesticide use and safety, organic gardening, ornamental gardening, and a variety of other topics.

In return for their training, Master Gardeners must volunteer a certain number of hours in public service. They may participate in plant clinics, assist with processing soil test reports, answer horticultural hotlines, conduct garden tours, or other activities that are aimed at disseminating reliable gardening information to the public.

Two hundred universities, public gardens, and nurseries throughout the United States and Canada are home to All America Selection (AAS) display gardens. These gardens provide visitors the opportunity to see how recent award-winning introductions (vegetables, flowers, and herbs) perform in a garden setting (see appendix for a list of AAS display gardens).

Close to home

Don't overlook a garden simply because it doesn't have a name: within your neighborhood there may be landscapes that deserve a closer look. Most gardeners love to show off the fruits of their labor, and some of the best advice available to you may be from the man or woman next door who shares both your growing conditions and your enthusiasm for gardening.

Observing the plants your neighbors grow, how they grow them, and how they tackle problems that arise can provide insight and ideas for your own yard. A gardening acquaintance may alert you to the arrival of a pest or show you a new plant that is just the ticket for your perennial border. Putting your heads together to find a solution for a problem multiplies your available resources.

As your garden comes of age, and neighbors can't help but observe your success, you are likely to be asked for advice from other interested gardeners. Be generous. Share your enthusiasm for gardening and your respect for the environment. You too are a valuable gardening resource.

Cutting edge
Faculty members at local and regional agricultural colleges often spend part of their time researching new techniques and breeding new plants. Their printed and electronic publications are a valuable resource.

EXTENSION SERVICE

While the Morrill Act served to establish and fund the land grant university system that began in earnest in the Northeast and Midwest in the 1860s and 1870s, it was 1887's Hatch Act and 1914's Smith Lever Act that created the foundation for the diverse network of resources that serve local gardeners in each northeastern state. The former established the Experiment Station program, originally dedicated to agricultural and mechanical research, while the latter created the Cooperative Extension Service, a vehicle for delivering the products of experiment station research and other valuable information to state residents.

Horticulturally speaking, land grant universities are very active in the Southeast, working in landscape plant selection, hybridization, evaluation, and production, as well as studying the organisms and conditions that dictate horticultural performance. More importantly, they target regional issues and offer results with genuine significance to state residents.

The Cooperative Extension Service delivers education and outreach to residents on a county level and tends to form specialties that reflect the characteristics of a given county's maekup. Urban counties will have a focus that differs a bit from those offices located in a rural, agrarian area. Southeastern Cooperative Extension Services distribute pertinent results of Experiment Station research and other valuable information to residents in the forms of lectures, bulletins, websites, telephone hotlines, and direct consultation. Topics include planting and maintenance techniques, farming information, plant pathology, and plant selection information. The Cooperative Extension Service also manages the Master Gardener program (see above).

HAVE FUN

Lots of people have yards; some have gardens. A yard is the area that surrounds your house. A garden, on the other hand, is a creation that enhances that space with sights, fragrances, and sounds that inspire and fulfill. The yard around your house is what you begin with; a garden is what it can become. Whether your garden is a woodland teeming with towering trees and flowering shrubs, a deep border of colorful perennials, a vegetable patch that stocks your table, or a simple windowbox overflowing with annuals, it should be fun for you and for those who visit.

The vision

Visualizing your dream garden can occupy many delightful hours looking through books and magazines for ideas, visiting botanical gardens, and imagining a bed here, a pond there, and over there, perhaps a trellis . . . it's a pleasant thing to daydream about your green activities. Planning for it to become a reality, and taking the measured steps necessary to assure success, is even more exciting. Witnessing the transformation of your yard into a SmartGarden™ through choosing great plants, maximizing efficient practices, and nurturing a friendly, healthy environment, is a thrill that grows over time.

The challenge

Achieving a SmartGarden™ is a challenge beyond simply planting a few perennials and trees around a patch of grass. It requires you to consider the question: how do you develop a garden, making the most of your landscape, while at the same time merging seamlessly into the rhythms and flow of nature? Your answer is both the task and the reward of its creation. Compromises will be necessary, and you may not see instant dividends on your investment, but over time you will enjoy the compounded benefits of a lovely garden and a healthy, balanced environment. Because you planned for it, your investment will continue to grow over time.

The gardening practices described in this book are designed to make the most of your gardening activities, using all available resources to streamline efforts so that you can concentrate on the gardening activities that you find particularly rewarding and have plenty of time to enjoy the fruits of your labor. Of course there will be some surprises. You will make changes as you go along, learning from and adapting to what works best for you. It is dynamic, challenging, and exciting, and, as every gardener comes to know, there is no such thing as a "finished" garden. The ongoing processes of planning, planting, maintaining, experiencing, refining, and sharing is part of the thrill.

The reward

Although many gardens are pleasant to look at, a SmartGarden™ is a delight to experience on many different levels. It harmonizes with its surroundings, and enhances its environment without dominating it. The soil is alive and teeming with beneficial organisms. The plants fit their site and space – and they flourish! Birds and butterflies are welcomed, encouraged by the diversity of vegetation and friendly habitat. It's exciting to know your plants intimately while taking pride in their performances and anticipating their changes through the seasons as well as the years.

People garden for many reasons: to enjoy nature, get some fresh air and spend time outdoors, cultivate particular plants, grow their own food, attract wildlife, and create a pleasing, comfortable environment. For most gardeners, it is a combination of such goals. Some people garden because they enjoy the solitude, while others consider it an opportunity to spend time productively in the company of friends or family. It is a perfect activity for intergenerational bonding: senior gardeners have a wealth of experience they can share with young garden enthusiasts. Whether alone or with company, most of us garden because it's fun.

Some gardeners find satisfaction in neat rows of plump tomatoes, while others take more pleasure in a casual meadow of wildflowers or an elaborate pond for night-blooming waterlilies. No matter which type of garden you choose, it can be grown following these ten tenets. This kind of garden affords you the opportunity to express your taste and style and then to watch it grow, knowing that it is a healthy and safe environment for all who visit. That knowledge will amplify the joy you derive from your garden.

Whether you are beginning from scratch or you are improving an existing garden, smart gardening will help you embrace the vision, meet the challenge, and enjoy the rewards of bringing plants, animals, and structures together into a green and living whole.

Lawn games
A well-planned and maintained garden that follows SmartGarden™ principles will bring endless pleasure to its owners, no matter the style or level of horticultural interest. The choices xare up to you!

PART II

PLANT CATALOG

including Woody Plants and
Herbaceous Plants

One of the three most critical factors for the
success of any SMARTGARDEN™ is choosing the
right plant for the right spot. In this section, more
than 4,000 plants that grow well in the Southeast
region are grouped by physical characteristics or
horticultural requirements, with information on
light and moisture needs, cold and heat
tolerance, and maximum height and width.
Below is a key of the symbols:

☼	Sun	◐ Moist	Zx–x	USDA hardiness zones
☼	Part shade	● Wet	Hx–x	AHS heat-range zones
☀	Shade	pH Acidic soil	↕ in/ft (cm/m)	Height of plant
◌	Dry	Ⓝ Native	↔ in/ft (cm/m)	Spread of plant

Plant catalog contents

WOODY

HERBACEOUS

WOODY PLANTS

OFTEN CALLED THE "the bones of the garden," trees and shrubs should be the first plants to go in once the hard landscaping is done. Slower growing than perennials or annuals, trees take longer to reach a good size, but they eventually make more impact on the landscape. Consider eventual size, hardiness and heat tolerance, foliage color and density, and flowering time. Because of their importance in the landscape, it pays to find just the right plant for every specific location. Trees play a dominant role and can influence the other plants you grow because of the shade they cast or their root systems. Shallow-rooted trees can take so much moisture from the soil that it is hard to grow even grass beneath them.

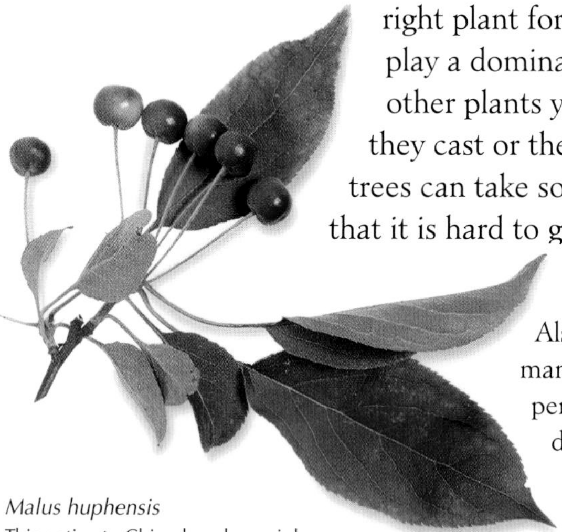

Malus huphensis
This native to China has deep pink buds that open to fragrant white flowers in mid- to late spring. Fast-growing and vase-shaped when young, it spreads later.

Also take into account the winter effect; many trees have brightly colored bark or persistent fruit, which may be the only decorative feature in the garden at that time of year.

There is a shrub for every location, soil type, and exposure. Low groundcover species can take the place of grass, tall upright forms make ideal hedges or screens, and spiny ones can make an intruder-proof barrier.

Different shrubs can provide colorful flowers from late winter through to fall, with fruits and berries to bridge the gap. In summer, leaves may be yellow, purple, variegated, or green, and colored stems can add winter interest.

The diversity of evergreens is equally broad. Most conifers have needle- or fanlike foliage that may be green, blue, or yellow, while broadleaved evergreens have flowers and fruit. They range from small, columnar plants to large, towering trees. Many make excellent hedges that filter the wind, rather than blocking it, while others are better as specimen plants. In general, they act as a quiet backdrop to more flamboyant, brightly colored perennials and annuals. Some broadleaved evergreens are grown mainly for their foliage, but in this region the majority are grown for their flowers, like rhododendrons, azaleas, and camellias.

Buddleia 'Pink Delight'
The Pink Delight prefers fertile soil and produces larger flower spikes and deeper green leaves than the species. Orange-eyed flowers bloom from summer to fall.

Abelia grandiflora
An evergreen or semi-evergreen shrub, its fragrant flowers are borne from midsummer to fall. Irresistible to many butterflies, it is also known as *A. rupestris.*

Viburnum macrocephalum
Many species and varieties are grown for their fragrant flowers, brightly colored fruits, and foliage which, if deciduous, turns a red or copper shade in fall.

Large shade trees

Plant these trees where they will have space to develop, like large estate lots, municipal parks, or golf courses, where space is not a consideration. Given suitable conditions, these trees will grow into graceful specimens but crowding may make them susceptible to problems. Plant them at least half their eventual spread away from the nearest tree or building.

Fagus grandifolia
AMERICAN BEECH
Ⓝ ☼ ◑ ◊ Z3–9 H9–1 ↕↔80ft (25m)
An imposing tree with smooth gray bark, even on older trees. Plant in slightly acidic soil that is neither compacted nor wet. Slow-growing, but worth it.

Cercidiphyllum japonicum
KATSURA TREE
☼ ◑ ◊ ♦ Z4–8 H8–1 ↕70ft (20m) ↔50ft (15m)
Pyramidal while young, becomes broader with age. Young foliage is pinkish, becoming blue-green and turning as shown in fall with a smell of burnt sugar.

Tilia americana
AMERICAN LINDEN, BASSWOOD
Ⓝ ☼ ◑ ◊ Z2–8 H8–1
↕80ft (25m) ↔40ft (12m)
Easy to grow in most soils, but shallow-rooted unless they are deep. Fragrant, pale yellow summer flowers attract bees and butterflies.

Fraxinus pennsylvanica
GREEN ASH
Ⓝ ☼ ♦ Z4–9 H9–4 ↕↔70ft (20m)
Upright and spreading tree with age. Shiny foliage turns yellow in autumn. Avoid seedling-grown trees; many bear nuisance fruit. Prone to borers and scale.

Acer rubrum
RED MAPLE
Ⓝ ☼ ◑ ♦ pH Z3–9 H9–1 ↕70ft (20m) ↔30ft (9m)
Tiny red flowers emerge before the leaves herald the arrival of spring in eastern North America. For the best display of vivid red fall color, grow in acidic soil.

Nyssa sylvatica
SOUR GUM
Ⓝ ☼ ◐ ● Z4–9 H9–2
↕70ft (20m) ↔30ft (9m)
Slow-growing, pyramidal tree that spreads and becomes more irregular with maturity. Leaves emerge late in spring. Females produce black fruit that birds devour.

Liriodendron tulipifera
TULIP TREE
Ⓝ ☼ ◐ ○ ◑ pH Z5–9 H9–1
↕100ft (30m) ↔50ft (15m)
Fast-growing tree with golden yellow foliage in fall. Aphids are a big problem, as are scale powdery mildew, and leaf spot. Native to the eastern United States.

Celtis occidentalis
COMMON HACKBERRY, SUGARBERRY
Ⓝ ☼ ○ Z2–9 H9–1 ↕70ft (20m) ↔50 ft (15m)
Very adaptable to soils and locations. Mature trees have a shape reminiscent of American elm. Spring flowers are not showy, but the brown-red fall fruit are sweet.

MORE CHOICES

- *Carya illinoiensis* Z5–9 H9–1
- *Celtis laevigata smallii* Z5-9 H9-3
- *Gymnocladus dioica* Z5-9 H9-2
- *Liquidambar styraciflua* 'Rotundiloba' Z6–9 H9–1
- *Pinus elliotii* Z8–9 H9–8
- *Pinus taeda* Z6–9 H9–6
- *Populus deltoides* Z3–9 H9–1
- *Quercus falcata* Z6–9 H9–5
- *Quercus stellata* Z5–8 H8–5
- *Sophora japonica* Z5-9 H9-5
- *Taxodium distichum* Z5–11 H12–5

Quercus alba
WHITE OAK
Ⓝ ☼ ◐ ○ pH Z5–9 H8–1 ↕↔60–100ft (18–30m)
A handsome oak with majestic, wide-spreading branches at maturity. Foliage turns a rich wine red in fall. Its acorns are relished by birds and mammals.

Quercus phellos
WILLOW OAK
Ⓝ ☼ ◐ ○ Z6–9 H9–3 ↕70ft (20m) ↔50ft (15m)
Fast-growing, with a cone-shaped growth habit. Smooth gray bark later develops shallow ridges. In warmer areas, dead leaves hang on through winter.

Medium-sized shade trees

Many of the trees shown here are suitable for the average city property, providing they are not in competition with similar trees close by. You need to consult with your neighbors to be sure you are not both intending to plant trees on either side of the property line. Trees of this type should be planted at least 20ft (6m) apart, and even more if they have a spreading habit of growth.

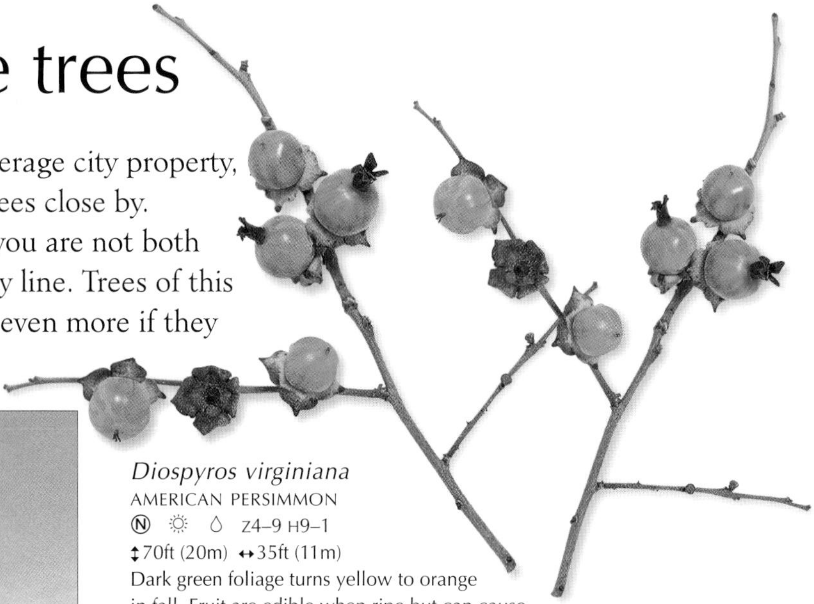

Diospyros virginiana
AMERICAN PERSIMMON
Ⓝ ☼ ◇ Z4–9 H9–1
↕70ft (20m) ↔35ft (11m)
Dark green foliage turns yellow to orange in fall. Fruit are edible when ripe but can cause litter if not picked. Fissured bark, showing orange inner bark, adds winter interest.

Morus rubra
RED MULBERRY
Ⓝ ☼ ◇◆ Z5–9 H9–5
↕40ft (12m) ↔50ft (15m)
The edible fruits are very attractive to birds who descend in large flocks and dispense seedlings. Crushed fruits will stain hard surfaces. Leaves turn yellow in fall.

Maclura pomifera
OSAGE-ORANGE
Ⓝ ☼ ◇ Z5–9 H9–5
↕50 ft (15m) ↔40ft (12m)
Fast-growing tree with low, rounded irregular head and stiff thorny branches. Deep orange-brown bark with wavy deep ridges. Very tough and durable.

Albizia julibrissin
SILK-TREE, MIMOSA
☼ ◇ Z6–9 H9–6 ↕↔30ft (10m)
Fluffy pink flowers give gray-brown seedpods that persist through the winter. Grows quickly but is not long-lived. Very susceptible to wilt and webworm. Self-sows strongly.

Robinia pseudoacacia 'Frisia'
FRISIA BLACK LOCUST
Ⓝ ☼ ◆ Z4–9 H9–3 ↕80ft (24m) ↔50 ft (15m)
Very fragrant flowers in late spring to early summer are followed by flat brown pods. Bees are very attracted to the flowers, producing a rich honey. The leaves keep their yellow color all summer.

MORE CHOICES

- *Catalpa bignoniodes* Z5–9 H9–5
- *Fagus sylvatica Atropurpurea* Z5–7 H7–5
- *Firmiana simplex* Z7–15 H12–8
- *Koelreuteria binpinnata* Z6–9 H9–1
- *Pistacia chinensis* Z6–9 H9–6
- *Pistacia serotina* Z6–9 H9–1
- *Prunus serotina* Z4–8 H8–1
- *Pyrus calleryana* 'Aristocrat' Z5–8 H8–1
- *Sapindus drummondii* Z8–11 H10–2
- *Ulmus alata* Z3–9 H9–1

Ginkgo biloba
MAIDENHAIR TREE
Z5–9 H9–3
↕100ft (30m) ↔25ft (8m)
Narrow to spreading young tree becomes umbrella-shaped. Slow-growing, tolerant of pollution and heat, and free of pests. Outstanding yellow fall foliage.

Gleditsia tricanthos var. *inermis* 'Skyline'
SKYLINE THORNLESS HONEYLOCUST
Ⓝ Z3–7 H7–1
↕45ft (12.5m) ↔35ft (10.5m)
An adaptable tree that grows well in most soils, and is pollution and salt-tolerant. Good yellow fall color. Susceptible to a pod-gall on the leaflets, but not serious.

Carpinus betulus
EUROPEAN HORNBEAM
Z4–8 H8–1
↕80ft (25m) ↔70ft (20m)
The smooth gray bark is fluted and muscly-looking. Leaves are yellow in fall and unusually free of pests. Excellent as a screening plant, as a hedge, or in large planters.

Koelreuteria paniculata
PANICLED GOLDEN RAIN TREE
Z6–9 H9–1 ↕↔30ft (10m)
Opening leaves are purplish red, become bright green, then turn golden yellow in fall. Yellow flowers appear in midsummer and become inflated fruit.

Salix babylonica var. *pekinensis* 'Tortuosa'
CORKSCREW WILLOW
Z5–9 H9–5 ↕50ft (15m) ↔25ft (8m)
Fast-growing, small to medium tree with twisted shoots with bright green bark. It is greatly prized by flower arrangers and adds winter interest to the garden.

Small trees

When choosing which tree to plant on your property, keep in mind certain factors. Flowers, fruit, foliage, fall color, and winter interest differ from one species to another. Trees shown here are suitable for small modern homes where garden space is limited, but can also be planted in groupings if you have a larger garden.

Ilex decidua
POSSUMHAW
Ⓝ ☼ ◐ ♦ Z5–9 H9–1
↕↔6–20ft (2–6m)
Foliage turns yellow in fall. Fruits ripen in September, hanging on to the tree throughout winter. The light gray stems stand out against an evergreen backdrop.

Asimina triloba
PAWPAW
☼ ◊ Z6–8 H8–6
↕12ft (4m) ↔12ft (4m)
Both females and males are required to produce fruit. When fully ripe, the banana-flavored interior is yellow and custardlike. Has few pest problems.

Halesia diptera var. *magniflora*
TWO-WINGED SILVERBELL
Ⓝ ☼ ◐ ♦ Z4–8 H8–1 ↕20ft (6m) ↔30ft (10m)
Larger flowers than the species. Winged green fruit appear after the flowers. Foliage on this rounded tree turns yellow in autumn. Protect from wind.

Ficus carica
COMMON FIG
☼ ♦ Z7–11 H12–1 ↕10ft (3m) ↔12ft (4m)
Most figs bear on the previous season's growth, so protect plants in winter in the northern part of their range. Rarely bothered by pests and diseases.

Cercis canadensis var. *alba*
WHITE EASTERN REDBUD
Ⓝ ☼ ◐ ♦ Z5–9 H9–5 ↕↔30ft (10m)
Early spring flowers often last two to three weeks. This appealing small tree is well used in a woodland border and other naturalized situations. The species has pink flowers.

Diospyros kaki
JAPANESE PERSIMMON
☼ ◊ Z7–10 H10–7
↕30ft (10m) ↔22ft (7m)
Spreading deciduous tree with foliage that turns orange to purple in fall. Small, pale yellow flowers in summer give edible fruits on female trees. Subject to powdery mildew.

Rhus copallina
DWARF SUMAC
Ⓝ ☼ ◊ Z5–9 H9–5
↕↔3–5ft (1–1.5m) or more
Compact in youth, this ages to an open irregular shrub with spreading branches and shiny, dark green foliage. Greenish yellow flowers occur in late summer.

Acer tataricum subsp. *ginnala*
AMUR MAPLE
☼ ☀ ◊ Z3–7 H7–1
↕30ft (10m) ↔25ft (8m)
A good small tree or large shrub with yellow flowers in spring, red-tinged fruit in summer, and excellent fall color.

Hamamelis virginiana
COMMON WITCH HAZEL
Ⓝ ☼ ◊ pH Z3–8 H8–1 ↕↔20ft (6m)
Bears small, spidery yellow flowers in fall, unlike its spring-blooming relatives. Grows well in the shade of a wall or fence. Native to Eastern North America.

MORE CHOICES

- *Acer palmatum* Z5–8 H8–2
- *Carpinus caroliniana* Z3–9 H9–1
- *Camellia japonica* Z7–8 H8–7
- *Cornus florida* Z5–8 H8–3
- *Crataegus marshallii* Z6–9 H9–1
- *Crataegus opaca* Z6–8 H8–3
- *Ilex cornuta* 'Burfordii' Z6–9 H9–1
- *Lagerstroemia fauriei* Z7–9 H9–7
- *Ligustrum lucidum* Z8–10 H10–8
- *Magnolia soulangiana* Z5–9 H9–5
- *Malus floribunda* 'Callaway' Z4–8 H8–1
- *Parkinsonia aculeata* Z11–12 H12–10
- *Prunus americana* Z3–8 H8–1
- *Prunus cerasifolia* Z5–9 H9–1
- *Rhamnus caroliniana* Z5–9 H9–4
- *Zizyphus jujube* Z5–10 H10–8

Chionanthus virginicus
WHITE FRINGETREE
Ⓝ ☼ ◊ Z4–9 H9–1 ↕↔20ft (6m)
A tree with a variable habit: some are open and spreading; others are denser. Lightly fragrant flowers precede dark blue, oval fruits with a white coating.

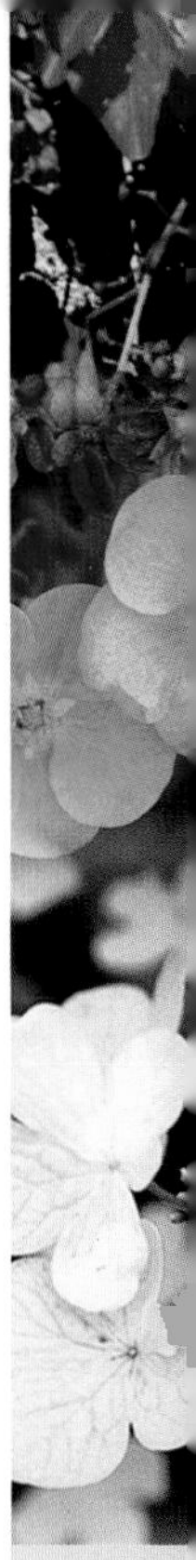
WOODY PLANTS

Evergreen coniferous trees

Coniferous evergreens play a special role in the garden. Those shown here all grow large in time, often with wide-spreading branches. They can be used individually or in groves to add color to winter gardens. Those with blue needles also add a cool tint to summer gardens. Some make good windbreaks or can be used as tall hedges.

Cunninghamia lanceolata
CHINESE FIR
◐ ◑ Z7–9 H9–7 ↕↔50ft (15m)
A conical tree that becomes more rounded or dome-topped as it ages. Growth rate is slow to moderate. Also known as *C. lanceolata* var. *sinensis.*

Picea pungens Glauca group
BLUE COLORADO SPRUCE
Ⓝ ☼ ◊ Z2–8 H8–1 ↕50ft (15m) ↔15ft (5m)
Attractive conical tree suited to gardens in higher elevations. Named forms, like 'Hoopsii' and 'Thompsen', are silvery blue.

Pinus strobus
EASTERN WHITE PINE
Ⓝ ☼ ◑ Z4–9 H9–1
↕100ft (30m) ↔75ft (22m)
A conical tree that becomes irregular and flat-topped with age. Smooth gray bark becomes black and cracked.

Chamaecyparis thyoides
WHITE FALSE CYPRESS
Ⓝ ☼ ◑ Z3–8 H8–1 ↕50ft (15m) ↔12ft (4m)
An excellent species for low-lying sites that tend to remain wet. Narrowly conical, the tree loses its lower branches over time. Female cones are angular; male cones are spherical. Native to swamps and bogs from Maine to Florida.

Thuja orientalis
CHINESE ARBORVITAE
☼ ◊◑ Z6–9 H9–6
↕to 50ft (15m) ↔to 20ft (6m)
The Oriental version of our native white cedar. The needles, in vertical not horizontal, fans turn bronzy in winter. There are several forms with yellow foliage but they do not grow as tall as the species.

Cedrus atlantica 'Glauca'
BLUE ATLAS CEDAR
☼ ◊ Z6–9 H9–3 ↕100ft (30m) ↔75ft (22m)
Scrawny when young but fills out as it matures with horizontally spreading branches. Moderate growth rate. Also known as *C. libani* subsp. *atlantica* f. *glauca*.

Pinus virginiana
VIRGINIA PINE
Ⓝ ☼ ◊ Z3–7 H7–1 ↕20–40ft (6–12m) ↔20–35ft (6–11m)
A two-needle pine that is good for poor dry soils where few other conifers will survive, including heavy clays. Does not grow well on shallow soils. May turn yellowish in winter.

MORE CHOICES

- *Araucaria araucana* Z7–11 H12–6
- *Cedrus deodara* Z6–9 H9–6
- *Cedrus libani* Z6–9 H9–3
- *Cupressus sempervirens* 'Glauca' Z8–10 H10–7
- *Juniperus chinensis* 'Kaizuka' Z3–9 H9–1
- *Juniperus virginiana* 'Canaertii' Z3–9 H9–1
- *Picea pungens* 'Koster' Z3–8 H8–1
- *Pinus glabra* Z8–9 H9–8
- *Pinus elliotii* Z8–9 H9–8
- *Pinus paulstris* Z8–11 H12–8
- *Pinus taeda* Z6–9 H9–6

x *Cupressocyparis leylandii*
LEYLAND CYPRESS
☼ ◊ Z6–9 H9–3 ↕120ft (35m) ↔15ft (5m)
A very fast-growing conifer often used for hedging and for Christmas trees in the South. It grows in most soils and withstands salt spray. Plant container grown, not ball and burlapped.

Cryptomeria japonica
JAPANESE CEDAR
☼ ♦ Z6–9 H9–4 ↕70ft (20m) ↔25ft (8m)
Cryptomeria is one of the few conifers that can be successfully coppiced (cut back severely). Normally a conical or columnar tree, it is a moderately fast grower.

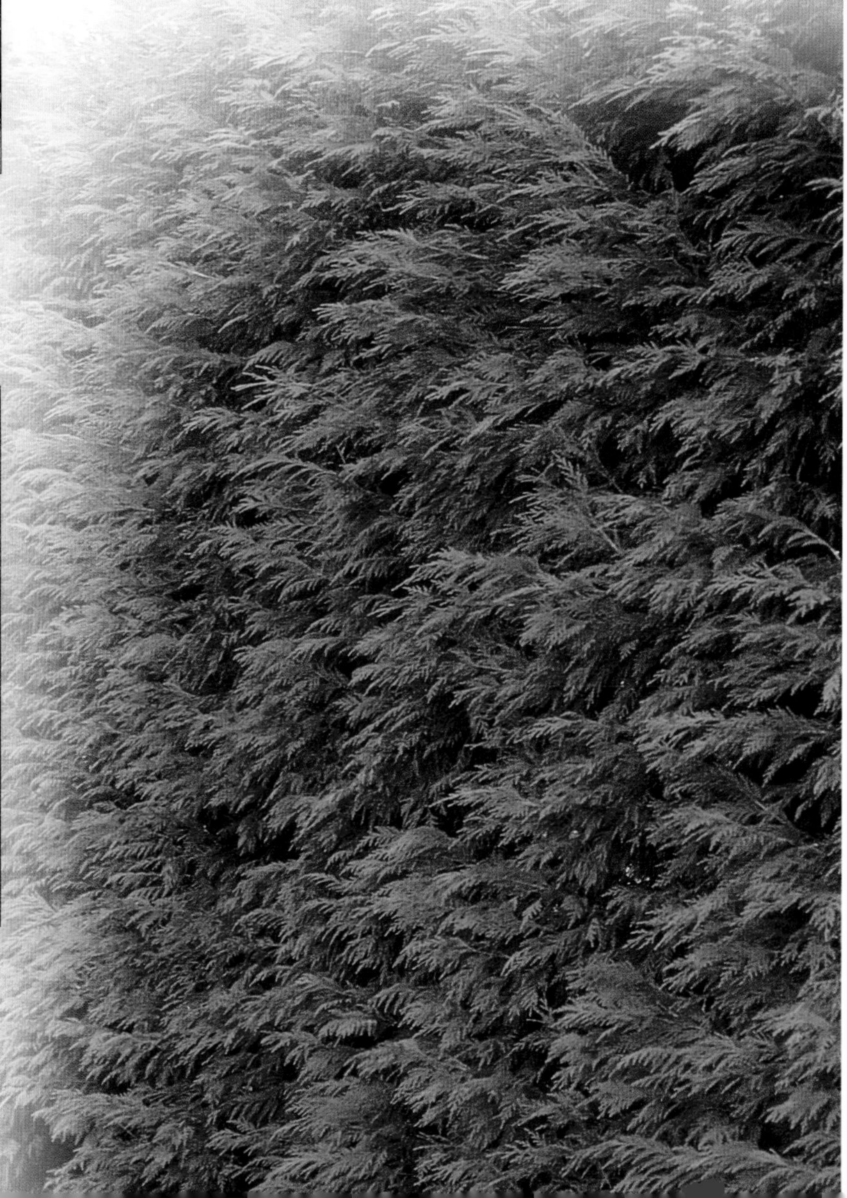

WOODY PLANTS

Shade-tolerant trees

Most trees provide shade for other plants, but some need to be planted in a building's permanent shade, or beneath the canopy of large trees that may show signs of age. Those shown here thrive in these conditions if they receive sufficient water until established. But remember, they may be competing with existing tree roots, or standing in a building's rain shadow.

Franklinia alatamaha
FRANKLIN TREE
Ⓝ ☼ ◑ Z6–9 H9–6 ↕↔15ft (5m)
Flowers from midsummer onward. Needs an acidic to neutral soil. Native to Georgia, it was collected in 1770, and has not been found in the wild since.

Chionanthus retusus
CHINESE FRINGE TREE
☼ ◯ Z5–9 H9–3 ↕↔10ft (3m)
Male and female flowers are on separate trees in spring; males are larger but females produce attractive fruit. Tolerates most soils, providing they are deep and fertile.

Carpinus betulus
EUROPEAN HORNBEAM
☼ ◐ ◯ Z4–8 H8–1
↕80ft (25m) ↔70ft (20m)
The smooth gray bark is fluted and brawny looking. Leaves are yellow in fall and unusually free of pests. Excellent as a screening plant, as a hedge, or in planters.

Amelanchier arborea
COMMON SERVICEBERRY
Ⓝ ☼ ◐ ◯ ◑ Z4–9 H9–4 ↕30ft (10m) ↔40ft (12m)
White spring flowers produce edible red to purple-black fruit. Fall color is bright yellow to red. Good for most soils, it forms a rounded, densely branched tree.

Cercidiphyllum japonicum
KATSURA TREE
☼ ◐ ◯ ◑ pH Z4–8 H8–1 ↕70ft (20m) ↔50ft (15m)
Spreading tree with dark green foliage in summer that smells of caramel in fall. Best when sheltered from strong winds. Small red flowers in early spring.

Acer palmatum
JAPANESE MAPLE
☼ 💧 Z5–8 H8–2
↕↔20ft (6m)
Leaves vary greatly in color and shape, and habit ranges from upright to weeping. This can be grown as a single-stemmed tree or multistemmed large shrub.

Davidia involucrata
DOVE TREE, HANDKERCHIEF TREE
☼ ◐ 💧 Z6–8 H8–6
↕50ft (15m) ↔30ft (10m)
Plant this in a soil rich in organic matter. A very showy tree when in flower, with leaves that persist until hard frost. Does not flower at a young age.

Tsuga caroliniana
CAROLINA HEMLOCK
Ⓝ ☼ ◐ 💧 Z3–8 H7–3 ↕50ft (15m) ↔25ft (8m)
An upright tree with short, often pendulous branches and a fissured, scaly brown bark. This is intolerant of drought and needs protection from strong winds.

MORE CHOICES

- *Acer palmatum* 'Garnet' Z5–8 H8–2
- *Asimina triloba* 'Rebecca's Gold' Z6–8 H8–6
- *Catalpa speciosa* Z5–9 H9–5
- *Cornus florida* Z5–8 H8–5
- *Halesia carolina* Z5–8 H8–4
- *Halesia diptera* Z5–8 H8–4
- *Ilex opaca* 'Jersey Delight' Z5–9 H9–5
- *Ilex opaca* 'Yellow Berry' Z5–9 H9–5
- *Illicium parviflorum* Z7–9 H9–7
- *Magnolia virginiana* Z6–9 H9–6
- *Ptelea trifoliata* Z5–9 H9–5
- *Sassafras albidum* Z4–8 H8–3
- *Vaccinium arboreum* Z9–10 H10–8

Stewartia pseudocamellia Koreana Group
KOREAN STEWARTIA
☼ ◐ 💧 💧 Z5–8 H8–4
↕70ft (20m) ↔25ft (8m)
Collective name for seed-raised plants that vary in form, flower shape, and intensity of fall color. Flowers open wider and fall color is brighter than on the Japanese species.

Styrax japonicus
JAPANESE SNOWBELL
☼ 💧 pH Z6–8 H8–6
↕↔50ft (15m)
This tree forms a broad crown with spreading branches, and has slightly fragrant flowers in late spring and attractive fruit in summer. Plant in early spring in humus-rich soil.

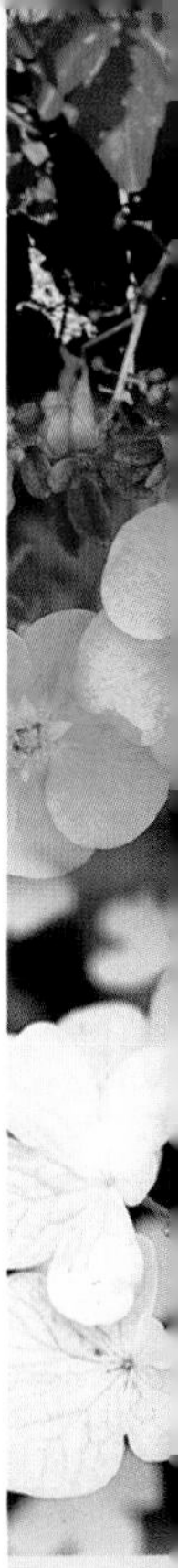

WOODY PLANTS

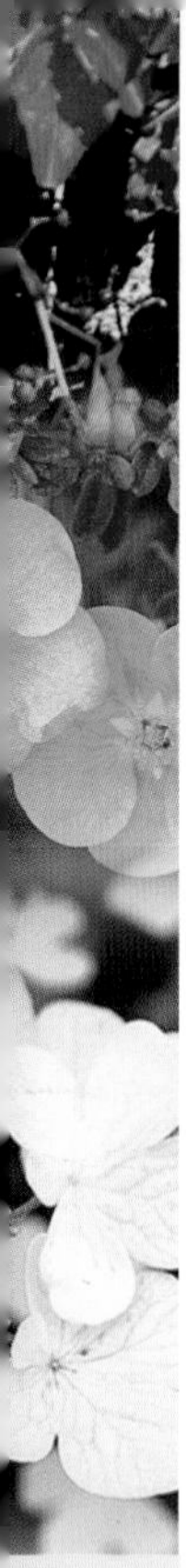

Specimen trees

These are trees with character that you will want to see at all times of the year. Their features warrant prominent placement in the garden, where they can be admired. While their main attraction may be their flowers or foliage, other attributes, such as attractive bark, persistent fruits, or bright fall color, will keep them interesting in every season of the year.

Chorisia speciosa
FLOSS SILK TREE
☼ ◊ Z13–14 H12–10 ↕to 50ft (15m) ↔5ft (1.5m)
Slow-growing, semi-evergreen tree with large spines on the trunk. Flowers open in late summer and give green fruits that turn brown and open to show seeds.

MORE CHOICES

- *Auraucaria heterophylla* Z9–11 H12–9
- *Camellia sasanqua* cvs. Z7–8 H8–7
- *Crataegus phaenopyrum* Z4–8 H8–1
- *Cryptomeria japonica* 'Lobbii' Z6–9 H9–4
- *Ginkgo biloba* 'Pendula' Z5–9 H9–3
- *Ilex vomitoria pendula* Z7–11 H12–7
- *Juniperus chinensis* 'Kaizuka' Z3–9 H9–1
- *Poncirus trifoliata* 'Flying Dragon' Z4–9 H9–1
- *Prunus yedoensis* Z5–8 H8–5
- *Sophora japonica* 'Pendula' Z5–9 H9–5

Chionanthus retusus
CHINESE FRINGE TREE
☼ ◊ Z5–9 H9–3 ↕↔10ft (3m)
Male and female flowers are on separate trees in spring; males are larger, but females produce attractive fruit. Tolerates most soils, providing they are deep and fertile.

Eucalyptus cinerea
SILVER DOLLAR TREE
☼ ♦ Z8–10 H10–8 ↕to 50ft (15m) ↔30–40ft (10–20m)
One of several Australian gums that are becoming increasingly popular as they become better known. White flowers open in summer. May get aphids and scale insects.

Prunus subhirtella 'Pendula'
WEEPING HIGAN CHERRY
☼ ◊ Z6–8 H8–6 ↕↔30ft (10m)
A graceful artistic weeper that grows quickly. The bark is particularly distinct, with gray-brown lenticels (corky pores) in stripes on the younger branches.

Salix caprea 'Kilmarnock'
KILMARNOCK WILLOW
☼ ◊♦ Z6–8 H8–6
↕5–6ft (1.5–2m) ↔6ft (2m)
Weeping tree, with gray male catkins that are produced on bare shoots in mid- and late spring. This is almost always grown as a grafted standard.

Trees for containers

Place beautiful containers where they will stand out and more homely ones where they are less conspicuous. For containers left outdoors year-round, select plants that are one or two zones hardier than your region – this is because plant roots in a container are exposed to colder temperatures than they would be in the ground.

Acer palmatum Dissectum Group
THREADLEAF JAPANESE MAPLE
☼ ◐ ♦ Z6–8 H8–6 ↕6ft (2m) ↔10ft (3m)
Mound-forming shrub with arching shoots bears finely cut red-purple leaves that turn gold in fall. Produces tiny purple-red flowers in late summer.

Rhus typhina 'Laciniata'
CUTLEAF STAGHORN SUMAC
☼ ◊ ♦ Z3–8 H8–1
↕6ft (2m) ↔10ft (3m)
Erect conical clusters of yellow-green flowers to 8in (20cm) long appear in summer. In fall, female plants produce dense clusters of bright crimson fruit.

Chionanthus virginicus
WHITE FRINGETREE
Ⓝ ☼ ♦ Z4–9 H9–1 ↕↔20ft (6m)
A tree with a variable habit: some are open and spreading; others are denser. Lightly fragrant flowers precede dark blue, oval fruits with a white coating.

MORE CHOICES

- *Acer buergerianum* Z5–9 H9–5
- *Acer palmatum* 'Burgundy Lace' Z5–8 H8–2
- *Amelanchier x grandiflora* 'Robin Hill' Z3–7 H7–1
- *Camellia sasanqua* cvs. Z7–8 H8–7
- *Ilex x attenuata* 'Fosteri' Z6–9 H9–4
- *Lagerstroemia indica* Z7–9 H9–6
- *Ligustrum japonicum* Z7–10 H10–7
- *Magnolia grandiflora* 'Little Gem' Z7–9 H9–3
- *Rhapis excelsa* Z14–15 H12–1

Malus 'Red Jade'
RED JADE CRABAPPLE
☼ ◐ ♦ Z4–8 H6–1 ↕12ft (4m) ↔20ft (6m)
Deep pink flower buds open white and then mature to glossy red fruit relished by birds and animals. Good container plant while young and not too widespread.

Magnolia stellata
STAR MAGNOLIA
☼ ◐ ◊ Z5–9 H9–5 ↕10ft (3m) ↔12ft (4m)
A bushy deciduous shrub that needs protection from winter winds and late frosts. Furry flower buds open before the leaves. Many cultivars and hybrids are available.

Trees with a columnar habit

In many cities, squeezing narrow homes into vacant lots means gardens are often long and narrow. A regular tree planted in such a spot would end up spreading over the neighbors' properties; one of the slender trees shown here might be a better fit. Even in a large garden, these different forms add to the overall interest and contrasts with more spreading forms.

Carpinus betulus 'Fastigiata'
FASTIGIATA HORNBEAM
☼ ◊ Z4–8 H8–3 ↕50ft (15m) ↔40ft (12m)
Upright when young, becoming more rounded later. Pollution-resistant, it grows well in urban locations. Good yellow color in fall and smooth bark in winter.

Populus alba 'Raket'
RAKET WHITE POPLAR
☼ ◑ Z4–9 H9–1 ↕25ft (8m) ↔50ft (15m)
Foliage is woolly-white beneath, showing in the slightest breeze. Salt-tolerant but tends to sucker and shed twigs and leaves in wind storms.

Populus nigra 'Italica'
LOMBARDY POPLAR
☼ ◊ Z3–9 H9–1 ↕100ft (30m) ↔15ft (5m)
Fast-growing, it is best used as a screen or windbreak to shelter more desirable species, then remove. Very prone to canker and dieback when mature.

MORE CHOICES

- *Acer rubrum* 'Columnare' Z3–9 H9–1
- *Cupressus sempervirens* 'Stricta' Z8–10 H10–8
- *Fagus sylvatica* 'Dawyck Purple' Z5–7 H7–5
- *Ginkgo biloba* 'Princeton Sentry' Z5–9 H9–2
- *Ilex vomitoria* 'Will Fleming' Z7–11 H12–7
- *Koelreuteria paninculata* 'Fastigiata' Z6–9 H9–1
- *Liriodendron tulipifera* 'Fastigiatum' Z5–9 H9–2
- *Prunus* 'Amanogawa' Z6–8 H8–6
- *Pyrus calleryana* 'Capital' or 'Chanticleer' Z4–8 H8–1
- *Sophora japonica* 'Fastigiata' Z5–9 H9–5
- *Taxodium ascendens* Z5–11 H12–5
- *Thuja orientalis* 'Elegantissima' Z6–8 H9–6
- *Tilia americana* 'Fastigiata' Z3–8 H8–1
- *Washingtonia robusta* Z13–15 H12–10

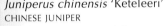

Juniperus chinensis 'Keteleeri'
CHINESE JUNIPER
☼ ◊ Z3–9 H9–1 ↕↔50ft (15m)
This cultivar is much more conical (and foliage is grayer) than the species. Brown bark peels in long strips. Needs very little pruning. Growth is moderate to slow.

Magnolia grandiflora 'Little Gem'
LITTLE GEM MAGNOLIA
Ⓝ ☼ ◐ ♦ Z7–9 H9–3 ↕20ft (6m) ↔10ft (3m)
A slow-growing, compact columnar tree. Leaves are dark green above, with a reddish down on the reverse. Flowers remain cup-shaped, rather than opening flat.

Chamaecyparis lawsoniana
LAWSON FALSE CYPRESS
Ⓝ ☼ ◊ Z5–9 H9–5 ↕130ft (40m) ↔15ft (5m)
Grows best in a slightly acidic soil but will also survive in a slightly alkaline one. Many named forms, some tall and slender, others best suited to a rock garden.

Acer saccharum 'Newton Sentry'
NEWTON SENTRY SUGAR MAPLE
Ⓝ ☼ ◊ Z4–8 H8–1 ↕30ft (10m) ↔8ft (2.5m)
This most slender sugar maple has short branchlets on the main branches. Leathery leaves have good yellow to orange fall color. May be sold as 'Columnare'.

Quercus robur 'Fastigiata'
UPRIGHT ENGLISH OAK
☼ ◐ ◊ Z5–8 H8–3 ↕↔50ft (15m)
Tolerant of alkaline soils but varies in size when grown from seed. Greenish catkins appear in spring before the leaves. Bark becomes deeply fissured with age.

Trees with interesting winter bark

Patterned, smooth, fissured, flaking, or brightly colored bark that reflects the winter sun, adds much to a garden's pleasure after the leaves fall. Plant these trees where they will be most visible during winter. Locate those with light-colored bark against a background of evergreens so they stand out, and those with bright bark where they catch the sun. Certain specimen trees on page 96 also have interesting bark.

Platanus occidentalis
SYCAMORE, BUTTONWOOD
Ⓝ ☼ ◊ Z5–8 H8–3
↕80ft (24m) ↔70ft (20m)
Brown bark flakes off irregularly, exposing whitish inner bark to produce a mottled appearance with age. Leafs out late. Used extensively as a street tree.

Pinus nigra
BLACK PINE, AUSTRIAN PINE
☼ ◊ Z5–8 H8–3
↕100ft (30m) ↔20–25ft (6–8m)
A conical, two-needle pine with a dense head of spreading branches at right-angles to the trunk. Does well in coastal locations. Makes a good screen or windbreak and will grow in most soils.

Betula nigra 'Heritage'
HERITAGE RIVER BIRCH
Ⓝ ☼ ◑● Z4–9 H9–1
↕60ft (18m) ↔40ft (12m)
This may be a single- or multi-stemmed tree and prefers acid soil. Needs moist soil in spring but will grow where soil is dryer in summer. Resistant to borers and leaf miners.

Arbutus unedo
STRAWBERRY TREE
☼ ◊ Z8–9 H9–6
↕↔25ft (8m)
Large shrub or small tree with white flowers in fall. The fruit persists until the following fall, so both are present together. Tolerates wind, alkaline soil, and coastal conditions.

Pseudocydonia sinensis
CHINESE QUINCE
☼ ◊ Z6–8 H8–4 ↕↔20ft (6m)
Dense upright tree with dark green foliage that turns yellow to red in fall. Light pink, early spring flowers precede egg-shaped, aromatic yellow fruit in autumn.

Lagerstroemia indica
COMMON CRAPE MYRTLE
☼ ◊ Z7–9 H9–6 ↕20ft (6m) ↔20ft (6m)
Upright habit and peeling gray and brown bark. Flowers may be white, red, or purple, blooming from summer to fall. Native to China.

Prunus serrula
ORIENTAL CHERRY
☼ ◑ Z6–8 H8–6 ↕↔30ft (10m)
A rounded tree with white flowers in spring as the foliage unfurls, followed by unshowy red fruit. Leaves turn yellow in fall. Polished, lined winter bark is the best feature. Susceptible to the usual cherry pests and diseases.

Broussonetia papyrifera
PAPER MULBERRY
☼ ◊ Z6–9 H9–6 ↕↔25ft (8m)
Grows well on poor soils, but needs protection from strong winds. Separate male and female flowers on same plant give orange-red edible fruits like mulberries in fall. Paper is made from shaggy bark.

MORE CHOICES

- *Acer buergerianum* Z5–9 H9–5
- *Arbutus menziesii* Z7–9 H9–7
- *Carpinus caroliniana* Z3–9 H9–1
- *Cornus mas* Z5–8 H8–5
- *Lagerstroemia* 'Natchez' Z6–9 H9–6
- *Oxydendrum arboreum* Z5–9 H9–3
- *Photinia villosa* Z4–9 H9–1
- *Poncirus trifoliata* 'Flying Dragon' Z4–9 H9–1
- *Salix babylonica var. pekinensis* 'Tortuosa' Z6–8 H9–6

Acer griseum
PAPERBARK MAPLE
☼ ◊ Z4–8 H8–1 ↕↔30ft (10m)
This slow-growing tree's bark character develops at a young age. Dark, bluish green leaves turn bronzy red and are held well into late fall. This native to central China is pest-free.

Spring-flowering trees

After winter's dark days, the sight of a tree bursting into flower in spring is one of the most wonderful of all garden displays. As an emotional pick-me-up, it rivals beds massed with annuals or the colorful sweep of a well-designed perennial border. Plant these trees where they can be seen from inside the house, to ensure full appreciation of their often-fleeting beauty.

Syringa vulgaris 'Charles Joly'
CHARLES JOLY LILAC
Z4–8 H8–1 ↕↔22ft (7m)
Produces conical clusters of sweetly scented, dark purple-red, double flowers. Requires little pruning. A small tree or large multistemmed shrub.

Cercis canadensis var. *alba*
EASTERN REDBUD
Ⓝ Z6–9 H9–3
↕↔30ft (10m)
Early spring flowers often last two to three weeks. This appealing small tree looks good in a woodland border and other naturalized situations. This spreading tree has heart-shaped leaves.

Syringa vulgaris 'Sensation'
SENSATION LILAC
Z4–8 H8–1 ↕↔22ft (7m)
Small tree or large shrub with very fragrant flowers freely produced. Deadhead the plant for the first few years and cut out weak shoots in winter. Suitable for heavy clay soils. Subject to mildew.

Cornus kousa
KOUSA DOGWOOD
Z5–8 H8–5 ↕22ft (7m) ↔15ft (5m)
A conical tree that grows best on sandy, organic, slightly acidic soils. Early summer flowers are followed by edible red fruit. Leaves turn red in fall.

MORE CHOICES

- *Aesculus pavia* Z5–9 H9–5
- *Aleurites fordii* Z11 H12–10
- *Amelanchier arborea* Z4–9 H9–4
- *Cercis siliquastrum* Z6–9 H9–3
- *Chionanthus virginicus* Z4–9 H9–1
- *Crataegus laciniata* Z6–8 H8–6
- *Gordonia lasianthus* Z8–11 H12–8
- *Laburnum alpinum* Z5–8 H8–5
- *Parkinsonia aculeata* Z11–12 H12–10
- *Prunus persica* Z4–8 H8–1

Cornus mas
CORNELIAN CHERRY
☼ ◐ ◊ Z5–8 H8–4 ↕↔15ft (5m)
Star-shaped flowers on bare branches precede edible, egg-shaped, bright red fruit that entice birds into the garden. Dark green leaves turn reddish purple in fall.

Poncirus trifoliata
HARDY ORANGE
☼ ◊ Z5–9 H9–5 ↕↔15ft (5m)
Vigorous spiny plant does best in acidic soils. Fragrant white flowers. Showy, orange-like fruits grow prolifically in warmer areas. Can be grown as a prickly hedge.

Cornus florida
FLOWERING DOGWOOD
Ⓝ ☼ ◐ ◊ Z5–8 H8–3 ↕20ft (6m) ↔25ft (8m)
Early flowering in pink or white, with clusters of glossy red fruit following in fall. Birds devour them. Excellent red to reddish purple fall color.

Prunus x *yedoensis*
YOSHINO CHERRY,
POTOMAC CHERRY
☼ ◊ Z5–8 H8–5 ↕↔30ft (10m)
Arching tree with almond-scented flowers in early spring before the leaves. Adaptable to most soils. Upright, weeping, and pink-flowered cultivars are available.

Prunus 'Kanzan'
JAPANESE FLOWERING CHERRY
☼ ◊◆ Z6–8 H8–6
↕↔30ft (10m)
Very popular form that spreads more with age. New foliage is copper-colored becoming dark green. This tree flowers in early spring as the leaves unfurl. May be sold as 'Kwanzan.'

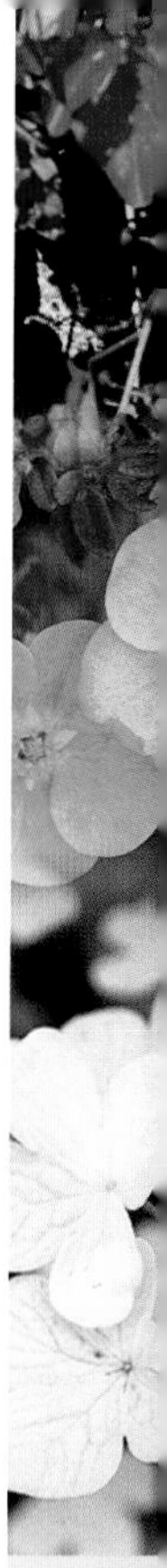

Malus baccata var. *mandshurica*
MANCHURIAN CRABAPPLE
☼ ◊ Z3–7 H7–1 ↕↔50ft (15m)
A geographical variety of the Siberian crab, this tree flowers earlier with pink buds and has more fragrant white flowers, as well as larger, long-stalked, reddish-yellow fruits. This tree is fast-growing and round.

Malus 'Almey'
ALMEY CRABAPPLE
☼ ◊ Z3–7 H7–1 ↕↔25ft (8m)
An old variety with fragrant flowers and edible, bright red fruits that are widest at the top and stay on the tree well into winter. An ideal speciman tree, it is also susceptible to diseases, especially apple scab.

MORE CHOICES

- *Rhododendron arboreum* Z7–9 H9–7
- *Rhododendron canescens* Z6–9 H9–4
- *Styrax americanum* Z6–8 H8–6
- *Viburnum prunifolium* Z3–9 H9–1

Laburnum x *watereri*
GOLDEN CHAIN TREE
☼ ◊ Z6–8 H8–3 ↕↔25ft (8m)
An adaptable spreading tree that grows in most soils, except very wet. Its young shoots are almost hairless and its dark green leaves are composed of three elliptic leaflets. It needs midday shade in the southern part of its hardiness range. Its seeds are poisonous.

Paulownia tomentosa
ROYAL PAULOWNIA, EMPRESS TREE
☼ ◇ Z5–8 H8–5 ↕40ft (12m) ↔30ft (9m)
Light brown, hairy flower buds are apparent all winter. A closeup of the vanilla-scented flowers reveals yellow stripes inside spotted, pale violet petals.

Aesculus x carnea
RED HORSE CHESTNUT
☼ ◑ ♦ Z7–8 H8–6 ↕70ft (20) ↔50ft (15)
Flowers appear late spring to early summer, followed by spiny fruit. Distinctive, rounded growth habit. Prone to canker, Japanese beetles, and scale insects.

Magnolia virginiana
SWEET BAY MAGNOLIA
Ⓝ ☼ ◑ ◇ Z6–9 H9–6 ↕28ft (9m) ↔20ft (6m)
Smallish lemon-scented flowers are produced throughout the summer. Grows well in soils ranging from dry to swampy, providing they are moderately acidic. Native from Massachusetts to Texas.

Magnolia salicifolia 'Wada's Memory'
WADA'S MEMORY MAGNOLIA
☼ ◇ Z6–8 HX–X ↕28ft (9m) ↔20ft (6m)
Conical tree with lemon-scented foliage. Its large-petalled flowers produce freely, even on young plants. Introduced from Japan.

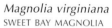

Davidia involucrata
DOVE TREE, HANDKERCHIEF TREE
☼ ◑ ♦ Z6–8 H8–6 ↕50ft (15m) ↔30ft (10m)
Plant this in a soil rich in organic matter. A very showy tree when in flower, its leaves persist until hard frost. Does not flower at a young age.

Summer-flowering trees

Although spring is the time of year when the majority of trees bloom, those that do flower in summer can add interest to the garden, and may tempt one to venture out of doors when the days are hot and humid. Many of those shown here are fragrant – an added bonus – as well as attractive to butterflies and hummingbirds.

Cladrastis kentukea
YELLOW WOOD
Ⓝ ☼ ◊ Z4–9 H9–1 ↕40ft (12m) ↔30ft (10m)
Long white trusses of slightly scented flowers hang from the branches in early summer and give small brown pea-like pods. It looks somewhat like a white laburnum.

Catalpa bignonioides 'Aurea'
GOLDEN SOUTHERN CATALPA
Ⓝ ☼ ◑ Z5–9 H9–3
↕↔30ft (10m)
Bright yellow when it unfurls in late spring, the foliage gradually turns green during summer. Fragrant white flowers produce long, persistent beanlike fruit.

Sophora japonica
JAPANESE PAGODA
☼ ◊ Z5–9 H9–5 ↕to 100ft (30m) ↔70ft (20m)
Spreading tree with glossy dark green leaves turning yellow in fall. Many small trusses of white flowers on shoot tips. Rust can be a problem.

Robinia neomexicana
NEW MEXICO LOCUST
Ⓝ ☼ ◊◑ Z5–9 H9–5 ↕20ft (6m) ↔15ft (5m)
Upright, spiny small tree or large shrub tolerant of poor, sandy soils. Early-summer flowers give brown pods in fall. Grow in a sheltered location, branches are brittle. All parts may cause discomfort if eaten.

MORE CHOICES

- *Albizia julibrissin* Z6–9 H9–6
- *Aralia spinosa* Z4–9 H9–1
- *Clerodendrum trichotomum* Z7–9 H9–7
- *Delonix regia* Z11–15 H10
- *Eucryphia glutinosa* Z8–11 H12–8
- *Lagerstroemia indica* 'William Toovey' Z7–9 H9–7
- *Kalopanax septemlobus* Z5–9 H9–4
- *Liriodendron tulipifera* Z5–9 H9–1
- *Oxydendrum arboreum* Z5–9 H9–3
- *Sophora secundiflora* Z7–11 H12–7

Bauhinia x *blakeana*
ORCHID TREE
☼ ◊◊ Z9–11 H12–10
↕20–40ft (6–12m) ↔15ft (5m)
Evergreen tropical tree or shrub with leaves divided in two at the top. Flowers are in small clusters in the leaf axils.

Koelreuteria paniculata
PANICLED GOLDEN RAIN TREE
☼ ◊ Z6–9 H9–1 ↕↔30ft (10m)
Opening leaves are purplish red, become bright green, then turn golden yellow in fall. Yellow flowers appear in midsummer and become inflated fruit.

Jacaranda mimosifolia
BLUE JACARANDA
☼ ◊ Z13–15 H12–10 ↕to 50ft (15m) ↔22–30ft (7–10m)
Spreading deciduous tree that flowers over a long period. Brown, circular, woody seed pods persist into winter. Very fine, thread-like foliage is bright green.

Lagerstroemia 'Natchez'
NATCHEZ CREPE MYRTLE
☼ ◊ Z6–9 H9–6
↕↔25ft (8m)
Glossy, dark green leaves turn red and orange in fall. From midsummer to fall, clusters of pure white flowers open in arching sprays.

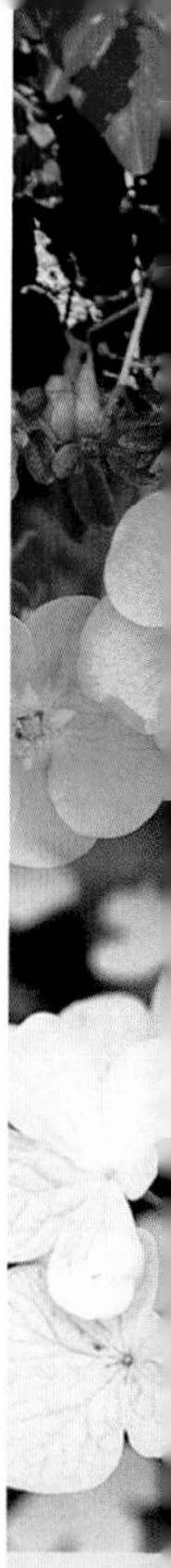

Trees with fragrant flowers

While fragrance in the garden can be enjoyable, not everyone reacts to floral scents the same way. A plant that is strongly scented to one, may seem almost without perfume to another. Before deciding what to plant, try to find it in flower at a local garden center or park to be sure the scent is one you can detect. If possible, plant fragrant trees upwind of the house.

Franklinia alatamaha
FRANKLIN TREE
Ⓝ ☼ 💧 Z6–9 H9–6 ↕↔15ft (5m)
Flowers from midsummer onward. Needs an acidic to neutral soil. Native to Georgia, it was collected in 1770, and has not been found in the wild since.

Oxydendrum arboreum
SOURWOOD
Ⓝ ☼ 💧 pH Z5–9 H9–3 ↕↔50ft (15m)
Slow-growing, pyramidal US native, rounded at the top. Flowers in summer, foliage turns yellow, red, and purple in autumn. Excellent as a specimen.

Magnolia grandiflora
SOUTHERN MAGNOLIA
Ⓝ ☼ ◑ 💧 Z7–9 H9–1 ↕↔30ft (9m)
Slow-growing, pyramidal evergreen that branches close to the ground. Fragrant, large white flowers bloom from late spring to early summer. Pest-free.

Styrax obassia
FRAGRANT SNOWBELL
☼ ◑ 💧 Z6–8 H8–6 ↕40ft (12m) ↔22ft (7m)
Wonderful winter shape has many winding, turning branches. Leaves are easily injured in spring, because they emerge very early.

Chionanthus virginicus
WHITE FRINGETREE
Ⓝ ☼ 💧 Z4–9 H9–1 ↕↔20ft (6m)
A tree with a variable habit: some are open and spreading, others are denser. Lightly fragrant flowers precede dark blue, oval fruits with a white coating.

Tilia americana
AMERICAN LINDEN, BASSWOOD
Ⓝ ☼ ◑ ◊ Z2–8 H8–1
↕80ft (25m) ↔40ft (12m)
Easy to grow, but tends to be shallow rooted unless soil is deep. Fragrant, pale yellow summer flowers attractive to bees and butterflies.

Prunus x *yedoensis*
YOSHINO CHERRY, POTOMAC CHERRY
☼ ◊ Z5–8 H8–5 ↕↔30ft (10m)
Arching tree with almond-scented flowers in early spring before the leaves. Adaptable to most soils. Upright, weeping, and pink-flowered cultivars are available.

Albizia julibrissin
SILK-TREE, MIMOSA
☼ ◊ Z6–9 H9–6 ↕↔30ft (10m)
Light gray-brown seedpods persist through the winter. Grows quickly and normally is not long-lived. Very susceptible to wilt and webworm. Self-sows strongly.

Malus sargentii
SARGENT'S CRABAPPLE
☼ ◊ Z4–8 H8–1 ↕10ft (3m) ↔15ft (5m)
Small tree with pink buds in spring and bright red, cherry-like fruits that last well into winter and are attractive to birds. Slightly disease prone.

MORE CHOICES

- *Cladrastis kentukea* Z4–9 H9–1
- *Clerodendrum trichotomum* Z7–9 H9–7
- *Hamamelis virginiana* Z3–8 H8–1
- *Lindera benzoin* Z4–9 H8–1
- *Magnolia stellata* 'Waterlily' Z6–9 H9–6
- *Magnolia virginiana* Z6–9 H9–6
- *Magnolia* x *soulangeana* Z5–9 H9–5
- *Osmanthus fragrans* Z8–11 H12–8
- *Paulownia tomentosa* Z5–8 H8–5

Robinia pseudoacacia
BLACK LOCUST
Ⓝ ☼ ◑ Z4–9 H9–3 ↕80ft (24m) ↔50 ft (15m)
Very fragrant flowers in late spring to early summer are followed by flat brown pods. Bees are very attracted to the flowers, producing a rich honey.

Tilia tomentosa
SILVER LINDEN
☼ ◑ ◑ Z6–9 H9–6 ↕100ft (30m) ↔70ft (20m)
A broadly pyramidal tree for a moist fertile soil, but tolerant of drought when established. The flowers are fragrant and can stupefy bees in summer.

Trees with fine, textured foliage

Narrow or needlelike foliage on trees allows light and water to penetrate to the grass or other groundcovers that grow below, allowing them to thrive. The foliage is also easier to clean up in fall and does not create solid mats of fallen leaves that may threaten to smother other plants unless removed promptly and thoroughly.

Gymnocladus dioica
KENTUCKY COFFEE TREE
Ⓝ ☼ ◊ Z5–9 H9–5 ↕70ft (20m) ↔50ft (15m)
Spreading tree with pink-edged young leaves, then yellow foliage in fall. Clusters of white flowers bloom in early summer, followed by hanging pods on females.

Cedrus deodara
DEODAR CEDAR
☼ ◐ Z6–9 H9–6
↕50–80ft (15–24m) ↔15–30ft (5–9m)
Starts out conical and becomes wide-spreading with age. Bark is dark brown to black. Moderate growth rate.

Juniperus virginiana 'Burkii'
BURK'S BLUE CEDAR
Ⓝ ☼ ☀ ◊ Z4–8 H8–1
↕20ft (6m) ↔3ft (1m)
Dense, upright small tree that produces attractive, blue-gray foliage, which takes on purple tints in winter. Like the species, it is susceptible to cedar rust. Brown-violet fruit ripens in the first fall.

Tsuga canadensis
EASTERN HEMLOCK, CANADA HEMLOCK
Ⓝ ☀ ◐ Z4–8 H8–1 ↕↔50ft (15m)
Grows on both alkaline and acidic soils, but not in wet soils or exposed locations. Excellent hedging plant. Many cultivars are upright, dwarf, or weeping.

Chamaecyparis pisifera 'Filifera'
THREADLEAVED SAWARA FALSE CYPRESS
☼ ◊ ◐ pH Z4–8 H8–1 ↕70ft (20m) ↔15ft (5m)
A slow-growing tree with narrow, whip-like, and mostly unbranched shoots, to which the scalelike leaves are closely pressed. Other forms have golden foliage.

Buddleja alternifolia
FOUNTAIN BUDDLEIA
Z4–9 H10–1 ↕↔12ft (4m)
Small tree or large shrub with arching branches and narrow leaves. The fragrant flowers cover the branches in early summer and are attractive to butterflies.

Pinus strobus
EASTERN WHITE PINE
Ⓝ Z4–9 H9–1 ↕100ft (30m) ↔25ft (8m)
Conical when young, this pine becomes irregular and flat-topped with age. The smooth gray bark becomes black and cracked.

MORE CHOICES

- *Cedrus atlantica* Z6–9 H9–6
- *Chamaecyparis obtusa* 'Filicoides' Z4–8 H8–1
- *Cryptomeria japonica* 'Yoshino' Z6–9 H9–6
- *Gleditsia triancanthos inermis* Z3–7 H7–1
- *Ilex* x *attenuata* 'Foster's #2' Z6–9 H9–4
- *Juniperus virginiana* 'Silver Spreader' Z3–9 H9–1
- x *Cupressocyparis leylandii* 'Naylor's Blue' Z6–9 H9–3

Metasequoia glyptostroboides
DAWN REDWOOD
Z4–11 H12–1
↕100ft (30m) ↔75ft (22m)
Foliage turns orange-brown before it sheds in late fall. Bark is orange-brown year round, and the trunk becomes inversely fluted with age. The tree's growth rate is fast.

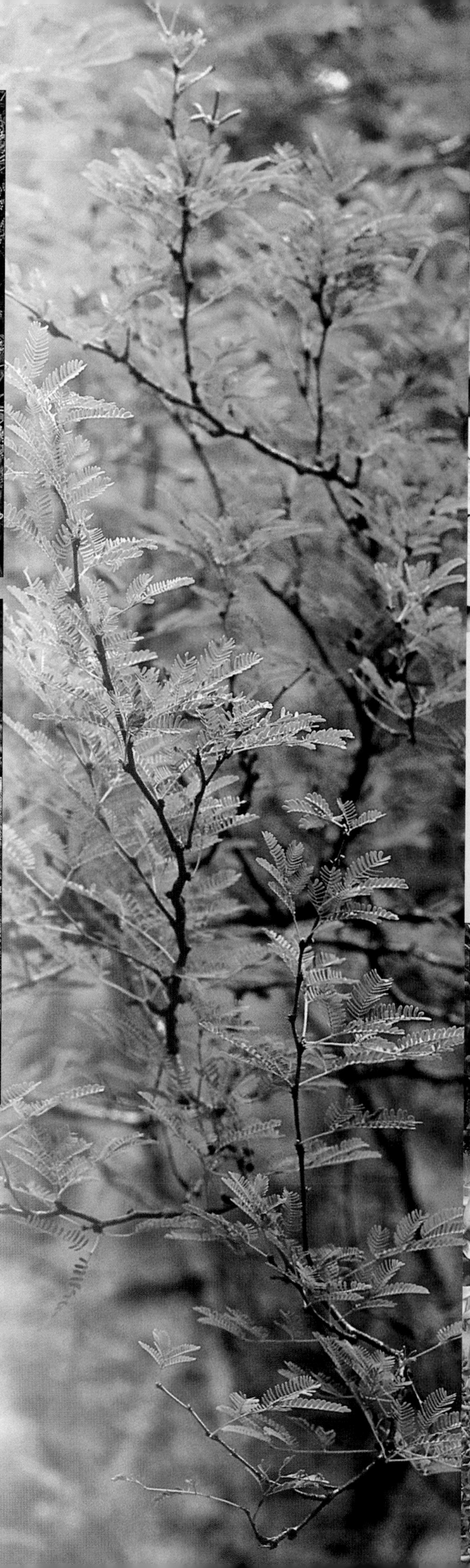

Acacia farnesiana
PERFUME ACACIA
Z10–11 H12–10
↕22ft (7m) ↔15–25ft (5–8m)
Fast-growing, thorny, many-branched small tree. Very fragrant small yellow flowers with long protruding stamens in clusters in early spring.

Trees with coarse, bold foliage

These trees make a bold statement in the landscape and are ideal as specimen trees, where their beauty can be fully appreciated. Because their large leaves cast a dense shade and shed rainfall, it is often difficult to grow other plants beneath them.

Magnolia macrophylla
BIGLEAF MAGNOLIA
☼ ◑ 🌢 Z6–9 H12–10
↕↔30ft (9m)
A rounded tree with huge fragrant flowers and large, oval, reddish conelike fruit. Immense leaves are sometimes over two feet long. Needs a large setting.

Magnolia grandiflora
SOUTHERN MAGNOLIA
Ⓝ ☼ ◑ 🌢 Z7–9 H9–1 ↕↔30ft (9m)
Slow-growing, pyramidal evergreen that branches close to the ground. Fragrant, large white flowers bloom from late spring to early summer. Pest-free.

Davidia involucrata
DOVE TREE, HANDKERCHIEF TREE
☼ ◑ 🌢 Z6–8 H8–6 ↕50ft (15m) ↔30ft (10m)
Plant this in a soil rich in organic matter. A very showy tree when in flower, its leaves persist until hard frost. Does not flower at a young age.

Cladrastis kentukea
YELLOWWOOD
Ⓝ ☼ ◊ pH Z4–9 H9–1
↕40ft (12m) ↔30ft (10m)
long trusses of white, slightly fragrant flowers, similar to a laburnum, appear in early summer and small brown seed pods in fall.

Pseudocydonia sinensis
CHINESE QUINCE
☼ ◊ Z6–8 H8–4 ↕↔20ft (6m)
Dense upright tree with dark green foliage that turns yellow to red in fall. Light pink, early spring flowers precede egg-shaped, aromatic yellow fruit in autumn.

Catalpa bignonioides 'Aurea'
GOLDEN SOUTHERN CATALPA
Ⓝ ☼ ◊ Z5–9 H9–5 ↕↔50ft (15m)
One of the last trees to leaf out in spring, this has a spreading growth habit. The early summer flowers become long, slender pods that persist all winter. Leaves turn green later where summers are hot.

Paulownia tomentosa
ROYAL PAULOWNIA, EMPRESS TREE
☼ ◊ Z5–8 H8–5 ↕40ft (12m) ↔30ft (9m)
Light brown, hairy flower buds are apparent all winter. A closeup of the vanilla-scented flowers reveals yellow stripes inside spotted, pale violet petals.

MORE CHOICES

- *Aesculus pavia* Z5–9 H9–5
- *Aralia spinosa* Z4–9 H9–1
- *Firmiana simplex* Z7–15 H12–8

Morus rubra
RED MULBERRY
Ⓝ ☼ ◊◊ Z5–9 H9–5
↕40ft (12m) ↔50ft (15m)
A rounded tree with dark green, broad leaves up to 5in (13cm) long that turn yellow in fall. Cylindrical, sweet-tasting fruit ripen to dark purple in late summer.

Platanus occidentalis
BUTTONWOOD, SYCAMORE
Ⓝ ☼ ◊ Z5–8 H8–3 ↕80ft (24m) ↔70ft (20m)
Wide-spreading tree with very attractive, flaking brown, gray, and cream bark. Produces green, then brown, fruit clusters that hang on in fall and winter.

Trees with outstanding fall color

Fall color is one of the glories of the northeastern forests, but there are many trees for the Southeast, as well, that have equally brilliant coloration. Use those shown here sparingly: one tree makes a statement, but if you plant too many, they can lose their impact. Remember that trees show their best color when grown in full sunlight.

Robinia pseudoacacia 'Frisia'
GOLDEN BLACK LOCUST
Ⓝ ☼ 💧 Z4–9 H9–4 ↕50ft (15m) ↔25ft (8m)
The leaves retain their color all summer. Long pendent tassels of fragrant white flowers open in late spring. A fast-growing, good tree for poor soils.

Gleditsia triacanthos
HONEYLOCUST
Ⓝ ☼ 💧💧 Z3–7 H7–1 ↕70ft (20m) ↔50ft (15m)
Very adaptable trees that grow in most soils. Many named forms have different growth habits or foliage colors. All are very salt-tolerant and easy to grow.

Parrotia persica
PERSIAN PARROTIA
☼ 💧 Z4–7 H7–1 ↕↔50ft (15m)
A useful accent tree with yellow, orange, and red fall color; peeling gray, green, white, and brown bark; and excellent pest and disease resistance. Native to Iran.

Amelanchier x *grandiflora*
'Autumn Brilliance'
AUTUMN BRILLIANCE APPLE SERVICEBERRY
☼ ◑ 💧 pH Z3–7 H7–1 ↕25ft (8m) ↔30ft (10m)
A spreading small tree or large shrub with white spring flowers. The blue-black fruit are edible and loved by birds. Emerging new foliage is bronze-tinted.

Pistacia chinensis
CHINESE PISTACHE
☼ ◊ Z6–9 H9–6 ↕80ft (25m) ↔30ft (10m)
Shiny, dark green leaves hold on late into fall before coloring up. Flowers (before the leaves) are followed by fruit that ripens from light blue to red. Pest-free.

Ginkgo biloba 'Autumn Gold'
AUTUMN GOLD MAIDENHAIR TREE
☼ ◊ Z3–9 H9–1
↕50 ft (15m) ↔30ft (9m)
Used extensively in city sites because of its tough constitution, its bright green, distinctly fan-shaped leaves turn gold in fall. Basically pest free.

Acer rubrum 'October Glory'
OCTOBER GLORY MAPLE
Ⓝ ☼ ◐ Z3–9 H9–1 ↕70ft (20m) ↔40ft (12m)
Forms a rounder profile and has glossier deeper green leaves than the species. One of the hardiest of the red maples, it is very fast-growing and nearly pest-free.

MORE CHOICES

- *Carya ovata* Z4–8 H8–1
- *Castanea mollissima* Z4–8 H8–1
- *Cercidiphyllum japonicum* Z4–8 H8–1
- *Cladrastis ketuckea* Z4–9 H9–1
- *Cornus florida* Z5–8 H8–3
- *Diospyros virginiana* Z4–9 H9–1
- *Fraxinus americana* Z6–9 H9–6
- *Hamamelis virginiana* Z3–8 H8–1
- *Liquidambar styraciflua* 'Lane Roberts' Z6–9 H9–6
- *Metasequoia glyptrostroboides* Z4–11 H12–1
- *Oxydendrum arboreum* Z5–9 H9–3
- *Quercus alba* Z5–9 H8–1
- *Quercus palustris* Z5–8 H8–5
- *Rhus glabra* Z2–8 H8–1
- *Sapindus drummondii* Z8–11 H10–2
- *Sassafras albidum* Z4–8 H8–3
- *Taxodium ascendens* Z5–11 H12–5

Nyssa sylvatica
SOUR GUM
Ⓝ ☼ ◐ Z4–9 H9–2
↕70ft (20m) ↔30ft (9m)
Has a cone-shaped head with a straight trunk and horizontal branches. Useful as a street tree or specimen. Tolerates coastal conditions, but not shade.

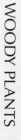

Taxodium distichum
BALD CYPRESS
Ⓝ ☼ ◐ Z5–11 H12–5
↕80ft (24m) ↔25ft (8m)
The needles turn rust-brown in fall before dropping. Pale brown, shallowly fissured bark. Distinctive aerial roots around the base in wet sites. Moderate growth rate.

Trees attractive to wildlife

While skunks and raccoons may not be the most desirable of garden visitors, they do pay nightly calls on many gardens to eat slugs, snails, and grubs. To encourage more welcome and attractive guests, plant trees that produce fruits appealing to birds, squirrels, and chipmunks, or have fragrant, nectar-rich flowers that attract moths and hummingbirds.

Ilex cornuta 'Burfordii'
BURFORD'S CHINESE HOLLY
Z6–9 H9–1 ↕12ft (4m) ↔8ft (2.5m)
Upright form with leaves that lack spiny margins. Very free-flowering and fruiting. The berries last well into winter if birds don't eat them first.

Cornus kousa 'Milky Way'
MILKY WAY KOUSA DOGWOOD
Z5–8 H8–3 ↕23ft (7m) ↔15ft (5m)
Showy white flowers are very freely produced in early summer. In the fall, pendulous, strawberry-like fruits ripen, and the leaves turn a crimson color.

Morus alba
WHITE MULBERRY
Z4–8 H8–1 ↕↔30ft (10m)
Adaptable, tough tree that is salt and pollution tolerant. Insignificant flowers give whitish edible fruits that turn red, then black, on some trees. Introduced from China to feed silkworms.

Malus sargentii
SARGENT'S CRABAPPLE
Z4–8 H8–1
↕6–10ft (2–3m) ↔8–15ft (2.5–5m)
White flowers open from red buds in late spring. Birds feed on long-lasting, dark red fruit $\frac{3}{8}$in (9mm) across. Native to Japan.

Myrica cerifera
WAX MYRTLE
Ⓝ ☼ ◐ ● ◇ ◑ ◆ Z6–9 H9–6 ↕↔15ft (5m)
This shrub produces small, yellow-green catkins in spring. Following these, dense clusters of waxy gray fruit appear along the shoots and last through winter.

Fagus grandifolia
AMERICAN BEECH
Ⓝ ☼ ◐ ◇ Z3–9 H9–1 ↕↔80ft (25m)
An imposing tree with smooth gray bark, even on older trees. Plant in slightly acidic soil that is neither compacted nor wet. Slow-growing, but worth it.

Ostrya virginiana
AMERICAN HOP HORNBEAM
Ⓝ ◐ ◇ Z5–9 H9–2
↕50ft (15m) ↔40ft (12m)
Conical, slow-growing tree with leaves that turn yellow in fall. Hop-like fruit is attractive. The "horn" in common name is for the wood that is as hard as horn; "beam" is old English for wood.

Sorbus x *thuringiaca*
GERMAN MOUNTAIN ASH
☼ ◐ ◇ Z5–8 H8–5
↕50ft (15m) ↔25ft (8m)
Small tree with oval head and closely held branches. Flat heads of white flowers in spring give fruits. Dark green leaves with gray hairs on underside turn orange in fall.

Crataegus viridis 'Winter King'
GREEN HAWTHORN
Ⓝ ☼ ◇ ◑ Z5–7 H7–5 ↕20ft (6m) ↔15ft (5m)
Rounded and very thorny, with gray-green, waxy stems. Fruits persist into winter and are larger than the species. Less rust-susceptible than other hawthorns.

MORE CHOICES

- *Carpinus caroliniana* Z3–9 H9–1
- *Celtis laevigata* Z5–9 H9–3
- *Magnolia grandiflora* Z7–9 H9–1
- *Photinia serrulata* Z4–8 H8–1
- *Prunus angustifolia* Z4–8 H8–1
- *Prunus caroliniana* Z4–10 H10–1
- *Prunus serotina* Z4–8 H8–1
- *Rhamnus caroliniana* Z5–9 H9–4
- *Vaccinium arboreum* Z9–10 H10–8

WOODY PLANTS

Drought-tolerant trees

Most plants prefer a moist, well-drained soil. In order to survive and grow well in gardens that are located on a hillside where water drains quickly, or in gardens with a very sandy soil, tough trees must be sought out. Given care until well-established, the trees shown here should thrive if healthy, despite a shortage of moisture.

Gleditsia triacanthos var. *inermis* 'Skyline'
SKYLINE HONEYLOCUST
Ⓝ ☼ 💧 Z3–7 H7–1 ↕to 50ft (15m) ↔70ft (20m)
One of several named forms of thornless honeylocust with foliage of green, yellow, or bronzish red. Subject to leaf gall that inflates leaf tips. Pollution tolerant.

Zelkova serrata
JAPANESE ZELKOVA
☼ ◑ 🌢 Z5–9 H9–5 ↕100ft (30m) ↔60ft (18m)
As it matures, smooth gray bark flakes off to reveal orange patches. Rough-textured, elmlike leaves have toothed edges. Native to Japan, Taiwan, and South Korea.

Quercus palustris
PIN OAK
Ⓝ ☼ ◑ 💧 Z5–8 H8–5 ↕70ft (20m) ↔40ft (12m)
Very striking growth form, with a clearly pyramidal outline and horizontal branching habit. Fall color can be an outstanding red. Tolerant of city conditions.

Quercus phellos
WILLOW OAK
Ⓝ ☼ ◑ 💧 Z6–9 H9–3 ↕70ft (20m) ↔50ft (15m)
Fast-growing, with a cone-shaped growth habit. Smooth gray bark ages with shallow ridges. In warmer areas, dead leaves hang on through winter.

MORE CHOICES

- *Callistemon rigidus* Z10–15 H12–10
- *Cassia leptophyllum* Z11–12 H12–10
- *Cedrus deodara* Z6–9 H9–6
- *Celtis occidentalis* Z2–9 H9–1
- *Chilopis linearis* Z8–9 H9–8
- x *Chitalpa tashkentensis* Z6–10 H10–5
- *Diospyros texana* Z9–11 H12–9
- *Juniperus virginiana* Z3–9 H9–1
- *Lagerstroemia indica* Z7–9 H9–6
- *Pinus* spp. Z2–10 H9–1
- *Prosopis glandulosa* Z8–11 H12–7
- *Rhus copallina* Z5–9 H9–5
- *Sophora japonica* Z5–9 H9–5

Ginkgo biloba
MAIDENHAIR TREE
☼ ◊ Z5–9 H9–3 ↕100ft (30m) ↔25ft (8m)
Narrow to spreading young tree becomes umbrella-shaped. Slow-growing, tolerant of pollution and heat, and free of pests. Outstanding yellow fall foliage.

Pistacia chinensis
CHINESE PISTACHE
☼ ◊ Z6–9 H9–6 ↕80ft (25m) ↔30ft (10m)
Shiny, dark green leaves hold on late into fall before coloring up. Flowers (before the leaves) are followed by fruit that ripens from light blue to red. Pest-free. Dolor sit amet, consectetur adipscing elit, sed diam nonnumy elusmod tempor incidunt ut labore et dolore magna allquam.

Fraxinus pennsylvanica
GREEN ASH
Ⓝ ☼ ◐ Z3–9 H9–4 ↕↔70ft (20m)
An upright tree that spreads with age. Its olive-green, shiny foliage turns yellow in autumn. The lance-shaped leaves can grow up to 12in (30cm) long. Avoid seedling-grown trees as many bear nuisance fruit. Prone to borers and scale, this is a deciduous and vigourous tree.

Carpinus betulus 'Fastigiata'
UPRIGHT EUROPEAN HORNBEAM
☼ ◊ Z4–8 H8–3 ↕50ft (15m) ↔40ft (12m)
Narrowly upright when young, more rounded with age. Mostly problem-free and tolerates city conditions. Flowers are in small catkins and fruits attract wildlife.

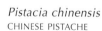

Salt-tolerant trees

With its long coastline, the Southeast is susceptible to salt-laden winds that can travel far inland. By altering the chemistry of the soil as it washes through, salt interferes with the uptake of minerals that plants need to survive. Also, salt can dry and burn the leaves of many species. The following trees can cope with these problems and show no effects.

Cryptomeria japonica
JAPANESE CEDAR
Z6–9 H9–4 ↕70ft (20m) ↔25ft (8m)
Cryptomeria is one of the few conifers that can be successfully coppiced (cut back severely). Normally a conical or columnar tree, it is a moderately fast grower.

MORE CHOICES

- *Araucaria heterophylla* Z9–11 H12–9
- *Ardisia paniculata* Z13–15 H12–10
- *Avicennia germinans* Z11–15 H12–10
- *Cocoloba uvifera* Z10–11 H12–9
- *Laguncularia racemosa* Z12–15 H12–10
- *Ligustrum ovifolium* 'Aureum' Z6–10 H10–9
- *Ligustrum ovifolium* 'Variegatum' Z7–11 H12–4
- *Pinus clausa* Z8–9 H9–8
- *Quercus virginiana* Z8–10 H10–7
- *Rhizophora mangle* Z11–15 H12–10
- *Salix alba* Z4–9 H9–1
- *Tamarix gallica* Z4–8 H8–2

Prunus maritima
BEACH PLUM
Z3–6 H6–1
↕6–8ft (2–2.5m) ↔indefinite
A small tree or large shrub that spreads by suckers. Its white flowers appear in late spring and give purple to crimson fruits that make excellent jelly. Native from Maine to Virginia.

Chamaecyparis pisifera 'Filifera'
THREADLEAVED SAWARA FALSE CYPRESS
Z4–8 H8–1
↕40ft (12m) ↔15ft (5m)
Slow-growing tree that prefers a slightly acidic, moist soil. It forms a large mound at first and eventually a tree. There is also a form with yellow foliage.

Hippophae rhamnoides
SEA BUCKTHORN
Z3–8 H8–1 ↕↔20ft (6m)
Small tree or large deciduous shrub with small yellow flowers in spring, followed by fruit, but only on female plants. It is very salt-tolerant.

Salix alba var. *vitellina*
GOLDEN WILLOW
☼ ◊ Z7–9 H9–7
↕80ft (25m) ↔30ft (10m)
This needs to be cut back hard in late winter or early spring to get the brightly colored new growth. May be grown as a small tree or a large shrub.

Ilex opaca
AMERICAN HOLLY
Ⓝ ☼ ◐ ● ◊ Z5–9 H9–5
↕45ft (14m) ↔4ft (1.2m)
Crimson (sometimes yellow or orange) berries enhance this evergreen in winter. Like most hollies, spiny leaves are occasionally smooth-edged. May be pruned hard once established.

Ulmus parvifolia
CHINESE ELM
☼ ◊ Z5–9 H9–5 ↕↔50ft (15m)
Spreading tree with flaking orange and brown bark. Very small red flowers appear in late summer, followed by green fruit and yellow to red leaves in late fall.

Butia capitata
JELLY PALM
☼ ◊ Z11–12 H12–10
↕12–20ft (4–6m) ↔10–15ft (3–5m)
Slow-growing, with stem clothed in old leaf bases. Sprays of yellow flowers up to 5ft (1.5m) long in summer give round, yellow to purple fruits. In dry soil, will survive temperatures close to freezing.

Pinus thunbergii
JAPANESE BLACK PINE
☼ ◗ Z5–8 H8–5 ↕↔50ft (15m)
Conical younger trees become more rounded and picturesquely irreglar with age. Bark is dark purplish gray, and the shoots and buds are covered with downy white scales. Moderate growth rate.

Trees for moist soils

Sometimes a garden can be wet without actually having swamplike conditions. If the water table is close to the surface, many deep-rooted trees can suffer. Those shown here will grow well in such conditions, and in land bordering a lake, pond, or stream.

Acer rubrum
RED MAPLE
Ⓝ ☼ ◑ 💧 pH Z3–9 H9–1 ↕70ft (20m) ↔30ft (9m)
Tiny red flowers emerge before the leaves herald the arrival of spring in eastern North America. For the best display of vivid red fall color, grow in acidic soil.

Salix alba var. *vitellina* 'Britzensis'
CORALBARK WILLOW
☼ 💧 Z4–9 H9–1 ↕100ft (30m) ↔75ft (22.5m)
Color is more intense on new growth, so cut shoots back almost to the base every second spring. Will grow in most soils except very alkaline.

Nyssa sylvatica
SOUR GUM
Ⓝ ☼ ◑ 💧 Z4–9 H9–2 ↕70ft (20m) ↔30ft (9m)
Has a cone-shaped head with a straight trunk and horizontal branches. Useful as a street tree or specimen. Tolerates coastal conditions, but not shade.

Metasequoia glyptostroboides
DAWN REDWOOD
◑ 💧 Z4–11 H12–1 ↕100ft (30m) ↔75ft (22m)
Foliage turns orange-brown before it sheds in late fall. Bark is orange-brown year round, and the trunk becomes inversely fluted with age. Growth rate is fast.

Quercus palustris
PIN OAK
Ⓝ ☼ ◑ 💧 Z5–8 H8–5 ↕70ft (20m) ↔40ft (12m)
Very striking growth form, with a clearly pyramidal outline and horizontal branching habit. Fall color can be an outstanding red. Tolerant of city conditions.

Ulmus americana
AMERICAN ELM
Ⓝ ☼ ◇ Z3–9 H9–1 ↕↔100ft (30m)
Although elms have been devastated by Dutch elm disease in many areas, new resistant hybrids like 'Homestead' and 'Pioneer' make reliable shade trees.

Celtis occidentalis
COMMON HACKBERRY, SUGARBERRY
Ⓝ ☼ ◇ Z2–9 H9–1 ↕70ft (20m) ↔50ft (15m)
Very adaptable to soils and locations. Mature trees have a shape reminiscent of American elm. Spring flowers are not showy, but the brown-red fall fruit are sweet.

Halesia diptera var. *magniflora*
TWO-WINGED SILVERBELL
Ⓝ ☼ ◐ ◆ Z4–8 H8–1 ↕20ft (6m) ↔30ft (10m)
Small tree or large shrub with early summer flowers and two-winged green fruit. This variety has larger flowers than the species. Foliage turns yellow in fall.

Betulus nigra
RIVER BIRCH
Ⓝ ☼ ◆◆ Z4–9 H9–1 ↕60ft (18m) ↔40ft (12m)
Tolerates dry soil in summer, providing the soil is wet in spring. 'Heritage' has attractive flaking bark and shows resistance to leaf miners and borers.

Liquidambar styraciflua
AMERICAN SWEET GUM
Ⓝ ☼ ◆ Z6–9 H9–6 ↕100ft (30m) ↔75ft (23m)
This species has fleshy roots and is slow to establish. Does not do well where root space is restricted. Named forms have superior fall color.

MORE CHOICES

- *Carpinus caroliniana* Z3–9 H9–1
- *Carya illinoinensis* Z5–9 H9–1
- *Gordonia lasianthus* Z8–11 H12–8
- *Salix bablonica* 'Tortuosa' Z5–9 H9–5
- *Liriodendron tulipifera* Z5–9 H9–1
- *Magnolia virginiana* Z6–9 H9–6
- *Taxodium distichum* Z5–11 H12–5

Trees for damp or heavy clay soils

Some southeastern areas have heavy clay soils that hold large quantities of water following rain. The fine particle structure of these soils makes them slow draining and, as a result, reduces the amount of oxygen available to plant roots. Still, they are rich in nutrients, and trees such as the ones shown here will survive and even thrive in these growing conditions.

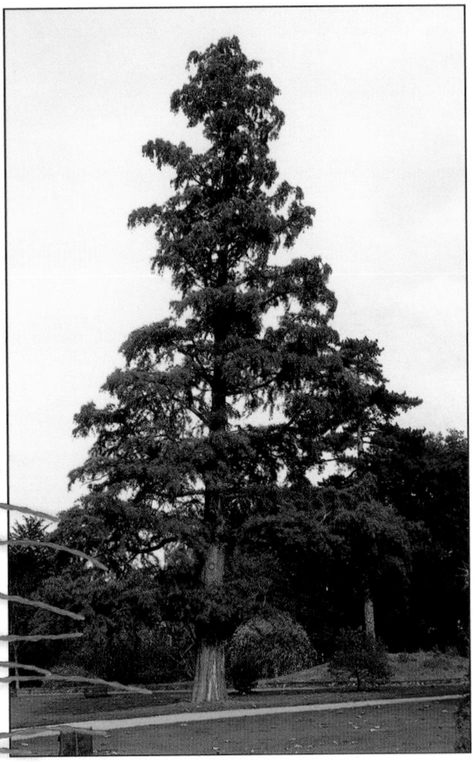

Taxodium distichum
BALD CYPRESS
Ⓝ ☼ ◑ ◈♦ Z5–11 H12–5 ↕80ft (24m) ↔25ft (8m)
Needles turn rust-brown in fall before dropping. Pale brown, shallowly fissured bark. Distinctive aerial roots ("knees") form around the base of the tree in wet sites.

Alnus incana
GRAY ALDER
☼ ◊◈♦ Z2–6 H6–1 ↕70ft (20m) ↔30ft (10m)
A small tree with mid-green leaves that are gray underneath, it is not very tolerant of alkaline soils. Its yellow catkins appear in late winter. A good tree for exposed locations.

Taxodium ascendens
POND CYPRESS
Ⓝ ☼ ◊◈♦ Z5–11 H12–5 ↕60ft (18m) ↔15ft (5m)
Narrowly conical, this deciduous conifer produces erect young shoots that become pendent with age. It has a moderate growth rate.

Magnolia virginiana
SWEET BAY MAGNOLIA
Ⓝ ☼ ◑ ◊ Z6–9 H9–6 ↕28ft (9m) ↔20ft (6m)
Small, lemon-scented flowers produced in summer. Grows well in soils ranging from dry to swampy, if moderately acidic. Native from New England to Texas.

Myrica cerifera
WAX MYRTLE
Ⓝ ☼ ◑ ● ◊◈♦ Z6–9 H9–6 ↕↔15ft (5m)
This shrub produces small, yellow-green catkins in spring. Following these, dense clusters of waxy gray fruit appear along the shoots and last through winter.

Acer rubrum
RED MAPLE
Ⓝ ☼ ◐ ◑ pH Z3–9 H9–1 ↕70ft (20m) ↔30ft (9m)
Tiny red flowers emerging before the leaves herald the arrival of spring. Named varieties have the brightest fall color, the main reason for growing them. Will grow in neutral soils.

Nyssa sylvatica
SOUR GUM
Ⓝ ☼ ◐ ● Z4–9 H9–2 ↕70ft (20m) ↔30ft (9m)
Has a cone-shaped head with straight trunk and horizontal branches. Useful as a street tree or specimen. Tolerates coastal conditions, but not shade.

Quercus bicolor
SWAMP WHITE OAK
Ⓝ ☼ ◐ ○ Z4–8 H8–1
↕70ft (20m) ↔50ft (15m)
Found in the wild in swampy areas, it develops into a fine specimen tree with yellow to red fall color. Very drought resistant. Native to the eastern half of the United States.

MORE CHOICES

- *Crataegus opaca* Z6–8 H8–3
- *Cyrilla racemiflora* Z6–9 H9–4
- *Gordonia lasianthus* Z8–11 H12–8
- *Ilex cassine* Z8–9 H9–7
- *Platanus occidentalis* Z5–8 H8–3
- *Quercus laurifolia* Z7–9 H9–7

Salix babylonica 'Crispa'
CURLY WEEPING WILLOW
☼ ○ ◑ Z6–8 H9–6 ↕↔40ft (12m)
Slow-growing upright form has unusual curled, spiral-shaped leaves. Do not plant near drains or septic systems (roots will clog them if they gain entry).

Betula nigra
RIVER BIRCH
Ⓝ ☼ ◑ ● Z4–9 H9–1 ↕60ft (18m) ↔40ft (12m)
Often multistemmed, this tree prefers acidic soil. Although it needs moist soil in the spring, it will grow where soil is dryer in summer. Its diamond-shaped, dark green leaves turn yellow in the fall. 'Heritage' is resistant to miners and borers.

WOODY PLANTS

Trees for compacted soils

Compacted soils are slow to drain and have a very limited amount of air between the soil particles – air that is essential for roots to function properly. If a spade easily penetrates the soil, it is not compacted. However, if a pick axe is necessary to create a hole, the soil is, indeed, compacted. The trees shown here are adapted to survive under such conditions.

Maclura pomifera
OSAGE ORANGE
Ⓝ ☼ ○ Z5–9 H9–5 ↕50 ft (15m) ↔40ft (12m)
Fast-growing tree with low, rounded irregular head and stiff thorny branches. Deep orange-brown bark with wavy deep ridges. Large round fruits form on females.

Acer negundo 'Flamingo'
FLAMINGO BOXELDER
Ⓝ ☼ ◐ ● Z5–8 H8–3
↕50ft (15m) ↔30ft (10m)
Pink young leaves age to green with white edges. To encourage production of more pink leaves, prune plants in late winter. Grows very quickly.

Gleditsia triacanthos var. *inermis* 'Sunburst'
SUNBURST HONEYLOCUST
☼ ○ Z3–7 H7–1 ↕40ft (12m) ↔30ft (10m)
Bright yellow in spring, the leaves gradually darken to green but new foliage opens all summer, giving a two-toned effect. A broadly pyramidal, fast-growing tree.

Liquidambar styraciflua
AMERICAN SWEET GUM
Ⓝ ☼ ● Z6–9 H9–6 ↕100ft (30m) ↔75ft (23m)
Narrow and upright when young, but lower limbs spread with age. Furrowed bark and corky wings on twigs add to its winter interest. Native to eastern US.

Ailanthus altissima
TREE OF HEAVEN
☼ ◐ ○ Z4–8 H8–1 ↕80ft (25m) ↔50ft (15m)
A tough spreading tree with many winged seeds in late summer. It can become weedy and self-sow, but will survive where few other trees can grow.

MORE CHOICES

- *Pyrus calleryana* Z5–8 H8–2
- *Quercus palustris* Z5–8 H8–5
- *Taxodium distichum* Z5–11 H12–5
- *Ulmus parviflora* Z5–9 H9–5
- *Zelkova serrata* Z5–9 H9–5

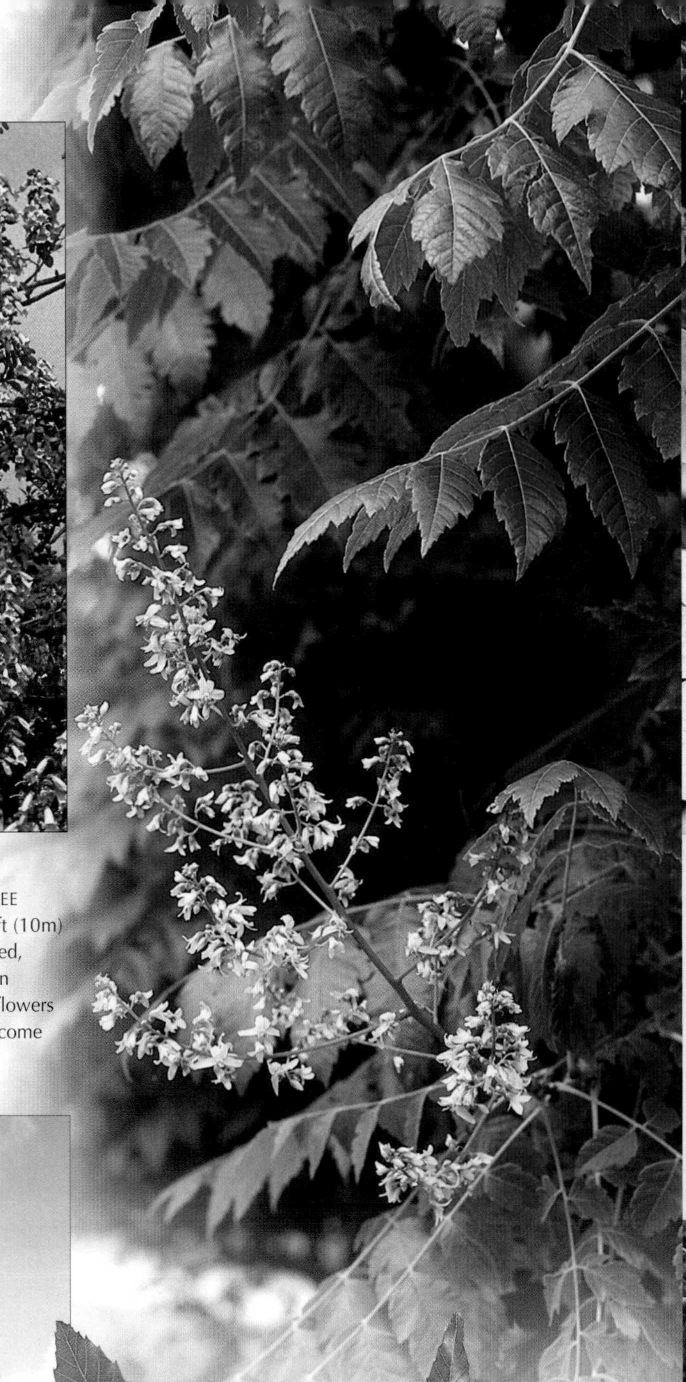

Paulownia tomentosa
ROYAL PAULOWNIA, EMPRESS TREE
☼ ◊ Z5–8 H8–5 ↕40ft (12m) ↔30ft (9m)
Flowers appear in early summer and have yellow stripes inside. Dark green leaves are densely hairy beneath. Grows quickly and has few problems.

Koelreuteria paniculata
PANICLED GOLDEN RAIN TREE
☼ ◊ Z6–9 H9–1 ↕↔30ft (10m)
Opening leaves are purplish red, become bright green, then turn golden yellow in fall. Yellow flowers appear in midsummer and become inflated fruit.

Ginkgo biloba
MAIDENHAIR TREE
☼ ◊ Z5–9 H9–3 ↕100ft (30m) ↔25ft (8m)
Narrow to spreading young tree becomes umbrella-shaped. Slow-growing, tolerant of pollution and heat, and free of pests, this tree has outstanding yellow fall foliage

Quercus robur fastigiata
UPRIGHT ENGLISH OAK
☼ ◐ ◊ Z5–8 H8–3
↕50ft (15m) ↔15ft (4.5m)
Greenish male flowers are in small catkins in spring. Bark becomes deeply fissured with age. Tolerant of alkaline soils. A useful tree for small gardens.

Quercus acutissima
SAWTOOTH OAK
☼ ◐ ◊ Z6–9 H8–3 ↕50 ft (15m) ↔70ft (20m)
Wide-spreading tree with foliage that emerges bright yellow in early spring and returns to yellow late in fall. Acorns have long recurving scales. Pest-free.

Trees for street planting

Street trees have to be tough. They have to withstand pollution from car and truck exhausts, be able to grow when most of their roots are covered with pavement, frequently suffer reflected heat from surrounding buildings, be subjected to streetlights that disrupt their natural rhythm, and survive with virtually no additional nutrients.

Acer buergerianum
TRIDENT MAPLE
☼ ◑ 💧 Z5–9 H9–5
↕30ft (10m) ↔25ft (8m)
A spreading tree with leaves that are blue-green beneath in summer and change to red or orange in fall. Drought resistant.

Juniperus chinensis 'Kaizuka'
HOLLYWOOD JUNIPER
☼ ◑ 💧 Z3–9 H9–1 ↕20ft (6m) ↔10–12ft (3–4m)
When grown as a tree rather than as a shrub, this is upright with slightly twisted branches and good heat and pollution tolerance. It may be sold as 'Torulosa'.

Betula nigra
RIVER BIRCH
Ⓝ ☼ 💧💧 Z4–9 H9–1 ↕60ft (18m) ↔40ft (12m)
Often a multistemmed tree, this prefers acidic soil. Needs moist soil in spring but will grow where soil is dryer in summer. 'Heritage' is resistant to miners and borers.

Tilia cordata 'Greenspire'
GREENSPIRE LITTLELEAF LINDEN
☼ ◑ 💧 Z4–8 H8–1 ↕50ft (15m) ↔22ft (7m)
A pollution-tolerant tree that will grow in a wide variety of soils and transplants easily. Fragrant flowers appear in midsummer. Other cultivars have broader outlines.

Taxodium distichum
BALD CYPRESS
Ⓝ ☼ ◑ 💧💧 Z5–11 H12–5
↕80ft (24m) ↔25ft (8m)
The needles turn rust-brown in fall before dropping. Distinctive aerial roots ("knees") form around the base of the tree in wet sites. Moderate growth rate.

MORE CHOICES

- *Acer rubrum* Z3–9 H9–1
- *Betula nigra* 'Heritage' Z4–9 H9–1
- *Fraxinus pennsylvanica* 'Marshall's Seedless' Z3–9 H9–1
- *Ginkgo biloba* 'Fairmount' Z5–9 H9–2
- *Ginkgo biloba* 'Saratoga' Z5–9 H9–3
- *Gleditsia tricanthos* 'Moraine' Z3–7 H7–1
- *Ilex x attenuata* 'Fosteri' Z6–9 H9–4
- *Lagerstroemia indica* 'Potomac' Z7–9 H9–7
- *Lagerstroemia indica* 'Watermelon Red' Z7–9 H9–7
- *Quercus virginiana* Z8–10 H10–7
- *Sophora japonica* 'Regent' Z4–9 H9–1
- *Tilia cordata* Z3–8 H8–1
- *Ulmus alata* Z3–9 H9–1
- *Ulmus crassifolia* Z8–9 H9–8
- *Ulmus parvifolia* 'Drake' Z6–9 H9–3
- *Zelkova serrata* 'Green Vase' Z5–9 H9–1

Gleditsia triacanthos 'Skyline'
SKYLINE THORNLESS HONEYLOCUST
Ⓝ ☼ ◊ Z3–7 H7–1 ↕45ft(12.5m) ↔35ft(10.5m)
A tough, pollution-tolerant tree that grows well in most soils. There are several other named forms but this is the most upright and suitable for street planting.

Washingtonia robusta
THREAD PALM
☼ ◊ Z13–15 H12–10 ↕80ft (25m) ↔15ft (5m)
Fast-growing palm with a slender tapering trunk. Old leaf-bases stay on the stem giving a shaggy look. A good conservatory plant where not hardy.

Sophora japonica
JAPANESE PAGODA TREE
☼ ◊ Z5–9 H9–5 ↕to 100ft (30m) ↔70ft (20m)
Spreading deciduous tree with good yellow fall color. Small, fragrant white flowers appear in drooping sprays in summer. 'Regent' is rounded, blooms while young.

Magnolias

The definitive trees and shrubs for the South, magnolias play a large role in southern landscaping. In addition to the often fragrant, showy flowers, leaves may have brown or whitish woolly hairs on the underside and the conelike fruits may open to reveal orange or scarlet seeds.

Magnolia ashei
ASHE MAGNOLIA
Ⓝ Z7–9 H9–7
↕30–70ft (10–20m)
↔25–50ft (8–15m)
Fragrant flowers open with the wavy-edged leaves. Free-flowering, even when young. Native to Florida.

Magnolia stellata 'Royal Star'
ROYAL STAR MAGNOLIA
Z5–9 H9–5 ↕10ft (3m) ↔12ft (4m)
Pink buds open in early spring to give fragrant flowers with up to 30 petals, over twice the number on the original species. Slow growing and densely branched.

Magnolia x *soulangeana*
SAUCER MAGNOLIA
Z4–9 H9–5 ↕20ft (6m) ↔20ft (6m)
Often grown as a low-branched, multistemmed tree, it flowers at an early age and early in the season, but is often damaged by frost. Tolerant of pollution.

Magnolia tripetala
UMBRELLA TREE
Ⓝ pH Z4–9 H9–5 ↕↔30ft (10m)
Terminal flowers are partly hidden by very large leaves, up to 3ft (90cm) long. Bright red fruits that follow are very showy and stand out against foliage.

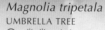

Magnolia acuminata
CUCUMBERTREE MAGNOLIA
Ⓝ Z4–8 H8–2 ↕70ft (20m) ↔30ft (9m)
Wide-spreading branches and freedom from pests make this tree perfect for parks, estates, and golf courses. Pinkish red, cucumber-like fruit in fall.

MORE CHOICES

- *M.* 'Anne' Z3–8 H8–1
- *M. grandiflora* 'Edith Bogue' Z6–9 H9–6
- *M. grandiflora* 'Little Gem' Z7–9 H9–6
- *M.* 'Jane' Z6–9 H9–6
- *M. kobus* Z5–9 H9–5
- *M.* x *loebneri* 'Merrill' Z5–9 H9–5
- *M. obovata* Z5–9 H9–5
- *M. salicifolia* 'Wada's Memory' Z6–9 H9–6
- *M.* 'Yellow Bird' Z4–8 H8–2

Magnolia macrophylla
BIGLEAF MAGNOLIA

☼ ◑ 💧 Z6–9 H12–10 ↕↔30ft (9m)

A rounded tree with huge fragrant flowers and large, oval, reddish conelike fruit. Immense leaves are sometimes over two feet long. Needs a large setting.

Magnolia fraseri
EAR-LEAVED UMBRELLA TREE

Ⓝ ☼ ◑ ◯ Z4–9 H9–6

↕30ft (10m) ↔25ft (8m)

Fast growing, often with multiple stems and decorative bark in winter. One of the first magnolias to flower, blooms are about 8in (20cm) wide.

Magnolia liliiflora
LILY-FLOWERED MAGNOLIA

☼ ◑ ◯ 💧 pH Z5–9 H9–1 ↕10ft (3m) ↔12ft (4m)

Flowering over a long period in early summer with some later flowering. This variety has redder flowers than the species, is more compact, and blooms at a younger age.

Magnolia virginiana
SWEET BAY MAGNOLIA

Ⓝ ☼ ◑ ◯ Z6–9 H9–6 ↕28ft (9m) ↔20ft (6m)

Smallish lemon-scented flowers are produced throughout summer. Grows well in soils ranging from dry to swampy, providing they are moderately acidic.

Magnolia denudata
YULAN MAGNOLIA

☼ ◑ 💧 Z5–9 H9–6 ↕↔30ft (9m)

Fragrant flowers on a rounded tree. Young plants are very upright but become open with age. Flowers are easily injured by late freezes. Native to central China.

Tree-sized hollies

Hollies are grown mainly for their berries, which brighten the landscape in winter. Evergreen species also play a role in the winter garden, especially those with variegated foliage. While many hollies are small to medium-sized shrubs, some will grow into large trees. Remember that male and female flowers are often on separate plants, so you need the occasional male of the same species nearby in order for berries to form.

Ilex cassine
DAHOON HOLLY
☼ ◐ ◇ ◆ Z8–9 H9–7 ↕30ft (10m) ↔15ft (5m)
A rounded, densely branched, evergreen tree with oblong, lance-shaped leaves that can grow to 2in (5cm) long. Bears abundant red to orange-yellow berries.

Ilex cornuta 'Burfordii'
BURFORD'S CHINESE HOLLY
Ⓝ ☼ ◐ ◇ ◆ Z6–9 H9–1 ↕15ft (5m) ↔12–15ft (4–5m)
A compact-growing variety with evergreen leaves tipped with a small spine. It fruits very heavily and berries can persist until spring. This variety originated in Atlanta, Georgia, in 1934.

Ilex opaca
AMERICAN HOLLY
Ⓝ ☼ ◐ ● ◇ Z5–9 H9–5 ↕45ft (14m) ↔4ft (1.2m)
In old age, the habit becomes more open and irregular. Fragrant white flowers in early summer are followed by small, persistent red fruit. Not for dry windy areas.

Ilex aquifolium 'Argentea Marginata'
WHITE-EDGED ENGLISH HOLLY
☼ 💧 Z7–9 H9–7 ↕50ft (15m) ↔12ft (4m)
New foliage is pink-tinged. A female clone, this will produce berries if a male form is nearby. Several other cultivars of English holly have white or gold variegation.

Ilex aquifolium 'Ferox Argentea'
SILVER HEDGEHOG HOLLY
☼ 💧 Z7–9 H9–7 ↕40ft (12m) ↔12ft (4m)
A male holly grown for its small, extremely prickly leaves that can even have spines on the leaf blade. Color varies from cream to pale yellow.

MORE CHOICES

Ilex aquifolium 'Angustifolia' Z7–9 H9–7
Ilex x attenuata 'Hume #2' Z6–9 H9–4
Ilex 'Emily Bruner' Z7–9 H9–7
Ilex opaca 'Carolina #2' Z5–9 H9–5
Ilex opaca 'Croonenberg' Z5–9 H9–5
Ilex opaca 'Merry Christmas' Z5–9 H9–5
Ilex opaca 'Morris Arboretum' Z5–9 H9–5

Ilex x *attenuata* 'Fosteri'
FOSTER'S HYBRID HOLLY
☼ ◐ 💧 Z6–9 H9–4
↕20–30ft (6–10m) ↔10–20ft (3–6m)
Three different forms have evergreen leaves, and are known as #2, (readily available) #3, and #4. The first two are females that fruit heavily; #4 is male.

Ilex x *attenuata* 'East Palatka'
EAST PALATKA HOLLY
☼ ◐ 💧 Z6–9 H9–4
↕30–45ft (10–14m) ↔10–15ft (3–5m)
Female and very free-fruiting with a more open habit than Foster #2. Dark green leaves with spines near the base. Found near East Palatka, Florida, in 1927.

Ilex vomitoria
YAUPON HOLLY
Ⓝ ☼ ◐ 💧
Z7–11 H12–7 ↕15–20ft (5–6m) ↔10–15ft (3–5m)
An upright small tree with evergreen foliage and very attractive, persistent fruits. It is fast growing, adaptable, and salt tolerant. The bark is whitish and attractive.

Sun-loving shrubs

These plants revel in a hot location in full sun. While they will probably grow in a location that only gets sun for half the day, their flowering will be reduced and their growth become leggy. Because of their exposed sites, watering will have to be carefully monitored for the first couple of years until they become established.

Hibiscus syriacus 'Helene'
ROSE OF SHARON
Z5–9 H9–1 ↕10ft (3m) ↔6ft (2m)
Flowers from midsummer until fall on new growth, so prune in early spring. Good as a border plant or hedge. Other varieties have pink, mauve, or blue flowers.

Ilex verticillata 'Red Sprite'
RED SPRITE WINTERBERRY
Z4–9 H9–1 ↕4ft (1.2m) ↔3ft (1.5m)
A deciduous holly with nonprickly leaves, plus fruit that remain for a long time. Can grow in swamps but will also thrive in much drier locations.

Hibiscus rosa-sinensis hybrid
ROSE OF CHINA
Z14–15 H12–1 ↕15ft (5m) ↔10ft (3m)
Large shrub or small tree with glossy, dark green foliage and flowers in a wide range of colors. Some named forms have double flowers. Susceptible to whiteflies.

MORE CHOICES

- *Acca sellowiana* Z8–11 H12–9
- *Cyrilla racemiflora* Z6–9 H9–4
- *Hypericum patulum* Z7–9 H9–7
- *Kolkwitzia amabilis* Z5–9 H9–5
- *Viburnum rhytidophyllum* 'Alleghany' Z5–8 H8–5

Philadelphus coronarius
MOCK ORANGE
Z4–9 H9–4 ↕10ft (3m) ↔8ft (2.5m)
Very fragrant flowers produced in small clusters in early summer. Makes a good addition to a mixed border where tall perennials can screen it when not in flower.

Spiraea x *vanhouttei*
VANHOUTTE SPIREA
☼ ◊ Z4–8 H8–1 ↕6ft (2m) ↔5ft (1.5m)
Flowers are borne in abundance in late spring and early summer and almost completely cover the dark green leaves. Very adaptable and tolerant.

Spiraea japonica 'Neon Flash'
NEON FLASH JAPANESE SPIREA
☼ ◐ ♦ Z3–9 H9–1 ↕4ft (1.2m) ↔5 (1.5m)
A bushy shrub that flowers over a long period, from early summer until fall and is attractive to butterflies. Foliage turns orange in fall. Rarely needs pruning.

Forsythia x *intermedia*
BORDER FORSYTHIA
☼ ◐ ♦ Z6–9 H9–3 ↕↔5ft (1.5m)
Profuse flowers are produced in early and midspring, before the leaves. Remove oldest stems after flowering to rejuvenate the plant. Useful as a hedge or screen.

Weigela florida 'Variegata'
VARIEGATED DWARF WEIGELA
☼ ◊ Z5–8 H8–1 ↕↔6–8ft (2–2.5m)
Dense, bushy shrub. Prune old, straggly plants hard. Can grow near roads and in urban environments, due to tolerance of air pollution. Easy to grow.

Caryopteris x *clandonensis* 'Arthur Simmonds'
BLUE MIST SHRUB
☼ ◐ ◊ Z6–9 H9–1 ↕3ft (1m) ↔5ft (1.5m)
A rounded shrub that grows best in poor soil and may becomes rampant in rich soil. Late summer flowers are on the new growth, so cut back hard in late winter.

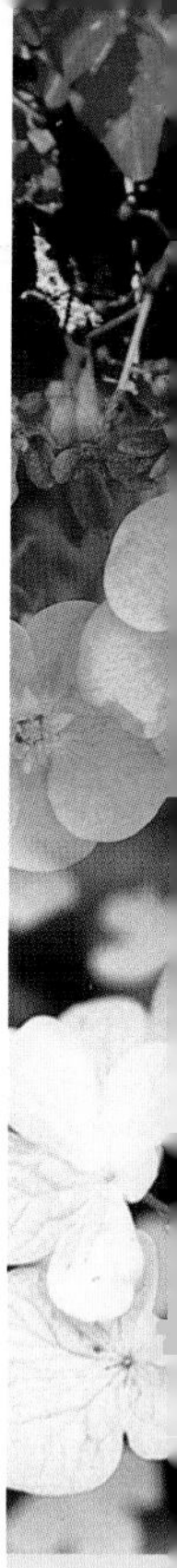

Viburnum dilatatum
LINDEN VIBURNUM
☼ ◑ ◊ Z5–8 H8–5 ↕10ft (3m) ↔6ft (2m)
Small, star-shaped white flowers are produced in late spring and early summer, preceding bright red berries. Dark green leaves turn bronze and red in fall.

Abelia x *grandiflora*
GLOSSY ABELIA
☼ ◊ Z6–9 H9–1 ↕10ft (3m) ↔12ft (4m)
Evergreen or semi-evergreen shrub. Fragrant flowers are borne from midsummer to fall. Irresistible to many butterflies. Also known as *A. rupestris.*

Leucophyllum frutescens
TEXAS RANGER
Ⓝ ☼ ◊ Z8–9 H9–8 ↕8ft (2.5m) ↔6ft (2m)
Compact, arching shrub. Tolerance to salt makes this ideal for seaside gardens. Bears rose-purple flowers in summer. Native to Mexico and Texas.

Deutzia gracilis
SLENDER DEUTZIA
☼ ◊ Z5–8 H8–1 ↕↔5ft (1.5m)
A bushy, deciduous shrub that grows in most soils. Makes a good informal hedge. Abundant, fragrant flowers are borne from spring into summer.

Kerria japonica 'Pleniflora'
DOUBLE JAPANESE KERRIA
☼ ◑ ◊ Z5–9 H8–3 ↕↔10ft (3m)
Long-blooming shrub that thrives in both poor soils and heavy clay. Prune out old growth occasionally. The bright green stems are attractive in winter.

Punica granatum 'Pleniflora'
DOUBLE-FLOWERED POMEGRANATE
☼ ◊ Z8–11 H12–1
↕↔12–39in (30–100cm)
An upright sometimes spiny shrub that is useful for the front of a border. It flowers over a long period but the double flowers rarely give rise to the edible fruits.

Hamamelis x intermedia 'Diane'
DIANE WITCH HAZEL
☼ ◑ ◊ ♦ Z5–9 H9–1
↕↔12ft (4m)
Fragrant yellow to orange flowers appear on the bare branches from early to midwinter. It grows well in acid soils but dislikes windy sites. Flowers withstand freezing well.

Buddleja 'Pink Delight'
PINK DELIGHT BUTTERFLY BUSH
☼ ◑ ◊ Z6–9 H9–1
↕8ft (2.5m) ↔6ft (2m)
Produces larger flower spikes and deeper green leaves than the species. Orange-eyed flowers bloom from summer to fall. Prefers fertile soil.

Chaenomeles speciosa 'Moerloosei'
MOERLOOSE FLOWERING QUINCE
☼ ◑ ◊ Z5–8 H8–5 ↕8ft (2.5m) ↔15ft (5m)
A rounded shrub with spiny branches that can also be used for a hedge or espalier. The fruit are yellow-green with black dots and can be used for jellies.

Shade-loving shrubs

Shady north sides of buildings and areas under large trees are often considered problem places in which to grow plants. In fact, they extend the range of plants you can grow by providing a specialized habitat. Many of the plants on these four pages will not survive if planted in full sun and require reflected light or dappled shade to thrive.

Clethra alnifolia 'Pink Spires'
PINK SPIRES SUMMERSWEET
☼ ◑ ○ ◑ pH Z3–9 H9–1 ↕↔8ft (2.5m)
Fragrant flowers appear from late summer to early fall when the foliage turns a good yellow. Salt-tolerance make this a good choice for seaside planting.

Clethra alnifolia
SUMMERSWEET
Ⓝ ◑ ● pH Z3–9 H9–1 ↕↔8ft (2.5m)
The fragrant, bell-shaped white flowers of this shrub form elegant spires. Upright shrub often increases through suckering. Leaves turn yellow in fall.

Aronia arbutifolia 'Brilliantissima'
BRILLIANT RED CHOKEBERRY
☼ ◑ ○ ◑ Z5–9 H9–4 ↕6ft (2m) ↔5ft (1.5m)
Early spring white flowers give the fruits seen here. The common name comes from the color of the fall foliage.

Kalmia polifolia
EASTERN BOG LAUREL
Ⓝ ☼ ◑ ◑ pH Z2–7 H7–1 ↕24in (60cm) ↔3ft (1m)
Blossoms in mid- to late spring. Glossy dark green leaves, arranged in opposite pairs or whorls of 3, have rolled-back margins and glandular hairs underneath.

Callicarpa americana var. *lactea*
WHITE BEAUTYBERRY
Ⓝ ☼ ◑ ○ Z5–9 H9–1 ↕to 6ft (2m) ↔5ft (1.5m)
An open shrub with leaves that are woolly beneath. Lavender flowers in spring and early summer give these fruits. In the species, the berries are violet, not white.

Illicium floridanum
PURPLE ANISE
Ⓝ pH Z7–9 H9–4 ↕↔8ft (2.5m)
An evergreen shrub with a bushy habit of growth and aromatic foliage. The flowers are borne in late spring and early summer but the fruits are not conspicuous.

Fothergilla major
LARGE WITCH ALDER
Ⓝ pH Z4–8 H9–2 ↕↔10ft (3m)
A multistemmed, erect shrub with dark green leaves that turn yellow, orange, and bright red in fall, with all three colors present at the same time.

Pieris japonica 'Christmas Cheer'
CHRISTMAS CHEER PIERIS
pH Z6–8 H8–7
↕12ft (4m) ↔10ft (3m)
Evergreen and one of the first pieris to flower, even on young plants. This vigorous variety will lose its color if planted in too much light. It originated in Japan.

Calycanthus floridus
CAROLINA ALLSPICE
Ⓝ Z5–9 H9–1
↕8ft (2.5m) ↔10ft (3m)
A spreading shrub that is tolerant of most soils and of sun. The fragrant flowers are produced from late spring into summer. Foliage is also fragrant when crushed.

Pieris japonica 'Compacta'
DWARF PIERIS
pH Z5–9 H9–1 ↕↔3–5ft (1–1.5m)
Compact, evergreen shrub with small leaves. Useful in the front of a woodland walk, it is very free-flowering and the blooms last for several weeks.

Michelia figo
BANANA SHRUB
☼ ◊ Z12–15 H12–10 ↕↔30ft (10m)
Bears flowers with a banana-like fragrance in spring and summer. Bushy, evergreen shrub with lightly hairy, yellow-brown stems. Slow-growing.

Itea virginica
VIRGINIA SWEETSPIRE
Ⓝ ☼ ◑ ♦ Z6–9 H10–7 ↕↔5ft (1.5m)
Fragrant white flowers bloom in dense, elongated clusters. Open shrub grows upright, then arching. Dark green leaves turn red to purple in fall.

Daphne odora
WINTER DAPHNE
☼ ◑ ◊ Z7–9 H9–7 ↕↔4ft (1.2m)
Very fragrant flowers blossom from midwinter to early spring and followed by fleshy red fruit. Grows best in a sheltered site.

Skimmia japonica
JAPANESE SKIMMIA
◑ ♦ Z7–8 H9–7 ↕↔5ft (1.5m)
Has slightly fragrant leaves as well as fragrant red- or pink-tinged white flowers. If both sexes are present, female plant bears red fruit.

Camellia japonica 'Betty Sheffield Supreme'
BETTY SHEFFIELD SUPREME JAPANESE CAMELLIA
◑ ◊ ♦ Z7–8 H8–7 ↕10–20ft (3–6m) ↔10ft (3m)
A winter-flowering variety with an open habit of growth. This variety tends to produce shoots that are not true to name. These need to be removed.

Styrax japonicus
JAPANESE SNOWBELL
Z6–8 H8–6 ↕↔50ft (15m)
This forms a broad crown with spreading branches. Slightly fragrant flowers in late spring, attractive fruit in summer. Plant in early spring in a humus-rich soil.

MORE CHOICES

- *Agarista populifolia* Z7–9 H9–7
- *Leucothoe axillaris* Z6–9 H9–6
- *Rhododendron maximum* Z4–9 H9–1
- *Stewartia ovata* Z3–9 H8–1
- *Viburnum alnifolium* Z4–7 H7–1

Aesculus parviflora
BOTTLEBRUSH BUCKEYE
Ⓝ Z5–9 H9–4 ↕10ft (3m) ↔15ft (5m)
Mound-forming. Leaves are bronze when young and turn dark green as they mature and yellow in fall. Slow to establish but eventually spreads widely.

Lindera benzoin
SPICE BUSH
Ⓝ Z4–9 H8–1 ↕↔10ft (3m)
A rounded shrub with upright branches and aromatic, bright green foliage. Yellow-green, star-shaped flowers blossom in midspring. Females bear red berries.

Myrica cerifera
WAX MYRTLE
Ⓝ Z6–9 H9–6 ↕↔15ft (5m)
This shrub produces small, yellow-green catkins in spring. Following these, dense clusters of waxy gray fruit appear along the shoots and last through winter.

Drought-tolerant shrubs

Many plants find it difficult to survive in areas that experience regular summer droughts, where a rain shadow is caused by a building or fence, or under high-limbed trees with a shallow root system. This situation is especially problematic close to a building where the reflected heat evaporates what little moisture there is. The shrubs shown here are tough and should thrive once established.

Cotoneaster dammeri
BEARBERRY COTONEASTER
☼ ◊ Z5–8 H8–3 ↕8in (20cm) ↔6ft (2m)
A low groundcover plant that makes a dense carpet of evergreen foliage turning dull purple in winter. The early summer flowers produce persistent red berries.

Hibiscus syriacus 'Pink Giant'
PINK GIANT ROSE OF SHARON
☼ ◊◑ Z5–9 H9–1 ↕10ft (3m) ↔6ft (2m)
The flowers are carried on the new growth from midsummer onwards. It can be used as a hedge or screen. Prune in early spring. There are varieties with white, blue, or mauve flowers.

Rapidophyllum hystrix
BLUE PALMETTO
Ⓝ ☼ ◊◑ Z6–10 H12–10
↕5–6ft (1.5–2m) ↔6–12ft (2–4m)
A slow-growing palm with a low branching habit of growth. The base of each leaf stalk is spiny. Reddish flowers in summer are hidden by the foliage.

Rhaphiolepis indica
INDIAN HAWTHORN
☼ ◊◑ Z8–11 H9–3 ↕5ft (1.5m) ↔6ft (2m)
Spreading evergreen shrub that is slow-growing and requires a moderately fertile soil. The flowers appear in spring and early summer. Protect from drying winds.

Lavandula angustifolia
ENGLISH LAVENDER
☼ ◊ Z5–8 H8–5 ↕3ft (1m) ↔4ft (1.2m)
Slow-growing, evergreen shrub with fragrant foliage. Summer flowers are white to blue-purple. Leaves and flowers can be dried for sachets.

Rosa rugosa
RUGOSA ROSE
Z2–9 H9–1
↕↔3–6ft (1–2m)
A vigorous, spiny species with leathery leaves and round, red fruit in winter. Flowers open from early summer to fall. There are many named forms.

Ligustrum japonicum
JAPANESE PRIVET
Z7–10 H10–7
↕10ft (3m) ↔8ft (2.5m)
Small white flowers forming large cones blossom in midsummer and early fall, followed by black fruit. Grows well along shady walls.

Lespedeza thunbergii
BUSHCLOVER
Z6–8 H8–6 ↕6ft (2m) ↔10ft (3m)
Although this is often killed almost to the ground in winter, it is fast-growing and soon regains its size. The flowers open in late summer on arching stems.

Pittosporum tobira
JAPANESE MOCK ORANGE
Z9–10 H10–9 ↕30ft (10m) ↔10ft (3m)
Rounded, dense, evergreen shrub or small tree with erect stems. The sweetly fragrant flowers open in spring and early summer and turn yellow as they age.

MORE CHOICES

- *Acca sellowiana* Z8–11 H12–9
- *Berberis thunbergii* Z5–8 H8–5
- *Berberis* x *mentorensis* Z5–8 H8–5
- *Callicarpa americana* Z5–9 H9–1
- *Chaenomeles speciosa* Z5–9 H9–1
- *Cycas revoluta* Z13–15 H12–6
- *Cytisus scoparius* Z6–8 H8–6
- *Euonymus alatus* Z4–9 H9–1
- *Ilex cornuta* Z6–9 H9–1
- *Ilex glabra* Z5–9 H9–1
- *Juniperus* spp. Z2–9 H9–1
- *Laurus nobilis* Z8–11 H12–1
- *Leucophyllum frutescens* Z8–9 H9–8
- *Podocarpus macrophyllus* Z7–11 H12–7
- *Pyrancantha coccinea* Z6–9 H9–6
- *Rhus typhina* Z3–8 H8–1

Nandina domestica
HEAVENLY BAMBOO
Z6–9 H9–3 ↕6ft (2m) ↔5ft (1.5m)
Upright shrub blooming in late spring to early summer. Bright red, round berries follow in early fall and hang on through winter. A pest-free native to China.

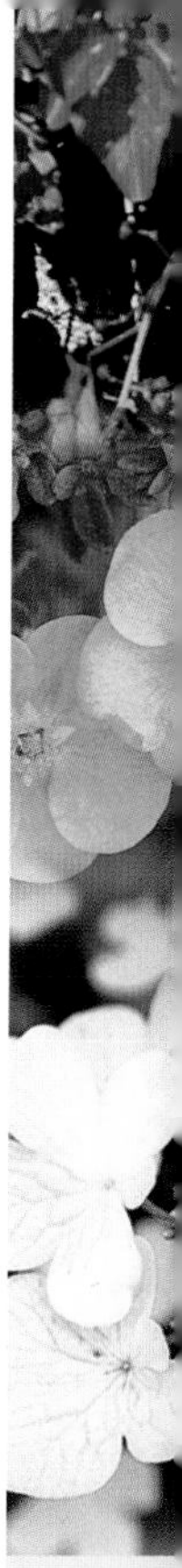

WOODY PLANTS

Salt-tolerant shrubs

With its long coastline, much of the Southeast is subject to occasional salt-laden gales which can be lethal to many plants. By altering the chemistry of the soil, salt interferes with the uptake of essential minerals that a plant needs to survive. The plants shown are able to cope with this and show no ill effects from high salt concentrations.

Rhus typhina
STAGHORN SUMAC
Ⓝ ☼ ◊ Z3–8 H8–1 ↕15ft (5m) ↔20ft (6m)
Erect conical clusters of yellow-green flowers to 8in (20cm) long appear in summer. In fall, female plants produce dense clusters of bright crimson fruit.

Ilex vomitoria
YAUPON HOLLY
Ⓝ ☼ ☼ ◊ ◐ Z7–11 H12–7 ↕20ft (6m) ↔15ft (5m)
This transplants easily and will grow in both wet and dry soils. It can be used as a specimen plant or as a hedge or screen to protect other species from salt spray.

Rhaphiolepis indica
INDIAN HAWTHORN
☼ ◊ ◐ Z8–11 H9–3 ↕5ft (1.5m) ↔6ft (2m)
Purchase this as a container-grown plant. It can be used in planters where its drought tolerance is an advantage, but should be located away from strong winds.

Callistemon citrinus 'Splendens'
CRIMSON BOTTLEBRUSH
☼ ◊ ◐ Z10–15 H12–10 ↕↔5–25ft (1.5–8m)
An arching shrub with broad leaves, pink when young and brighter than the species. Cut back hard if overgrown. Flowers open in spring and summer.

Myrica cerifera
WAX MYRTLE
Ⓝ ☼ ☼ ☼ ◊ ◐ ● Z6–9 H9–6 ↕↔15ft (5m)
This shrub produces small, yellow-green catkins in spring. Following these, dense clusters of waxy gray fruit appear along the shoots and last through winter.

Viburnum suspensum
SANDANKWA VIBURNUM
☼ ☼ ◐ Z8–9 H9–8 ↕↔6–12ft (2–4m)
An evergreen shrub widely used for screens and hedges in Florida. Fragrant flowers open in spring and give rise to rounded red fruits. Grows well on sandy soils.

Pittosporum tobira
JAPANESE MOCK ORANGE
☼ ☼ ◊ ◐ Z9–10 H10–9 ↕30ft (10m) ↔10ft (3m)
An adaptable plant that will grow well in dry sandy soils or in clay. The flowers, produced in spring and summer, are very fragrant, and age to a pale yellow.

Ixora coccinea
FLAME OF THE WOODS
Z14–15 H12–10 ↕8ft (2.5m) ↔6ft (2m)
Bushy, rounded evergreen shrub that blooms from early summer until fall. It makes a good container plant where not hardy if given winter protection.

Nerium oleander
OLEANDER
Z13–15 H12–1
↕↔20ft (6m)
Red, pink, white, apricot, or yellow flowers, often on dark red stalks, are produced in summer and followed by beanlike seed pods. Evergreen, upright shrub.

Lantana camara 'Dwarf White'
SNOW WHITE SHRUB VERBENA
Z9–15 H12–1 ↕↔3–6ft (1–2m)
A prickly-stemmed shrub with strongly scented leaves. There are many other named forms, in shades of salmon, yellow, orange, red, or with two-toned flowers.

Juniperus conferta 'Blue Pacific'
SHORE JUNIPER
Z5–9 H9–1 ↕12in (30cm)
This cultivar is more trailing than the species and has a deeper blue cast to the foliage. Produces black fruit with a silvery white coating. Growth rate is moderate.

MORE CHOICES

- *Baccharis halminifolia* Z3–7 H7–1
- *Cocculus uvifera* Z10–11 H12–9
- *Erythrina coccinea* Z9–10 H10–9
- *Hippophae rhamnoides* Z3–8 H8–1
- *Yucca gloriosa* Z7–11 H12–7

Agave americana 'Marginata'
VARIEGATED CENTURY PLANT
Z9–11 H12–5 ↕to 6ft (2m) ↔to 10ft (3m)
New leaves are edged in yellow which turns to white with age. Yellowish flowers are produced in summer after which that rosette dies, but side-shoots survive.

Shrubs tolerant of wet soils

Wet areas occur at the base of a slope, close to rivers and streams, and anywhere the water table is high. Soil with a high water content has very little air in the spaces between its particles. Most plants need oxygen in these spaces for roots to function properly. This is why shrubs die in areas that are flooded for an extended period. The shrubs here will tolerate moist soil.

Clethra alnifolia
SUMMERSWEET

Ⓝ ◑ 💧 pH Z3–9 H9–1 ↕↔8ft (2.5m)

Fragrant, bell-shaped white flowers form elegant spires. An upright shrub, it readily increases by suckering. Leaves turn yellow in fall.

Fothergilla gardenii
WITCH ALDER

Ⓝ ☼ ◑ 💧 pH Z4–9 H9–1 ↕↔3ft (1m)

Bears spikes of fragrant flowers in spring, before the leaves. Dark blue-green leaves turn orange, red, and purple in fall. Good for a woodland garden.

Physocarpus opulifolius
NINEBARK

Ⓝ ☼ 💧💧 pH Z3–7 H7–1 ↕10ft (3m) ↔15ft (5m)

Upright, with small spikes of light pink flowers in early summer, and nutlike fruits. Grows well in dry soils. Varieties with yellow or bronze foliage are preferable.

Ilex verticillata
WINTERBERRY

Ⓝ ☼ 💧 Z5–8 H8–5 ↕↔15ft (5m)

Deciduous shrub bears bright green, saw-toothed leaves. White flowers are followed by fruit that may be dark red to scarlet, or sometimes orange or yellow.

MORE CHOICES

- *Agarista populifolia* Z7–9 H9–7
- *Cephalanthus occidentalis* Z5–11 H12–3
- *Cornus amomum* Z5–8 H8–5
- *Cyrilla racemiflora* Z6–9 H9–4
- *Hydrangea arborescens* Z4–9 H9–1
- *Ilex glabra* 'Shamrock' Z3–7 H7–1
- *Ilex glabra* 'Nigra' Z3–9 H9–1
- *Ilex glabra* 'Nordic' Z3–9 H9–1
- *Leucothoe fontanesiana* Z5–8 H8–5
- *Neviusia alabamensis* Z4–8 H8–1
- *Rhododendron viscosum* Z3–9 H9–1

Sambucus canadensis
AMERICAN ELDER
Z4–9 H9–1 ↕↔12ft (4m)
Freely suckering shrub that flowers in early summer. Black fruits are good for jellies, wine, or to feed birds. 'Aurea' has red fruits and golden foliage that stays yellow all summer.

Ilex glabra 'Compacta'
DWARF INKBERRY
Z5–9 H9–5 ↕↔4–6ft (1.2–2m)
An upright, suckering female shrub that forms colonies and makes a good hedge. It may eventually become bare at the base but can be cut back to rejuvenate it.

Aronia arbutifolia
RED CHOKEBERRY
Z5–9 H9–4 ↕↔10ft (3m)
The spring flowers become very astringent, decorative, shiny red fruits that last well into winter. Leaves turn glowing red to purple in fall.

Itea virginica
VIRGINIA SWEETSPIRE
Z6–9 H10–7 ↕↔5ft (1.5m)
Fragrant white flowers bloom in dense elongated clusters. Open shrub grows upright, then arching. Dark green leaves turn red to purple in fall.

Lindera benzoin
SPICE BUSH
Z4–9 H8–1 ↕↔10ft (3m)
Grown for its aromatic foliage, which turns yellow in fall, this rounded deciduous shrub bears tiny, yellow-green, star-shaped flowers in early and midspring, followed by red berries on female plants.

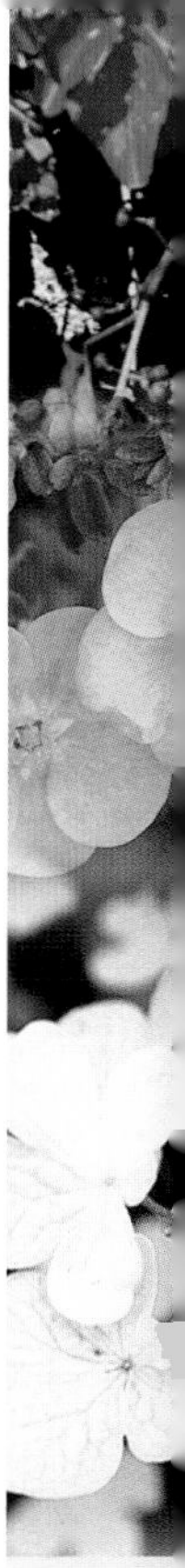

Shrubs for hedges or screening

Hedges and screens serve several purposes in the garden. They can give privacy, hiding a patio from neighbors for example. They can act as a wind barrier, giving shelter where slightly tender plants may thrive. Or they can act as a physical block, preventing people from cutting across your lot. Those shown here can also add color to your garden.

Viburnum odoratissimum
SWEET VIBURNUM
☼ ◑ ◊ ♦ Z8–9 H9–7 ↕↔15ft (5m)
A vigorous, bushy evergreen shrub with large heads of fragrant white flowers in spring and red fruits turning black later. Leaves are glossy and can be 8in (20cm) long. Best used as a screen that is not closely clipped.

Viburnum suspensum
SANDANKWA VIBURNUM
☼ ◑ ♦ Z8–9 H9–8
↕↔6–12ft (2–4m)
Also evergreen, this is much used for both screen and hedges in Florida. It grows well on sandy soils. Flowers are often tinged pink, fruits are red.

Osmanthus heterophyllus
FALSE HOLLY
☼ ◑ ◊ Z7–9 H9–7
↕↔15ft (5m)
Grows best on acidic soils; also okay in soils that are close to neutral. Young leaves are hollylike; on mature plants they are oval and spineless. Good hedge plant.

Berberis julianae
WINTER BARBERRY
☼ ◊ Z6–9 H9–4 ↕↔10ft (3m)
Dense bushy shrub. Leaves are dark green and glossy above and pale green underneath. Yellow or red-tinged flowers are followed by egg-shaped black fruits.

Photinia x *fraseri* 'Red Robin'
RED ROBIN RED TIP
☼ ◑ ◊ ♦ Z8–9 H9–8 ↕↔15ft (5m)
When used as a hedge, frequent clipping gives constant, brightly colored new growth, the main attraction of this popular plant. 'Birmingham' is more copper-colored.

Rhodendron simsii
INDIAN AZALEA
◑ 💧💧 Z5–8 H8–5 ↕↔6–8ft (2–2.5m)
Evergreen screening shrub with hairy leaves and flowers in small clusters in late spring. The parent of many forms of "Indian azaleas" in a range of pinks and reds.

Abelia x *grandiflora*
GLOSSY ABELIA
☼ 💧 Z6–9 H9–1 ↕10ft (3m) ↔12ft (4m)
Evergreen or semi-evergreen shrub. Fragrant flowers are borne from midsummer to fall. Irresistible to many butterflies, this is also known as *A. rupestris.*

Ilex opaca
AMERICAN HOLLY
Ⓝ ☼ ◑ ● 💧 Z5–9 H9–5 ↕45ft (14m) ↔4ft (1.2m)
Crimson (sometimes yellow or orange) berries enhance this evergreen in winter. Like most hollies, spiny leaves are occasionally smooth-edged.

Aucuba japonica
JAPANESE LAUREL
☼ 💧 Z6–15 H12–6 ↕↔10ft (3m)
Rounded evergreen shrub with long, glossy, dark green leaves. Female plants produce round to egg-shaped red berries in fall.

Prunus laurocerasus
CHERRY LAUREL
☼ 💧 Z6–9 H9–6 ↕20ft (6m) ↔30ft (10m)
Spreading shrub that is best used as an informal hedge. Hand-prune in fall, removing only the shoots that are growing away from the general shape.

MORE CHOICES

- *Agarista populifolia* Z7–9 H9–7
- *Berberis thunbergii* Z5–8 H8–5
- *Buxus microphylla* Z6–9 H9–6
- *Camellia sinsensis* Z7–10 H8–7
- *Eleagnus pungens* Z7–9 H9–7
- *Forsythia* x *intermedia* Z6–9 H9–3
- *Ilex cornuta* Z7–9 H9–7
- *Ilex crenata* 'Convexa' Z5–7 H7–5
- *Illicium anisatum* Z7–9 H9–7
- *Laurus nobilis* Z8–11 H12–1
- *Ligustrum japonicum* Z7–10 H10–7
- *Lonicera nitida* 'Baggesen's Gold' Z6–9 H9–6
- *Osmanthus* x *fortunei* Z8–9 H9–8
- *Osmanthus fragrans* Z8–11 H12–8
- *Ternstroemia gymnanthera* Z8–10 H10–8
- *Viburnum* x *rhytidophylloides* Z5–8 H8–5
- *Viburnum tinus* Z8–10 H10–8

Shrubs for accent

The shrubs shown here can be used on their own. They are all striking in some way and make good specimen plants, where their individual characteristics can be seen to full advantage. They may also be planted in small groups, but keep in mind that they can lose their individuality if used in a mixed border.

x Fatshedera lizei
TREE IVY
☼ ◊ Z8–11 H12–8 ↕4–6ft (1.2–2m) ↔10ft (3m)
Spreading shrub with five to seven pointed leaves and greenish-white sterile flowers that are produced in fall. Makes a good house plant.

Acer palmatum 'Dissectum'
THREADLEAF JAPANESE MAPLE
☼ ◐ ◆ Z6–8 H8–6 ↕6ft (2m) ↔10ft (3m)
Mound-forming shrub with arching shoots bears finely cut red-purple leaves that turn gold in fall. Produces tiny purple-red flowers in late summer.

Corylus avellana 'Contorta'
CORKSCREW HAZEL
☼ ◐ ◊ Z3–9 H9–1 ↕↔25ft (5m)
An upright large shrub, this does best in a neutral to alkaline soil. The catkins open in late winter and the twisted branches are prized by flower arrangers.

Cycas revoluta
JAPANESE SAGO PALM
☼ ◊ Z13–15 H12–6 ↕↔3–6ft (1–2m) or more
A very ancient genus from the time of dinosaurs that is often grown as a conservatory plant. When mature, pineapple-scented male flowers grow from the center.

Rhus typhina 'Dissecta'
CUTLEAF STAGHORN SUMAC
☼ ◊ ▲ z3–8 H8–1 ‡6ft (2m) ↔10ft (3m)
Spreading shrub with mid-green foliage that forms small thickets. Red, conical flower spikes appear in summer and attract birds later. Good fall color.

Mahonia bealei
LEATHERLEAF MAHONIA
☼ ◊ z7–8 H8–7 ‡↔10ft (3m)
Mildly fragrant, pale yellow flowers appear in early spring. Fruits ripen to blue-purple. Prefers moderately fertile, organic soil. Oldest leaves turn orange in fall.

Aralia spinosa
DEVIL'S WALKING STICK
Ⓝ ☼ ☼ ◊ z4–9 H9–1
‡30ft (10m) ↔15ft (5m)
Makes an impenetrable thicket in time, with spiny stems and leaves. Has white flowers in July and fruit that attract birds. Grows well in poor soils.

MORE CHOICES

- *Abeliophyllum distichum* z5–9 H9–1
- *Acer palmatum* 'Waterfall' z5–8 H8–2
- *Cotinus* 'Grace' z5–8 H8–5
- *Magnolia x soulangeana* z5–9 H9–5
- *Mahonia lomariifolia* z8–9 H9–5
- *Viburnum marcocephalum* 'Snowball' z7–9 H9–7
- *Yucca gloriosa* z7–11 H12–7

Nandina domestica
HEAVENLY BAMBOO
☼ ▲ z6–9 H9–3
‡6ft (2m) ↔5ft (1.5m)
Upright shrub blooming in late spring to early summer, Bright red, round berries follow in early fall and hang on through winter. Pest-free. Native to China.

Fatsia japonica
JAPANESE ARALIA
☼ ☼ ◊ ▲ z8–11 H12–8
‡5–12ft (1.5–4m)
Fall-flowering shrub with a spreading habit that increases slowly by underground suckers. Small black berries form later. Varieties with gold and with variegated foliage.

WOODY PLANTS

Spring-flowering shrubs

A welcome sight after the dark weeks of winter, these early flowering plants are best located where they can be seen from inside the house. Locate those with a scent next to a walkway where their cheerful blooms and fragrance can be fully appreciated. Plant them is groups of the same species for the greatest visual impact.

Magnolia stellata 'Royal Star'
ROYAL STAR MAGNOLIA
Z5–9 H9–5 ↕10ft (3m) ↔12ft (4m)
A bushy, deciduous shrub that needs protection from winter winds and late frosts. Furry flower buds open before the leaves.

Weigela 'Red Prince'
RED PRINCE WEIGELA
Z4–8 H8–1 ↕5–6ft (1.5–2m) ↔5ft (1.5m)
An upright, free-flowering variety that blooms over a long period in spring and early summer. It is probably the brightest of all the red-flowered weigela's.

Kerria japonica 'Pleniflora'
DOUBLE JAPANESE KERRIA
Z5–9 H8–3 ↕↔10ft (3m)
Long-blooming shrub, with bright green stems that are attractive in winter. It will grow in both poor sandy soils and heavy clay. Prune out old growth occasionally.

Kalmia latifolia
CALICO BUSH, MOUNTAIN LAUREL
Ⓝ pH Z5–9 H9–5 ↕↔10ft (3m)
Dense evergreen shrub that does well in woodland gardens in similar conditions to rhododendrons and azaleas. Modern varieties have shades of red and pink.

Rhododendron 'Fireball'
FIREBALL AZALEA
Z5–9 H9–3 ↕↔3ft (1m)
An Exbury hybrid raised in England, this vigorous plant has bronze new foliage, turning green then yellow in fall. Best in cooler climates.

Calycanthus floridus
CAROLINA ALLSPICE
Ⓝ Z5–9 H9–1 ↕8ft (2.5m) ↔10ft (3m)
A spreading shrub that is tolerant of most soils and of sun. The fragrant flowers are produced from late spring into summer. Foliage is also fragrant when crushed.

Pieris japonica
JAPANESE PIERIS
Z6–8 H8–6 ↕↔20ft (6m)
This species needs a slightly acidic soil with additional organic matter. New leaves are usually bronze, and some cultivars have been selected for this trait.

Rhododendron catawbiense
MOUNTAIN ROSEBAY
Ⓝ Z4–8 H8–1 ↕↔10ft (3m)
A very tough species that will take both winter cold and summer heat, and direct sunlight.

Forsythia x intermedia
BORDER FORSYTHIA
Z6–9 H9–3 ↕↔5ft (1.5m)
Profuse flowers are produced in early and midspring, before the leaves. Remove oldest stems after flowering to rejuvenate the plant. Useful as a hedge or screen.

Fothergilla major
LARGE WITCH ALDER
Ⓝ ☀ 💧 pH Z4–8 H9–2 ↕↔10ft (3m)
A multistemmed, erect shrub with dark green leaves that turn yellow, orange, and bright red in fall, with all three colors present at the same time. It may become chlorotic if grown on even slightly alkaline soils.

Mahonia aquifolium
OREGON GRAPE HOLLY
Ⓝ ☀ 💧 Z6–9 H9–6
↕↔5ft (1.5m)
This slow-growing, upright evergreen shrub turns purplish bronze in fall. Blue-black, wax-coated berries ripen in early fall and hang on through winter.

Daphne x *burkwoodii*
BURKWOOD DAPHNE
☼ 💧 Z4–7 H7–1 ↕↔5ft (1.5m)
Densely branched, semi-evergreen shrub bears fragrant flowers in clusters in late spring and sometimes in fall, especially if given water in summer.

Deutzia gracilis
SLENDER DEUTZIA
☼ 💧 Z5–8 H8–1 ↕↔5ft (1.5m)
A bushy, deciduous shrub that grows in most soils. Makes a good informal hedge. Abundant, fragrant flowers are borne from spring into summer.

MORE CHOICES

- *Cyrilla racemiflora* Z6–9 H9–4
- *Exochorda racemosa* Z5–9 H9–5
- *Fothergilla gardenii* Z4–9 H9–1
- *Genista lydia* Z6–9 H9–3
- *Neviusua alabamensis* Z4–8 H8–1
- *Philadelphus coronarius* Z4–9 H9–4
- *Rhododendron canescens* Z6–9 H9–4
- *Rhododedron kurume* Z6–9 H9–5
- *Rhododedron indicum* Z8–9 H9–7
- *Spiraea thunbergii* Z5–8 H8–5
- *Syringa* x *lacinata* Z4–8 H8–1
- *Viburnum* x *carlcephalum* Z6–8 H8–5

Spiraea x *vanhouttei*
VANHOUTTE SPIREA
☼ 💧 Z4–8 H8–1 ↕6ft (2m) ↔5ft (1.5m)
Flowers are borne in abundance in late spring and early summer and almost completely cover the dark green leaves. Very adaptable and tolerant.

Genista pilosa 'Vancouver Gold'
VANCOUVER GOLD BROOM
☼ ◊ Z5–9 H9–3 ↕18in (45cm) ↔3ft (1m)
A spreading, mounded plant that makes a good groundcover. Free-flowering and stays in bloom for a long time. Leaves are lance-shaped and silky beneath.

Prunus glandulosa
DWARF FLOWERING ALMOND
☼ ◊◆ Z5–8 H8–3 ↕↔5ft (1.5m)
A somewhat sprawling shrub that is grown for its abundant display of flowers. Best hidden by tall perennials after blooming.

Corylopsis glabrescens
FRAGRANT WINTERHAZEL
◐ ◆ pH Z6–9 H9–6 ↕↔15ft (5m)
A spreading, multi-stemmed shrub that blooms in very early spring before the leaves. It prefers a soil rich in humus. Shelter from late frosts that damage flowers.

Viburnum carlesii
KOREAN SPICE VIBURNUM
☼ ◊ Z5–8 H8–5 ↕↔5ft (1.5m)
Rounded upright shrub blooms in midspring. Foliage turns dark red in fall. Best on slightly acidic soil. 'Compactum' grows to only half the size indicated.

Viburnum macrocephalum
CHINESE SNOWBALL VIBURNUM
☼ ◐ ◊◆ Z7–9 H9–7 ↕↔15ft (5m)
A dense rounded shrub with evergreen foliage in the South. May also flower in fall in warm locations. Protect from winter winds in the northern part of its range.

WOODY PLANTS

Summer-flowering shrubs

In the South, color and fragrance do not end with spring; shrubs which bloom in our hot, humid summers keep monotony at bay, and when planted in strategic spots where their interest and bouquet can catch our attention, they may even lure us outside into the garden. Many of these summer blooms also serve to attract butterflies and hummingbirds to brighten the garden.

Cotinus coggygria
SMOKE TREE
Z5–9 H9–3 ↕↔15ft (5m)
While the flowers are attractive, it is the fluffy stems on the seeds that give this its common name. The foliage often turns a bright yellow in fall.

Hydrangea paniculata 'Grandiflora'
PEEGEE HYDRANGEA
Z4–8 H8–1 ↕22ft (7m) ↔8ft (2.5m)
A tough, somewhat leggy plant that will thrive in most locations. The heads of bloom turn pink as they age and then brown. They can be cut at any stage for drying.

Hydrangea quercifolia
OAKLEAF HYDRANGEA
Ⓝ Z5–9 H9–1
↕6ft (2m) ↔8ft (2.5m)
Mounds of flowers dry intact and extend the season of display. The foliage contrasts well with nearby perennials and shrubs and turns an attractive copper in fall.

Buddleja davidii 'Harlequin'
HARLEQUIN BUTTERFLY BUSH
Z6–9 H10–4 ↕↔20ft (6m)
One of many named forms, this is distinctive with its variegated foliage. Encourage constant blooming, and more butterflies, by deadheading spent flower spikes.

Hypericum 'Hidcote'
HIDCOTE ST. JOHN'S WORT
Z6–9 H9–6 ↕↔5ft (1.5m)
Flowers from midsummer to early autumn. This dense and bushy hybrid bears evergreen to semi-evergreen foliage and prefers moderately fertile soil.

Clethra alnifolia 'Ruby Spice'
RUBY SPICE SUMMERSWEET
Ⓝ ☼ ◐ 💧 Z3–9 H9–1 ↕↔6–8ft (2–2.5m)
An upright, deciduous, clump-forming shrub that grows equally well from mountains to the coast. Long-lasting fragrant flowers appear in late summer and early fall, and attract butterflies and hummingbirds.

Clethra alnifolia
SUMMERSWEET
Ⓝ ◐ 💧 pH Z3–9 H9–1 ↕↔8ft (2.5m)
Grow in highly organic soil. Late to leaf out in spring, the foliage turns golden in fall. Very fragrant flowers last about a month.

Vitex agnus-castus
CHASTE TREE
☼ 💧 (outline) Z6–9 H9–6 ↕↔8ft (2.5m)
Long-lasting spikes of fragrant flowers appear for most of the summer. Deadhead to encourage more blooms. This grows best where summers are hot.

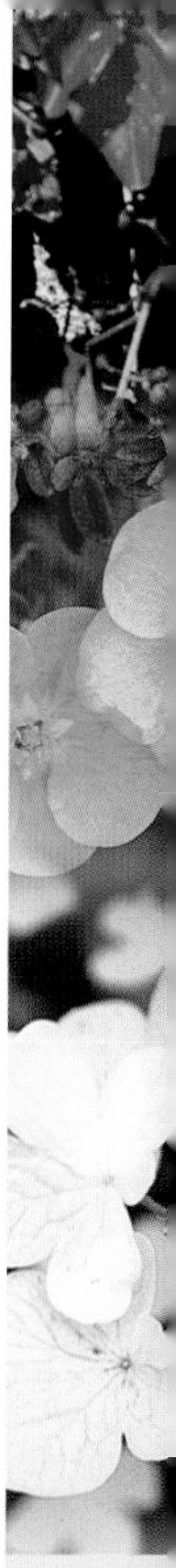

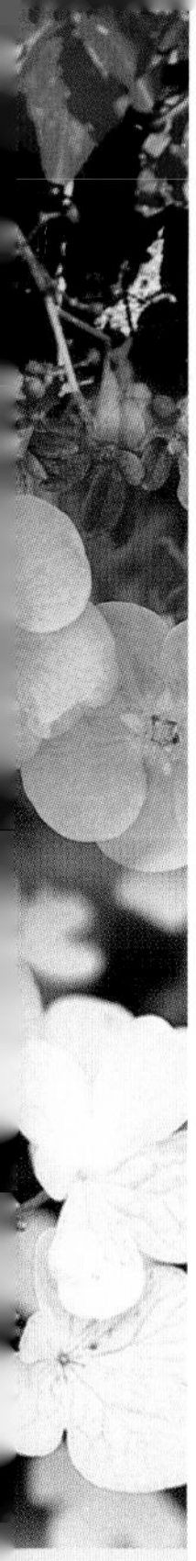

WOODY PLANTS

Abelia 'Edward Goucher'

EDWARD GOUCHER ABELIA

☼ ◑ ◊ Z6–9 H9–1 ↕5ft (1.5m) ↔6ft (2m)

A semi-evergreen shrub with leaves, often in whorls, that are bronzy when young. The flowers are produced over a long period, well into fall, and attract butterflies.

Itea virginica

VIRGINIA SWEETSPIRE

Ⓝ ☼ ◑ Z6–9 H10–7 ↕10ft (3m) ↔5ft (1.5m)

Spikes of fragrant flowers persist into summer. The plant forms a thicket and spreads slowly by underground stems. Foliage turns garnet red in fall.

Ixora coccinea

FLAME OF THE WOODS

☼ ◊◑ Z14–15 H12–10 ↕8ft (2.5m) ↔5–6ft (1.5–2m)

Frequently grown along the Florida coast as a decorative hedge, this forms a rounded, evergreen shrub. There are varieties in other colors. Good container plant.

MORE CHOICES

- *Brunsfelsia australis* Z12–15 H12–10
- *Clerodendrum speciosissimum* Z13–15 H12–10
- *Clerodendrum trichotomum* var. *fargesii* Z7–9 H9–7
- *Gardenia augusta* Z8–11 H12–8
- *Hydrangea arborescens* Z4–9 H9–1
- *Indigofera kirilowii* Z6–9 H9–5

Spiraea japonica
'Anthony Waterer'
ANTHONY WATERER SPIREA
☼ ◊♦ Z3–9 H9–1 ↕↔to 5ft (1.5m)
An old favorite that blooms over a long period. It makes a good informal hedge or can be mass-planted as a groundcover. New foliage is red-tinged and turns wine red in fall.

Hibiscus syriacus
'Collie Mullens'
COLLIE MULLENS ROSE OF SHARON
☼ ◊ Z5–9 H9–1 ↕8–10ft (2.5–3m) ↔6–8ft (2–2.5ft)
A new sterile hybrid to replace older varieties that seed freely and can become invasive. Flowers are on new growth so prune in spring. Can be used as a hedge.

Aesculus parviflora
BOTTLEBRUSH BUCKEYE
Ⓝ ☼ ◐ ◊♦ Z5–9 H9–4
↕10ft (3m) ↔15ft (5m)
Young bronze leaves turn dark green in summer and yellow in fall. Sometimes slow to establish, this shrub is best grown in a large or medium-sized garden.

Hibiscus rosa-sinensis
Hybrid
ROSE OF CHINA
☼ ◊♦ Z14–15 H12–1 ↕8–15ft (2.5–5m) ↔5–10ft (1.5–3m)
Favorite tropical container or bedding shrub with fist-size flowers favored by hummingbirds. Constant flowers shine against very glossy, dark green foliage.

Nerium oleander
OLEANDER
☼ ◊ Z13–15 H12–1 ↕↔20ft (6m)
A free-flowering shrub that also comes with red or white flowers. Frequently grown as a house plant but needs bright light to flower well. All parts are toxic if eaten.

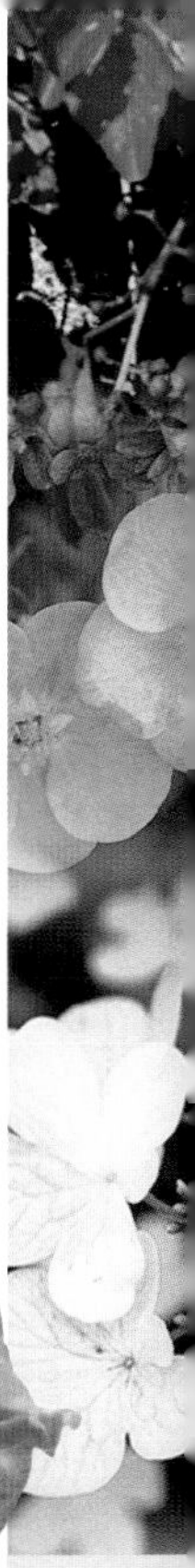

Fall-flowering shrubs

As the summer draws to a close, perennials tend to dominate the garden. To add diversity, plant some late-blooming shrubs that will give a contrast in texture and height to your garden. Combine the shrubs shown here with those that flower in spring and summer to create a garden that is almost ever-blooming.

Caryopteris x *clandonensis* 'Arthur Simmonds'
ARTHUR SIMMONDS BLUE MIST SHRUB
☼ ◐ ◊ Z6–9 H9–1
↕3ft (1m) ↔5ft (1.5m)
Aromatic, gray-green foliage is silvery beneath. A rounded and deciduous shrub, it flowers in late summer/ early fall.

Osmanthus heterophyllus 'Goshiki'
VARIEGATED FALSE HOLLY
☼ ◐ ◊ Z7–9 H9–7 ↕↔15ft (5m)
White flowers bloom in small clusters in late summer and fall, followed by egg-shaped, blue-black berries. This is excellent as a hedge or topiary, but trim in spring.

Buddleja 'Pink Delight'
PINK DELIGHT BUTTERFLY BUSH
☼ ◐ ◊ Z6–9 H9–1 ↕8ft (2.5m) ↔6ft (2m)
Produces larger flower spikes and deeper green leaves than the species. Orange-eyed flowers bloom from summer to fall. Prefers fertile soil.

Buddleia davidii 'White Ball'
WHITE BALL BUTTERFLY BUSH
☼ ◊ Z5–9 H9–3 ↕↔3ft (1m)
A new miniature variety from Holland that flowers on the current growth and should be cut back in spring. The flowers appear in late summer and fall.

Tibouchina urvilleana
BRAZILIAN SPIDER FLOWER
☼ ◆ Z13–15 H12–10 ↕20ft (6m) ↔10ft (3m)
Spreading evergreen shrub with pairs of opposite leathery leaves. Flowers occur in threes from summer to fall. A good greenhouse plant where not hardy.

Hamamelis virginiana
COMMON WITCH HAZEL
Ⓝ ☼ ◊ pH Z3–8 H8–1 ↕↔20ft (6m)
Unlike its spring-blooming relatives, this shrub bears small, fragrant, spidery yellow flowers in the fall. Grows well in the shade of a wall or fence.

Camellia sansanqua 'Yuletide'
YULETIDE CAMELLIA
◐ ◊◑ pH Z8–10 H8–7 ↕20ft (6m) ↔10ft (3m)
This group of camellias differs from the more commonly grown Japanese type because it flowers in late fall and early winter. It needs similar conditions.

MORE CHOICES

- *Abelia* 'Edward Goucher' Z6–9 H9–1
- *Lagerstroemia* spp. Z7–9 H9–7

Rosmarinus officinalis
ROSEMARY
☼ ◊ Z8–11 H12–8 ↕↔5ft (1.5m)
Aromatic leaves used as a culinary herb. Grow outdoors or in a container inside. Tolerant of drought, and unappealing to rabbits.

Osmanthus fragrans
FRAGRANT OLIVE
☼ ◐ ◊ Z7–10 H10–7 ↕↔20ft (6m)
Has sweet-smelling flowers from fall to spring. Prune in spring to remove winter injury if required. Makes a good combination with camellias.

Fatsia japonica
JAPANESE ARALIA
☼ ◐ ◊◑ Z8–11 H12–8 ↕5–12ft (1.5–4m)
Somewhat open bushy shrub spreads by underground runners. Small black fruits in early winter. Varieties with gold or variegated foliage may be more attractive.

Winter-flowering shrubs

Only the Tropics out-bloom the South when it comes to winter color, thanks to evergreen and deciduous shrubs that flower before, during, and after sudden hard freezes and rare snow. Everyone should have one or two of these to add color to the winter garden and brighten up the three months when other plants don't bloom.

Daphne odora
WINTER DAPHNE
☼ ◐ ◊ Z7–9 H9–7 ↕↔4ft (1.2m)
A neat, evergreen shrub whose fragrance spreads on the slightest breeze. It can be a bit finicky to grow and requires a perfectly drained soil or the roots will rot.

Prunus mume
JAPANESE APRICOT
☼ ◊ ◆ Z6–8 H8–6 ↕↔28ft (9m)
Although the yellowish fruit are not edible, this is worth growing for its midwinter fragrant flowers. Prune soon after flowering to ensure a good crop of blooms the following year.

Chimonanthus praecox
WINTERSWEET
☼ ◊ Z7–9 H9–7
↕8ft (2.5m) ↔10ft (3m)
Plant this near a walk or porch where its delicate spicy fragrance can be enjoyed. It needs a period of cold to induce flowering. The glossy leaves are in opposite pairs.

Jasminum nudiflorum
WINTER JASMINE
☼ ◊ Z6–9 H9–6 ↕↔10ft (3m)
The willowlike, bright green stems on this slender deciduous shrub stand out in early winter, before the flowers open. A somewhat rampant grower, it needs severe pruning every few years to rejuvenate.

Chaenomeles speciosa 'Moerloosei'
MOERLOOSE FLOWERING QUINCE
☼ ◐ ◊ Z5–8 H8–5 ↕8ft (2.5m) ↔15ft (5m)
A rounded shrub with spiny branches that can also be used for a hedge or espalier. The fruit are yellow-green with black dots and can be used for jellies.

Lonicera fragrantissima
WINTER HONEYSUCKLE
☼ ◑ ◇ Z4–8 H8–3 ↕6ft (2m) ↔12ft (4m)
Very fragrant flowers are welcomed by bees. This is widely planted along interstate embankments in the southeast. The dull red berries are food for birds.

Hamamelis x *intermedia* 'Jelena'
JELENA HYBRID WITCH HAZEL
☼ ◑ ◑ ● Z5–9 H9–1 ↕↔12ft (4m)
Large, slightly fragrant flowers appear on zigzag branches that can be cut for forcing indoors. Foliage turns bright orange and red in fall. Protect from wind.

MORE CHOICES

- *Hamamelis japonica* Z5–9 H9–5
- *Hamamelis mollis* Z5–9 H9–5
- *Mahonia bealei* Z7–8 H8–7
- *Mahonia lomarlifolia* Z8–9 H9–5
- *Prunus glandulosa* Z5–8 H8–3

Camellia japonica 'Sensation'
SENSATION JAPANESE CAMELLIA
◑ ◇ ◑ Z7–8 H8–7 ↕10–12ft (3–4m) ↔8ft (2.5m)
This is one of many named forms of the Japanese camellia that come in a range of flower colors and types. Shelter slightly to protect the open flowers.

Abeliophyllum distichum
WHITE FORSYTHIA, KOREAN ABELIALEAF
☼ ◇ Z5–9 H9–1 ↕↔4ft (1.2m)
Open spreading shrub with long stems covered with spikes of fragrant, sometimes pink-tinged flowers with purple-tinged stems. Foliage turns purple in fall.

Osmanthus fragrans
FRAGRANT OLIVE
☼ ◑ ◇ Z8–11 H12–8 ↕↔20ft (6m)
Very sweet-smelling flowers from fall to spring. Prune in spring if required to remove winter injury. Makes a good combination with camellias.

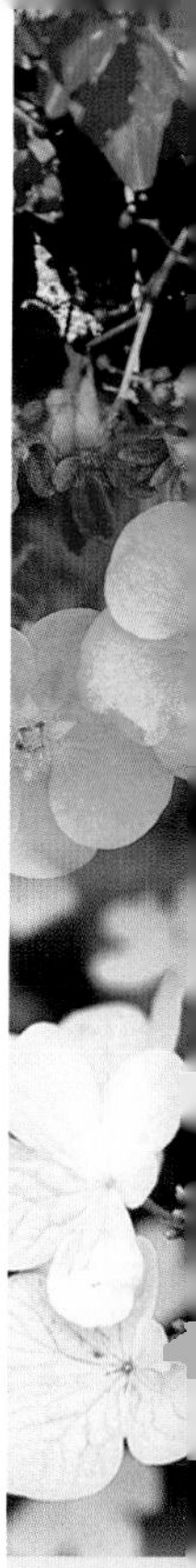

Shrubs with fragrant flowers

Fragrance adds a pleasurable dimension to the garden. By selecting plants with careful consideration, you can have a fragrant shrub or perennial in flower almost year-round. Plant some of those shown here by a walkway, or under a window, where their fragrance can be appreciated easily. Before planting, however, test their scent in a local nursery.

Daphne x *burkwoodii* 'Carol Mackie'
CAROL MACKIE DAPHNE
☼ ◐ 💧 Z5–8 H8–4 ↕↔3–5ft (1–1.5m)
Fragrant, light pink flowers in early summer. May be evergreen in the South. Though there are other variegated forms of this hybrid, this is the most common.

Michelia figo
BANANA SHRUB
☼ 💧 Z12–15 H12–10 ↕↔30ft (10m)
Bears flowers with a banana-like fragrance in spring and summer. Bushy evergreen shrub with lightly hairy, yellow-brown stems. Slow growing.

Viburnum x *burkwoodii*
BURKWOOD VIBURNUM
☼ ◐ 💧💧 Z5–8 H8–1 ↕↔8ft (2.5m)
A good evergreen viburnum with glossy leaves, dark green above, gray-felted below. Flowering in late winter, it has red fruits later that turn black when ripe.

Calycanthus floridus
CAROLINA ALLSPICE, COMMON SWEETSHRUB
Ⓝ ◐ 💧 Z5–9 H9–1 ↕8ft (2.5m) ↔10ft (3m)
A spreading shrub that is tolerant of most soils and of sun. The fragrant flowers are produced from late spring into summer. Foliage is also fragrant when crushed.

Osmanthus fragrans
FRAGRANT OLIVE
☼ ◐ 💧 Z8–11 H12–8 ↕↔20ft (6m)
Evergreen shrub with sweet-smelling flowers from fall to spring. Prune in spring to remove winter injury if required. Makes a good combination with camellias.

MORE CHOICES

- *Choisya ternata* Z8–10 H10–8
- *Hamamelis virginiana* Z3–8 H8–1
- *Magnolia ashei* Z7–9 H9–7
- *Myrtus communis* Z8–9 H9–8
- *Osmanthus americanus* Z7–10 H10–7
- *Osmanthus* x *fortunei* Z8–9 H9–8
- *Osmanthus heterophyllus* Z7–9 H9–7
- *Rhododendron arborescens* Z5–9 H9–4
- *Styrax obassia* Z6–8 H8–6
- *Viburnum x carlcephalum* Z6–8 H8–5
- *Viburnum carlesii* Z5–8 H8–5

Syringa vulgaris 'Ami Schott'
AMI SCHOTT FRENCH LILAC
☼ ◊ Z4–8 H8–1 ↕↔22ft (7m)
One of several hundred named varieties of French lilac in shades from white to dark red. Most have single flowers but some, like this one, are double. All are very fragrant.

Gardenia jasminoides
CAPE JASMINE
◐ ◊◆ Z8–11 H12–8 ↕6–40ft (2–12m) ↔3–10ft (1–3m)
Evergreen shrub with leathery leaves. Grows best in a slightly acid soil, rich in organic matter. Highly fragrant flowers open for much of the summer and can be over-powering en masse. Prone to whitefly attack.

Chimonanthus praecox
WINTERSWEET
☼ ◊ Z7–9 H9–7
↕8ft (2.5m) ↔10ft (3m)
In winter, this shrub produces fragrant, pendent, cup-shaped flowers. Leaves are lance shaped and glossy, arranged in opposite pairs.

Lonicera nitida
BOXLEAF HONEYSUCKLE
☼ ◊ Z6–9 H9–5 ↕6ft (2m) ↔10ft (3m)
This evergreen honeysuckle produces fragrant flowers up to ½in (1.5cm) long, followed by round purple berries. Makes a good hedge.

Sarcococca hookeriana var. *digyna*
SLENDER SWEETBOX
◐ ◊◆ Z6–9 H9–6 ↕5ft (1.5m) ↔6ft (2m)
Dense, clump-forming evergreen groundcover. Sweetly scented white flowers are followed by round black fruits. Male flowers have cream anthers.

Daphne odora
WINTER DAPHNE
☼ ◐ ◊ Z7–9 H9–7 ↕↔4ft (1.2m)
A rounded evergreen shrub with very fragrant flowers that blossom from midwinter to early spring, followed by fleshy red fruit.

Shrubs with white flowers

There are more shrubs with white flowers than any other color. White gardens or borders are very popular, and the wide range of growth habits, flower forms, and bloom times available in these shrubs makes the design process relatively simple. Using these as a background for white-flowered perennials, bulbs, and annuals will create a unified theme garden.

Styrax obassia
FRAGRANT SNOWBELL
☼ ◐ ● Z6–8 H8–6 ↕40ft (12m) ↔22ft (7m)
Wonderful winter shape has many winding, turning branches. Leaves are easily injured in early spring, because they emerge very early.

Spiraea x *vanhouttei*
VANHOUTTE SPIREA
☼ ○ Z4–8 H8–1 ↕6ft (2m) ↔5ft (1.5m)
Flowers are borne in abundance in late spring and early summer and almost completely cover the dark green leaves. Very adaptable and tolerant.

Exochorda racemosa
COMMON PEARLBUSH
☼ ◐ ○ ◑ Z5–9 H9–5 ↕↔10–12ft (3–4m)
A dense rounded shrub with arching branches that survives heat and drought well. The pearl-like flower buds give this its common name and open in spring.

Deutzia crenata var. *nakaiana* 'Nikko'
NIKKO DEUTZIA
☼ ○ Z4–8 H8–1 ↕24in (60cm) ↔4ft (1.2m)
A dwarf selection that does well in a large rock garden or as a groundcover. The leaves turn burgundy red in fall.

Hydrangea paniculata 'Tardiva'
LATE HYDRANGEA
Z3–8 H8–1 ↕22ft (7m) ↔8ft (2.5m)
This form of the panicle hydrangea flowers in late summer, long after others have finished. It needs little pruning, just the removal of old flower heads in spring.

Fothergilla major
LARGE WITCH ALDER
N pH Z4–8 H9–2
↕↔10ft (3m)
A multistemmed erect shrub with dark green leaves that turn yellow, orange, and bright red in fall, with all three colors present at the same time. It may become chlorotic if grown on even slightly alkaline soils.

Magnolia stellata 'Royal Star'
ROYAL STAR MAGNOLIA
Z5–9 H9–5 ↕10ft (3m) ↔12ft (4m)
A very free-flowering form of the star magnolia that has more petals than the species. Plant where it will be protected from late frosts and chilling winds.

Virburnum plicatum f. *tomentosum* 'Shasta'
SHASTA DOUBLEFILE VIBURNUM
Z4–8 H8–1 ↕6ft (2m) ↔10–12ft (3–4m)
Showy flower clusters are carried on top of horizontal branches to give a stunning display. Unfortunately, many inferior strains are being offered under this name.

Leptospermum scoparium
NEW ZEALAND TEA TREE
Z12–15 H12–3 ↕↔10ft (3m)
A compact shrub with arching shoots covered with silver-haired aromatic leaves that turn dark green with age. The flowers appear in spring and early summer.

MORE CHOICES

- *Aronia arbutifolia* Z5–9 H9–4
- *Neviusia alabamensis* Z4–8 H8–1
- *Rhododendron alabamense* Z7–9 H9–7
- *Rhus chinensis* Z8–10 H10–8
- *Spiraea nipponica* Z4–8 H8–1
- *Styrax americanus* Z6–8 H8–6

Shrubs with cool flowers

Cool-colored flowers are restful, especially when the weather becomes hot and humid. Pale pinks, blues, and whites are particularly good in the shade, bringing a sense of peace. Use the variety of plant shapes and leaf forms shown here to give a contrast in textures that is held together by the blending of cool tones.

Buddleja 'Lochinch'
LOCHINCH BUTTERFLY BUSH
☼ ◊ Z6–9 H9–6 ↕8ft (2.5m) ↔10ft (3m)
A hybrid, with the common *B. davidii* as one parent. The fragrant summer flower spikes are up to 12in (30cm) long. Flowers on new growth, so cut back hard in spring.

Chaenomeles speciosa 'Moerloosei'
MOERLOOSE FLOWERING QUINCE
☼ ◑ ◊ Z5–8 H8–5 ↕8ft (2.5m) ↔15ft (5m)
A rounded shrub with spiny branches that can also be used for a hedge or espalier. The fruit are yellow-green with black dots and can be used for jellies.

Plumbago auriculata
CAPE LEADWORT
☼ ◊ Z12–15 H12–10 ↕10–20ft (3–6m) ↔10ft (3m)
A sprawling woody plant that is often treated as a climber, it is commonly grown as a tender houseplant where not hardy and planted out for the summer. Its flowers are sticky.

Abelia 'Edward Goucher'
EDWARD GOUCHER ABELIA
☼ ◑ ◊ Z6–9 H9–1 ↕10ft (3m) ↔12ft (4m)
An evergreen or semi-evergreen shrub with arching branches that have fragrant flowers from midsummer to fall. It is irresistible to many butterflies.

Spiraea japonica 'Little Princess'
LITTLE PRINCESS JAPANESE SPIREA
Z4–9 H9–1 ↕↔5ft (1.5m)
A deciduous shrub that blooms profusely in mid- to late summer on a dense mound, but it is slower growing and less tolerant of severe pruning than many other spireas.

Kolkwitzia amabilis
BEAUTYBUSH
Z5–9 H9–5
↕12ft (3.5m) ↔10ft (3m)
This suckering deciduous shrub has masses of blooms with yellow throats in early summer. Grow at the back of a border where it is not prominent when not in flower.

Hydrangea macrophylla 'Blue Wave'
BLUE WAVE LACECAP HYDRANGEA
Z6–9 H9–2 ↕6ft (1m) ↔8ft (2.5m)
Sterile flowers in the center of the flowerhead are surrounded by the showier fertile flowers. Color varies in intensity, depending on soil pH.

Clethera alnifolia 'Ruby Spice'
RUBY SPICE SUMMERSWEET
Z3–9 H9–1
↕↔6–8ft (2–2.5m)
This cultivar has pink flowers; the species often have a pink tinge. Fragrant flowers appear from late summer to early fall. Tolerant of seaside conditions.

Tibouchina urvilleana
BRAZILIAN SPIDER FLOWER
Z13–15 H12–10 ↕10–20ft (3–6m) ↔10ft (3m)
Spreading evergreen shrub with pairs of opposite leathery leaves. Flowers occur in threes from summer to fall. Makes a good greenhouse plant where not hardy.

MORE CHOICES

- *Brunsfelsia australis* Z12–15 H12–10
- *Caryopteris x clandonensis* 'Blue Billows' Z6–9 H9–1
- *Hydrangea marcophylla* 'Nikko Blue' Z6–9 H9–3
- *Raphiolepis umbellata* 'Springtime' Z7–11 H12–7
- *Rhododendron canescens* Z6–9 H9–4
- *Robinia hispida* Z6–11 H12–6
- *Syringa* x *laciniata* Z4–8 H8–1
- *Syringa patula* 'Miss Kim' Z3–8 H8–1

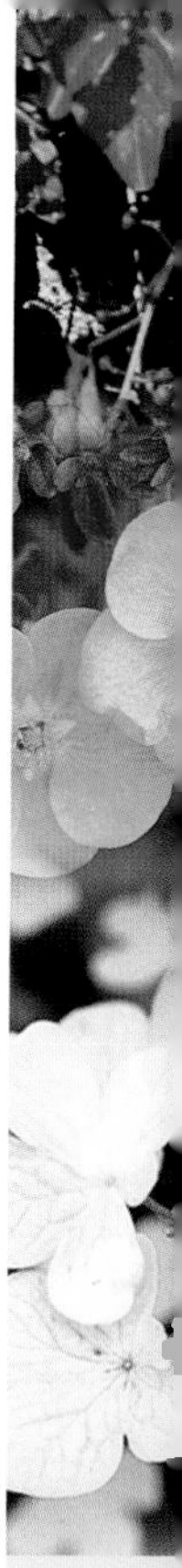

Shrubs with hot flowers

Hot-colored flowers are the ones that shout at you, the ones that grab your attention even when seen from a great distance. They tend to clash more readily than cool colors and should be located with careful consideration. But keep in mind the season of bloom – two hot colors that flower at different times cannot clash.

Rosa rugosa
RUGOSA ROSE, JAPANESE ROSE
Z2–9 H9–1 ↕↔3–6ft (1–2m)
A vigorous spiny species with leathery leaves and round red fruit in winter. Flowers open from early summer to fall. There are many named forms available.

Forsythia x *intermedia*
BORDER FORSYTHIA
Z6–9 H9–3 ↕↔5ft (1.5m)
Profuse flowers are produced in early and midspring, before the leaves. Remove oldest stems after flowering to rejuvenate the plant. Useful as a hedge or screen.

Hypericum calycinum
AARON'S BEARD, ROSE OF SHARON
Z5–9 H9–4
↕24in (60cm) ↔indefinite
A semi-evergreen shrub that thrives in sandy soil, spreads by underground shoots, and forms a dense carpet. Flowers from midsummer onward.

Hibiscus rosa-sinensis hybrid
ROSE OF CHINA
Z14–15 H12–1 ↕8–15ft (2.5–5m) ↔5–10ft (1.5–3m)
Large shrub or small tree with glossy, dark green foliage and flowers in a wide range of colors. Some named forms also have double flowers. Susceptible to whiteflies.

Mahonia aquifolium
OREGON GRAPE HOLLY
Ⓝ Z6–9 H9–6 ↕↔5ft (1.5m)
This slow-growing, upright evergreen shrub turns purplish bronze in fall. Blue-black, wax-coated berries ripen in early fall and hang on through the winter.

Cystisus scoparius
SCOTCH BROOM
Z6–8 H8–6 ↕5ft (1.5cm) ↔5ft (1.5cm)
Upright bushy shrub with arching branches and eye-catching flowers in late spring. Similar to gorse (*Ulex*) in appearance but not spiny and not as invasive.

Erythrina crista-galli
COCK'S COMB
☼ ◊ Z11–15 H12–8 (1.5–6m)
↕5–20ft (1.5–6m) ↔3–100ft (1–3m)
Tropical plant that may be a tree in the Deep South. Branches and leaf stalks are spiny. Flowers open from midsummer to fall above leathery foliage. A good conservatory plant where not hardy.

Kerria japonica 'Golden Guinea'
GOLDEN GUINEA JAPANESE KERRIA
☼ ◊ Z5–9 H9–1 ↕6ft (2m) ↔8ft (2.5m)
An arching shrub that is easy to grow and will survive in most soils. This cultivar has larger flowers. There is also a double-flowered cultivar that is not quite as hardy.

MORE CHOICES

- *Cassia alata* Z9–11 H12–9
- *Cassia bicapsularis* Z11–12 H12–9
- *Chaenomeles speciosa* Z5–9 H9–1
- *Genista tinctoria* Z2–8 H8–1
- *Mahonia bealei* Z7–8 H8–7
- *Malvaviscus arborescens* Z14–15 H12–6
- *Rhododendron austrinum* Z6–10 H10–6
- *Rhododendron* 'Vulcan' Z5–8 H8–5

Callistemon citrinus 'Splendens'
CRIMSON BOTTLEBRUSH
☼ ◊◊ Z10–15 H12–10 ↕↔5–25ft (1.5–8m)
An arching shrub with broad leaves that are pink when young. It can be cut back hard if it becomes overgrown. The flowers open in spring and summer. This variety is brighter than the species.

Buddleja globosa
ORANGE BALL TREE
☼ ◊ Z7–9 H9–7 ↕15ft (3m) ↔15ft (3m)
Erect arching shrub with lance-shaped deep green leaves that may be evergreen in the South. Striking flowers appear in early summer. Do not cut back hard in spring as you would a butterfly bush.

Shrubs attractive to butterflies

Many of the shrubs that flower from early summer onwards are attractive to butterflies and hummingbirds. Generally it is those with tubular, but not necessarily red, flowers that the hummingbirds enjoy, while butterflies will feed on a much wider range of flower shapes like those shown here, providing they have nectar.

Aesculus parviflora
BOTTLEBRUSH BUCKEYE
Ⓝ ☼ ☀ ◊ ♦ Z5–9 H9–4 ↕10ft (3m) ↔15ft (5m)
Young bronze leaves turn dark green in summer and yellow in fall. Sometimes slow to establish. Best grown in a large or medium-sized garden.

Plumbago auriculata
CAPE LEADWORT
☼ ◊ Z12–15 H12–10
↕10–20ft (3–6m) ↔3–10ft (1–3m)
A sprawling woody plant, often treated as a climber, with sticky flowers. Commonly grown as a tender houseplant where not hardy and planted out for the summer.

MORE CHOICES

- *Caryopteris* 'Arthur Simmonds' Z7–9 H9–1
- *Cephalanthus occidentalis* Z5–11 H12–3
- *Clerodendrum speciosissimum* Z13–15 H12–10
- *Clerodendrum trichotomum* Z7–9 H9–7
- *Hamelia patens* Z11–12 H9
- *Jatropha integerrima* Z9–11 H12–9

Clethra alnifolia
SUMMERSWEET
Ⓝ ☀ ♦ pH Z3–9 H9–1 ↕↔8ft (2.5m)
Fragrant, bell-shaped white flowers form elegant spires. An upright shrub, it readily increases by suckering. Leaves turn yellow in fall.

Abelia 'Edward Goucher'
EDWARD GOUCHER ABELIA
☼ ☀ ◊ Z6–9 H9–1 ↕5ft (1.5m) ↔6ft (2m)
Semi-evergreen shrub with leaves, often in whorls, that are bronzy when young. Flowers are produced over a long period, well into fall, and attract butterflies.

Callistemon citrinus 'Splendens'
CRIMSON BOTTLEBRUSH
☼ ◊ ♦ Z10–15 H12–10 ↕↔5–25ft (1.5–8m)
An arching shrub with broad leaves that are pink when young. Can be cut back if overgrown. The flowers open in spring and summer. Brighter than the species.

Hibiscus rosa-sinensis
ROSE OF CHINA
☼ 💧 Z14–15 H12–1 ↕15ft (5m) ↔10ft (3m)
Blooming from mid-summer to fall, this is one of many named varieties in a wide range of colors. They are commonly grown as houseplants where not hardy.

Vitex agnus-castus
CHASTE TREE
☼ 💧 Z6–9 H9–6
↕↔8ft (2.5m)
Fragrant flowers appear throughout much of the summer. Deadhead to encourage repeat bloom. This deciduous spreading shrub prefers hot weather, and is native to southern Europe and western Asia.

Lantana camara
SHRUB VERBENA
Ⓝ ☼ 💧 Z11 H12–1 ↕↔3–6ft (1–2m)
A prickly stemmed plant with strongly scented leaves. There are many forms in shades of white, salmon, yellow, orange, red, or with two-toned flowers.

Weigela florida 'Variegata'
VARIEGATED WEIGELA
☼ 💧 Z5–8 H8–1 ↕↔6–8ft (2–2.5m)
A dense bushy shrub. Prune old straggly plants hard. Easy to grow and can grow near roads and in urban environments, due to tolerance of air pollution.

Buddleja davidii 'White Profusion'
WHITE PROFUSION BUTTERFLY BUSH
☼ 💧 Z6–9 H10–4 ↕10ft (3m) ↔15ft (5m)
Long spikes of fragrant flowers attract butterflies and bees. Best planted in groups in a border. Has no serious pests. Transplants easily and can self-sow profusely.

Buddleja davidii 'Fascinating'
FASCINATING BUTTERFLY BUSH
☼ 💧 Z6–9 H10–4 ↕10ft (3m) ↔15ft (5m)
This shrub attracts many insects, especially butterflies. Tubular flowers with a sweet fragrance form dense clusters 4in (10cm) or more across.

Shrubs with fruits or berries

Colorful fruits add another dimension to the garden. Many last for weeks, or even months, as they slowly ripen, and the range of colors they change through is interesting to watch. Once ripe, they may be fleeting if birds enjoy them, but birds are also worth encouraging. Consider the color before planting. White or yellow fruits look best against a dark background, and dark fruits against pale siding.

Callicarpa bodinieri
BODINIER BEAUTYBERRY
☼ ◐ ◊ Z4–7 H7–1 ↕10ft (3m) ↔8ft (2.5m)
An upright, deciduous shrub that needs a fertile soil to flower well. Small pink flowers open in midsummer. Grown mostly for the clusters of small, bright fruit. Variety 'Profusion' is shown above.

Callicarpa japonica
JAPANESE BEAUTYBERRY
☼ ◐ ◊ Z5–8 H12–3 ↕↔6ft (2m)
A more compact shrub with white to pale pink flowers in late summer. Cut back hard in spring to promote new growth, which bears the flowers. Do not over-fertilize. Variety 'Leucantha' has white fruit.

Cotoneaster horizontalis
ROCKSPRAY COTONEASTER
☼ ◊ Z4–7 H7–3 ↕↔5ft (1.5m)
A prostrate plant with congested branches that will follow the contours of a rock and flow down its face. Small white flowers in summer produce persistent fruit.

Cotoneaster lacteus (C. parneyi)
MILKFLOWER COTONEASTER
☼ ◐ ◊ Z7–9 H9–7 ↕↔12ft (4m)
This evergreen shrub produces clusters of up to 100 white flowers in early to mid-summer, followed by fruit that last through winter. Makes a good hedge.

Ardisia crenata
CORALBERRY, SPICE BERRY
◐ 💧 Z13–15 H12–10 ↕8ft (2.5) ↔6ft (2m)
A common pot plant, also useful as a container plant outdoors in summer where it is not hardy. Long-lasting fruit may survive until the plant is in flower again.

Hippophae rhamnoides
SEA BUCKTHORN
Z3–8 H8–1 ↕↔20ft (6m)
A large deciduous shrub or small tree with small yellow flowers in spring, followed by fruit, but only on female plants. It is very salt-tolerant.

Duranta erecta
PIGEON BERRY, SKYFLOWER
Z11–12 H12–10 ↕10–20ft (3–6m) ↔10ft (3m)
Shrub or small tree with pendulous sprays of white, purple, blue, or lilac flowers with spreading petals, followed by these fruits. Good conservatory plant.

Fatsia japonica
JAPANESE ARALIA
Z8–11 H12–8 ↕5–12ft(1.5–4m)
A spreading shrub that suckers slowly. Flowers open in fall and give small black berries. Forms with gold and with variegated foliage are even more attractive.

MORE CHOICES

- *Berberis thunbergii* cvs. Z4–8 H8–1
- *Clerodendrum trichotomum* Z7–9 H9–7
- *Danae racemosa* Z6–9 H9–2
- *Elaegnus pungens* Z7–9 H9–7
- *Feijoa sellowiana* Z8–11 H12–8
- *Nandina domestica 'Alba'* Z6–11 H12–4
- *Rosa* spp. Z4–9 H9–3
- *Ruscus aculeatus* Z7–9 H9–7
- *Vaccinium ashei* Z5–9 H9–2
- *Viburnum davidii* Z7–9 H9–3

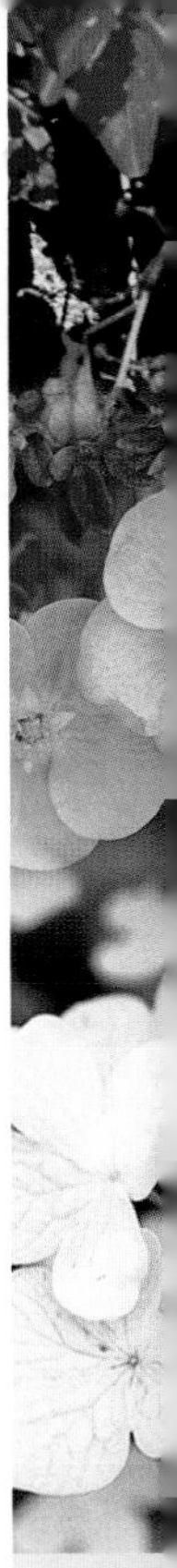

Ilex verticillata 'Red Sprite'
RED SPRITE WINTERBERRY
Ⓝ ☼ ◐ ◑ Z4–9 H9–1 ↕4ft (120cm) ↔3ft (1.5m)
A deciduous holly with nonprickly leaves, plus fruit that remain for a long time. Can grow in swamps but will also thrive in much drier locations.

Ilex x *meserveae* 'Blue Princess'
BLUE PRINCESS HOLLY
☼ ◑ Z5–9 H9–5 ↕10ft (3m) ↔4ft (1.2m)
A hybrid holly with slightly prickly leaves. The spring flowers are small and white. A male pollinator is needed nearby for fruit set. Grows in most soils.

Mahonia japonica Bealei Group
LEATHERLEAF MAHONIA
◐ ◑ Z7–8 H8–7 ↕↔10ft (3m)
A collection of similar plants that may differ slightly in the time of flowering in winter, and the intensity of blue sheen on the leaves and fruit. Fragrant flowers.

Euonymus hamiltonianus
HAMILTON'S SPINDLE TREE
☼ ◐ ◯ Z6–8 H8–6 ↕↔20ft (6m)
Deciduous shrub or small tree similar to the European spindle tree. Leaves turn a brilliant pink-red in fall. Fruits open to reveal scarlet red seeds.

Ligustrum 'Vicaryi'
VICARY GOLDEN PRIVET
☼ ◐ ◯ Z4–8 H8–1 ↕↔10ft (3m)
A semi-evergreen, upright shrub with leaves that turn a bronzy purple in winter. The summer flowers produce black fruit. Makes a good hedging plant.

Aronia arbutifolia 'Brilliantissima'
BRILLIANT RED CHOKEBERRY
Ⓝ ☼ ◐ ◯ Z5–9 H9–4 ↕10ft (3m) ↔5ft (1.5m)
An upright, suckering shrub that thrives in most soils. White flowers in spring bear fruit. Foliage turns bright red in fall. This variety is brighter and grows fruit more prolifically.

Viburnum plicatum
f. *tomentosum* 'Mariesii'
MARIESII DOUBLEFILE VIBURNUM
☼ ◊ Z4–8 H8–1 ↕↔20ft (6m)
Bushy, spreading shrub with distinctively tiered branches. Blooms in late spring and early summer.

Viburnum opulus 'Xanthocarpum'
YELLOW-FRUITED CRANBERRY BUSH
☼ ◑ ♦ Z4–8 H8–1 ↕↔12ft (4m)
An arching shrub with dark green leaves that turn red in fall. Flowers in flat platelike heads, showy sterile flowers around the outside. Fruit last well into winter.

Pyracantha 'Golden Charmer'
GOLDEN CHARMER FIRETHORN
☼ ◊ Z7–9 H9–7 ↕↔10ft (3m)
Vigorous, with thorny, arching branches. Flat heads of white flowers open in early summer. Does well trained against a wall as an espalier, or as an informal hedge.

Shrubs attractive to birds

Planting a diverse array of plants that bear fruits and berries will help attract birds to your garden. In addition to the enjoyment you will get from the sound of birdsong, creating a bird-friendly garden will draw insect-eating species that help control insects and other pests. Fruiting shrubs also provide cover and nesting sites for birds and other beneficial wildlife.

Cotoneaster lacteus
MILKFLOWER COTONEASTER
Z7–9 H9–7 ↕↔12ft (4m)
This evergreen shrub produces clusters of up to 100 white flowers in early to midsummer, followed by fruit that last through winter. Makes a good hedge.

Lindera benzoin
SPICE BUSH
Ⓝ Z4–9 H8–1 ↕↔10ft (3m)
Rounded deciduous shrub with aromatic, bright green leaves that turn yellow in fall. Tiny, star-shaped, yellow flowers are followed by red fruits on female plants.

Cotoneaster adpressus
CREEPING COTONEASTER
Z5–7 H7–1
↕1ft (30cm) ↔6ft (2m)
A low deciduous shrub that makes a good groundcover because branches root where they touch the soil. Fruits color early and persist into winter.

Mahonia aquifolium
OREGON GRAPE HOLLY
Ⓝ Z6–9 H9–6 ↕↔5ft (1.5m)
This slow-growing, upright evergreen shrub turns purplish bronze in fall. Blue-black, wax-coated berries ripen in early fall and hang on through winter.

Ilex verticillata 'Red Sprite'
RED SPRITE WINTERBERRY
☼ ◑ ♦ Z4–9 H9–1
↕4ft (120cm) ↔3ft (1.5m)
A deciduous holly with nonprickly leaves, plus fruit that remain for a long time. Can grow in swamps but will also thrive in much drier locations.

MORE CHOICES

- *Berberis x mentorensis* Z5–8 H8–5
- *Callicarpa bodinieri* Z4–7 H7–1
- *Cornus mas* Z5-8 H8–5
- *Prunus caroliniana* Z4–10 H10–1
- *Pyracantha coccinea* Z6–9 H9–6
- *Rosa glauca* Z2-8 H8–1
- *Symphoricarpus orbiculatus* Z2–7 H7–1
- *Vaccinium corymbosum* Z3–7 H7–1
- *Viburnum x burkwoodii* Z5–8 H8–1
- *Viburnum plicatum* f. *tomentosum* Z4–8 H8–1

Callicarpa americana
AMERICAN BEAUTYBERRY
Ⓝ ☼ ◑ ◊ Z5–9 H9–1
↕6ft (2m) ↔5ft (1.5m)
A hairy-leaved, deciduous shrub with pale lavender flowers in summer gives fruits that ripen slowly and persist well into winter. Good for naturalizing or mass planting.

Viburnum wrightii
WRIGHT VIBURNUM
☼ ◑ ◊ Z5–8 H8–4
↕10ft (3m) ↔6ft (2m)
Similar to the linden viburnum but without the hairy stems and with better, deep red, fall color. Very free-fruiting with berries that keep their bright red color.

Aronia melanocarpa
BLACK CHOKEBERRY
Ⓝ ☼ ◑ ♦ Z3–8 H8–1 ↕6ft (2m) ↔10ft (3m)
A small upright shrub with glossy, dark green leaves in summer. Small clusters of slightly fragrant white flowers in spring produce tart black berries.

Callicarpa dichotoma
PURPLE BEAUTYBERRY
☼ ◑ ◊ Z5–8 H8–7 ↕↔4ft (1.2m)
Slender arching branches curve to the ground, and leaves grow in a single plane. Flowers and fruit are carried above the foliage in summer and fall.

Myrica cerifera
WAX MYRTLE
Ⓝ ☼ ◑ ● ◊ ♦ ♦ Z6–9 H9–6 ↕↔15ft (5m)
This shrub produces small, yellow-green catkins in spring. Following these, dense clusters of waxy gray fruit appear along the shoots and last through winter.

WOODY PLANTS

Shrubs with fine, textured foliage

As you become more involved in gardening, you will begin to appreciate the range of different foliage shapes and textures, in both woody and perennial plants. Use these differences to bring diversity to your garden year-round, mixing evergreen plants with deciduous, fine foliage with coarse, green leaves with colored.

Taxus baccata 'Repandens'
DWARF ENGLISH YEW
☼ ◐ ● ◊ Z7–8 H8–7
↕24in (60cm) ↔15ft (5m)
A wide shrub with drooping branch tips. New growth is as shown, darkening later in summer to a midgreen. It grows equally well on alkaline and acidic soils.

Syringa laciniata
NARROW-LEAF LILAC
☼ ◊ Z4–8 H8–1 ↕6ft (2m) ↔10ft (3m)
Dark green leaves with from three to nine leaflets on a spreading shrub. Lightly fragrant late spring flowers, after the French lilacs have finished, attract early butterflies.

Spiraea thunbergii
THUNBERG'S SPIREA
☼ ◊ Z5–8 H8–5
↕5ft (1.5m) ↔6ft (2m)
Arching branches are covered with small clusters of blooms in early and mid-spring. Often one of the first spireas to flower. Makes a dense shrub that seldom needs pruning.

Juniperus conferta 'Blue Pacific'
SHORE JUNIPER
☼ ◐ ◊ Z5–9 H9–1
↕12in (30cm)
This cultivar is more trailing than the species and has a deeper blue cast to the foliage. Produces black fruit with a silvery white coating. Growth rate is moderate.

Rhus typhina
STAGHORN SUMAC
Ⓝ ☼ ◊ Z3–8 H8–1 ↕15ft (5m) ↔20ft (6m)
A thicket-forming shrub that spreads by underground runners. It thrives on poor soil and will often turn color in late summer in a dry year. Felty new shoots.

MORE CHOICES

- *Caesalpinia pulcherrima* Z9–11 H12–9
- *Cephalotaxus harringtonia* Z6–9 H9–3
- *Cotoneaster salicifolius* 'Repens' Z6–8 H8–3
- *Cytisus scoparius* Z6–8 H8–6
- *Podocarpus macrophyllus* Z7–11 H12–7
- *Russelia equisetiformis* Z11–12 H12–1
- *Sambucus nigra* 'Laciniata' Z5–6 H8–6
- *Sarcococca humilis* Z6–9 H9–6
- *Spiraea x bumalda* 'Crispa' Z4–9 H9–1
- *Taxus x media* Z5–7 H7–5

Shrubs with coarse, bold foliage

On any of the shrubs shown here, their foliage can be as attractive as the flowers. They make a visual impact all summer long, and a good contrast to those shrubs shown on the opposite page. Try to locate these where they are protected from the prevailing winds since their large leaves can be damaged if exposed.

Aesculus parviflora
BOTTLEBRUSH BUCKEYE
Ⓝ ☼ ◐ ◊ ◆ Z5–9 H9–4 ↕10ft (3m) ↔15ft (5m)
Young bronze leaves turn dark green in summer and yellow in fall. Sometimes slow to establish. Best grown in a large or medium-sized garden.

MORE CHOICES

- *Aralia spinosa* Z4–9 H9–1
- *Asimina triloba* Z6–8 H8–6
- *Aucuba japonica* Z6–15 H12–6
- *Hydrangea arborescens* 'Annabelle' Z4–9 H9–1
- *Hydrangea macrophylla* Z6–9 H9–6
- *Jatropha multifida* Z8–9 H9–5
- *Mahonia lomariifolia* Z8–9 H9–5
- *Prunus laurocerasus* Z6–9 H9–6
- *Tetrapanax papyriferus* Z6–11 H12–6
- *Viburnum rhytidophyllum* Z5–8 H8–5

Styrax obassia
FRAGRANT SNOWBELL
☼ ◐ ◆ Z6–8 H8–6 ↕40ft (12m) ↔22ft (7m)
Wonderful winter shape has many winding, turning branches. Leaves are easily injured in early spring, because they emerge very early.

Fatsia japonica
JAPANESE ARALIA
☼ ◐ ◊ ◆ Z8–11 H12–8 ↕5–12ft (1.5–4m)
Fall-flowering shrub with spreading habit that increases by underground suckers. Small black berries form later. Varieties with gold and variegated foliage.

Hydrangea quercifolia
OAKLEAF HYDRANGEA
Ⓝ ☼ ◐ ◆ Z5–9 H9–1 ↕6ft (2m) ↔8ft (2.5m)
Bears flowers from midsummer through midfall that become pink-tinged with age. Leaves turn red and purple in fall. Distinctive, peeling, orange-brown bark.

Aucuba japonica
JAPANESE LAUREL
☼ ◐ ◊ Z6–15 H12–6 ↕10ft (3m) ↔10ft (3m)
Glossy-leaved evergreen shrub produces small red-purple flowers in midspring. In fall, female plants produce red berries. Disliked by rabbits.

Clerodendrum trichotomum
HARLEQUIN GLORYBOWER
☼ ◆ Z7–9 H9–7
↕↔20ft (6m)
A small shrub best grown as a perennial at the northern end of its range. Flowering starts in summer and continues into fall; fruit and flowers often occur together.

Shrubs with variegated foliage

Most shrubs are grown chiefly for their flowers or fruit; by choosing those with variegated foliage, you gain a plant that has garden interest throughout the growing season. However, they stand out best when grown with, and particularly in front of, shrubs and trees that have single-colored leaves, because too much variegation can be visually overpowering.

Buxus sempervirens 'Elegantissima'
VARIEGATED COMMON BOXWOOD
Z6–8 H8–6 ↕↔5ft (1.5m)
A compact, dense-growing, dome-shaped shrub that makes an attractive specimen or can be used for low hedging. This is the best silver-variegated form but is slower-growing than the green-leaved forms.

Buddleja davidii 'Harlequin'
HARLEQUIN VARIEGATED BUTTERFLY BUSH
Z6–9 H10–4 ↕↔20ft (6m)
Expanding leaves are yellow, old leaves almost white. Less vigorous and smaller than many butterfly bushes. Flowers can be cut, but they do not last long.

Daphne x *burkwoodii* 'Carol Mackie'
CAROL MACKIE DAPHNE
Z5–8 H8–4 ↕↔3–5ft (1–1.5m)
Semi-evergreen, retaining its leaves until the end of winter. New foliage is yellow-edged at first, becoming white later. The flowers open in early summer.

Pieris japonica 'White Rim'
WHITE RIM JAPANESE PIERIS
pH Z6–8 H8–4 ↕12ft (4m) ↔10ft (3m)
A slow-growing shrub with leaves flushed with pink when young. The spring flowers are sweetly scented and last a long time. This may be sold as 'Variegata'.

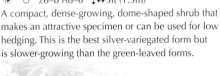

Cornus alba 'Elegantissima'
VARIEGATED RED TWIG DOGWOOD
Z2–8 H8–1 ↕↔10ft (3m)
Gray-green leaves have irregular white margins. White flowers appear in late spring and early summer, followed by white fruit. Shoots are bright red in winter.

MORE CHOICES

- *Abelia x grandiflora 'Variegata'* Z6–9 H9–1
- *Cornus mas 'Variegata'* Z5–8 H8–3
- *Eleutherococcus sieboldianus 'Variegatus'* Z4–8 H9–3
- *Euonymus fortunei 'Silver Queen'* Z5–9 H9–5
- *Hibiscus syriacus 'Purpureus Variegatus'* Z5–9 H9–1
- *Kerria japonica 'Picta'* Z4–9 H9–1
- *Ligustrum sinense 'Variegata'* Z7–11 H12–4
- *Philadelphus coronarius 'Variegatus'* Z5–8 H8–3
- *Pittosporum tobira 'Variegata'* Z9–11 H12–3
- *Sanchezia speciosa* Z14–15 H12–10

Syringa vulgaris 'Dappled Dawn'
DAPPLED DAWN LILAC
☼ ◊ Z4–8 H8–1 ↕↔15ft (5m)
Although the flowers are not quite as sweetly scented as some other named varieties, this continues to look attractive once the flowers have faded. Not as mildew-prone as some varieties.

Hydrangea macrophylla 'Maculata'
VARIEGATED LACECAP HYDRANGEA
☼ ☀ ◊ ◆ Z6–9 H9–3 ↕3ft (1m) ↔8ft (2.5m)
An erect shrub grown mainly for its attractive foliage. Flowers are sparsely produced when compared to other lacecap hydrangeas. May be sold as 'Variegata'.

Pittosporum 'Turner's Variegated Dwarf'
TURNER'S DWARF PITTOSPORUM
☼ ◊ ◆ Z9–10 H10–9 ↕30in (75cm) ↔3ft (100cm)
Developed in Texas with pendent branches that forms a low creeping mound. Leaves are small, about the size of a quarter.

Osmanthus heterophyllus 'Variegatus'
VARIEGATED FALSE HOLLY
☼ ☀ ◊ Z7–9 H9–4 ↕20ft (6m) ↔6–10ft (2–3m)
A slow-growing shrub that can become a small tree, with fragrant white flowers in fall. Distinguished from holly by its opposite, rather than alternate, leaves.

WOODY PLANTS

Shrubs with bronze or purple foliage

Whether used as foundation plants or in a mixed border, these shrubs add contrast and diversity. They vary from pale to deep bronzish purple, so by careful selection, one can find the perfect shade to complement or tone with neighboring plants or structures. Some can be used for hedging, making an eye-catching change from the usual green.

Cotinus coggygria 'Royal Purple'
ROYAL PURPLE SMOKETREE
☼ ◑ ◊ ♦ Z5–8 H8–3 ↕↔15ft (5m)
A small deciduous tree or bushy shrub. Foliage turns scarlet in fall. Plumelike flower stalks turn a smoky grayish pink as they age.

Berberis thunbergii 'Crimson Pygmy'
CRIMSON PYGMY BARBERRY
☼ ◑ ◊ Z5–8 H8–5 ↕24in (60cm) ↔30in (75cm)
A mounding form that makes an excellent low, impenetrable hedge or can be used for a groundcover. The color is best in full sun.

Berberis thunbergii 'Atropurpurea Nana'
DWARF PURPLE JAPANESE BARBERRY
☼ ◊ Z5–8 H8–5 ↕↔24in (60cm)
This densely branched, dwarf shrub can be grown in a container or rock garden or as a small hedge. Attractive reddish purple leaves turn red-orange in fall.

Berberis thunbergii var. *atropurpurea* 'Rose Glow'
ROSE GLOW JAPANESE BARBERRY
☼ ◑ ◊ Z5–8 H8–5
↕3ft (1m) ↔8ft (2.5m)
A spreading form that makes a rounded bush. The first flush of leaves in spring does not show the characteristic pale mottling; it develops later.

Corylus maxima 'Purpurea'
PURPLE-LEAVED FILBERT
☼ ◑ ◊ Z4–9 H9–1
↕20ft (6m) ↔15ft (5m)
An upright deciduous shrub or small tree. Purple-tinged yellow catkins hang in clusters before the leaves open, follwed by purple-husked, edible nuts.

Prunus x *cistena*
PURPLELEAF SANDCHERRY
Z3–8 H8–1 ↕↔5ft (1.5m)
A widely grown, upright, relatively slow-growing, deciduous shrub. Spring flowers are followed by dark red edible fruit that are hard to see against the foliage, but birds usually find them.

Acer palmatum 'Garnet'
GARNET JAPANESE MAPLE
Z5–8 H8–2
↕6ft (2m) ↔10ft (3m)
This is one of the fern-leaved Japanese maples that keeps its deep red foliage color all summer, turning a brighter, coppery red in fall. Grow in a sheltered location.

Physocarpus opulifolius 'Diablo'
DIABLO NINEBARK
Z3–7 H7–1
↕6ft (2m) ↔8ft (2.5m)
A new introduction. Pinkish-white flowers in summer are followed by bright red, eye-catching fruit. Leaf color lightens to a burgundy in fall.

Sambucus nigra 'Guincho Purple'
GUINCHO PURPLE EUROPEAN ELDER
Z6–8 H8–6 ↕↔20ft (6m)
The leaves open green and change color as they age, turning red in fall. Flowers are bright pink in bud and are borne on purple stalks. It grows well in most soils.

MORE CHOICES

- *Berberis thunbergii* var. *atropurpurea 'Darts Red Lady'* Z4–8 H8–3
- *Berberis thunbergii* var. *atropurpurea 'Red Chief'* Z4–8 H8–1
- *Itea virginica* 'Henry's Garnet' Z6–9 H10–7
- *Leucothoe fontanesiana 'Zeblid'* Z5–8 H8–5
- *Loropetalum chinense var. rubrum 'Burgundy'* Z7–9 H12–1

Shrubs with golden foliage

The unique tones of yellow- or golden-leaved shrubs make them invaluable for adding contrast in the garden. Some of these retain their bright color all summer and deserve to be in a prominent location; others gradually fade in intensity and should be sited where their spring brilliance can be seen but where other shrubs will assume center stage later in the year.

Spiraea japonica 'Goldflame'
GOLDFLAME SPIREA
Z4–9 H9–1 ↕↔3ft (1m)
A very popular mounded shrub with foliage that opens an orange-red and turns yellow with age. Colors stay bright all summer. Remove shoots that revert to green.

Ligustrum 'Vicaryi'
VICARY GOLDEN PRIVET
Z4–8 H8–1
↕↔10ft (3m)
A semi-evergreen, upright shrub with leaves that turn a bronzy purple in winter. The summer flowers produce black fruit. Makes a good hedging plant.

Lonicera nitida 'Baggesen's Gold'
BOXLEAF HONEYSUCKLE
Z6–9 H9–6 ↕↔5ft (1.5m)
Mounded shrub with white, fragrant flowers in summer but grown mainly for its foliage which turns a pale green as it matures. Color is best in maritime climates.

Berberis thunbergii 'Aurea'
YELLOW-LEAVED JAPANESE BARBERRY
Z5–8 H8–5 ↕↔5ft (1.5m)
Foliage is bright yellow when young. Leaves turn orange and red in fall, especially if the plant is in sun. Small flowers are followed by glossy red fruit.

Viburnum opulus 'Aureum'
GOLDEN-LEAVED GUELDER ROSE
Z3–8 H8–1
↕↔5–10ft (1.5–3m)
White flowerheads of clustered, tubular fertile flowers, surrounded by flat sterile flowers, are of secondary interest. Be careful as foliage may scorch in strong sun and dry soil.

Elaeagnus pungens 'Maculata'
MACULATA THORNY ELAEAGNUS
Z7–9 H9–7
↕12ft (4m) ↔15ft (5m)
A spreading evergreen shrub with fragrant flowers in fall. It makes a good shelter plant with a moderate growth rate. Watch for shoots reverting to green and prune out as soon as found.

Spiraea japonica 'Magic Carpet'
MAGIC CARPET SPIREA
Z4–9 H9–1
↕3ft (1m) ↔6ft (2m)
An upright plant with bright pink to red flowers in flat clusters all summer long. Tolerant of most soils, this is a new variety that is brighter-flowered than most.

Physocarpus opulifolius 'Dart's Gold'
DART'S GOLDEN NINEBARK
Z3–7 H7–1
↕6ft (2m) ↔8ft (2.5m)
This compact shrub features attractively peeling bark with age. Clusters of shallow, cup-shaped flowers in white or pale pink blossom in late spring.

MORE CHOICES

- *Abelia x grandiflora* 'Francis Mason' Z6–9 H9–1
- *Aucuba japonica* 'Gold Dust' Z6–15 H12–6
- *Aucuba japonica* 'Picturata' Z6–15 H12–6
- *Calluna vulgaris* 'Gold Haze' Z5–7 H7–5
- *Chamaecyparis obtusa* 'Nana Lutea' Z4–8 H8–1
- *Daphne odora* 'Aueromarginata' Z7–9 H9–7
- *Elaeagnus pungens* 'Aurea Dicksonii' Z7–9 H9–7
- *Ilex crenata* 'Golden Gem' Z5–7 H7–3
- *Osmanthus heterophyllus* 'Aureomarginata' Z7–9 H9–7

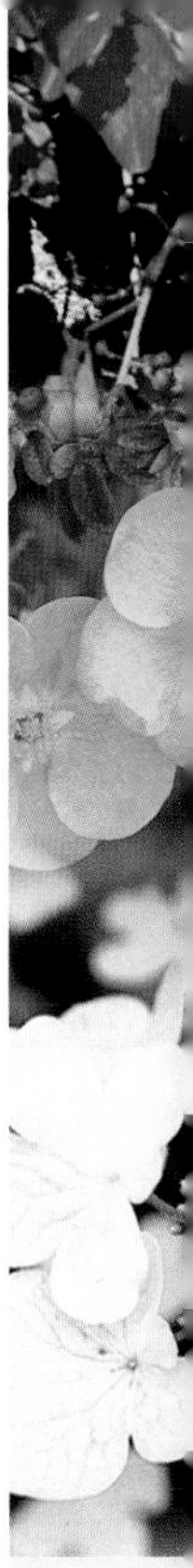

Shrubs with gray or blue foliage

Gray or bluish foliage looks cool, especially during the hot days of midsummer. It also makes a good contrast to plants with dark red or purple foliage, showing both off to advantage, and forms a good backdrop for brightly colored flowers. Use this foliage color with moderation, because it will have a greater visual impact than when overused.

Leucophyllum frutescens 'Compactum'
DWARF SILVERLEAF
Ⓝ ☼ 💧 Z8–9 H9–8
↕3–5 (1–1.5in) ↔3 (1m)
Dense, arching evergreen that thrives in hot dry summers, when flowers open. Makes a good low hedge or front plant for a shrub border.

Ruta graveolens
RUE
☼ ◐ 💧 Z5–9 H9–5
↕3ft (1m) ↔30in (75cm)
Flowers borne in summer. Prefers moderately fertile soil. Seedpods can be used in dried designs and wreaths. Contact with leaf oils can cause severe dermatitis.

Hippophae rhamnoides
SEA BUCKTHORN
☼ 💧 Z3–8 H8–1 ↕↔20ft (6m)
This grows best in a poor, very well-drained soil. The yellow flowers open in early spring, before the leaves. Berries are produced on female plants only.

Lavandula stoechas
SPANISH LAVENDER
☼ 💧 Z8–9 H9–8 ↕↔5ft (1.5m)
Grown for its aromatic silver-gray leaves and fragrant purple flowers borne in late spring and summer. Adaptable and easy to care for.

Acacia baileyana 'Cootamundra'
COOTAMUNDRA WATTLE
☼ ◊ Z10–11 H12–10 ↕15–25ft (5–8m) ↔10–20ft (3–6m)
A large shrub or small tree with spreading branches and flowers that open from late winter to spring. Prune, if needed, immediately after flowering.

Cistus 'Peggy Sammons'
PEGGY SAMMONS ROCK ROSE
☼ ◊ Z9–11 H12–9 ↕↔3ft (1m)
A bushy upright plant that does best on poor soils, low in nutrients, becoming spindly on rich ones. The flowers open in early summer. May become chlorotic on very alkaline soils.

MORE CHOICES

- *Buddleja 'Pink Delight'* Z6–9 H9–1
- *Cornus racemosa* Z4–8 H8–3
- *Fothergilla gardenii* 'Blue Mist' Z4–8 H8–1
- *Genista pilosa* Z9–11 H12–9
- *Juniperus chinensis* 'Pfitzerana Glauca' Z4–9 H9–1
- *Juniperus virginiana* 'Silver Spreader' Z3–9 H9–1
- *Salix elaeagnos* Z4–7 H7–1
- *Santolina chamaecyparissus* Z6–9 H9–6

Rosmarinus officinalis
ROSEMARY
☼ ◊ Z8–11 H12–8
↕↔5ft (1.5m)
Evergreen, aromatic leaves. Rosemary is a popular culinary herb and an attractive garden plant. Flowers are produced mostly at or near shoot tips .

Juniperus horizontalis 'Blue Chip'
BLUE CHIP CREEPING JUNIPER
Ⓝ ☼ ◐ ◊ ◊ Z3–9 H9–1 ↕8–10in(20-25cm) ↔8-10ft (2.5-3m)
Of the several named forms of this juniper, this is one of the bluest. The foliage turns a purple shade at the tips in cold weather. Makes a good groundcover.

Juniperus scopulorum 'Blue Star'
BLUE STAR ROCKY MOUNTAIN JUNIPER
☼ ◐ ◊ Z4–8 H8–1 ↕16in (40cm) ↔3ft (1m)
Most of the Rocky Mountain Junipers are upright trees, but a few selections are dwarf, slowly spreading plants, such as this, suitable for small spaces.

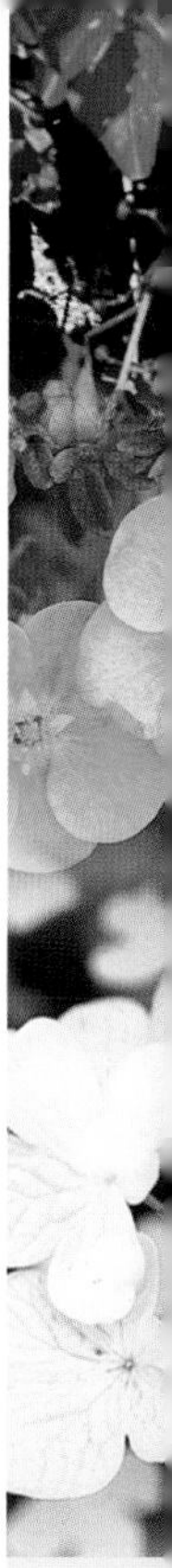

Shrubs with good fall color

One tends to think of trees in conjunction with fall color, but there are also many shrubs that can rival their larger relatives for brilliance of autumn hue. As the growing season comes to a close, the subtle to incandescent colors of fall foliage on shrubs complement the hues of surrounding grasses and fall-blooming perennials. Those shown here present a nice variety of overall size and foliage shape.

Viburnum x *rhytidophylloides* 'Alleghany'
ALLEGHANY VIBURNUM
☼ ◑ ◊ Z5–8 H8–5 ↕↔12ft (4m)
Good introduction from the US National Arboretum with semi-evergreen foliage and large heads of creamy-white flowers in spring, followed by red, then black fruits.

Cotinus 'Grace'
GRACE SMOKEBUSH
☼ ◑ ♦ Z5–8 H8–3 ↕↔15ft (5m)
A vigorous, tall, deciduous hybrid smokebush with conical purplish flowers in summer. The pinkish flower stems that remain later give the effect of pink smoke.

Fothergilla gardenii
WITCH ALDER
Ⓝ ☼ ◑ ♦ pH Z4–9 H9–1 ↕↔3ft (1m)
Bears spikes of fragrant flowers in spring, before the leaves. Dark blue-green leaves turn orange, red, and purple in fall. Good for a woodland garden.

Euonymous alatus
BURNING BUSH
☼ ◑ ◊ Z4–9 H9–1
↕6ft (2m) ↔10ft (3m)
A deciduous shrub with dark green leaves that turn red in fall. Also produces orange fruit. Tolerant of many soil types. 'Compacta' is more compact, with pinker fall color.

Hamamelis x *intermedia* 'Jelena'
JELENA HYBRID WITCH HAZEL
☼ ◐ 💧💧 Z5–9 H9–1 ↕↔12ft (4m)
Bright green leaves turn orange and red in fall and drop off before large, coppery blossoms appear in early to midwinter. This deciduous shrub dislikes dry soils and very windy sites.

Hamamelis x *intermedia* 'Diane'
DIANE HYBRID WITCH HAZEL
☼ ◐ 💧💧 Z5–9 H9–1 ↕↔12ft (4m)
A vase-shaped shrub with foliage that lasts well into early winter. The bright coppery-red, lightly fragrant flowers begin to open in mid- to late winter and continue until early spring. Grows well in acidic soil.

Aronia melanocarpa
BLACK CHOKEBERRY
Ⓝ ☼ ◐ 💧 Z3–8 H8–1
↕6ft (2m) ↔10ft (3m)
A small upright shrub with glossy, dark green leaves in summer that turn dark purple-red in fall. Small clusters of slightly fragrant white flowers, up to an inch across, appear in spring and produce tart black berries.

MORE CHOICES

- *Berberis* x *mentorensis* Z5–8 H8–5
- *Hydrangea quercifolia* Z5–9 H9–1
- *Itea virginica* 'Henry's Garnet' Z6–9 H10–7
- *Rhododendron luteum* Z7–9 H9–7
- *Vaccinium corymbosum* Z3–7 H7–1

Berberis thunbergii 'Rose Glow'
ROSE GLOW JAPANESE BARBERRY
☼ ◐ ◊ Z5–8 H8–5 ↕3ft (1m) ↔8ft (2.5m)
A spreading form that makes a rounded bush. The first flush of leaves in spring does not show the characteristic pale mottling; it develops later.

Rhus typhina 'Dissecta'
CUTLEAF STAGHORN SUMAC
Ⓝ ☼ ◊ Z3–8 H8–1 ↕15ft (5m) ↔20ft (6m)
A thicket-forming shrub spreading by underground runners. Showy, conical red female flowers in summer give seed heads that attract birds.

Carissa marcrocarpa
NATAL PLUM
☼ ◊ Z9–11 H12–9 ↕6–10ft (2–3m) ↔10ft (3m)
A many-branched spiny shrub with fragrant flowers in late spring. These give red to purple plum-like fruit that persist into winter.

Skimmia japonica
JAPANESE SKIMMIA
◐ ◑ Z7–8 H9–7 ↕↔5ft (1.5m)
Has slightly fragrant leaves as well as fragrant red- or pink-tinged white flowers. If both sexes are present, female plant bears red fruit.

MORE CHOICES

- *Ardisia crenata* Z13–15 H12–10
- *Camellia sinensis* Z7–10 H8–7
- *Cephalotaxus harringtonia* Z6–9 H9–3
- *Danae racemosa* Z6–9 H9–2
- *Leucothoe axillaris* Z6–9 H9–6

Acca sellowiana
PINEAPPLE GUAVA
☼ ◐ ◊ Z8–11 H12–9 ↕↔10–15ft (3–4.5m)
A bushy shrub with leaves that are woolly beneath. The flowers open in midsummer and give red-tinged berries. There is also a form with variegated leaves.

Evergreen shrubs

Evergreen shrubs play an important role in the landscape in the Southeast. They act as a foil for more flamboyant perennials and deciduous plants, but really come into their own during the winter when they are the main focus of the garden. Many have attractive, often fragrant flowers, while others are grown chiefly for their foliage effect.

Osmanthus heterophyllus 'Goshiki'
VARIEGATED FALSE HOLLY
☼ ◑ ◊ Z7–9 H9–7 ↕↔15ft (5m)
White flowers bloom in small clusters in late summer and fall, followed by egg-shaped, blue-black berries. Excellent as a hedge or topiary. Trim hedges in spring.

Osmanthus fragrans
FRAGRANT OLIVE
☼ ◑ ◊ Z8–11 H12–8 ↕↔20ft (6m)
Very sweet-smelling flowers open from fall to spring. Prune back in spring if needed to remove any winter injury. Makes a good combination with camellias.

Ardisia crispa
CHRISTMAS BERRY
◑ ● ◊ ◊ Z8–15 H12–10 ↕5ft (1.5m) ↔18–24in (45–60cm)
An erect shrub that flowers in summer. The berries are very long-lived and are often still present when flowers appear the following year.

Aucuba japonica
JAPANESE LAUREL
☼ ◑ ◊ Z6–15 H12–6 ↕10ft (3m) ↔10ft (3m)
Glossy-leaved evergreen shrub produces small, red-purple flowers in midspring. In fall, female plants produce red berries. Disliked by rabbits.

Fatsia japonica
JAPANESE ARALIA
☼ ◑ ◊ ◊ Z8–11 H12–8 ↕5–12ft (1.5–4m)
A spreading shrub that suckers slowly. The flowers open in fall and give small black berries. There are forms with gold and with variegated foliage.

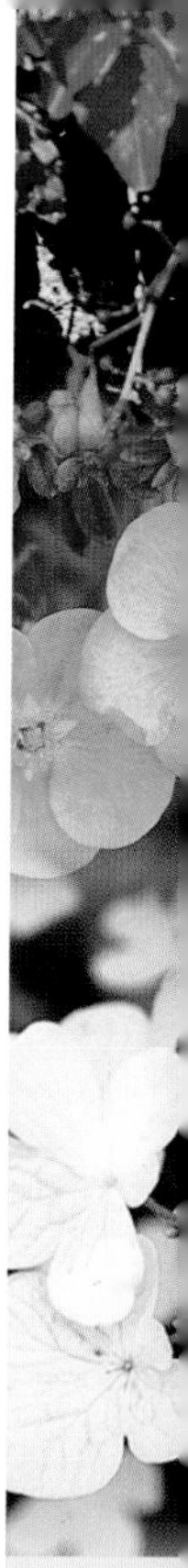

Arbutus unedo
STRAWBERRY TREE
☼ 💧 Z8–9 H9–6 ↕↔25ft (8m)
A large shrub or small tree with attractive, rough reddish bark. The fall flowers give warty red fruit that persist until the following autumn.

Ilex aquifolium
ENGLISH HOLLY
☼ ◐ ● 💧 Z7–9 H9–7 ↕70ft (20m) ↔20ft (6m)
Upright evergreen with dense foliage and gray bark. Berries are prized for winter decorations. Grows best in well-drained soil. Native to Europe, N Africa, Asia.

Viburnum tinus
LAURUSTINUS
☼ ◐ 💧💧 Z8–10 H10–8 ↕↔10ft (3m)
An upright species that is attractive all year. Flowers open in winter in the South, in early spring farther north. Makes a good hedge and is salt-resistant.

Illicium floridanum
PURPLE ANISE
Ⓝ ☼ ◐ 💧💧 Z7–9 H9–4 ↕↔8ft (2.5m)
Has a bushy habit of growth and aromatic foliage that is pale green when young, darkening later. The flowers are borne in late spring and early summer.

Ilex opaca
AMERICAN HOLLY
Ⓝ ☼ ◐ ● 💧 Z5–9 H9–5 ↕45ft (14m) ↔4ft (1.2m)
Crimson (sometimes yellow or orange) berries enhance this evergreen in winter. Like most hollies, spiny leaves are occasionally smooth-edged.

Gardenia jasminoides 'Veitchii'

VEITCH CAPE JASMINE

◐ ◊ ◆ Z14–15 H12–1

↕6–40ft (2–12m) ↔3–10ft (1–3m)

Grow in a slightly acid soil rich in organic matter. Highly fragrant flowers open for much of the summer. Prone to whitefly attack.

Gardenia jasminoides 'Klehm's Hardy'

KLEHM'S HARDY CAPE JASMINE

☼ ◐ ◊ ◆ Z8–11 H12–1

↕↔3–4ft (1–1.3m)

A slightly tougher variety that needs a sheltered location at the northern limit of its hardiness. A good container plant that should be grown near a patio.

Prunus caroliniana

CAROLINA CHERRY LAUREL

Ⓝ ☼ ◐ ◊ ◆ Z4–10 H10–1 ↕30ft (10m) ↔25ft (8m)

Large shrub or small tree that can be used for a hedge or screen, but grows quickly and may prove invasive. Fragrant spring flowers give these fruits, which birds eat.

Prunus laurocerasus

CHERRY LAUREL

☼ ◊ Z6–9 H9–6 ↕20ft (6m) ↔30ft (10m)

Spreading shrub that is best used as an informal hedge. Hand-prune in fall, removing only the shoots that are growing away from the general shape.

Large shrubs

Although large shrubs may be as tall as small trees, their branching habit gives them a very different outline in the landscape. Since most shrubs come from forests and forest edges, they do better in partial shade than many comparably sized trees. In medium-sized yards these shrubs make fine specimen plants that will complement the scale of the landscape.

Ligustrum lucidum 'Excelsum Superbum'
EXCELSUM SUPERBUM CHINESE PRIVET
☼ ◑ ◊ Z8–11 H12–8 ↕↔30ft (10m)
Tall open shrub, similar to the Japanese privet but with larger clusters of later flowers. The species is widely grown in the South and tolerates many different soils.

Rhus typhina
STAGHORN SUMAC
Ⓝ ☼ ◊ Z3–8 H8–1 ↕15ft (5m) ↔20ft (6m)
Erect conical clusters of yellow-green flowers to 8in (20cm) long appear in summer. In fall, female plants produce dense clusters of bright crimson fruit.

Elaeagnus pungens 'Variegata'
VARIEGATED THORNY ELAEAGNUS
☼ ◑ ◊ Z3–11 H12–1 ↕12ft (4m) ↔15ft (5m)
A very adaptable shrub that is tolerant of salt and air pollution. Often used along highways to provide a screen. Not suitable for small gardens.

Viburnum plicatum var. *tomentosum*
DOUBLEFILE VIBURNUM
☼ ◑ ◊ ♦ Z4–8 H8–1 ↕10ft (3m) ↔12ft (4m)
Excellent plant with flat heads of white flowers carried above the branches in spring. These give the red fruit seen here that turn black if the birds don't eat them first.

MORE CHOICES

- *Cornus mas* Z5–8 H8–4
- *Cotinus coggygria* Z5–9 H9–3
- *Ilex cornuta* 'Burfordii' Z6–9 H9–1
- *Loropetalum chinense* Z8–9 H9–8
- *Magnolia x soulangeana* Z5–9 H9–5
- *Myrica cerifera* Z6–9 H9–6
- *Nerium oleander* Z13–15 H12–1
- *Osmanthus fragrans* Z8–11 H12–8
- *Prunus laurocerasus* Z6–9 H9–6

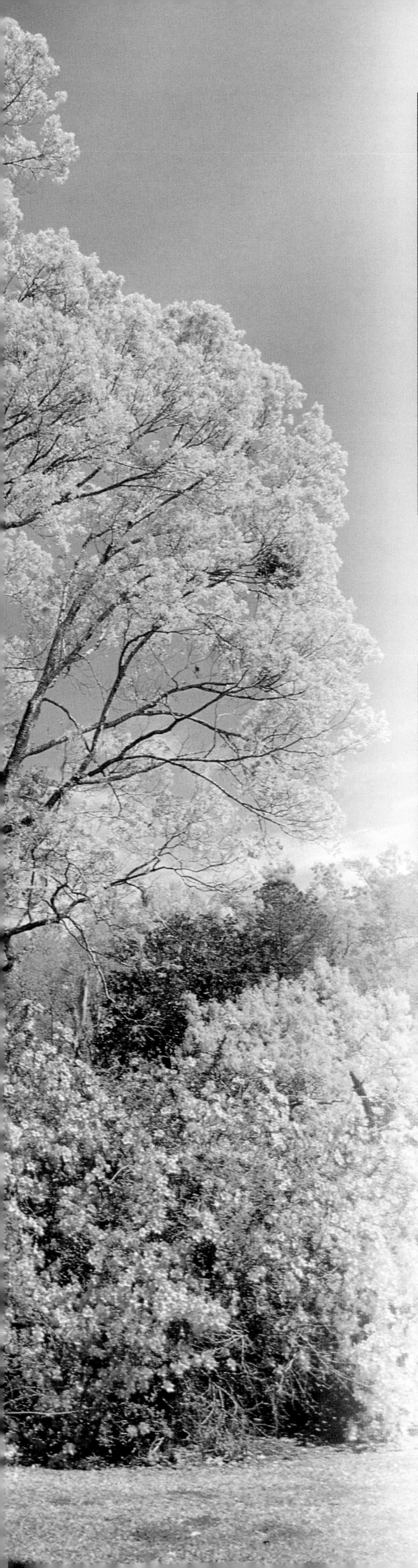

Camellia sasanqua 'Appleblossom'
APPLEBLOSSOM CAMELLIA
Z7–8 H8–7 ↕15ft (5m) ↔10ft (3m)
A broad, densely branched tree with smaller leaves than the Japanese camellia. Flowers open during late fall and early winter and plants need a sheltered site.

Photinia x *fraseri* 'Red Robin'
RED ROBIN RED TIP
Z8–9 H9–8 ↕↔15ft (5m)
The common name comes from the color of the new foliage, which turns green later. Widely used as a hedge and screen, it is susceptible to leaf spot.

Rhododendron indicum
SATSUKI AZALEA
Z8–9 H9–7 ↕↔3–10ft (1–3m)
A spring flowering species that is one parent of several widely grown evergreen azaleas. While it will take full sun in spring, it needs part shade during summer.

MORE CHOICES

- *Rhodendron maximum* Z4–9 H9–1
- *Viburnum rhytidophyllum* Z5–8 H8–5
- *Vitex agnus-castus* Z6–9 H9–6

Pittosporum tobira
JAPANESE MOCK ORANGE
Z9–10 H10–9 ↕to 30ft (10m) ↔10ft (3m)
An adaptable plant that will grow well in dry sandy soils or in clay. The flowers are produced in spring and summer, are very fragrant, and age to a pale yellow.

Hamamelis x *intermedia* 'Jelena'
JELENA HYBRID WITCH HAZEL
Z5–9 H9–1 ↕↔12ft (4m)
Bright green leaves turn orange and red in fall and drop off before blossoms appear in early to midwinter. Dislikes dry soils and very windy sites.

Medium-sized shrubs

These midsized woody plants should be considered the backbone of well-designed landscapes. They mix well with smaller shrubs as well as perennials in large mixed borders. They hold their own as specimen plants in a small lawn or other open garden area, and they can be used to face down larger shrubs or even trees.

Cotoneaster salicifolius
WILLOWLEAF COTONEASTER
☼ ◑ ◊ Z6–8 H8–6
↕↔15ft (3m)
A spreading, arching shrub with shiny foliage that turns purplish in winter. Small white flowers in flattened heads in early summer produce berries that persist all winter.

Callicarpa japonica
JAPANESE BEAUTYBERRY
☼ ◑ ◊ Z5–8 H12–3 ↕↔6ft (2m)
A deciduous shrub with arching stems. The white flowers in midsummer give these fruits that persist well into winter. Foliage turns a pinkish shade in fall.

Calycanthus floridus
CAROLINA ALLSPICE, COMMON SWEETSHRUB
Ⓝ ◑ ♦ Z5–9 H9–1 ↕8ft (2.5m) ↔10ft (3m)
A spreading shrub that is tolerant of most soils and of sun. The fragrant flowers are produced from late spring into summer. Foliage is also fragrant when crushed.

Forsythia x *intermedia*
BORDER FORSYTHIA
☼ ◑ ♦ Z6–9 H9–3
↕↔5ft (1.5m)
Profuse flowers are produced in early and midspring, before the leaves. Remove oldest stems after flowering to rejuvenate the plant.

Lindera benzoin
SPICE BUSH
Ⓝ ◑ ♦ pH Z4–9 H8–1 ↕↔10ft (3m)
A rounded shrub with upright branches and aromatic, bright green foliage. Yellow-green, star-shaped flowers blossom in midspring. Females bear red berries.

MORE CHOICES

- *Berberis julianae* Z6–9 H9–4
- *Buddleja davidii* Z6–9 H10–4
- *Buxus sempervirens* Z6–8 H8–6
- *Cephalanthus occidentalis* Z5–11 H12–3
- *Fothergilla major* Z4–8 H9–2
- *Hydrangea paniculata* Z4–8 H8–1
- *Ilex glabra* Z5–9 H9–1
- *Ilex verticillata* Z5–8 H8–5
- *Lonicera tatarica* Z3–9 H9–1
- *Magnolia stellata* Z5–9 H9–5
- *Mahonia fortunei* Z8–9 H9–4
- *Spiraea cantonensis* Z5–9 H9–1
- *Viburnum tinus* Z8–10 H10–8

Pieris japonica
JAPANESE PIERIS
Z6–8 H8–6 ↕↔20ft (6m)
This species needs a slightly acidic soil with additional organic matter. New leaves are usually bronze, and some cultivars have been selected for this trait.

Hibiscus syriacus 'Minerva'
MINERVA ROSE OF SHARON
Z5–9 H9–1 ↕8ft (2.5m) ↔7ft (2.2m)
This transplants best as a small plant. Grow in a soil rich in organic matter. The mid- to late summer flowers are on the new wood, so prune hard in early spring

Clethra alnifolia
SUMMERSWEET
Z3–9 H9–1 ↕↔8ft (2.5m)
The fragrant, bell-shaped white flowers of this shrub form elegant spires. Upright shrub often increases through suckering. Leaves turn yellow in fall.

Spiraea x *vanhouttei*
VANHOUTTE SPIREA
Z4–8 H8–1 ↕6ft (2m) ↔5ft (1.5m)
Flowers are borne in abundance in late spring and early summer and almost completely cover the dark green leaves. Very adaptable and tolerant.

Small shrubs

Shrubs fill the niche between herbaceous flowers and stately trees – and small shrubs make the first step. Accent a small space, group for a groundcover-like mass, or simply add year-round emphasis or texture to a flowerbed, and enjoy the multiple-season effect of foliage, form, flowers, fruit – and even fragrance.

Yucca filamentosa
ADAM'S NEEDLE
Ⓝ ☼ ◊ Z4–11 H12–5 ↕30in (75cm) ↔5ft (1.5m)
Its major value is as a foliage plant where the soft-tipped leaves contrast well in flower or shrub beds. The waxy summer flowers are a bonus.

MORE CHOICES

- *Ardisia crenata* Z13–15 H12–10
- *Buxus microphylla* Z6–9 H9–6
- *Euonymus fortunei* var. *coloratus* Z5–9 H9–2
- *Genista pilosa* 'Vancouver Gold' Z9–11 H12–9
- *Hypericum frondosum* Z9–11 H12–9
- *Spiraea japonica* Z3–9 H9–1

Caryopteris x *clandonensis* 'Worcester Gold'
WORCESTER GOLD BLUE MIST SHRUB
Ⓝ ☼ ◐ ◊ Z6–9 H9–1 ↕3ft (1m) ↔5ft (1.5m)
A low mound that grows best in poor soils. The late summer flowers are on new growth. Cut back almost to the ground in late winter or spring if overgrown.

Cotoneaster horizontalis
ROCKSPRAY COTONEASTER
☼ ◊ Z4–7 H7–3 ↕↔5ft (1.5m)
An excellent groundcover that will follow the contours of the ground. White flowers in spring give these persistent fruits. Use on banks and walls.

Cuphea hyssopifolia
FALSE HEATHER
☼ ◊ Z12–15 H12–10 ↕12–24in (30–60cm) ↔8–32in (20–80cm)
Tidy, compact border plant, evergreen only along the South's coastal areas. Tiny flowers attract butterflies and hummingbirds. Pinch tips to thicken plant.

Leucophyllum frutescens
TEXAS RANGER, SILVERLEAF TEXAS SAGE
Ⓝ ☼ ◑ Z8–9 H9–8 ↕8ft (2.5m) ↔6ft (2m)
This compact arching shrub is an excellent choice for hot dry sites, but must have drainage, especially in high rainfall areas. It flowers in midsummer.

Prunus glandulosa 'Rosea Plena'
DOUBLE DWARF FLOWERING ALMOND
Z5–8 H8–3 ↕↔5ft (1.5m)
This forms a multistemmed shrub with arching branches that are best hidden by perennials once the showy spring flowers have fallen.

MORE CHOICES

- *Hypericum* 'Hidcote' Z6–9 H9–6
- *Ilex crenata* 'Helleri' Z5–7 H7–5
- *Ilex glabra* 'Compacta' Z5–9 H9–5
- *Ilex vomitoria* 'Nana' Z7–11 H12–7
- *Nandina domestica* 'Nana' Z6–11 H12–4
- *Pittosporum tobira* 'Wheeler's Dwarf' Z9–11 H12–3
- *Skimmia japonica* Z7–9 H9–7
- *Stephanandra incisa* 'Crispa' Z3–8 H8–4
- *Zamia pumila* Z11–15 H12–10

Deutzia crenata var. *nakaiana* 'Nikko'
NIKKO DEUTZIA
Z4–8 H8–1 ↕24in (60cm) ↔4ft (1.2m)
Dwarf that does well on a large rock garden or as a groundcover. Leaves turn burgundy red in fall.

Juniperus conferta
SHORE JUNIPER
Z6–9 H9–1 ↕6in (15cm) ↔3–6ft (1–2m)
Evergreen groundcover for impossibly hot dry sites, especially around parking areas and patios. Interplant with daffodils for seasonal flowers.

Berberis thunbergii 'Crimson Pygmy'
CRIMSON PYGMY BARBERRY
Z5–8 H8–5 ↕24in (60cm) ↔30in (75cm)
Dense small leaves on a durable shrub used for accent or mass planting. Sharp needles make this a good choice for foot-traffic control.

Large azaleas

Azaleas are one of the mainstays of Southern gardens. Few other shrubs put on the magnificent floral display that these do; many have so many blooms that the foliage cannot be seen at all. By selecting varieties that flower in succession, this display can last for many weeks. However, their foliage is still attractive and the evergreen varieties add color to the winter garden.

Rhododendron calendulaceum
FLAME AZALEA
Z5–8 H9–4 ↕↔6–10ft (2–3m)
Produces yellow, scarlet, or orange flowers in early summer, with or just after the leaves. Midgreen leaves are softly hairy both above and underneath.

Rhododendron arborescens
SWEET AZALEA
Z5–9 H9–4
↕↔20ft (6m)
Forms an upright shrub with scented flowers in early summer. The dark green, shiny leaves turn red in fall. Native from Pennsylvania to Georgia.

Rhododendron 'Daphne Salmon'
DAPHNE SALMON AZALEA
Z7–9 H9–7 ↕↔4–6ft (1.2–2m)
This midseason, evergreen azalea is one of a group known as the Southern Indian hybrids which grow well in areas with a high light intensity. It may also be sold as 'Lawsal'.

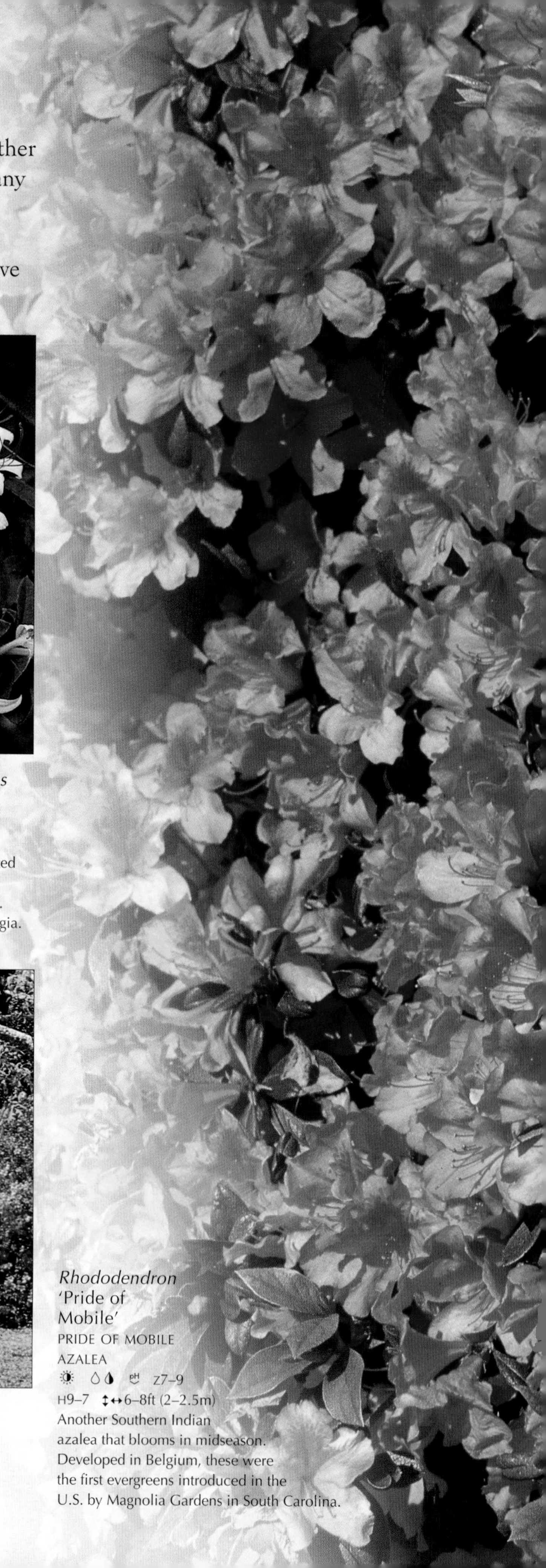

Rhododendron 'Pride of Mobile'
PRIDE OF MOBILE AZALEA
Z7–9 H9–7 ↕↔6–8ft (2–2.5m)
Another Southern Indian azalea that blooms in midseason. Developed in Belgium, these were the first evergreens introduced in the U.S. by Magnolia Gardens in South Carolina.

MORE CHOICES

- *Rhododendron* 'Amy' Z7–9 H9–6
- *Rhododendron* 'Fielder's White' Z7–9 H9–7
- *Rhododendron* 'Koromo Shikibu' Z5–8 H8–5
- *Rhododendron* 'Mrs. GG Gerbing' Z7–9 H9–7
- *Rhododendron* 'President Clayes' Z7–9 H9–7
- *Rhododendron* 'Red Formosa' Z7–9 H9–7
- *Rhododendron* 'Sunglow' Z7–9 H9–7

Rhododendron 'George Lindley Tabor'

GEORGE LINDLEY TABOR AZALEA

☼ ◊♦ pH Z8–9 H9–7 ↕10–12ft (3–4m) ↔10ft (3m)

An evergreen, early to midseason, Southern Indian azalea. This variety is hardier than others of this group and less likely to lose its buds during a hard winter.

Rhododendron prunifolium

PLUMLEAF AZALEA

(N) ☼ ◊ pH Z6–9 H9–5 ↕10ft (3m) ↔8ft (2.5m)

A hairless shrub with medium-sized, elliptic leaves. Orange-red to red flowers blossom in summer, much later than most azaleas. Sometimes semi-evergreen.

Rhododendron 'Southern Charm'

SOUTHERN CHARM AZALEA

☼ ◊♦ pH Z8–9 H9–7 ↕x (x) ↔x (x)

An open-shaped, midseason variety of Southern Indian azalea. These azaleas have a complex parentage involving species from Japan, China, and Burma and are normally fast growing.

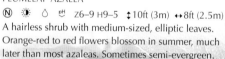

Medium-sized azaleas

Azaleas may be evergreen or deciduous and tend to have their flowers in small clusters. Those shown here can be used as fillers under large shrubs where they will benefit from the shade. Like all rhododendrons, they need an acid soil to grow well. Because they are shallow-rooting, they should not be allowed to become too dry in summer.

Rhododendron 'Hino-crimson'
HINO-CRIMSON AZALEA
Z5–9 H9–5
↕↔24in (60cm)
One of the group of azaleas known as Kurume Hybrids, these have been cultivated in Japan for centuries and were first brought to North America by E.H. Wilson in 1914.

Rhododendron 'Hinode-giri'
HINODE-GIRI AZALEA
Z6–9 H9–6 ↕↔24in (60cm)
Also a Kurume azalea, this has evergreen foliage that turns wine-red in fall and over winter. Kurume azaleas are more cold tolerant than Southern Indian types and less likely to suffer bud damage.

Rhododendron 'Coral Bells'
CORAL BELLS AZALEA
Z7–9 H9–7 ↕3ft (1m) ↔4ft (1.2m)
An older Kurume hybrid that may also be sold as 'Kirin'. The small flowers have a second set of petals inside the outer ones, a form known as hose-in-hose.

Rhododendron 'Fashion'
FASHION AZALEA
Z7–9 H9–6
↕3–5ft (1–1.5m) ↔4–6ft (1.2–2m)
The early to midseason hose-in-hose flowers are 2in (5cm) across. Buds are reliably hardy to 0°F (118°C).

MORE CHOICES

- *Rhododendron* 'Aphrodite' Z7–9 H9–6
- *Rhododendron* 'Arctic Pearl' Z3–8 H8–1
- *Rhododendron* 'Christmas Cheer' Z7–8 H9–6
- *Rhododendron* 'Copperman' Z7–9 H9–6
- *Rhododendron* 'Eureka' Z7–9 H9–7
- *Rhododendron* 'Geisha' Z7–9 H9–6
- *Rhododendron* 'Glacier' Z7–9 H9–6
- *Rhododendron* 'Glory' Z5–9 H9–5
- *Rhododendron* 'H.H. Hume' Z6–9 H9–6
- *Rhododendron* 'Hershey Red' Z5–9 H9–5
- *Rhododendron* 'Mother's Day' Z7–9 H9–7
- *Rhododendron* 'Pink Pearl' Z7–9 H9–7
- *Rhododendron* 'Radiant' Z6–8 H8–6
- *Rhododendron* 'Sherwood Red' Z7–9 H9–7
- *Rhododendron* 'Snow' Z7–9 H9–7

Dwarf azaleas

These are mostly low or spreading azaleas that can be used under taller varieties to extend the flowering season and to act as a groundcover when not in bloom. They need a location in dappled shade with protection from the strong early afternoon sunlight. A few will take full sun; your local nursery can best advise you on suitable varieties in your area.

Rhododendron 'Higasa'
HIGASA AZALEA
Z7–9 H9–4 ↕3ft (1m) ↔4ft (1.2m)
A Japanese variety from a group known collectively as Satsuki, meaning fifth month, because that is when they bloom, thus extending the flowering season.

Rhododendron 'Pink Ruffles'
PINK RUFFLES AZALEA
Z8–11 H12–9
↕↔4–6ft (1.2–2m)
This is a Rutherford Hybrid, developed originally as greenhouse pot plants by Bobinks and Atkins Nursery in New Jersey around 1930.

Rhododendron 'Amagasa'
AMAGASA AZALEA
Z7–9 H9–7 ↕↔2–3ft (60cm–1m)
Another Satsuki hybrid with large 3.5in (8cm) flowers freely produced. These are not quite as bud-hardy as the Kurume azaleas and may need a sheltered location in the North.

Rhododendron 'Gumpo White'
GUMPO WHITE AZALEA
Z7–10 H10–7 ↕18in (45cm) ↔x (x)
Also a Satsuki hybrid. The flowers may have purple flecks inside and are late to open. This and 'Gumpo Pink' are very popular garden plants.

Rhododendron 'Red Ruffles'
RED RUFFLES AZALEA
Z9–11 H12–9 ↕↔4–6ft (1.2–2m)
This has the same background as 'Pink Ruffles'. Many of these hybrids were later found to be suitable for outdoor use in the milder parts of the country but are still grown as pot plants in the North.

MORE CHOICES

- *Rhododendron* 'Gumpo Pink' Z7–10 H10–7
- *Rhododendron* 'Shynnyo No Tanki' Z7–10 H10–7

Rhododendrons

Rhododendrons are very distinctive plants and even the most novice gardener can usually identify them by their leaves alone. These selections are evergreen, need a slightly acidic soil, and most require dappled shade. Because rhododendrons are shallow rooted, try to plant them in a sheltered location to protect them from strong winds that could uproot them.

Rhododendron maximum
ROSEBAY RHODODENDRON
Ⓝ ☀ 💧 pH Z4–9 H9–1
↕15ft (5m) ↔indefinite
Spreading shrub that can become almost treelike, with leathery leaves with rolled edges. Flowers, which can shade to white, open in summer. Native from Canada to Georgia.

Rhododendron 'Scintillation'
SCINTILLATION RHODODENDRON
☼ 💧 pH Z5–9 H9–5 ↕5ft (1.5m) ↔4–5ft (1.2–1.5m)
Spreading shrub with large, waxy, shiny, deep green leaves up to 6in (15cm) long. Large trusses of 12-15 scented flowers open in late spring and are freely produced. Flowers well each year.

Rhododendron 'Vulcan'
VULCAN RHODODENDRON
☼ 💧 pH Z4–9 H9–5 ↕↔4ft (1.2m)
More compact than many varieties and with a good mounded shape. Dome-shaped trusses of flowers with wavy-edged petals open in late spring. Cold-resistant buds still open at limits of hardiness.

Rhododendron 'Anna Rose Whitney'
ANNA ROSE WHITNEY RHODODENDRON
☼ 💧 pH Z5–9 H9–5 ↕↔12ft (4m)
Large vigorous shrub with leaves up to 4.5in (11cm) long. Rounded trusses of blooms open in late spring or early summer. Individual flowers can be 4in (10cm) across.

Rhododendron 'English Roseum'
ENGLISH ROSEUM RHODODENDRON
☼ 💧 pH Z4–8 H9–5 ↕5ft (1.5m) ↔4–5ft (1.2–1.5m)
An older "ironclad" rhododendron that stands up to both summer heat and humidity, and cold winters. It forms an upright plant, fast growing, with glossy, dark green leaves.

Rhododendron 'Yaku Princess'
YAKU PRINCESS RHODODENDRON
Z5–9 H9–5 ↕↔5ft (1.5m)
This dense, compact, low-growing, evergreen has a similar habit of growth to *R. yakushimanum*, but the leaves lack the white reverse. Sphreical trusses of funnel-shaped pinkish flowers are borne in midseason and fade to white at maturity.

Rhododendron 'Nova Zembla'
NOVA ZEMBLA RHODODENDRON
Z4–8 H9–5
↕5–10ft (1.5–3m)
Heat-tolerant, this is another of the older "ironclad" varieties that grows equally well in humid and cold climates. It blooms in early summer and does well in this region.

Rhododendron 'Catawbiense Album'
WHITE MOUNTAIN ROSEBAY
Ⓝ Z4–8 H9–5 ↕↔10ft (3m)
This variety of the native mountain rosebay (*R. catawbiense*) will take considerable direct sunlight without burning. Lilac buds open in early summer. Another "ironclad" (see 'English Roseum', opposite).

MORE CHOICES

- *Rhododendron* 'America' Z5–9 H9–5
- *Rhododendron* 'Besse Howells' Z4–7 H7–1
- *Rhododendron* 'Blue Ensign' Z6–9 H9–6
- *Rhododendron* 'Chinoides' Z5–9 H9–4
- *Rhododendron minus* Z6–9 H9–6
- *Rhododendron* 'Sappho' Z6–9 H9–1

Rhododendron 'Gomer Waterer'
GOMER WATERER RHODODENDRON
Z5–9 H9–5 ↕↔6ft (2m)
Another sun-, heat-, and wind-tolerant variety. Introduced before 1900, it makes a very dense shrub with large trusses of fragrant flowers in early summer.

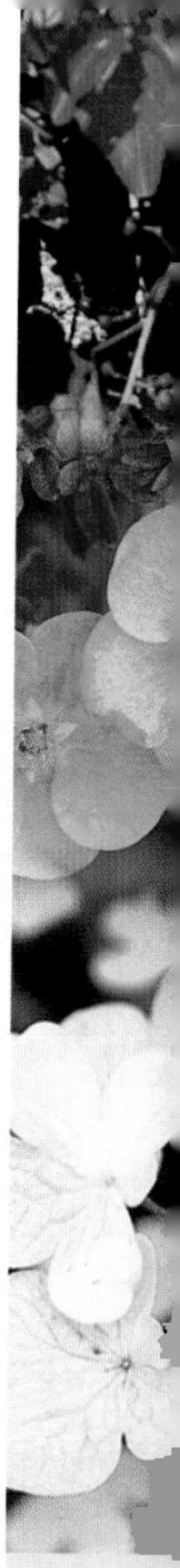

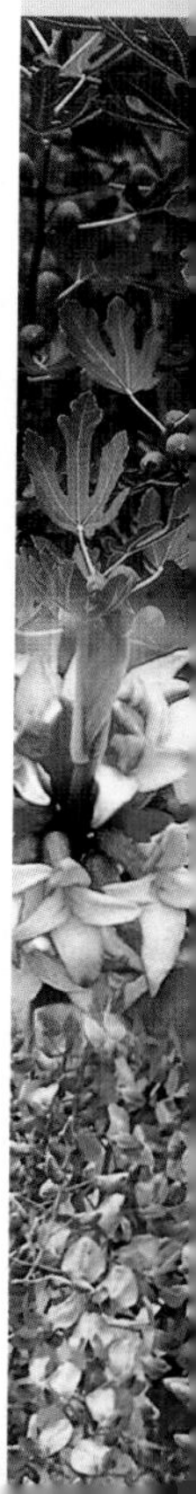

Native azaleas and hybrids

The eastern half of North America is home to many species of azaleas that make good garden plants. Ghent, Belgium, was the source of prominent hybrid introductions in the 1800s, followed by Knap Hill Nursery and Exbury Gardens in England in the 1900s. Most of these species and hybrids are deciduous, and many have sweetly fragrant flowers.

Rhododendron 'Danger'
DANGER AZALEA
◐ ◊ Z5–8 H8–5 ↕↔4ft (1.2m)
A Knap Hill introduction with early spring blooms, a spicy fragrance, and deciduous leaves that turn an orange-yellow in fall. Grow in a highly organic soil.

Rhododendron arborescens
SWEET AZALEA
Ⓝ ◐ ◊ pH Z5–9 H9–4 ↕↔20ft (6m)
Forms an upright shrub with scented flowers in early summer. The dark green, shiny leaves turn red in fall. Native from Pennsylvania to Georgia.

Rhododendron 'Ginger'
GINGER AZALEA
◐ ◊ Z5–8 H8–5 ↕↔5ft (1.5m)
One of many fine deciduous azaleas Lionel de Rothschild at Exbury introduced. They are all fragrant to a degree and do best in light dappled shade.

Rhododendron 'Homebush'
HOMEBUSH AZALEA
☼ ◐ ◊ Z5–8 H8–5 ↕↔5ft (1.5m)
A very popular variety originating at Knap Hill Nursery in 1926, this is a vigorous upright shrub that covers itself with the unusual rounded heads of double flowers.

Rhododendron calendulaceum
FLAME AZALEA
Ⓝ ☼ ◐ ◊ pH Z5–8 H9–4
↕↔6–10ft (2–3m)
Produces yellow, scarlet, or orange flowers in early summer, with or just after the leaves. Midgreen leaves are softly hairy both above and underneath.

Rhododendron 'George Reynolds'
GEORGE REYNOLDS AZALEA
☼ ◐ ◊ Z5–8 H8–5 ↕↔6ft (2m)
Like all these azaleas, this needs a slightly acidic, woodsy soil. Where soil is neutral or slightly alkaline, grow in a raised bed and mulch with pine needles.

MORE CHOICES

- *Rhododendron alabamense* Z7–9 H9–7
- *Rhododendron canescens* Z6–9 H9–4
- *Rhododendron serrulatum* Z4–8 H8–1
- *Rhododendron vaseyi* Z5–8 H8–4
- *Rhododendron viscosum* Z3–9 H9–1

Rhododendron 'Oxydol'
OXYDOL AZALEA
Ⓝ ☼ ◐ ◊ Z5–8 H8–5 ↕↔5ft (1.5m)
Spreading shrub with bronzy foliage that turns copper in fall. It is named for a British soap powder that got clothes whiter, but the yellow blotch doesn't wash out.

Rhododendron prunifolium
PLUMLEAF AZALEA
Ⓝ ◐ ◑ Z6–9 H8–6 ↕8–10ft (2.5–3m) ↔6–8ft (2–2.5m)
A hairless evergreen shrub with medium-sized, elliptic leaves. Orange-red to red flowers blossom very late in the rhododendron season.

Rhododendron austrinum
FLORIDA AZALEA
Ⓝ ☼ ◐ ◊ pH Z6–10 H10–6 ↕↔4–6ft (1.2–2m)
Deciduous azalea with elliptic green leaves that are hairy underneath. Fragrant, tubular-funnel-shaped flowers with red-tinged tubes.

WOODY PLANTS

Fall-flowering camellias

Where they survive, camellias are a “must have” plant to give color in the garden over a long period. They need a slightly acid soil and some protection from winter winds that can scorch the foliage. The winter flowering type is the most commonly grown (see the following pages) but the hybrids shown here are generally more slender.

Camellia x hiemalis 'Chansonette'

CHANSONETTE CAMELLIA

☼ ○◐ Z7–9 H8–7 ↕10–12ft (3–4m) ↔6–12ft (2–4m)

A strong growing, upright shrub with small, oval, dark green leaves. It flowers best during long hot summers and is possibly not as hardy as the others shown here.

Camellia sasanqua 'Setsugekka'

SETSUGEKKA CAMELLIA

☼ ○◐ Z8–10 H8–7 ↕10ft (3m) ↔6–8ft (2–2.5m)

Originating on Kyushu, the most southerly of the Japanese islands, this has many varieties in Japan, of which this is one and can be used as hedging.

Camellia sasanqua 'Mine No Yuki'

MINE NO YUKI CAMELLIA

☼ ○ Z7–9 H8–7 ↕10ft (3m) ↔4–6ft (1.2–2m)

A compact plant with a slightly spreading habit of growth. The profuse rose-form flowers have outer petals that overlap in rings, like the shingles on a roof.

Camellia sasanqua 'Shishi Gashira'

SHISHI GASHIRA CAMELLIA

☼ ○◐ Z8–10 H8–7 ↕to 20ft (6m) ↔to 10ft (3m)

Vigorous with rounded foliage. May make a small tree in the South of this region. Flowers are semi-double and the bright yellow stamens make this distinctive.

Camellia sasanqua 'Bonanza'

BONANZA CAMELLIA

☼ ○◐ Z7–10 H8–7 ↕10ft (3m) ↔3–6ft (1–2m)

An upright shrub with dark green, shiny foliage and small peony-like flowers. Like all these camellias this makes a good container.

MORE CHOICES

- *C. sasanqua* 'Hana Jiman' Z8–10 H8–7
- *C. sasanqua* 'Little Pearl' Z0–0 H8–7
- *C. sasanqua* 'Pink Snow' Z0–0 H8–7
- *C. sasanqua* 'Polar Ice' Z7–11 H8–7
- *C. sasanqua* 'William Lanier Hunt' Z7–10 H8–7
- *C. sasanqua* 'Winter's Star' Z7–10 H8–7

Camellia sansanqua 'Jean May'
JEAN MAY CAMELLIA
☼ ◊◑ Z7–8 H8–7 ↕8–10ft (2.5–3m) ↔6–10ft (2–3m)
A slightly spreading shrub with large fragrant flowers and small, dark green leaves. This makes a good wall shrub where it benefits from the reflected warmth on cool days.

Camellia sasanqua 'Sparkling Burgundy'
SPARKLING BURGUNDY CAMELLIA
☼ ◊◑ Z7–8 H8–7 ↕5–10ft (1.5–3m) ↔3–6ft (1–2m)
A vigorous variety that can even be used as a screen. The fragrant flowers have a lavender sheen overlaying the rose petals and last reasonably well in water.

Camellia sasanqua 'Appleblossom'
APPLEBLOSSOM CAMELLIA
☼ ◊◑ Z7–8 H8–7 ↕20ft (6m) ↔10ft (3m)
A bi-colored form with fragrant flowers on an upright shrub. Where not hardy, grow in a container and bring into a well-lit, frost-proof building for the winter.

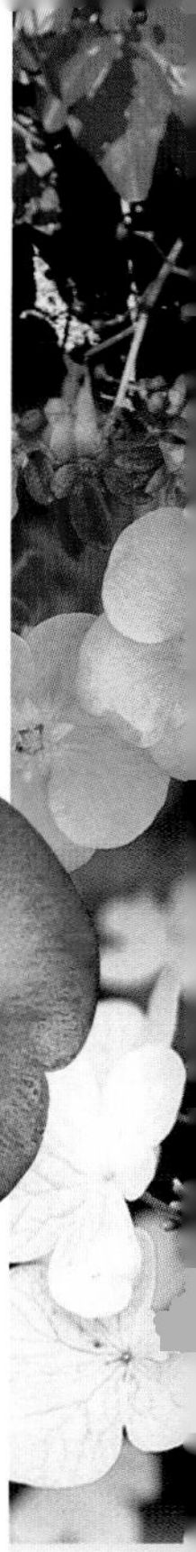

WOODY PLANTS

Camellia sasanqua 'Cleopatra'
CLEOPATRA CAMELLIA
☼ ◊◑ Zx–x Hx–x ↕to 12ft (4m) ↔to 10ft (3m)
A spreading variety with semi-double flowers that open over a long period. Like most camellias shown here, their blooms do not last well if cut.

Camellia x *vernalis* 'Yuletide'
YULETIDE CAMELLIA
☼ ◊◑ Z8–10 H8–7 ↕to 20ft (6m) ↔to 10ft (3m)
A hybrid between *C. sasanqua* and *C. japonica,* this keeps the early flowering habit of the seed parent. An upright shrub with a slower growth than others here.

Winter-flowering camellias

These camellias need a sheltered location to protect not only the foliage but also the flower buds. Once open, the flowers are remarkably tough and can withstand lower temperatures, but the buds are susceptible to cold winds and, if chilled too much, can either fail to open or become distorted. All camellias should be given an annual topdressing of leaf mold.

Camellia japonica 'Elegans'
ELEGANS CAMELLIA
☼ ◊ ♦ z7–8 H10–7 ↕6ft (2m) ↔6–8ft (2–2.5m)
An old variety that was first introduced in 1822, this shape of flower is known as "Anemone Form" with a central boss of small petals called petalodes.

Camellia japonica 'Bernice Boddy'
BERNICE BODDY CAMELLIA
☼ ◊ ♦ z7–8 H10–7 ↕↔6–7ft (2–2.2m)
A vigorous upright shrub with an arching habit of growth. The semidouble flowers open in midseason and are delicately scented. Has exceptionally cold-hardy buds.

Camellia japonica 'Betty Sheffield Supreme'
BETTY SHEFFIELD CAMELLIA
☼ ◊ ♦ z7–8 H8–7 ↕10ft (3m) ↔6–8ft (2–2.5m)
Midseason blooming variety with semidouble flowers on an upright plant. Distinctive picotee-edged petals darken on the edges as the flowers age.

Camellia japonica 'Guilio Nuccio'
GUILIO NUCCIO CAMELLIA
☼ ◊ ♦ z7–8 H8–7 ↕10ft (3m) ↔6–8ft (2–2.5m)
Vigorous erect shrub with long, narrow pointed leaves. The midseason, semidouble blooms are notable for their very prominent bright yellow stamens.

MORE CHOICES

- *Camellia japonica* 'Adolphe Audusson' z7–8 H8–7
- *Camellia japonica* 'Betty Sheffield Blush' z7–8 H8–7
- *Camellia japonica* 'Daikagura' z7–8 H8–7
- *Camellia japonica* 'Dr. Tinsley' z7–8 H8–7
- *Camellia japonica* 'Elegans Champagne' z7–8 H8–7
- *Camellia japonica* 'Faith' z7–8 H8–7
- *Camellia japonica* 'Fashinata' z7–8 H8–7
- *Camellia japonica* 'Fimbriata' z7–8 H8–7
- *Camellia japonica* 'Herme' z7–8 H8–7
- *Camellia japonica* 'Lady Clare' z7–8 H8–7
- *Camellia japonica* 'Pink Perfection' z7–8 H8–7
- *Camellia japonica* 'R. L. Wheeler' z7–8 H8–7
- *Camellia japonica* 'Rev. John G. Drayton' z7–8 H8–7
- *Camellia japonica* 'Rose Dawn' z7–8 H8–7
- *Camellia japonica* 'Sawada's Dream' z7–8 H8–7

Camellia japonica
'Professor Charles S. Sargent'
PROFESSOR SARGENT CAMELLIA
☼ ◊♦ Z7–8 H8–7
↕12–15ft (4–5m) ↔8–10ft (2.5–3m)
Upright and compact with broad, dark green foliage. Flowers resemble the garden peony in form.

Camellia japonica
'Mathotiana'
MATHOTIANA CAMELLIA
☼ ◊♦ Z7–8 H8–7
↕10–11ft (3–3.5m) ↔8–10ft (2.5–3m)
Late, rose-like flowers with overlapping petals, on an upright vigorous shrub. The buds are fairly susceptible to cold and it needs a sheltered location.

Camellia japonica 'Nuccio's Gem'
NUCCIO'S GEM CAMELLIA
☼ ◊♦ Z7–8 H8–7 ↕10–15ft (3–5m) ↔6–10ft (2–3m)
An upright dense shrub with perfectly formed double flowers, each with concentric rings of overlapping petals when grown with good protection. May only be semidouble in more exposed sites.

Camellia japonica
'Alba Plena'
ALBA PLENA
CAMELLIA
☼ ◊♦ Z7–8 H8–7
↕30ft (9m) ↔25ft (8m)
Fully double, 4in (10cm), flowers open early in the winter on a compact, erect bushy shrub. This foliage is a paler green than most other camellias.

Camellia japonica 'Bob Hope'
BOB HOPE CAMELLIA
☼ ◊♦ Z7–8 H8–7
↕10–15ft (3–5m) ↔3–6ft (1–2m)
Possibly the darkest red of all camellias, these semidouble flowers appear on an upright, medium-sized bush with dense growth.

No-spray shrub roses

Roses are grouped into three main categories: bush roses, shrub roses, and climbing roses. Bush roses are the most popular but have many pest and disease problems that may require frequent spraying. Shrub, and most climbing, roses are not as problem-prone, seldom needing to be sprayed. The varieties shown here are particularly problem-free.

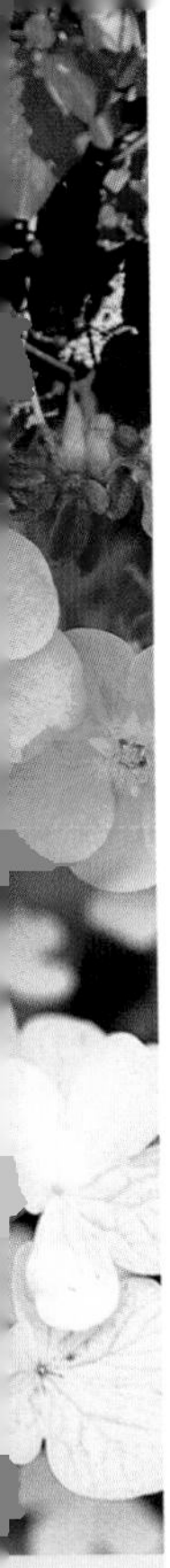

Rosa bonica 'Meidomonac'
BONICA ROSE
☼ ◊ Z4–9 H9–1 ↕3–4ft (1–1.2m) ↔3.5ft (1.1m)
A justifiably popular rose with arching stems and glossy, coppery green foliage. It is very free-flowering and continues to bloom late in the year.

Rosa 'The Fairy'
THE FAIRY ROSE
☼ ◊ Z5–9 H9–5
↕↔24–36in (60–90cm)
A small polyantha rose first introduced in 1932. It is repeat flowering and will carry clusters of blooms from early summer to fall. Makes a good edging plant or low hedge.

Rosa 'Lady Penzance'
LADY PENZANCE ROSE
☼ ◊◊ Z5–9 H9–5 ↕↔6ft (2m)
A dense, vigorous shrubby rose with strongly apple-scented foliage. The sweetly fragrant summer flowers give bright red fruits that last well into winter.

Rosa 'Cécile Brunner'
CÉCILE BRUNNER ROSE
☼ ◊◊ Z5–9 H9–1 ↕30in (75cm) ↔24in (60cm)
The delicately fragrant blooms are produced freely throughout the summer. One of the China class of roses with sparse foliage, there is also a climbing form.

Rosa 'Dortmund'
DORTMUND ROSE
☼ ◊ Z5–9 H9–5 ↕10ft (3m) ↔6ft (2m)
Slightly fragrant flowers are carried in large clusters on a vigorous thorny plant for most of the summer. Can be used as a climbing rose if tied to a pillar or trellis.

Rosa 'La Marne'
LA MARNE ROSE
☼ ◐ 💧 Z4–11 H12–1 ↕to 5ft (1.5m) ↔3ft (90cm)
A bushy polyantha rose with very few thorns, flowers in clusters and repeat bloomer. The fragrance is slight. Makes a good container plant. Introduced in 1915.

Rosa 'Old Blush'
OLD BLUSH CHINA ROSE
☼ ◐ 💧 Z6–9 H9–1 ↕6ft (2m) ↔4ft (1.2m)
A very fragrant rose with almost thornless, upright stems. This can be grown as a small climber and is well worth growing for its repeated flushes of blooms.

Rosa 'Ramona'
RAMONA ROSE
Ⓝ ☼ 💧💧 Z7–9 H9–1
↕8ft (2.5m) ↔10ft (3m)
This variety has the Cherokee rose *(R. laevigata)* as one parent. A vigorous climber with sharply recurved thorns and repeat blooming, flowers are fragrant.

Rosa 'Belinda's Dream'
BELINDA'S DREAM SHRUB ROSE
☼ 💧💧 Z5–9 H9–5 ↕5ft (1.5m) ↔4ft (1.2m)
A fast growing shrub rose, developed in Texas. Prune in spring when all danger of frost is passed. It is a heavy feeder but blooms almost continuously all summer. Makes a good cut flower.

Rosa x *odorata* 'Mutabilis'
CHINA ROSE
☼ 💧 Z7–9 H9–7 ↕↔3ft (1m)
Flowers from summer to fall, changing from light yellow to copper-pink then to deep pink. Will climb if given support. Also known as *R. chinensis* 'Mutabilis'.

MORE CHOICES

- *Rosa* 'Aloha' Z5–9 H9–5
- *Rosa* 'Carefree Delight' Z4–9 H9–1
- *Rosa* 'Duchesse de Brabant' Z7–9 H9–7
- *Rosa* 'Europeana' Z4–11 H12–1
- *Rosa* 'Knock Out' Z4–9 H9–1
- *Rosa* 'Louis Philippe' Z7–9 H9–7
- *Rosa* 'Mister Lincoln' Z6–9 H9–1
- *Rosa* 'Petite Pink Scotch' Z5–9 H9–1
- *Rosa* 'Red Cascades' Z5–9 H9–1

Climbing roses

Although they are called climbing roses, in fact they don't really climb. These roses are sprawlers that, in nature, would grow up through other plants and hang on with their backward-pointing thorns. In the garden, however, these plants can climb if you tie them to the framework of a trellis, arch, or arbor.

Rosa 'Zéphirine Drouhin'
THORNLESS ZEPHRINE DROUHIN ROSE
☼ ◊ Z5–9 H9–5 ↕to 8ft (2.5m) ↔to 6ft (2m)
Popular for its lack of thorns and long-flowering, this has new shoots of a bronzy red that turn green as they mature. Grows in part shade and poor soils. Very fragrant.

Rosa 'Paul Lédé'
PAUL LEDE CLIMBING ROSE
☼ ◊ Z5–9 H9–5 ↕ 120ft (3.5m) ↔ 8ft (2.5m)
A climbing form of an older Hybrid Tea rose with non-fading, very fragrant flowers that open from typical pointed buds to give an almost flat bloom.

Rosa 'Veilchenblau'
VEILCHENBLAU ROSE
☼ ◊ Z5–9 H9–5 ↕12ft (4m) ↔7ft (2.2m)
Vigorous rambler that flowers on the previous year's wood with large trusses of scented flowers in summer. Prune soon after flowering. Will grow in part shade.

Rosa laevigata
CHEROKEE ROSE
☼ ◊◆ Z7–9 H9–7 ↕↔15–20ft (5–6m)
Originally native to China, with large hooked thorns, this has naturalized itself in many parts of the South. Slightly fragrant flowers give bristly orange hips.

Rosa 'Lamarque'
LAMARQUE ROSE
☼ ◊ Z7–9 H9–7
↕to 15ft (5m) ↔8ft (2.5m)
An old, slightly tender rose with very fragrant flowers on long stems. The shoots are almost thornless. This Noisette hybrid was introduced in France in 1830.

Rosa 'Handel'
HANDEL CLIMBING ROSE
☼ ◊ Z5–9 H9–5 ↕10ft (3m) ↔7ft (2.2m)
Modern climber introduced in 1956 in Ireland. The foliage is glossy and dark, showing off the flowers. The picotee edging to the petals darkens as it ages.

Rosa 'Don Juan'
DON JUAN CLIMBING ROSE
☼ ◊ Z5–9 H9–1 ↕10ft (3m) ↔6ft (2m)
Very fragrant flowers are borne in clusters on a branching upright plant with dark green, leathery foliage. 'New Dawn' is one parent of this variety.

Rosa 'Climbing Iceberg'
ICEBERG CLIMBING ROSE
☼ ◊◑ Z5–9 H9–5 ↕↔10ft (3m)
One of the best white-flowered climbing roses, this is a climbing version on the popular floribunda rose of the same name. Both are almost thornless but have only slight fragrance.

Rosa 'New Dawn'
NEW DAWN ROSE
☼ ◊ Z5–9 H9–5 ↕10ft (3m) ↔8ft (2.5m)
One of the most popular pale pink climbers, this is fragrant and exceptionally free-flowering over a long period. Glossy, dark green foliage is disease resistant.

Rosa 'Mrs Sam McGredy' *climbing*
CLIMBING MRS SAM MCGREDY ROSE
☼ ◊ Z5–9 H9–5 ↕20ft (6m) ↔15ft (4.5m)
A vigorous climbing form of the popular Hybrid Tea rose with young foliage tinged with orange-red. The fragrant flowers are carried in recurring waves, not continuously.

MORE CHOICES

- *Rosa* 'America' Z5–9 H9–1
- *Rosa* 'Cornelia' Z6–9 H9–6
- *Rosa* 'Fortune's Double Yellow' Z8–9 H9–8
- *Rosa* 'Sombreuil' Z4–9 H9–3
- *Rosa* 'White Cockade' Z5–9 H9–5

WOODY PLANTS

Antique roses

Roses have long been a favored garden flower. Early plant hunters brought new species back to Europe and these, when combined with the existing cross-bred superior native roses, opened the way to modern roses that are still being grown today – a tribute to their beauty and ruggednesss. Those shown here were all introduced at least 140 years ago.

Rosa palustris (1726)
SWAMP ROSE
Ⓝ ☼ ◐ 💧💧 Z5–9 H9–1 ↕6ft (2m) ↔4ft (1.2m)
A vigorous, upright suckering rose, native to eastern North America. Flowers open over a long period and are followed by oval hips that turn red in fall.

Rosa 'Duchesse de Brabant' (1857)
DUCHESSE DE BRABANT ROSE
☼ 💧 Z7–9 H9–7 ↕↔5ft (1.5m)
Very fragrant flowers are borne over a long period on a spreading bush. The flowers are double so no hips are produced. Classed as a "tea" rose.

Rosa x odorata 'Mutabilis' (1840)
CHINA ROSE
☼ 💧 Z7–9 H9–7 ↕↔3ft (1m)
Flowers from summer to fall, changing from light yellow to copper-pink then to deep pink. Will climb if given support. Also known as *R. chinensis* 'Mutabilis'.

Rosa 'Souvenir de la Malmaison' (1843)
SOUVENIR DE LA MALMAISON ROSE
☼ 💧 Z6–9 H9–6 ↕↔3ft (1m)
One of the most beautiful of the Bourbon roses, especially when grown in a dry climate as the flowers do not open properly when wet. Very fragrant and long flowering.

Rosa 'Fortuniana' (1850)
FORTUNIANA ROSE
☼ 💧 Z6–9 H9–1 ↕16ft (5m) ↔6ft (2m)
An evergreen rose that may be a cross between the Lady Banks and the Cherokee roses, both originally from China. The latter is now naturalized in the South.

Rosa 'Céline Forestier' (1858)
CÉLINE FORESTIER ROSE
☼ ◊ Z6–9 H9–6 ↕13ft (4m) ↔6ft (2m)
This is a Noisette rose, a class first raised by John Champney in Charleston, South Carolina, but made popular by Noisette Nursery in France. This climber has a strong spicy scent.

Rosa glauca (1830)
REDLEAF ROSE
☼ ◊ Z2–8 H8–1 ↕6ft (2m) ↔5ft (1.5m)
An eyecatching rose with arching stems and foliage tinged dark red. The smallish flowers are followed by round, bright red hips that last through winter.

MORE CHOICES

- *Rosa banskiae* 'Alba Plena' (1807) Z8–9 H9–4
- *Rosa banksiae 'Lutea'* (1824) Z8–9 H9–8
- *Rosa* 'Blush Noisette' (1817) Z6–9 H9–6
- *Rosa* 'Celestial' (1759) Z3–9 H9–1
- *Rosa* 'Champney's Pink Cluster' (1811) Z5–9 H9–1
- *Rosa* 'Cramoisi Superieur' (1832) Z7–9 H9–7
- *Rosa* 'Félicité Parmentier' (1834) Z3–9 H9–3
- *Rosa gallica* 'Versicolor' (1581) Z3–9 H9–1
- *Rosa* 'Königen von Dänemark' (1809) Z3–9 H9–1
- *Rosa* 'Louis Odier' (1851) Z3–9 H9–1
- *Rosa* 'Louis Philippe' (1834) Z7–9 H9–7
- *Rosa* 'Maiden's Blush' (1797) Z3–9 H9–1
- *Rosa* 'Marechal Niel' (1864) Z7–9 H9–7
- *Rosa* 'Mme Isaac Pereire' (1881) Z6–9 H9–6
- *Rosa moschata* (1540) Z7–9 H9–7
- *Rosa roxburghii* (1814) Z6–9 H9–5
- *Rosa* 'Sombreuil' (1850) Z4–9 H9–3
- *Rosa* 'Stanwell Perpetual' (1838) Z3–9 H9–1

Rosa 'Old Blush' (1752)
OLD BLUSH ROSE
☼ ◊ Z6–9 H9–1 ↕6ft (2m) ↔4ft (1.2m)
One of the best of the China roses, this is an almost thornless, upright shrub that can be used as a small climber. Long flowering but only slight fragrance.

Palms

Palms add a tropical look to the garden. In form, they are so completely different from other plants that they really stand out in the landscape. Some get very tall and are suitable only for large properties. Even where not fully hardy, the smaller species make good container plants if protected in winter by wrapping or by moving into a well-lit, frost-proof building.

Chamaerops humilis
EUROPEAN FAN PALM
☼ ◊ Z12–14 H12–10 ↕6–10ft (2–3m) ↔3–6ft (1–2m)
This bushy suckering palm makes a good container plant where not hardy. Will stand temperatures down to freezing for short periods. Native to sandy soils.

Ptychosperma macarthurii
MACARTHUR PALM
☀ ◊◊ Z11–12 H12–10 ↕22ft (7m) ↔12ft (4m)
This multistemmed palm makes a good specimen plant in a lawn. Yellowish flowers are produced in summer, followed by red fruits.

Cocos nucifera
COCONUT PALM
☼ ◊ Z11–12 H12–10 ↕100ft (30m) ↔to 40ft (12m)
An interesting palm that rarely grows upright, generally leaning sideways. Fragrant, cream-colored flowers are produced several times each year and give the fruits.

MORE CHOICES

- *Arecastrum romanzoffianum* Z15 H10–1
- *Chrysalidocarpus lutescens* Z11–12 H12–10
- *Lantana loddigesii* Z13–15 H12–10
- *Phoenix canariensis* Z11–15 H12–10
- *Ptychosperma elegans* Z11–12 H12–10
- *Washingtonia filifera* Z8–11 H12–8

Phoenix roebelenii

MINIATURE DATE PALM

☼ ◊♦ Z11–12 H12–10 ↕6ft (2m) ↔8ft (2.5m)

A useful small palm for containers or as a specimen. Old leaves tend to hang on giving an untidy look. Creamy flowers in summer give edible black fruits.

Phoenix dactylifera

DATE PALM

☼ ◊♦ Z11–12 H12–10 ↕100ft (30m) ↔40ft (12m)

Old foliage tends to hang on like a skirt below the fresh, green new leaves. Long spikes of cream flowers open in spring or summer and give edible fruits.

Livistona chinensis

CHINESE FAN PALM

☼ ◐ ◊♦ Z11–12 H12–10

↕to 40ft (12m) ↔15ft (5m)

An upright palm with a trunk that is swollen at the base and covered with fibrous leaf bases at the top. In summer, sprays of cream flowers open and give rise to pinkish fruits.

Caryota mitis

BURMESE FISHTAIL PALM

◐ ◊♦ Z11–12 H12–10 ↕40ft (12m) ↔22ft (7m)

A multiple-stemmed tree with broad leaves up to 12ft (4m) long with as many as 60 fishtail-like leaflets. A related species is the source of sago and palm wine.

Roystonea regia
ROYAL PALM
☼ ◊♦ Z11–12 H12–10 ↕80ft (25m) ↔30ft (10m)
Slender palms with leaves up to 15ft (5m) long with the leaflets arranged in several rows. Cup-shaped white flowers in short sprays appear in summer. Like all palms, subject to mites and scale insects.

Rhapidophyllum hystrix
BLUE PALMETTO
Ⓝ ◐ ◊♦ Z6–10 H12–10 ↕6ft (2m) ↔12ft (4m)
A clump-forming palm with stems branching just below the soil surface. The base of each leaf sheath carries long upright spines.

Sabal palmetto
CABBAGE PALMETTO
☼ ◊ Z12–15 H12–10 ↕100ft (30m) ↔22ft (7m)
The rough trunk may be up to 2ft (60cm) in diameter and is topped with a head of 6ft (2m) long, fan-shaped leaves with thread-like filaments between the leaflets.

Trachycarpus fortunei
CHUSAN PALM
☼ ◊ Z8–11 H12–8 ↕↔50ft (15m)
Long clusters of small yellow flowers hang from the leaf bases in early summer, followed by round, blue-black fruit on females. Protect from strong or cold winds.

Serenoa repens
SAW PALMETTO

Ⓝ ☀ ◐ ◊ Z8–11 H12–9
↕2–3ft (60cm–1m) ↔6ft (2m)
A small, clump-forming, spiny palm
that forms dense thickets from
underground, with prostrate stems.
and fragrant solitary or paired flowers
in summer. Native to the coastal
southeastern US.

Washingtonia robusta
THREAD PALM

☀ ◊ Z13–15 H12–10 ↕80ft (25m) ↔8–15ft (2.5–5m)
Slender palms with heads of fan-shaped leaves that
leave a thatch on the trunk as they die, becoming a fire
hazard. Used as street trees where hardy.

Butia capitata
JELLY PALM

☀ ◐ ◊ Z11–12 H12–10 ↕12–20ft (4–6m) ↔15ft (5m)
Slow-growing palm with stems covered in old leaf
bases. Yellow flowers in 5ft (1.5m) sprays in summer
give yellow to purple fruits. Good container specimen.

Veitchia merrillii
CHRISTMAS PALM

☀ ◊◊ Z11 H12–10 ↕20ft (6m) ↔6–11ft (2–3.5m)
Very slender palm with leaves scaly beneath. Summer
flowers are yellow-green and in 3ft (1m) sprays.
The fruits seen here color well and last into winter.

Rhapis excelsa
MINIATURE FAN PALM

◐ ◊◊ Z14–15 H12–1 ↕↔5–15ft (1.5–5m)
Slender, clump-forming palm with bamboo-like stems
and long stalked leaves. Short spikes of small cream
flowers open in summer.

Coniferous shrubs

Not all conifers are large trees, many are more shrublike in growth and well-suited to smaller gardens. Even tall-growing species often have dwarf or spreading forms and some enthusiasts collect these and have gardens with little else. Often slow-growing, these add contrast in foliage and form and give color in the garden in winter where this may be lacking.

Pinus mugo
MUGO PINE
Z3–7 H7–1 ↕10–15ft (3–5m)
↔15–25 ft (5–8m)
Resinous green stems age to brown. Bark is scaly and gray. Many of the cultivars are small shrubs that grow slowly and are suitable for city gardens.

Chamaecyparis obtusa
HINOKI CYPRESS
Z4–8 H8–3
↕70ft (20m) ↔15ft (5m)
An open irregular shrub to small tree, depending on the cultivar. Small cones start green and turn brown as they ripen in fall. Growth rate is moderate.

Cephalotaxus harringtonia
PLUM YEW
Z6–9 H9–3 ↕15ft (5m) ↔10ft (3m)
Can be a large shrub or small tree as it ages. Female plants produce small, egg-shaped, olive-green fruit in fall. Prefers fertile soil. Resistant to deer browsing.

Juniperus x *media* 'Pfitzeriana Aurea'
GOLDEN PFITZER JUNIPER
Z4–9 H9–1 ↕7ft (2m) ↔15ft (4m)
A widely planted juniper that is large at maturity and needs room to develop. It does well in clay soils. The color of new growth is intense in spring and summer.

Juniperus horizontalis 'Plumosa'
ANDORRA JUNIPER
Ⓝ Z3–9 H9–1
↕2ft (60cm) ↔10ft (3m)
A dense shrub with branches that grow at a 45-degree angle, flattening later. The foliage turns purplish in winter. A very popular variety.

Taxus cuspidata
JAPANESE YEW
Ⓝ Z5–7 H7–1 ↕50ft (15m) ↔25ft (8m)
Soft-textured conifer that can be grown as a shrub or a small tree. Fleshy fruit are scarlet, and dark green needles turn red-green in winter. Slow growing.

MORE CHOICES

- *Juniperus chinensis* 'Hetzii' Z4–9 H9–1
- *Juniperus chinensis* 'Sea Green' Z4–9 H9–1
- *Juniperus horizontalis* Z3–9 H9–1
- *Thuja occidentalis* 'Little Gem' Z3–7 H7–1
- *Thuja orientalis* 'Compacta' Z6–9 H9–6

Thuja orientalis 'Semperaurea'
OREINTAL ARBORVITAE
Z6–9 H9–6 ↕10ft (3m) ↔6ft (2m)
The new growth of this cultivar is golden yellow. Foliage may turn bronze in winter. Slower growing and more compact than the species.

Thuja occidentalis 'Globosa'
GLOBE WHITE CEDAR, GLOBE ARBORVITAE
Ⓝ Z2–8 H8–1 ↕↔6ft (2m)
One of several, slow-growing globe forms of this popular plant. It withstands clipping well, providing it is not too severe, and can easily be kept as a neat small globe.

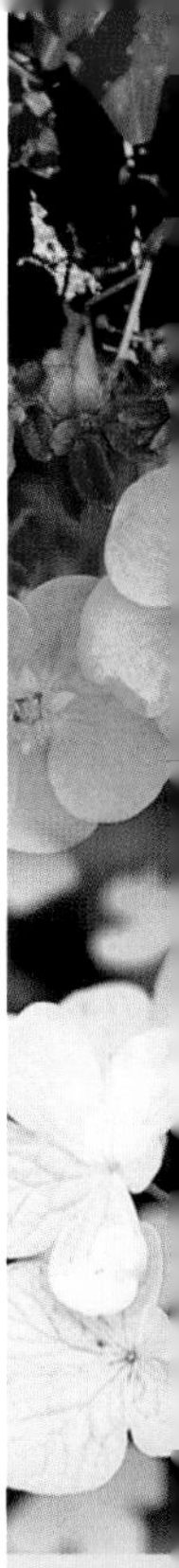

Coniferous groundcovers

Planted through cuts made in the landscape's fabric, which is then mulched with bark chips or coarse gravel, spreading conifers can make a very effective, low-maintenance groundcover. Remember to allow them room at planting time – many have an indefinite spread, and close planting means heavy pruning later.

Juniperus conferta 'Blue Pacific'
BLUE PACIFIC SHORE JUNIPER
Z5–9 H9–1 ↕12in (30cm) ↔indefinite
This cultivar is more trailing than the species and has a deeper blue cast to the foliage. Produces black fruit with a silvery white coating. Growth rate is moderate.

Juniperus conferta 'Emerald Sea'
EMERALD SEA SHORE JUNIPER
Z5–9 H9–1 ↕10in (25cm) ↔indefinite
Makes a very dense mat with small pointed needles in whorls of three. Turns a greenish yellow in winter. Very salt tolerant so a good choice for coastal regions.

MORE CHOICES

- *Cephalotaxus harringtonia* 'Prostrata' Z6–9 H9–6
- *Juniperus conferta* 'Compacta' Z6–9 H9–1
- *Juniperus conferta 'Silver Mist'* Z6–9 H9–1
- *Juniperus horizontalis 'Bar Harbor'* Z3–9 H9–1

Juniperus conferta
SHORE JUNIPER
Z5–9 H9–1 ↕12in (30cm) ↔indefinite
Prostrate shrub with pointed needles that turn from bright green to grayed green in their second year. Black fruits have bluish dusty coating. Japanese native.

Juniperus conferta 'Sunsplash'
SUNSPLASH SHORE JUNIPER
Z5–9 H9–1 ↕12in (30cm) ↔indefinite
A recent introduction, this has bright yellow new foliage that turns green as it matures. It is not as dense as 'Emerald Sea' but is more striking. Fruit are similar to the species.

Juniperus horizontalis
CREEPING JUNIPER
Ⓝ ☼ ◐ ◊ Z3–9 H9–1
↕12in (30cm) ↔indefinite
A very adaptable plant that will grow in most soils, including dry and alkaline. Named varieties may have blue or bright green needles and grow to varying heights.

Juniperus x *pfitzeriana* 'Old Gold'
OLD GOLD JUNIPER
☼ ◐ ◊ Z4–9 H9–1
↕3ft (1m) ↔4ft (1.2m)
Forms a neat golden mound that keeps its color well and makes a good contrast to the more spreading forms. May be listed as a variety of *J. chinensis* in garden centers.

Juniperus horizontalis 'Blue Chip'
BLUE CHIP CREEPING JUNIPER
Ⓝ ☼ ◐ ◊ ◆ Z3–9 H9–1
↕8–10in(20–25cm) ↔8–10ft (2.5–3m)
More prostrate than the species, this is also a brighter blue in summer, becoming purple-tinged in winter. 'Wiltoni', the blue rug juniper, is as blue but even more prostrate.

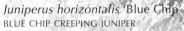

Juniperus procumbens 'Nana'
JAPANESE GARDEN JUNIPER
☼ ◊ Z3–9 H9–1 ↕6–8in (15–20cm) ↔30in (75cm)
A dwarf compact form of an already procumbent shrub resulting in a low, mat-forming plant. Foliage turns slightly purple in winter. Growth rate is rather slow.

Pinus mugo var. *pumilo*
PUMILO MOUNTAIN PINE
☼ ◊ Z3–7 H7–1 ↕5ft (1.5m) ↔10ft (3m)
Very variable group of plants usually grown from seed. Plants with shortest new growth are slowest growing. Pinch out half new "candles" to restrict growth.

Vines with attractive fruit

Of the many vines that are grown to provide a screen or to cover a blank wall or fence, those that have attractive flowers are the most widely used. The vines shown here have fairly insignificant flowers, but more than make up for this by their fruit, which brighten the garden in fall and may persist into winter.

Actinidia arguta
HARDY KIWI VINE, TARA VINE
☼ ◊ Z3–8 H8–1 ↕22ft (7m)
A vigorous twining vine with fragrant flowers in early summer. Male and female flowers are on separate plants; both are usually needed to produce the edible fruit. 'Issai', however, is self-fertile.

Akebia quinata
CHOCOLATE VINE
☼ ◐ ◊ Z5–9 H9–5 ↕30ft (10m)
Semi-evergreen climber with foliage tinged purple in winter. Spicy-smelling flowers borne in early spring and give small violet-colored fruits in late summer.

Celastrus scandens
AMERICAN BITTERSWEET
Ⓝ ☼ ◐ ◆ Z3–8 H8–1
↕30ft (10m)
A deciduous climber with clusters of small yellow flowers in summer that give these fruits that open to show the red seeds. Vigorous grower that can strangle trees it climbs into.

Parthenocissus quinquifolia
VIRGINIA CREEPER
Ⓝ ◐ ● ◆ Z7–9 H9–1 ↕50ft (15m) or more
Grows vigorously and climbs over and onto anything in its path. Brilliant red fall foliage and dark blue fruits are additional virtues.

MORE CHOICES

- *Actinidia deliciosa* Z7–9 H9–7
- *Clematis paniculata* Z4–7 H9–1
- *Hydrangea anomola subsp. petiolaris* Z4–9 H9–1
- *Passiflora caerulea* Z6–9 H9–6
- *Smilax lanceolata* Z9–11 H12–9
- *Vitis lanceolata* Z4–8 H8–3

Vines for small arbors

These vines are not necessarily slow growing, but generally do not get too large and heavy. They are suitable for small arbors, for growing up a garden trellis, and other similar locations where the structure would not support a rampant heavy vine such as wisteria.

Pyrostegia venusta
FLAME VINE
☼ ◊ Z14–15 H12–10 ↕30ft (10m)
Tropical vine with slender stems that climbs by means of tendrils. Dark green, lance-shaped, opposite leaves about 3in (8cm) long. Flowers in late fall and winter.

Clytostoma callistegioides
ARGENTINE TRUMPET VINE
◑ ◊ Z13–15 H12–9 ↕30ft (10m)
Vigorous South American climber with bronze young foliage. Very free-flowering in summer. Makes a good container plant. Prune back hard to keep within bounds.

Mandevilla x amoena 'Alice duPont'
ALICE DUPONT DIPLADENIA
☼ ◑ ◊ Z13–15 H12–2 ↕22ft (7m)
Woody twining climber that is good for sheltered locations or as a conservatory plant. Flowers, 3-4in (8-10cm) across are freely produced in summer. Withstands hard pruning.

Trachelospermum jasminoides
CONFEDERATE JASMINE
☼ ◑ ◊ Z9–10 H12–6 ↕28ft (9m)
Woody, evergreen twining climber with glossy, dark green leaves, bronze-red in winter. Fragrant flowers in summer. 'Variegatum' has leaves marked with white.

MORE CHOICES

- *Campsis radicans* Z5–9 H9–3
- *Clematis armandii* Z7–9 H9–7
- *Clematis paniculata* Z4–9 H9–1
- *Decumaria barbara* Z6–9 H9–6
- *Gelsemium sempervirens* Z7–9 H9–1
- *Hydrangea anomala subsp. petiolaris* Z4–9 H9–1
- *Jasminum polyanthum* Z8–10 H10–8
- *Lonicera sempervirens* 'Sulphurea' Z4–9 H9–1
- *Rosa banksiae* Z8–9 H9–8
- *Schizophragma hydrangiodeoides* Z6–9 H9–6
- *Wisteria frutescens* Z6–9 H9–6

Bignonia capreolata
CROSS VINE
Ⓝ ☼ ◊ Z6–9 H9–5 ↕30ft (10m)
Vigorous climber that may be evergreen in the South. Small clusters of fragrant flowers open in late spring and early summer. Makes a good conservatory plant.

Vines with fragrant flowers

It is always pleasant to sit out on a vine-covered porch and listen to the rustle of the leaves, especially when the experience includes perfume. If the porch is not feasible, these vines will grow equally well on a fence, and some can be trained up against a wall. Try to site them upwind of the main outdoor sitting area, so their fragrance will drift down and surround you.

Clematis armandii
EVERGREEN CLEMATIS
☼ ◑ ◊ Z7–9 H9–7 ↕15ft (5m) ↔10ft (3m)
The wonderfully scented flowers are produced in early spring on last season's growth, so prune immediately after flowering.

Jasminum officinale
COMMON WHITE JASMINE
☼ ◊ Z8–10 H12–8 ↕10–15ft (3–5m)
A semi-evergreen climber that blooms from mid- to late summer with very fragrant flowers. This has been cultivated in European gardens for centuries.

Lonicera x *heckrottii*
GOLDFLAME HONEYSUCKLE
☼ ◊ Z5–9 H9–6 ↕10–20ft (3–6m)
Flower buds are red, opening with yellow inner petals that gradually turn the pink seen here. The flowers appear from late spring to fall. Evergreen in the South.

Akebia quinata
CHOCOLATE VINE
☼ ◊ Z5–9 H9–5
↕30ft (10m) or more
Spicily scented flowers appear in early spring, followed by sausage-shaped, purple-fleshed fruits. Prefers fertile soil. Prune after flowering to restrict growth.

Gelsemium sempervirens
CAROLINA YELLOW JESSAMINE
Ⓝ ☼ ◑ ◊ Z6–9 H9–7
↕10–20ft (3–6m)
The spring flowers often reappear in fall. A very useful climber that has a multitude of roles and can climb into small trees. It can even be used as a groundcover.

MORE CHOICES

- *Ipomoea alba* Z12–15 H12–10
- *Jasminum nitidum* Z10–11 H12–7
- *Polygonum aubertii* Z5–9 H9–3
- *Rosa banksiae* 'Alba Plena' Z8–9 H9–4
- *Stephanotis floribunda* Z14–15 H12–10
- *Trachelospermum jasminoides* Z8–13 H12–6

Evergreen vines

One tends to think of vines as needing support, but sometimes they can be used as groundcovers as well. The periwinkle shown here is a case in point: it is usually grown in this way and would need constant tying to use it as an upright vine. The ivy can be used for either purpose. Evergreen vines are best appreciated of course in winter, once other vines have lost their foliage.

MORE CHOICES

- *Bignonia capreolata* Z6–9 H9–5
- *Euonymus fortunei* 'Coloratus' Z5–9 H9–2
- *Gelsemium sempervirens* Z7–9 H9–7
- *Hedera canariensis* Z6–11 H12–6
- *Millettia reticulata* Z7–10 H10–7

Hedera helix 'Manda's Crested'
MANDA'S CRESTED ENGLISH IVY
☼ ◐ ● ◊ Z5–11 H12–6 ↕↔6ft (2m)
This cultivar's foliage takes on coppery tints in cold weather. Good for growing on a wall or fence or as a groundcover.

Vinca major 'Maculata'
SPOTTED GREATER PERIWINKLE
☼ ◐ ◊ ◑ Z7–9 H9–6
↕18in (45cm) ↔indefinite
This cultivar's leaves sport yellow-green centers. Flowers from midspring to autumn. Can also be grown in containers.

Ficus pumila
CLIMBING FIG
☼ ◐ ◊ Z8–10 H12–1
↕10–15ft (3–5m)
This climbs by aerial roots and clings firmly to any porous surface. Juvenile leaves are wider at the base while adult leaves are wider at the top. Can be rampant in the South.

x *Fatshedera lizei*
FATSHEDERA
◐ ● ◊ Z8–10 H12–8
↕4–6ft (1.2–2m)
A good subject for training on a wall where the large leaves are very distinctive. Pale green flowers are produced in large clusters in fall. There is also a variegated form.

HERBACEOUS PLANTS

HERBACEOUS PLANTS – by definition, those that die down to ground level each year – are the multifaceted components of almost every gardener's palette. Whatever the size of your garden, you can use them to produce infinite combinations of colors, textures, scents, and shapes and to provide interest throughout most of the year (all year round, in the case of evergreen herbaceous plants). They often require more time investment than woody plants but repay rich dividends.

The backbone of the herbaceous garden is often the bulbs – the crocuses and snowdrops, narcissus and tulips, to just name a few. Among the first and most dependable harbingers of spring, some bloom well into summer.

Chrysanthemum rubellum 'Clara Curtis'
There are many plants with daisy-like flowers, such as these, and most of them give color to the late summer and fall garden. Most are also good cut flowers, lasting for several days in water.

Narcissus 'Geranium'
The many forms of narcissus and daffodil are indispensable, sweetly scented additions to the spring garden. By growing different varieties, their bloom time can last for several weeks.

Many bulbous plants last for years, often naturalizing and, in many cases, spreading well beyond the area where they were originally planted.

At the other end of the spectrum are the decorative grasses, whose leaves and seedheads remain until they are pruned back in spring. Some of these grasses can be used on the edge of a pond or in any particularly damp areas.

Another group of perennials well suited to difficult growing conditions are the alpine plants, those that are native to regions of high altitude. They do well in dry, windy sites and are often used in rock gardens because of their small size and creeping habit.

Garden ponds are becoming increasingly popular and give the opportunity to grow an entirely new range of plants, like water lilies for the pond and march marigolds for the wet areas surrounding it.

Regardless of any limitations of your garden, you will be able to find many herbaceous plants to provide a kaleidoscope of color and texture.

Zinnia 'Elegans' Thumbelina Series
Some annuals thrive in the heat of summer, while others are best in the cool weather of spring and fall. They are invaluable for filling gaps in a perennial display and for hiding dying foliage.

Geranium 'Anna Folkard'
Hardy perennial geraniums are increasingly popular with their long flowering ability. Many make good groundcovers when not in bloom.

Perennials attractive to butterflies

With the exception of the cabbage white, gardeners enjoy seeing butterflies flitting about the garden. Butterflies feed mainly on nectar, and the plants shown here are attractive to them for this reason. They also appreciate an area of wet sand or soil from which they can drink. To encourage butterflies, one must occasionally put up with the damage their caterpillars do.

Asclepias tuberosa
BUTTERFLY WEED
Ⓝ ☼ ◊ Z4–9 H9–2
↕30in (75cm) ↔18in (45cm)
Blooms in midsummer. Prefers fertile, well-drained, loamy soil. Susceptible to aphids and mealybugs when in bloom.

Echinacea purpurea
PURPLE CONEFLOWER
Ⓝ ☼ ◊ Z3–9 H9–1 ↕to 5ft (1.5m) ↔18in (45cm)
Flowers from midsummer to early autumn and prefers deep organic soil. The cultivars bred from this native plant are often more suitable for the garden border.

MORE CHOICES

- *Castilleja coccinea* Z6–9 H9–6
- *Coreopsis lanceolata* Z4–9 H9–1
- *Erythrina herbacea* Z8–10 H10–9
- *Eupatorium purpureum* Z3–9 H9–1
- *Geum coccineum* Z5–8 H8–5
- *Lobelia cardinalis* Z2–8 H8–1
- *Lychnis coronaria* Z4–8 H8–1
- *Monarda didyma* Z4–10 H10–1
- *Oenothera missouriensis* Z4–9 H9–2
- *Verbena bonariensis* Z8–11 H12–8

Agastache foeniculum
ANISE HYSSOP
Ⓝ ☼ ◊ Z6–10 H9–5 ↕5ft (1.5m) ↔12in (30cm)
Blooms from midsummer to early autumn. Flowers can also be white. Good at the back of borders. Leaves have the scent and flavor of licorice.

Crocosmia x *crocosmiflora*
MONTBRETIA
☼ ◐ ♦ Z6–9 H9–3
↕24in (60cm) ↔3in (8cm)
Summer flowers vary from yellow to orange to red. Prefers moderately fertile, organic soil. Hybrid cross between *C. aurea* and *C. pottsii*.

Foeniculum vulgare
FENNEL
☼ ◊ ◑ Z4–9 H9–1 ↕6ft (1.8m) ↔18in (45cm)
This summer-flowering herb is most attractive to butterflies who feed on the nectar in the flowers. It is also food for the caterpillars of swallowtail butterflies.

MORE CHOICES

- *Salvia greggii* 'Cherry Queen' Z7–10 H9–7
- *Salvia leucantha* Z9–11 H12–4
- *Sedum spectabile* Z4–9 H9–1
- *Lantana camara* Z11 H12–1
- *Tecomaria capensis* Z12–15 H12–10

Heuchera sanguinea 'Splendens'
SPLENDENS CORAL BELLS
Ⓝ ☼ ☀ ◑ Z3–8 H8–1 ↕28in (70cm)
Clump-forming perennial with flowers carried in summer well above the kidney-shaped leaves. Prefers fertile organic soil. Can be grown as a groundcover.

Liatris spicata
DENSE GAYFEATHER
Ⓝ ☼ ◊ Z4–9 H9–5 ↕24in (60cm) ↔12in (30cm)
Long-lasting flowers bloom from late summer to early fall. Prefers light, moderately fertile, well-drained, organic soil. In cooler areas, mulch during winter.

Salvia guaranitica
ANISE SAGE
☼ ☀ ◊ ◑ Z7–10 H12–8 ↕5ft (1.5m) ↔24in (60cm)
Shrubby perennial with hairy, wrinkled, slightly aromatic leaves that is grown as an annual in the north of this region. The flowers appear in late summer.

Solidago 'Goldenmosa'
GOLDENMOSA GOLDENROD
☼ ◊ Z5–9 H9–5 ↕30in (75cm) ↔18in (45cm)
Blooms in late summer. Other cultivars vary in height and flowering time. Although considered a weed by some, goldenrods are excellent butterfly plants.

Perennials attractive to hummingbirds

Everyone's favorite birds, hummingbirds are easy to attract into the garden by growing plants that are rich in nectar. A supplemental feeder will keep them coming even when their favored plants are not in bloom. Despite everything you may have read, hummingbirds do not feed only on red flowers, as the plants shown here demonstrate.

Salvia guaranitica
ANISE SAGE
☼ ☀ ◊ ♦ Z7–10 H12–8 ↕5ft (1.5m) ↔24in (60cm)
This late-summer flowering, shrubby perennial is grown as an annual in the north of this region. Flowers are in long spikes above wrinkled foliage.

Salvia elegans
PINEAPPLE SCENTED SAGE
☀ ◊ ♦ Z8–11 H12–1 ↕4ft (1.2m) ↔3ft (1m)
An open-branched, woody perennial with foliage that smells of fresh pineapples when crushed. It flowers in late summer and may be evergreen in the South.

Lychnis coronaria 'Flore Pleno'
PERUVIAN LILY
☼ ☀ ◊ ♦ Z4–7 H7–1 ↕3ft (1m) ↔18in (45cm)
A branching plant with gray, woolly stems and leaves. Flowers in summer. It is fairly short-lived, but will leave behind a multitude of seedlings.

Monarda 'Cambridge Scarlet'
CAMBRIDGE SCARLET BEE BALM
Ⓝ ☼ ☀ ◊ Z4–8 H8–1 ↕3ft (1m) ↔24in (60cm)
Blooms from mid- to late summer. Best in a soil with high organic content. Divide every two or three years to keep clumps small and reduce risk of mildew.

Lobelia cardinalis
CARDINAL FLOWER
Ⓝ ☼ ♦ Z2–8 H8–1 ↕3ft (1m) ↔9in (23cm)
Flowers from summer to early autumn. Foliage is lance-shaped, bright green, and tinged with bronze. Best if grown in fertile, organic soil. Short-lived.

Aquilegia canadensis
CANADIAN COLUMBINE
Ⓝ ☼ ◐ 💧 Z3–8 H8–1 ↕3ft (1m) ↔12in (30cm)
A delicate-looking perennial with dark green leaves divided into leaflets. Prefers fertile soil, but too much fertility causes lanky growth. Often self-sows.

Phlox paniculata 'Norah Leigh'
NORAH LEIGH GARDEN PHLOX
☼ ◐ 💧 Z4–8 H8–1 ↕4ft (1.2m) ↔2ft (60cm)
Plant this where it will receive some shade during the middle of the day. An excellent choice for the middle to front of the border, where its foliage can be admired.

MORE CHOICES

- *Alstroemeria* spp. Z8–11 H12–7
- *Castilleja coccinea* Z6–9 H9–6
- *Cuphea micropetella* Z11–12 H12–1
- *Malvaviscus arboreus* Z14–15 H12–6
- *Monarda didyma* Z4–10 H10–1
- *Penstemon smallii* Z5–9 H9–1
- *Physostegia* spp. Z2–8 H8–4
- *Silene virginica* Z4–8 H9–3

Mertensia pulmonarioides
VIRGINIA BLUEBELLS
Ⓝ ◐ ◊ Z3–7 H7–1 ↕24in (60cm) ↔18in (45cm)
Flowers open from pink-tinted buds in mid- to late spring. Grow in well-drained, organic soil. Prone to problems but usually outgrows them.

Hedychium coronarium
WHITE GINGER LILY
☼ ◐ 💧 Z9–10 H12–7
↕6ft (2m) ↔3ft (1m)
The lance-shaped leaves are downy beneath. Highly fragrant, late-summer flowers open from a narrow spike and are 4in (10cm) across. Native to India.

Mirabilis jalapa
FOUR O'CLOCK, MARVEL OF PERU
☼ ◊ Z11–15 H12–9
↕24in (60cm) ↔30in (75cm)
Although grown as an annual, this bushy plant will form swollen storage roots reminiscent of dahlias. Keep soil on the dry side during winter.

Heuchera sanguinea 'Splendens'
CORAL BELLS
Ⓝ ☼ ◐ ◊ 💧 Z3–8 H8–1 ↕↔12in (30cm)
Clump-forming perennial with flowers carried in summer well above the kidney-shaped leaves. Prefers fertile organic soil. Can be grown as a groundcover.

Perennials for alkaline soils

In areas where the underlying rock is limestone, soils tend to be alkaline, and acid-loving perennials such as anemone (*Anemone* x *hybrida*) and bugbane (*Cimicifuga*) may not thrive. Given such conditions, there is still a wide variety of plants you can grow to give a colorful display throughout the year in sun or shade.

Gaura lindheimeri
WHITE GAURA
Ⓝ ☼ ♦ Z6–9 H9–6 ↕5ft (1.5m) ↔3ft (1m)
In a rich soil this is free-flowering, especially in the south of this region. It is very drought tolerant. In the north, it may be an annual but can self-seed.

Bergenia x *schmidtii*
SCHMIDT'S BERGENIA
☼ ◊ Z3–9 H9–1 ↕18–24in (45–60cm) ↔12in (30cm)
Excellent groundcover that spreads slowly by creeping rhizomes. Useful in front of a border. Flowers open in late winter or early spring.

Oenothera speciosa
SHOWY EVENING PRIMROSE
Ⓝ ☼ ◊ Z5–8 H8–1
↕↔12in (30cm)
If grown in a rich soil, the spreading roots make this plant invasive. It is less so in poor soils. The summer flowers turn pale pink as they age. There is also a form with light pink blooms.

Geranium 'Brookside'
BROOKSIDE CRANESBILL
Ⓝ ☼ ♦ Z3–9 H9–2 ↕5ft (1.5m) ↔18in (45cm)
A cultivar that blooms in midsummer and produces coiled pods that scatter seeds far and wide when they burst. Bees visit the flowers, and birds eat the seeds.

Helleborus orientalis
LENTEN ROSE
◐ ♦ Z4–8 H8–3 ↕↔to 18in (45cm)
Leathery, deep green overwintering leaves. Flowers, most often white or greenish cream aging to pink, bloom from midwinter to midspring.

Amsonia tabernaemontana
WILLOW BLUE-STAR
Ⓝ ☼ ◊ Z3–9 H9–1 ↕24in (60cm) ↔12in (30cm)
An erect, clump-forming perennial. Will grow in most soil types but prefers sandy soil. Cut plant back by one-third after it finishes flowering in spring.

MORE CHOICES

- *Cortaderia selloana* Z7–11 H12–7
- *Echinacea purpurea* Z3–9 H9–1
- *Euphorbia epithymoides* Z5–9 H9–5
- *Mirabilis jalapa* Z11–15 H12–9
- *Oenothera stricta* 'Sulphurea' Z5–8 H8–5
- *Phytolacca polyandra* Z5–9 H9–5
- *Solidago* spp. Z3–10 H9–6
- *Thalictrum aquilegifolium* Z5–9 H9–5
- *Veronicastrum virginicum* Z3–8 H8–1

Hemerocallis 'Lavender Tonic'
LAVENDER TONIC DAYLILY
☼ ◊ Z3–10 H12–2
↕23in (58cm) ↔18in (45cm)
A semi-evergreen, midseason bloomer with very pleated edges to the reflexed petals. Flowers open for almost a day.

Dianthus alpines 'Joan's Blood'
ALPINE PINK
☼ ◊ Z4–8 H8–1 ↕3in (8cm) ↔ to 4in (10cm)
Alpine pinks form a loose clump that eventually can cover a large area. It grows best in an alkaline soil. The scentless, early summer flowers almost hide the foliage.

Liatris spicata
CAT-TAIL GAYFEATHER
☼ ◑ ♦ Z5–8 H8–1 ↕↔2ft (60cm)
Long-lasting flowers bloom from late summer to early fall. Prefers light, moderately fertile, well-drained, organic soil. In cooler areas, mulch during winter.

Physostegia virginiana 'Vivid'
VIVID OBEDIENT PLANT
☼ ◊ Z4–8 H8–1 ↕12–24in (30–60cm) ↔12in (30cm)
Late summer bloom. Common name comes from the flowers that can be moved on the stem and stay there. Other pink-flowered varities are taller.

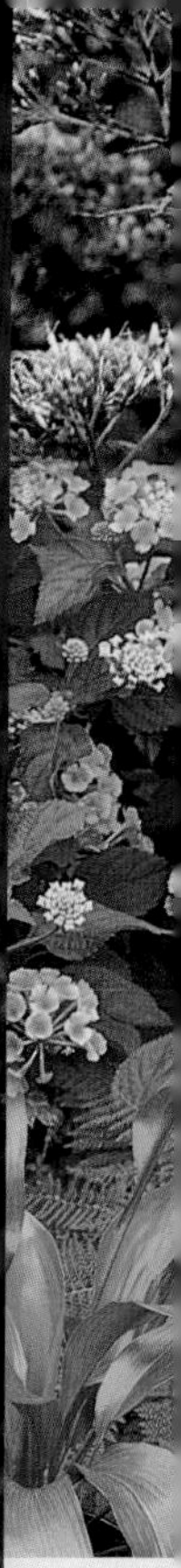

Perennials for acid soils

The soil in much of the Southeast is ideal for growing shrubs like rhododendrons and camellias. If these thrive in your area, it is an indication that the soil is acid and the perennials shown here will also grow well. This is also a good soil for many woodland plants like ferns and some shade-loving grasses.

Dicentra spectabilis 'Alba'
BLEEDING HEART
◑ ○ Z3–9 H9–1 ↕30in (75cm) ↔20in (50cm)
Flowers appear from late spring to early summer. Plants normally die back to the thick, fleshy roots in midsummer. Prefers fertile, organic soil.

Iris ensata 'Variegata'
VARIEGATED JAPANESE WATER IRIS
☼ ◑ ○ Z5–8 H8–4 ↕3ft (1m) ↔indefinite
Blooms in early summer. Leaves and stems are attractively white-striped. Prefers well-drained, fertile soil and dislikes high levels of nitrogen. Plant from midsummer to early fall.

MORE CHOICES

- *Erythronium americanum* Z3–9 H9–2
- *Keringeshoma palmate* Z5–8 H8–5
- *Mertensia pulmonarioides* Z3–7 H7–1
- *Osmunda regalis* Z2–10 H9–1
- *Polygonatum odoratum* Z3–8 H9–1
- *Tricyrtis formosana* Z6–9 H9–6

Viola cornuta
HORNED VIOLET
☼ ◑ ○ Z6–9 H9–1 ↕6in (15cm) ↔16in (40cm)
A vigorous plant often used as a groundcover. The slightly fragrant flowers open in spring but may be produced throughout the summer.

Trillium erectum
PURPLE TRILLIUM
Ⓝ ◑ ○ Z4–9 H7–3 ↕20in (50cm) ↔12in (30cm)
Outward-facing flowers appear in spring. Prefers acidic to neutral soil rich in organic matter. Mulch in fall with leaf mold.

Cimicifuga racemosa
BLACK BUGBANE, BLACK COHOSH
Ⓝ ◑ ● Z3–8 H12–1 ↕4–7ft (1.2–2.2m) ↔24in (60cm)
A clump-forming perennial that blooms in midsummer. Flowers are scented, but many people find them disagreeable. Prefers moist, fertile, organic soil.

Physostegia virginiana 'Miss Manners'
MISS MANNERS OBEDIENT PLANT
Z4–8 H8–1 ↕3ft (1m) ↔24in (60cm)
A new variety that is very free-flowering in late summer. It spreads slowly and will need dividing every few years to keep it under control.

Amsonia tabernaemontana
WILLOW BLUE-STAR
Z3–9 H9–1 ↕18–24in (45–60cm) ↔12in (30cm)
An erect, clump-forming perennial. Will grow in most soil types but prefers sandy soil. Cut plant back by one-third after it finishes flowering in spring.

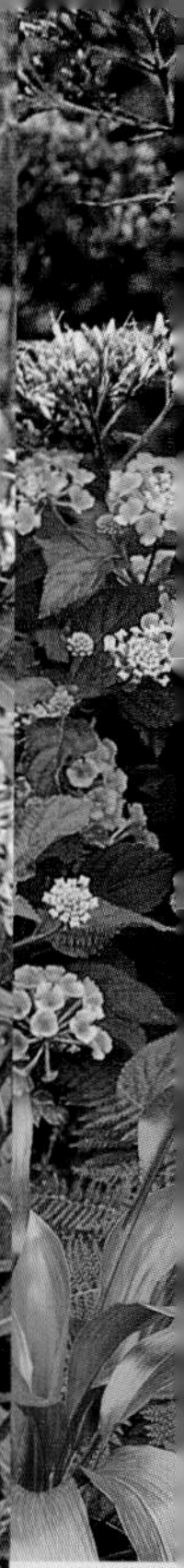

Phlox divaricata subsp. *laphamii*
MAUVE WOODLAND PHLOX
Z4–8 H8–1 ↕12in (30cm) ↔8in (20cm)
This form of the common woodland or blue phlox has much pinker flowers. It forms a creeping mat and makes an attractive groundcover with spring bulbs.

Lobelia cardinalis
CARDINAL FLOWER
Z2–8 H8–1 ↕3ft (1m) ↔9in (23cm)
Flowers from summer to early autumn. Foliage is lance-shaped, bright green, and tinged with bronze. Best if grown in fertile organic soil. Short-lived.

Podophyllum peltatum
MAYAPPLE
Z3–9 H8–2
↕18in (45cm) ↔12in (30cm)
A good groundcover with solitary flowers in spring, partly hidden in the fork of twin leaves. This plant grows best in a deep woodsy soil with high organic content.

Perennials for clay soils

Clay soils present special problems to both the gardener and plants. Because they are composed of very fine particles, water is very slow to drain through, which greatly reduces the amount of air in the soil. Only plants such as these, that are adapted to the low levels of oxygen available at root level, can survive in heavy clay.

Aster novae-angliae 'Andenken an Alma Pötschke'
ALMA PÖTSCHKE NEW ENGLAND ASTER
☼ ☀ ◆ Z4–8 H8–1 ↕4ft (1.2m) ↔24in (60cm)
One on the mainstays of the fall border, the varieties of this aster come in a range of heights and colors. Tall varieties should be staked to fully enjoy them.

Hemerocallis fulva
COMMON DAYLILY, TIGER LILY
☼ ◆ Z3–9 H12–1 ↕3ft (1m) ↔4ft (1.2m)
The single- and double-flowered forms of this are very common. They thrive on neglect and grow almost anywhere. Flowers in midsummer.

Helianthus salicifolius
WILLOW-LEAVED SUNFLOWER
Ⓝ ☼ ◇ Z6–9 H9–6 ↕8ft (2.5m) ↔36in (90cm)
The upright stems have narrow leaves up to 8in (20cm) long. The flowers open in late summer and are so numerous they bow the plant unless it is staked.

Asclepias tuberosa
BUTTERFLY WEED
Ⓝ ☼ ◇ Z4–9 H9–2 ↕30in (75cm) ↔18in (45cm)
Blooms in midsummer. Prefers fertile, well-drained, loamy soil. Susceptible to aphids and mealybugs when in bloom.

MORE CHOICES

- *Achillea millefolium* Z4–9 H9–2
- *Artemisia* spp. Z5–11 H12–1
- *Aruncus dioiscus* Z3–7 H7–1
- *Aspidistra elatior* Z7–11 H12–4
- *Iris germanica* Z3–9 H9–1
- *Liatris* spp. Z3–9 H9–2
- *Prunella vulgaris* Z5–8 H8–5
- *Silphium terebinthinaceum* Z3–9 H9–1

Aster x *frikartii*
MICHAELMAS DAISY, FRIKART'S ASTER
☼ ◇ Z4–8 H8–1 ↕28in (70cm) ↔18in (45cm)
Flowers from late summer to early fall. This hybrid of *A. amellus* and *A. thomsonii* prefers moderately fertile soil. Susceptible to *Verticillium* wilt and other diseases.

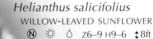

Vernonia noveboracensis
IRONWEED
Ⓝ Z4–8 H8–3 ↕6ft (2m) ↔24in (60cm)
An upright, branching plant with toothed leaves. Blooms from late summer into fall. The common name comes from the rusty color of the old flowers.

Achillea millefolium 'Paprika'
PAPRIKA YARROW
Ⓝ Z3–9 H8–2 ↕↔24in (60cm)
Blooms from early to late summer. Seedheads persist through the winter if not cut back, but yarrows tend to self-sow, producing possibly unwanted "volunteers."

Rudbeckia fulgida var. *sullivantii* 'Goldsturm'
GOLDSTURM BLACK-EYED SUSAN
Ⓝ Z4–9 H9–1
↕2ft (60cm) ↔18in (45cm)
Front-of-the-border plant that flowers freely on much-branched stems in late summer. Drought-tolerant.

Eupatorium purpureum
PURPLE JOE PYE WEED
Ⓝ Z3–9 H9–1 ↕7ft (2.2m) ↔3ft (1m)
Blooms from midsummer to early autumn. Leaves smell like vanilla when bruised. Prone to rust, powdery mildew, white smut, and leaf spots.

Drought-tolerant perennials

These are plants that thrive in full sun and on well-drained soils. Some of these will make good groundcovers for a sandy bank while others can be used to soften the edges of gravel paths or between dry-stone paving. Because of their dry habitat, growth is very rarely lush and even tall plants seldom need staking.

Gaura lindheimeri 'Siskiyou Pink'
SISKIYOU PINK GAURA
Ⓝ ☼ ◊ Z6–9 H9–6 ↕3–4ft (1–1.3m) ↔3ft (1m)
A good perennial for the south of this region that may be a self-seeding annual in the north. It is very free-flowering over a long period.

Rudbeckia fulgida var. *sullivantii* 'Goldsturm'
GOLDSTURM BLACK EYED SUSAN
Ⓝ ☼ ◑ ◊ Z4–9 H9–1 ↕2ft (60cm) ↔18in (45cm)
Front-of-the-border plant that flowers freely on much-branched stems in late summer. The seed heads are very attractive to birds, especially finches.

Verbena bonariensis
BRAZILIAN VERBENA
☼ ◊ Z7–11 H12–7 ↕6ft (2m) ↔18in (45cm)
Dainty, upright stems grow from a cluster of basal leaves. Makes an excellent accent plant when grown singly. Probably a self-seeding annual in the North.

Artemisia ludoviciana 'Silver King'
CUDWEED, WHITE SAGE
Ⓝ ☼ ◊ Z5–9 H12–8 ↕4ft (1.2m) ↔24in (60m)
A clump-forming perennial with foliage that turns red in fall. Flower heads are borne from midsummer to autumn. Best in well-drained, low-fertility soil.

Helianthus 'Lemon Queen'
LEMON QUEEN SUNFLOWER
☼ ◊◐ Z5–9 H9–5 ↕5.5ft (1.7m) ↔4ft (1.2m)
Good background plants for late summer flowers. Pinch the tips out of new growth in spring to encourage branching. May need some support if not grown in full sun.

Stokesia laevis
STOKES' ASTER
Ⓝ ☼ ◐ pH Z5–9 H9–5
↕24in (60cm) ↔18in (45cm)
Flowers appear from midsummer to early fall above the rosettes of oval-shaped to lance-shaped, evergreen leaves. Prefers light, fertile soil.

Salvia greggii 'Dark Dancer'
DARK DANCER AUTUMN SAGE
Ⓝ ☼ ◊ Z7–10 H9–7 ↕↔12–20in (30–50cm)
Woody-based perennial, evergreen in the South, with hairy stems. Flowers are borne in pairs and open in late summer. Pink- and white-flowered varieties.

Lychnis coronaria
ROSE CAMPION
☼ ◐ ◊ Z4–8 H8–1 ↕32in (80cm) ↔18in (45cm)
A branching plant with gray, woolly stems and leaves. Flowers in summer. It is fairly short-lived, but will leave behind a multitude of seedlings that are easy to remove while small.

Solidago 'Golden Wings'
GOLDEN WINGS GOLDENROD
☼ ◊ Z5–9 H9–5 ↕6ft (1.8m)
↔36in (90cm)
Blooms in late summer. Cultivars vary in height and flowering time. Although considered a weed by some, goldenrods are good butterfly plants.

MORE CHOICES

- *Aster oblongifolia* Z4–8 H8–1
- *Baptisia australis* Z3-9 H9-1
- *Coreopsis verticillata* Z4-9 H9-1
- *Echinacea* spp. Z3–9 H12–1
- *Echinops ritro* Z3-9 H12-1
- *Eryngium bourgatii* Z5-9 H9-5
- *Hemerocallis* cvs. Z3–10 H12–2
- *Iris* cvs. Z4–8 H8–1
- *Knautia macedonica* Z5-9 H9-5
- *Lantana* spp. Z9–15 H12–1
- *Sedum* spp. Z6–9 H9–6
- *Setcreasea pallida* Z11 H12–10
- *Verbascum* spp. Z5–9 H9–2
- *Verbena rigida* Z8–15 H12–1

Oenothera speciosa
SHOWY EVENING PRIMROSE
Ⓝ ☼ ◊ Z5–8 H8–1 ↕↔12in (30cm)
If grown in a rich soil, the spreading roots make this plant invasive. It is less so in poor soils. The summer flowers turn pale pink as they age.

Perennials for moist soils

In our typically wet winter, spring, and "hurricane season," water often puddles around plants far longer than most can tolerate, especially in heavy or unimproved clay soils. Use these perennials in low areas where water stands more than two or three hours after a hard rain, under building eaves, and beside ponds and splashy water gardens.

Aruncus dioicus
GOATSBEARD
Ⓝ ☼ ◊ Z3–7 H7–1 ↕6ft (2m) ↔4ft (1.2m)
Blooms from early to midsummer and makes good cut flowers. Fernlike, alternately pinnate, midgreen leaves can grow 3ft (1m) long. Best grown in fertile soil.

Monarda didyma
BEE BALM, SWEET BERGAMOT
Ⓝ ☼ ◐ ◑ ● Z4–10 H10–1
↕3ft (1m) ↔24in (60cm)
Summer-blooming wildflower favored by butterflies that spreads by runners. Powdery mildew may be a problem. Also tolerates dry soils.

Arisaema triphyllum
JACK-IN-THE-PULPIT
Ⓝ ◐ ◑ Z4–9 H9–1
↕24in (60cm) ↔6in (15cm)
A tuberous plant that increases slowly and needs a woodland-type soil. Once the spring flowers have faded, clusters of green fruit enlarge and turn bright red by fall.

Helianthus angustifolius
SWAMP SUNFLOWER
Ⓝ ☼ ◑ Z6–9 H9–4 ↕6ft (1.8m) ↔4ft (1.2m)
One of the best fall-blooming sunflowers for the south, they need plenty of moisture and feeding. Grows taller than shown in part-shade and needs staking.

Aster novae-angliae 'Barr's Pink'
BARR'S PINK NEW ENGLAND ASTER
Ⓝ ☼ ☀ ◑ Z4–8 H8–1 ↕54in (1.3m) ↔24in (60cm)
This is just one of a large number of named forms of this species. They are excellent garden plants with an upright habit, and add color to the border in fall.

MORE CHOICES

- *Angelica atropurpurea* Z4–9 H9–1
- *Asarum* spp. Z4–9 H9–3
- *Astrantia major* Z4–7 H7–1
- *Brunnera macrophylla* Z3–7 H7–1
- *Caltha palaustris* Z3–7 H7–1
- *Cleome glabra* Z3–8 H9–1
- *Eupatorium maculatum* Z5–11 H9–1
- *Galium odoratum* Z5–8 H8–5
- *Hibiscus coccineus* Z6–15 H12–1
- *Iris versicolor* Z3–9 H9–1
- *Lobelia siphilitica* Z4–8 H8–1
- *Lysimachia punctata* Z4–8 H8–1
- *Physostegia virginiana* Z4–8 H8–1
- *Primula denticulata* Z2–8 H8–1
- *Smilacina racemosa* Z4–9 H9–1
- *Tradescantia* spp. Z3–10 H12–1
- *Zantedeschia aethiopica* Z8–10 H10–8

Lobelia cardinalis
CARDINAL FLOWER
Ⓝ ☼ ◑ Z2–8 H8–1 ↕3ft (1m) ↔9in (23cm)
Brilliantly colored flowers in late summer. May be short-lived but self-seeds. Excellent cut flowers. Attracts hummingbirds. Foliage is bronze-tinged.

Filipendula rubra
QUEEN OF THE PRAIRIE
Ⓝ ☀ ● Z3–9 H9–1
↕6–8ft (2–2.5m) ↔4ft (1.2m)
Large, fernlike foliage topped in summer with tall plumes. Use in borders, naturalistic settings, and along ponds, or in low areas of perennial borders.

Asclepias incarnata
SWAMP MILKWEED
Ⓝ ☼ ◑ Z3–8 H8–1 ↕4ft (1.2m) ↔24in (60cm)
Showy flowers from midsummer to early fall become attractive, pointed seed pods. Foliage is food for butterflies. Susceptible to aphids, especially in bloom.

Iris pseudacorus
YELLOW FLAG
☼ ● Z5–8 H8–3 ↕6ft (2m) ↔indefinite
Flowers early in spring. Foliage is evergreen or nearly so, and adds an important linear effect in garden. Can become invasive in natural areas.

Salt-tolerant perennials

Given the long coastline of this region, it is not surprising that salt-tolerance is a concern. Even in summer, winds off the sea can leave a fine deposit of salt on leaves and stems. The seashore is the native habitat for some of the plants shown, but most are inland plants that just happen to be able to withstand high salt concentrations.

Gaillardia x *grandiflora* 'Lollipop'
BLANKET FLOWER
☼ ◊ Z10–11 H12–1 ↕2ft (60cm) ↔18in (45cm)
A sometimes short-lived perennial that can be raised from seed. Several named forms have single or double flowers in shades of yellow and red.

Artemisia vulgaris
COMMON WORMWOOD
Ⓝ ☼ ◊ Z4–8 H8–1 ↕↔2–3ft (60–90cm)
The gray foliage makes a useful foil against brightly colored plants, especially to separate two strong colors. Varying heights, with similar foliage.

Achillea filipendulina 'Gold Plate'
GOLD PLATE YARROW
☼ ◊◊ Z3–9 H9–1 ↕4ft (1.2m) ↔2ft (60cm)
A stiff, well-branched, upright hybrid. Flowering begins in early summer and continues for many weeks. Dries well, keeping its color.

Nepeta catarica
CATNIP
☼ ☀ ◊ Z3–7 H7–1 ↕to 36in (90cm) ↔18in (45cm)
Purple-spotted white flowers appear in summer and fall above woolly aromatic foliage. Grows well in most soils. Neighborhood cats may flatten your plants.

Asclepias tuberosa
BUTTERFLY WEED
Ⓝ ☼ ◊ Z4–9 H9–2 ↕30in (75cm) ↔18in (45cm)
Blooms in midsummer. Prefers fertile, well-drained, loamy soil. Susceptible to aphids, mealybugs, rust, and bacterial and fungal leaf spots.

Stachys byzantina
LAMB'S EARS, WOOLY BETONY
☼ ◊ Z4–8 H8–1 ↕18in (45cm) ↔24in (60cm)
An excellent edging plant that makes a good foil for brighter flowers. Flowers detract from the foliage; the flowerless variety 'Silver Carpet' may be preferable.

Plumbago auriculata 'Alba'
WHITE CAPE LEADWORT
☼ ◊ Z12–15 H12–10 ↕20ft (6m) ↔10ft (3m)
Sprawling, somewhat woody plant with sticky flowers, sky-blue in species. Commonly grown as a houseplant where not hardy. May be sold as *P. capensis*.

MORE CHOICES

- *Agapanthus africanus* Z7–10 H12–1
- *Coreopsis verticillata* Z4–9 H9–1
- *Cortadera selloana* Z7–11 H12–7
- *Crinum* spp. Z7–10 H10–7
- *Eryngium alpinum* Z6–9 H9–6
- *Hemerocallis* cvs. Z3–10 H12–2
- *Hibiscus moscheutos* Z5–10 H12–1
- *Oenothera speciosa* Z5–8 H8–1
- *Tulbaghia violacea* Z7–10 H10–7
- *Uniola paniculata* Z8–10 H10–8
- *Verbena rigida* Z8–15 H12–1

Senecio cineraria
DUSTY MILLER
☼ ◊ Z8–11 H12–1 ↕↔to 24in (60cm)
Commonly used as an edging plant, this is grown for its foliage, flowers are best removed. It is treated as an annual where not hardy and raised from seed.

Santolina chamaecyparissus
LAVENDER COTTON
☼ ◊ Z6–9 H9–4 ↕20in (50cm) ↔3ft (1m)
Spreading evergreen mound bears summer flowers, best removed after they fade. Use in a mass planting, in rock gardens, or as a low hedge. Salt-tolerant.

Lantana camara 'Snow White'
SNOW WHITE SHRUB VERBENA
☼ ◊ Z9–15 H12–1 ↕↔3–6ft (1–2m)
A prickly-stemmed shrubby plant with strongly scented leaves. Other named forms in shades of salmon, yellow, orange, red, or two-toned flowers.

Low-maintenance perennials

Some plants are so attractive that we grow them even though they need a lot of work, like frequent staking and tying, or being divided and replanted often to keep them vigorous. The plants on these two pages are not like that. Once planted, they will take care of themselves and reappear each year better than ever.

Kniphofia 'Strawberries & Cream'
STRAWBERRIES AND CREAM RED-HOT POKER
Z6–9 H9–4 ↕24in (60cm) ↔12in (30cm)
This is one of the many named forms of red-hot poker. It flowers in early summer. After flowers fade, the spikes should be cut off to prevent seed formation.

Saponaria officinalis
BOUNCING BET
Z3–9 H9–1 ↕24in (60cm) ↔20in (50cm)
Spreads rapidly by underground runners but flowers over a long period from summer to fall. 'Dazzler' has pink flowers, variegated leaves, and is less invasive.

Begonia grandis
HARDY BEGONIA
Z6–9 H9–5 ↕3ft (1m) ↔4ft (1.2m)
A bulbous begonia that needs a slightly acidic soil rich in organic matter. Where not hardy, lift in fall after frost has killed stems and overwinter in a frost-free place

MORE CHOICES

- *Amsonia tabernaemontana* Z3–9 H9–1
- *Artemisia ludoviciana* Z4–9 H9–1
- *Aster x frikartii* Z4–8 H8–1
- *Chrysanthemum leucanthemum* Z6–9 H9–6
- *Chrysanthemum maximum* Z5–8 H8–5
- *Coreopsis lanceolata* Z4–9 H9–1
- *Echinacea purpurea* Z3–9 H9–1
- *Gaillardia spp.* Z3–8 H8–1

Liatris spicata
DENSE GAYFEATHER
Ⓝ Z4–9 H9–5 ↕24in (60cm) ↔12in (30cm)
Long-lasting flowers bloom from late summer to early fall. Prefers light, moderately fertile, well-drained, organic soil. In cooler areas, mulch during winter.

Hemerocallis flava
LEMON LILY
Z3–10 H12–2 ↕↔3ft (1m)
One of the first daylilies to flower and one parent of many hybrids. The lemon-scented flowers open over a long period, although each only lasts a day.

Achillea millefolium
YARROW
Ⓝ Z3–9 H9–1 ↕↔24in (60cm)
Blooms from early to late summer. Tolerates a wide range of soil conditions. Self-sows, so deadhead after blooming if you don't want volunteers popping up.

Phlox divaricata 'Fuller's White'
FULLER'S WHITE PHLOX
Ⓝ Z4–8 H8–1 ↕8in (20cm) ↔20in (50cm)
Free-flowering variety that covers itself with blooms in spring. Spreads slowly and makes a good groundcover. Shear off old flower stems after blooming.

MORE CHOICES

- *Hosta sp.* Z3–9 H9–2
- *Iris germanica* Z3–9 H9–1
- *Iris pseudacorus* Z5–8 H8–3
- *Kniphofia uvaria* Z6–9 H9–1
- *Lobelia cardinalis* Z2–8 H8–1
- *Paeonia* hybrids Z3–8 H8–1
- *Perovskia atriplicifolia* Z4–9 H9–4

Iris sibirica 'Illini Charm'
ILLINI CHARM SIBERIAN IRIS
Z3–9 H9–1 ↕24in (60cm) ↔12in (30cm)
These flower later than the tall bearded iris and don't have the prominent beard. They are adaptable and can grow in dry or wet soils.

Physostegia virginiana 'Vivid'
VIVID OBEDIENT PLANT
Ⓝ Z4–8 H8–1
↕12-24in (30-60cm) ↔12in (30cm)
A useful plant for late summer bloom. Other, pink-flowered varieties are taller.

Perennials for rock gardens

Rock gardening is a very intensive and addictive form of gardening. It is ideal for the avid gardener who has limited space, enabling a wide variety of interesting and sometimes challenging plants to be grown in a small area. The number of possible plants is enormous, and there are national and local rock garden societies able to give advice (see p. 385).

Gentiana acaulis
TRUMPET GENTIAN
Z5–8 H8–5 ↕3in (8cm) ↔12in (30cm)
Sometimes difficult species that needs an alkaline soil. Once established, it forms a low mat with many solitary flowers in spring. Native to the Alps.

Geranium cinereum 'Ballerina'
BALLERINA CRANESBILL
Z4–9 H9–3 ↕4in (10cm) ↔12in (30cm)
Flowers from late spring to early summer. This cultivar has grayer leaves than the species. Excellent in a rock or alpine garden, it also grows well in a container.

Ceratostigma plumbaginoides
LEADWORT, PLUMBAGO
Z6–9 H9–6 ↕18in (45cm) ↔12 in (30cm)
Flowers in late summer. A rhizomatous, spreading, woody-based perennial. Prefers moderately fertile soil. Prune in early to midspring.

MORE CHOICES

- *Campanula poscharskyana* Z3–9 H9–1
- *Coreopsis auriculata* 'Nana' Z4–9 H9–1
- *Heuchera* spp. Z4–8 H8–1
- *Iberis sempervirens* Z5–9 H9–3
- *Lysimachia nummularia* 'Aurea' Z4–8 H8–1
- *Nepeta* spp. Z3–9 H12–2
- *Ophiopogon planiscapus* 'Nigrescens' Z6–11 H12–1
- *Oxalis adenophylla* Z6–8 H8–6
- *Veronica spicata* Z3–8 H8–1

Phlox subulata 'Candy Stripes'
CANDY STRIPE MOSS PHLOX
Z3–8 H8–1
↕2–6in (5–15cm) ↔20in (50cm)
Flowers from late spring to early summer and sometimes again in fall. Evergreen. Prefers fertile soil.

0Dianthus deltoides
MAIDEN PINK
☼ ◊ Z3–10 H10–1 ↕to 8in (20cm) ↔12in (30cm)
Scentless flowers borne in summer. Flower colors can range from white to deep pink and red. A mat-forming plant that makes a good groundcover. Self-sows.

Arabis ferdinandi-coburgi 'Variegata'
VARIEGATED ROCK CRESS
☼ ☀ ◊◆ Z5–8 H8–3 ↕↔3–4in (7.5–19cm)
Flowers are borne from spring to early summer. This mat-forming perennial is good in rock gardens and as a groundcover. Also called *A. procurrens* 'Variegata'.

Sedum kamtschaticum
ORANGE STONECROP
☼ ◊ Z3–8 H8–1 ↕3in (8cm) ↔8in (20cm)
Late summer-blooming clump-former, good at the front of a bed or in a rock garden. Cut back after flow-ering to keep compact. Prefers moderately fertile soil.

Dianthus gratianopolitanus 'Bath's Pink'
BATH'S CHEDDAR PINK
☼ ◊ Z3–9 H9–1 ↕8–12in (20–30cm) ↔18–24in (45–60cm)
One of many named forms of pink, this has sweetly scented flowers from spring to early summer. Flowering is prolonged if plants do not seed.

Sempervivum tectorum 'Pacific Hawk'
PACIFIC HAWK HOUSELEEK
☼ ◊ Z4–9 H8–1 ↕6in (15cm) ↔20in (50cm)
There are several hundred named varieties of houseleek that differ in size, color, and leaf shape. The individual rosettes die after flowering, but make offsets first.

Armeria maritima
SEA PINK
Ⓝ ☼ ◊ Z3–9 H9–1 ↕4in (10cm) ↔6in (15cm)
Flowers from late spring to summer. Prefers marginally to moderately fertile soil and will tolerate almost pure sand. Divide every 4 to 5 years as center dies out.

Sun-loving perennials

These are plants that thrive in full sun and will not grow properly in even part shade. Many will thrive in well-drained locations, or even gravelly soils, and these rarely grow very lush and seldom need staking. A few are better suited to wetter conditions and will not survive prolonged drought although short periods of dryness are not detrimental.

Boltonia asteroides 'Snowbank'
SNOWBANK BOLTONIA
Ⓝ Z4–9 H9–1 ↕5ft (1.5m) ↔3ft (1m)
Strong-stemmed plant with blue-green leaves and flowers from late summer to early fall in white, lilac, or pinkish purple. Divide every few years.

Monarda didyma 'Marshall's Delight'
MARSHALL'S DELIGHT BEE BALM
Z4–8 H8–1 ↕3ft (1m) ↔24in (60cm)
Blooms from mid- to late summer. Prefers moderately fertile, organic, well-drained soil. Highly resistant to powdery mildew. Susceptible to leaf spots and rust.

Coreopsis verticillata 'Zagreb'
ZAGREB THREAD-LEAVED TICKSEED
Z4–9 H9–1 ↕↔12in (30cm)
If the first flush of flowers in summer is trimmed off, this variety will bloom again in early fall. It forms an attractive mound with threadlike foliage.

MORE CHOICES

- *Achillea x* 'Coronation Gold' Z3–9 H9–1
- *Artemisia* spp. Z5–11 H12–1
- *Baptisia australis* Z3–9 H9–1
- *Campanula persicifolia* Z3–8 H8–1
- *Dictamnus albus* Z3–8 H8–1
- *Echinacea* spp. Z3–9 H12–1
- *Erigeron speciosus* Z2–8 H8–1
- *Foeniculum vulgare* Z6–9 H9–6
- *Hibiscus moscheutos* Z5–10 H12–1
- *Iris* cvs. Z4–8 H8–1
- *Phlox paniculata* Z4–8 H8–1
- *Rudbeckia laciniata* Z3–9 H9–1
- *Salvia* spp. Z4–10 H12–1
- *Solidago* cvs. Z3–10 H9–6
- *Stachys byzantina* Z4–8 H8–1
- *Stokesia laevis* Z5–9 H9–5
- *Verbena canadensis* Z7–11 H12–1

Solidago 'Goldenmosa'
GOLDENMOSA GOLDENROD
Z5–9 H9–5 ↕30in (75cm) ↔18in (45cm)
Blooms in late summer. Other cultivars vary in height and flowering time. Although considered a weed by some, goldenrods are excellent butterfly plants.

Helianthus 'Lemon Queen'
LEMON QUEEN SUNFLOWER
☼ ◊ ◑ Z5–9 H9–5 ↕to 5.5ft (1.7m) ↔4ft (1.2m)
Good background plant for late summer flowers. Pinch the tips out of new growth in spring to encourage branching. May need some support if not grown in full sun.

Leucanthemum vulgare
OX-EYE DAISY
☼ ◐ ◊ ◑ Z3–8 H8–1
↕12–36in (30–90cm) ↔24in (60cm)
A European native that has naturalized itself in North America. It forms a slow-spreading clump that flowers freely in late spring and early summer. Deadhead to prevent seeding.

Platycodon grandiflorus 'Sentimental Blue'
SENTIMENTAL BLUE BALLOON FLOWER
☼ ◐ ◊ ◑ Z7–9 H9–1 ↕18–36in (45–90cm) ↔18–24in (45–60cm)
Late to start growing in spring so do not damage when cultivating. Does best in light shade in the South. An excellent cut-flower, this can be raised from seed.

Hemerocallis 'Red Rum'
RED RUM DAYLILY
☼ ◊ ◑ Z4–11 H12–1
↕16in (40cm)
Most daylilies are summer bloomers, providing color for a few to several weeks. As their name suggests, each flower lives only a single day.

HERBACEOUS PLANTS

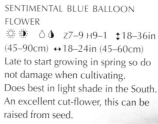

Penstemon digitalis 'Husker Red'
HUSKER RED PENSTEMON
Ⓝ ☼ ◐ ◊ Z3–8 H8–1
↕30in (75cm) ↔12in (30cm)
Flowers appear from early to late summer. Tolerant of high humidity. Grow in moderately fertile to marginally fertile soil. Prone to foliage diseases and slugs and snails.

Filipendula rubra
QUEEN OF THE PRAIRIE
Ⓝ ◐ ♦ Z3–9 H9–1
↕6–8ft (2–2.5m) ↔4ft (1.2m)
Fragrant flowers in midsummer. A spreading plant, it forms large clumps of irregularly cut, pinnate leaves. Prefers moderately fertile, leafy soil.

Shade-loving perennials

These are plants that will grow well in a regular garden bed that is shaded during the hottest part of the day. They will take early morning or late afternoon sun, but their foliage may scorch badly if exposed to full, strong hot sunlight. Other than this, they need no special care and should be treated like most perennials.

Phlox divaricata 'Dirigo Ice'
DIRIGO ICE BLUE PHLOX
Z4–8 H8–1
↕8–12in (20–30cm) ↔20in (50cm)
Spreads slowly and makes a good groundcover with blooms for several weeks in spring.

Trillium grandiflorum
WAKE ROBIN
Ⓝ Z4–7 H7–3 ↕18in (45cm) ↔12in (30cm)
Flowers bloom in midspring and often turn pink as they age. Prefers acidic to neutral soil rich in organic matter. Mulch in fall with leaf mold.

Spigelia marilandica
INDIAN PINK
Ⓝ Z5–9 H9–2 ↕24in (60cm) ↔18in (45cm)
The flowers appear above dark green paired leaves in early summer. Plant this in large clumps to gain the best effect. Native to this region.

Iris cristata
DWARF CRESTED IRIS
Ⓝ Z4–10 H10–1 ↕4in (10cm) ↔indefinite
Grows from a shallow rhizome that creeps on the surface and spreads fairly rapidly. Blooms in spring. There is a white-flowered form, plus other color variants.

MORE CHOICES

- *Alstroemeria pulchella* Z8–11 H12–7
- *Amsonia* spp. Z3–9 H8–4
- *Aquilegia canadensis* Z3–8 H8–1
- *Arisaema triphyllum* Z4–9 H9–1
- *Asarum shuttleworthii* Z5–9 H9–1
- *Bergenia* hybrids Z4–8 H8–1
- *Chelone lyonii* Z3–9 H9–3
- *Chrysogonum virginianum* Z5–9 H9–2
- *Epimedium* x *youngianum* Z5–9 H9–5
- *Geranium maculatum* Z4–8 H8–1
- *Helleborus orientalis* Z4–8 H8–3
- *Heuchera sanguinea* Z3–8 H8–1
- *Lobelia siphilitica* Z4–8 H8–1
- *Mertensia pulmonarioides* Z3–7 H7–1
- *Primula denticulata* Z2–8 H8–1
- *Rheum palmatum* Z5–9 H9–1
- *Rhodea japonica* Z7–9 H9–7
- *Sanguinaria canadensis* Z3–9 H8–1
- *Silene* spp. Z4–8 H9–3
- *Tradescantia virginica* Z5–9 H9–5
- *Viola odorata* Z6–8 H8–6

Hosta sieboldiana var. *elegans*
ELEGANT SIEBOLD'S HOSTA
Z3–9 H9–1 ↕3ft (1m) ↔4ft (1.2m)
Possibly the very first hosta exported from Japan, this is the parent of many hybrids. The puckered leaves and elegant flower spikes are loved by flower arrangers.

Tiarella cordifolia
FOAMFLOWER
Z3–8 H7–1 ↕8in (20cm) ↔12in (30cm)
A gently spreading plant that makes an excellent groundcover and flowers in late spring. T. wherryi is similar with maroon-tinted leaves and pinkish flowers.

Astilbe x *arendsii* 'Fanal'
FANAL ASTILBE
Z3–9 H9–1 ↕24in (60cm) ↔18in (45cm)
Flowers appear in midsummer above very dark green, pinnate foliage. Prefers organic rich soil. Divide every 4 years to maintain bloom quality.

Polygonatum odoratum 'Variegatum'
VARIEGATED FRAGRANT SOLOMON'S SEAL
Z4–8 H8–1
↕34in (85cm) ↔12in (30cm)
Creeping perennial that slowly forms a large clump. The arching stems have single or paired, pendulous greenish flowers on the underside in late spring.

Dicentra spectabilis 'Alba'
WHITE BLEEDING HEART
Z3–9 H9–1 ↕4ft (1.2m) ↔18in (45cm)
Flowers appear from late spring to early summer. Plants normally die back to the thick fleshy roots in midsummer. Prefers fertile organic soil.

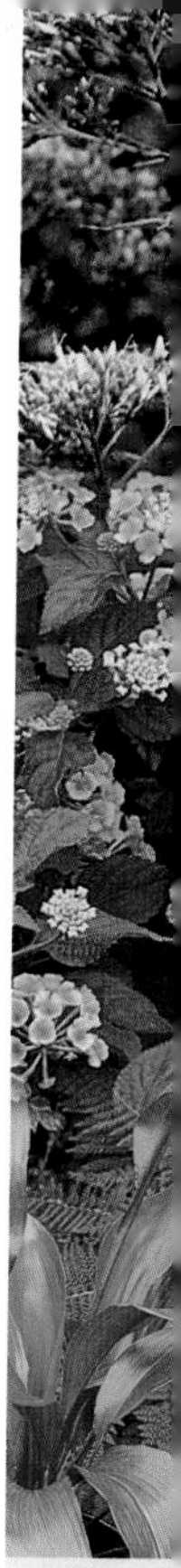

Spring-flowering perennials

Since they grow from ground level each spring, most perennials are summer- to fall-flowering. The ones here either initiate their flower buds the previous fall (evergreens), or grow and bloom rapidly when warm weather comes. They add early color to the garden when combined with spring-flowering bulbs, and compliment trees and shrubs when planted beneath them.

Epimedium x *versicolor* 'Sulphureum'
YELLOW BARRENWORT
◐ ◊ ◆ Z5–8 H8–5 ↕12in (30cm) ↔3ft (1m)
Other cultivars of this hybrid cross have pink to copper-red flowers. Prefers fertile, organic, well-drained soil. Susceptible to vine weevil and mosaic virus.

Dicentra spectabilis
BLEEDING HEART
◐ ◊ Z3–9 H9–1 ↕30in (75cm) ↔20in (50cm)
A very showy plant when in flower. Foliage lasts all summer in cooler climates and moist soil, but dies down soon after flowering in hotter regions or drier soil.

Iris pumila 'Dwarf Blue'
DWARF BLUE IRIS
☼ ◊ Z3–9 H9–1 ↕6in (15cm) ↔3ft (30cm)
One of many forms of dwarf bearded iris, which range in height from 4–18in (10–45cm) and come in almost every color. Divide every few years in late summer when the clumps no longer bloom freely.

Astilbe x arendsii 'Fanal'
FANAL ASTILBE
☼ ◐ ◆ Z3–9 H9–1
↕24in (60cm) ↔18in (45cm)
Flowers appear in midsummer above very dark green, pinnate foliage. Prefers organic rich soil. Divide every four years to maintain bloom quality.

Aquilegia canadensis
CANADIAN COLUMBINE
Ⓝ ☼ ◐ ◆ Z3–8 H8–1
↕3ft (1m) ↔12in (30cm)
A delicate-looking perennial with dark green leaves divided into leaflets. Prefers fertile soil, but too much fertility causes lanky growth. Often self-sows.

Oenothera fruticosa 'Fyrverkeri'
FIREWORKS SUNDROPS
Ⓝ ☼ 💧 Z4–8 H8–1
↕3ft (1m) ↔12in (30cm)
This differs from the species by having red-tinged stems, larger flowers, and less height. A good border plant with leaves that turn red in fall.

Phlox divaricata
WOODLAND PHLOX
Ⓝ ☀ 💧 Z4–8 H8–1
↕12in (30cm) ↔8in (20cm)
A slowly spreading, low plant with creeping stems. Spring flowers are on upright stems that rise above the mats. Cultivars have flowers in white, pale blue, and purple.

Euphorbia myrsinites
MYRTLE SPURGE
☼ 💧 Z5–8 H8–5 ↕4in (10cm)
↔12in (30cm)
The spirally arranged, blue-green leaves make this attractive even when not in flower. It makes a dense mat with prostrate stems that flower in spring.

MORE CHOICES

- *Anemone coronaria* Z8–11 H12–8
- *Convallaria majalis* Z2–7 H7–1
- *Cyclamen coum* Z5–9 H9–5
- *Dianthus barbatus* Z5–9 H8–1
- *Geranium macrorrhizum* Z4–8 H8–1
- *Iberis sempervirens* Z5–9 H9–3
- *Iris virginica* Z6–9 H10–7
- *Lathyrus vernus* Z5–7 H7–5
- *Paeonia lactiflora* 'Festiva Maxima' Z3–8 H8–1
- *Primula auricula* Z3–8 H8–1
- *Ranunculus asiaticus* Z7–11 H12–7
- *Thalictrum aquilegifolium* Z5–9 H9–5
- *Tiarella cordifolia* Z3–8 H7–1
- *Trillium cuneatum* Z6–9 H9–6
- *Veronica gentianoides* Z4–7 H7–1
- *Verbena tenuisecta* Z8–11 H12–8

Potentilla nepalensis
NEPAL CINQUEFOIL
☼ 💧 Z4–8 H9–4 ↕↔12–36in (30–90cm)
Mounding plant that flowers over a long period, from spring to midsummer. Tends to be short lived and should be divided every two to three years. 'Miss Willmott' variety has redder flowers.

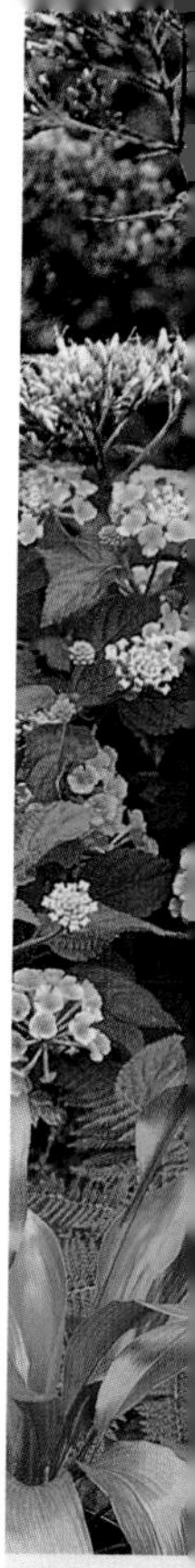

Summer-flowering perennials

Spring perennials tend to be fleeting and, in fall, the colors are predominantly yellow and copper, but the perennials that bloom in summer give us the greatest range of colors. Use the colors like an artist's palette, but take foliage texture and form into account as well, so that the garden is still interesting once the flowers have faded.

Lantana montevidensis
WEEPING SHRUB VERBENA
Z13–15 H12–9 ↕8–39in (20–100cm) ↔2–4ft (60–120cm)
A prostrate plant that forms a solid mat. It is mainly grown as an annual and is used for planters and hanging baskets where it is not hardy.

Cuphea hyssopifolia
FALSE HEATHER
Z12–15 H12–10 ↕12–24in (30–60cm) ↔8–32in (20–80cm)
Small neat plant with tiny flowers in late summer that attract butterflies. Evergreen in southern coastal areas and often grown as a houseplant.

Monarda didyma 'Jacob Cline'
JACOB CLINE BEE BALM
Z4–9 H9–1 ↕18in (45cm) ↔2ft (60cm)
Blooms mid- to late summer. Grow in moderately fertile, organic, well-drained soil. More resistant to powdery mildew and rust than the species.

Verbena bonariensis
BRAZILIAN VERBENA
Z7–11 H12–7 ↕6ft (2m) ↔18in (45cm)
Dainty, upright stems grow from a cluster of basal leaves. Makes an excellent accent plant when grown singly. Probably a self-seeding annual in the north.

Begonia grandis
HARDY BEGONIA
☼ ☀ ◇ Z6–9 H9–5 ↕3ft (1m) ↔4ft (1.2m)
A bulbous begonia that needs a slightly acidic soil rich in organic matter. Where not hardy, lift in fall after frost has killed stems and overwinter in a frost-free place.

Liatris spicata 'Alba'
WHITE GAYFEATHER
☼ ◇ Z4–9 H9–1 ↕24in (60cm) ↔12in (30cm)
Long-lasting flowers bloom from late summer to early fall. Prefers light, moderately fertile, well-drained, organic soil. In cooler areas, mulch during winter.

Saponaria officinalis 'Rosea Plena'
DOUBLE PINK BOUNCING BET
☼ ◇ Z2–8 H9–1 ↕24in (60cm) ↔20in (50cm)
Spreads rapidly by underground runners but flowers over a long period from summer to fall. 'Dazzler' has single flowers, variegated leaves, and is less invasive.

Phlox paniculata 'Fujiyama'
FUJIYAMA GARDEN PHLOX
☼ ☀ ◑ Z4–8 H8–1
↕30in (75cm) ↔24–39in (60–100cm)
Deliciously fragrant plant for butterflies and hummingbirds but prone to mildew in humid climates. This variety grows fast and needs frequent division.

MORE CHOICES

- *Canna generalis* 'Pfitzer's Dwarf' Z7–11 H12–1
- *Echinacea* spp. Z3–9 H12–1
- *Hemerocallis* cvs. Z3–10 H12–2
- *Penstemon pinifolius* Z4–10 H10–1
- *Persicaria bistorta* 'Superbum' Z4–8 H9–1
- *Rudbeckia fulgida* 'Goldsturm' Z4–9 H9–1
- *Ruellia brittoniana* 'Katie' Z7–12 H12–10
- *Setcreasea pallida* Z11 H12–10
- *Tulbaghia* spp. Z9–11 H12–4
- *Veronica alpina* 'Goodness Grows' Z3–8 H8–1

Kniphofia 'Green Jade'
GREEN JADE RED-HOT POKER
☼ ☀ ◇ ◑ Z6–9 H9–4 ↕to 5ft (1.5m) ↔24–30in (60–75cm)
One of many varieties of red-hot poker, this has an unusual color. Remove flower heads as they fade to prevent seeding. Prefers a soil rich in organic matter.

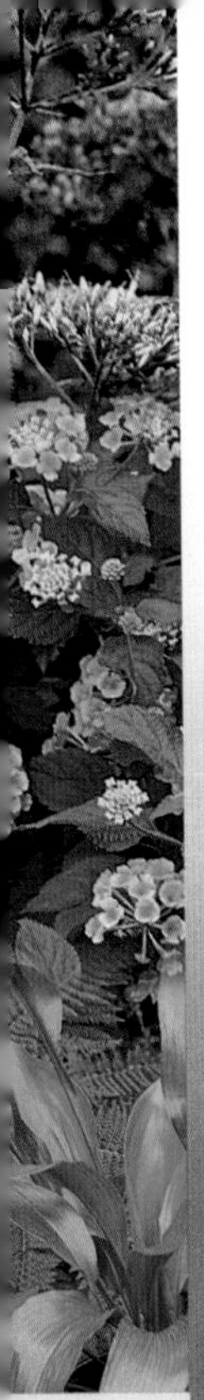

Perennials for winter gardens

One of the most anxious times of the horticultural year for avid gardeners comes right after the Christmas break, as they wait for some evidence of the approaching spring to lift them out of the winter doldrums. Here are some spirit-lifting plants that flower just when the winter-weary gardener is most in need of a boost to get ready for the season ahead.

Helleborus niger
CHRISTMAS ROSE
☼ ◊ Z3–8 H8–1 ↕↔12in (30cm)
A clump-forming plant with overwintering, dark green, leathery leaves. Flowers can also be flushed with pink. Prefers fertile organic soil. Very early blooming.

Helleborus orientalis
LENTEN ROSE
☼ ♦ Z4–8 H8–3
↕↔18in (45cm)
An elegant plant with leathery, deep green overwintering leaves. Flowers, most often white or greenish cream aging to pink, bloom from midwinter to midspring.

Helleborus foetidus
STINKING HELLEBORE
☼ ◊ Z6–9 H9–6 ↕↔18in (45cm)
Flowers from midwinter to midspring. Although the foliage smells rank when bruised, the flower can have a pleasant aroma. Readily self-sows.

MORE CHOICES

- *Dianthus plumarius* Z4–9 H9–1
- *Iris danfordiae* Z5–8 H8–4
- *Iris foetidissima* Z7–9 H9–2
- *Mazus japonicus* Z5–8 H8–5

Eranthis hyemalis
WINTER ACONITE
Z4–9 H9–1 ↕3in (8cm) ↔2in (5cm)
One of the first flowers to bloom in spring, this can self-seed freely in a woodland situation but is seldom a pest. The foliage dies down soon after flowering.

Anemone blanda 'Violet Star'
GRECIAN WINDFLOWER
Z4–8 H8–1 ↕↔6in (5cm)
This grows best in a woodland location. The flowers close at night or on cloudy days. Soak new bulbs overnight before planting to improve survival.

Iberis sempervirens 'Little Gem'
LITTLE GEM CANDYTUFT
Z5–9 H9–1 ↕6in (15cm) ↔10in (25cm)
Really a tiny shrub with woody stems so do not cut back after flowering. A good rock garden plant or as edging along a path. Attractive even when not in flower.

Bergenia 'Ballawley'
BALLAWLEY BERGENIA
Z6–9 H9–6
↕24in (60cm) ↔18–24in (45–60cm)
Leathery evergreen leaves become bronzy in winter and red flowers open in spring. Good groundcover.

Iris reticulata
NETTED IRIS
Z5–9 H8–4 ↕4–6in (10–15cm) ↔indefinite
Charming bulbous iris that blooms in late winter. They need a soil that dries out in summer so do not irrigate. Named forms come in blue and mauve shades.

Galanthus nivalis
COMMON SNOWDROP
Z3–8 H8–1 ↕4–6in (10–15cm) ↔2–3in (5–8cm)
A bulbous perennial native from the Pyrenees to Ukraine. Naturalizes in grass or in a woodland. When overcrowded, divide immediately after flowering.

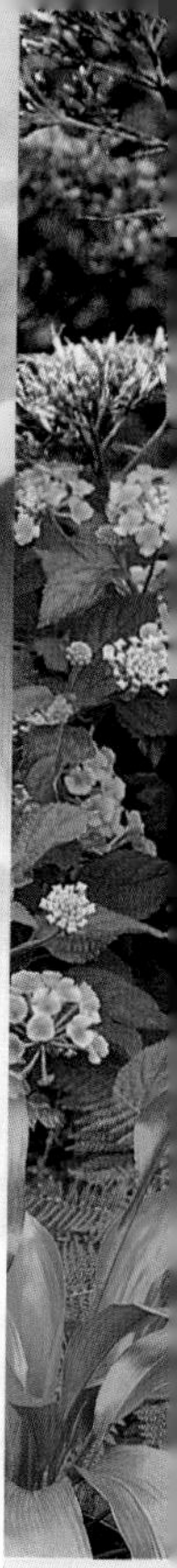

Long-flowering perennials

These are plants that will grow well in a regular garden bed that is shaded during the hottest part of the day. They will take early morning or late afternoon sun, but their foliage may scorch badly if exposed to full, strong hot sunlight. Other than this, they need no special care and should be treated like most perennials.

Phlox paniculata 'David'
DAVID GARDEN PHLOX
☼ ◑ ♦ Z4–8 H8–1 ↕↔42in (1.2m)
This robust variety blooms from midsummer to early autumn and is mildew resistant, which is unusual for this species. Grows best in fertile soil.

Veronica spicata 'Red Fox'
RED FOX SPIKE SPEEDWELL
☼ ◊ Z3–8 H8–3 ↕↔12in (30cm)
Flowers from late spring to early summer. Attracts bees and butterflies. It makes a good midground perennial and can also be used as a focal point in a bed.

Lantana camara
SHRUB VERBENA
Ⓝ ☼ ◊♦ Z11 H12–1 ↕↔3–6ft (1–2m)
A prickly-stemmed shrubby plant with strongly scented leaves. There are many named forms in shades of white, salmon, yellow, orange, red, or two-toned.

Hibiscus moscheutos
ROSE MALLOW, SWAMP HIBISCUS
Ⓝ ☼ ♦ Z5–10 H12–1 ↕8ft (2.5m) ↔3ft (1m)
Blooms during summer. Prefers well-drained, organic soil, in which it will grow rapidly to shrub size. Watch out for Japanese beetle infestations in summer.

Mirabilis jalapa
FOUR O'CLOCK, MARVEL OF PERU
☼ ◊ Z11–15 H12–9 ↕24in (60cm)
The fragrant flowers come in magenta, yellow, red, pink, and white and are often striped or mottled. Prefers a moderately fertile, well-drained soil.

Boltonia asteroides
BOLTONIA
Ⓝ ☼ ◐ ♦ Z4–8 H9–1
↕6ft (2m) ↔3ft (1m)
A strong-stemmed plant with blue-green leaves and flowers from late summer into early fall in white, lilac, or purple. Divide every few years.

Perovskia atriplicifolia 'Blue Spire'
BLUE SPIRE RUSSIAN SAGE
Ⓝ ☼ ◊ Z6–8 H9–6
↕↔5ft (1.5m)
This cultivar is much more floriferous than the species. The flower spikes create a purple haze of color above the foliage. Flowers in late summer and early autumn.

Gaura lindheimeri
WHITE GAURA
Ⓝ ☼ ♦ Z6–9 H9–6 ↕5ft (1.5m) ↔3ft (1m)
In a rich soil this is free-flowering, especially in the south of this region. It is very drought tolerant. In the north, it may be an annual but can self-seed.

MORE CHOICES

- *Begonia grandis* Z6–9 H9–5
- *Echinacea purpurea* Z3–9 H9–1
- *Hamelia patens* Z11–12 H9
- *Helleborus orientalis* Z4–8 H8–3
- *Hemerocallis spp.* Z3–10 H12–2
- *Monarda punctata* Z4–9 H9–2
- *Nepeta* x *faassenii* 'Dropmore' Z4–8 H8–1
- *Patrinia scabiosifolia* Z5–8 H8–5
- *Plumbago auriculata* Z12–15 H12–10
- *Rudbeckia laciniata* 'Herbstone' Z3–9 H9–1
- *Salvia farinacea* Z8–11 H12–1
- *Salvia greggii* Z7–9 H9–4
- *Salvia uliginosa* Z8–11 H12–7
- *Sedum spectabile* Z4–9 H9–1
- *Setcreasea pallida* 'Purple Heart' Z11–11 H12–10
- *Veronica spicata* 'Sunny Border Blue' Z3–8 H8–1

Ruellia brittoniana 'Chi Chi'
MEXICAN PETUNIA
Ⓝ ☼ ◐ ◊ ♦ Z7–12 H12–10
↕4ft (1.2m) ↔12–18in (30–45cm)
A tall, robust upright plant with a constant scattering of petunia-shaped flowers. Forms a solid backdrop with the deep green foliage and is great with yellows.

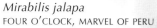

Perennials with spiky flowers

In both floral arrangements and the garden itself, tall or pointy flowers are "exclamation points" – dramatic lines that draw attention to and complement surrounding flowers. Many spiky flowers tend to get floppy in our rain and humidity, and require staking or being planted behind smaller sturdier plants for support.

Liatris spicata
DENSE GAYFEATHER
Ⓝ ☼ 💧 Z4–9 H9–5 ↕24in (60cm) ↔12in (30cm)
Long-lasting flowers bloom from late summer to early fall. Prefers light, moderately fertile, well-drained, organic soil. In cooler areas, mulch during winter.

Verbascum nigra
DARK MULLEIN
☼ 💧 Z3–8 H8–1 ↕3ft (1m) ↔2ft (60cm)
This perennial forms rosettes with long-stalked, dark green leaves that are hairy underneath. The spikes of flowers grow in mid- to late summer. May be invasive if not deadheaded.

Verbascum 'Helen Johnson'
HELEN JOHNSON MULLEIN
☼ 💧 Z6–9 H9–5 ↕36in (90cm) ↔12in (30cm)
Hybrid mullein that is not as invasive as the species. Many named forms come in a range of shades from white, through orange, to brick red. Good border specimen.

Baptisia australis
FALSE INDIGO
Ⓝ ☼ 💧 Z3–9 H9–1 ↕30in (75cm) ↔24in (60cm)
Blooms in early summer. Seedpods are ornamental. Best used in the back of a border or as a specimen plant. This member of the pea family attracts birds.

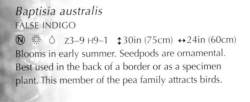

Kniphofia uvaria
RED-HOT POKER
☼ ☼ 💧 Z6–9 H9–1 ↕4ft (1.2m) ↔24in (60cm)
Blooms appear from late summer to early fall. Flowers are red in bud, open orange, and turn yellow. Best if grown in fertile, organic, rich sandy soil.

MORE CHOICES

- *Delphinium x elatum* Z3–8 H7–3
- *Digitalis purpurea* Z4-8 H9–1
- *Galtonia candicans* Z7–10 H10–7
- *Gladiolus communis* Z8–10 H9–1
- *Iris germanica cvs* Z4–9 H9–2
- *Lilium* cvs. Z3–8 H8–1
- *Polianthes tuberosa* Z7–11 H11–7
- *Salvia mexicana* 'Tula' Z9–11 H12–10
- *Salvia* superba Z5–9 H9–5
- *Verbena peruviana* Z9–11 H12–9
- *Veronica spicata* 'Red Fox' Z3–8 H8–1

Solidago 'Goldenmosa'
GOLDENMOSA GOLDENROD
Z5–9 H9–5 ↕30in (75cm) ↔18in (45cm)
Blooms in late summer. Other cultivars vary in height and flowering time. Although considered a weed by some, goldenrods are excellent butterfly plants.

Justicia brandegeeana
SHRIMP PLANT
Z14–15 H12–1
↕36in (90cm) ↔24–36in (60–90cm)
Familiar spring border plant is often massed along woodland edges. Cut spent flowers for a second summer show, and expect the short-lived perennial to reseed.

Physostegia virginiana 'Vivid'
VIVID OBEDIENT PLANT
Ⓝ Z4–8 H8–1
↕4ft (1.2m) ↔24in (60cm)
The common name comes from how individual midsummer flowers are hinged on the stem, and can be pointed in any direction. Can be invasive.

Salvia leucantha
MEXICAN BUSH SAGE
Z9–11 H12–4 ↕24–39in (60–100cm) ↔16–36in (40–90cm)
Narrow, often-branched spikes light up a summer border, and can be cut for reblooming in the fall. Tough and drought-tolerant; resent frequent watering. The foliage is woolly-white on the underside.

Perennials with fragrant flowers

Nothing rounds out a garden better than plants that engage the sense of smell. Some plants have delightful fragrance during the day when the sun is warm and the air is still, while others often emit powerful fragrances as evening approaches or at night. These flowers attract not only the human nose but also pollinating insects, including butterflies and moths.

Nepeta x *faassenii*
FAASSEN'S CATMINT
☼ ◊ Z4–8 H8–1 ↕↔18in (45cm)
Flowers from early summer to early autumn. Cut back scented foliage after flowering to keep plants tight and encourage repeat flowering. Also known as *N. mussinii*.

Dianthus gratianopolitanus
CHEDDAR PINK
☼ ◊ Z3–9 H9–1 ↕6in (15cm) ↔16in (40cm)
When not in flower, this is an attractive gray-green hummock. The flowers start to open in late spring and will continue well into summer if deadheaded.

Paeonia 'Edulis Superba'
EDULIS SUPERBA PEONY
☼ ◐ ♦ Z3–8 H8–1 ↕32in (80cm) ↔36in (90cm)
Peony varieties never seem to age and old varieties like this, introduced in 1824, are still widely available. This is an early flowered, very fragrant variety.

Centranthus ruber
JUPITER'S BEARD, RED VALERIAN
☼ ◊ Z5–8 H8–5 ↕3ft (1m) ↔2ft (60cm)
Fragrant flowers appear spring to late summer. Also available with white and rose-pink flowers. Self-sows freely. Prefers minimally to moderately fertile soil.

Convallaria majalis
LILY-OF-THE-VALLEY
◐ ♦ Z2–7 H7–1 ↕6in (15cm) ↔indefinite
Bears sweetly scented spring flowers. A handful of cultivars show varying flower color and leaf variegation. Prefers moist, organic soil and leaf mold mulch.

Phlox paniculata 'David'
GARDEN PHLOX
Ⓝ Z4–8 H8–1
↕4ft (1.2m) ↔24–39in (60–100cm)
This robust variety blooms from midsummer to early autumn and is mildew resistant, which is unusual for this species. Grows best in fertile soil.

Lilium candidum
MADONNA LILY
Z6–9 H9–6 ↕↔3–6ft (1–2m)
A shiny, bright green basal leaf rosette gives rise to a tall flower stalk in summer. The flowers are sweetly fragrant. Susceptible to *Botrytis* (gray mold).

Narcissus 'Pipit'
PIPIT DAFFODIL
Ⓝ Z3–9 H9–1 ↕↔10in (25cm)
A small, mid-season daffodil with several sweetly scented flowers on each stem. The trumpet fades to cream as it ages, giving a two-toned effect.

Hedychium coronarium
WHITE GINGER LILY
Z7–11 H12–7
↕10ft (3m) ↔3ft (1m)
The lance-shaped leaves are downy beneath. Highly fragrant, late-summer flowers open from a narrow spike and are 4in (10cm) across. Native to India.

Lilium speciosum var. *rubrum*
RUBRUM LILY
Z3–8 H8–1 ↕6ft (18.m)
Once widely grown for cutting, it has been surpassed by modern hybrid trumpet lilies, but is still beautiful with raised whiskers toward the center of the petals.

MORE CHOICES

- *Acidanthera bicolor* Z0–0 H12–4
- *Hemerocallis* 'Gentle Shepherd' Z3–10 H12–2
- *Hosta plantaginea* Z3–9 H9–1
- *Lavandula angustifolia* Z5–8 H8–5
- *Lobularia maritime* Z10–11 H12–1
- *Lycoris squamigera* Z6–11 H12–6
- *Nicotiana alata* Z10–11 H12–1
- *Paeonia lactiflora* Z3–8 H8–1
- *Polianthes tuberosa* Z7–11 H11–7
- *Polygonatum odoratum* Z3–8 H9–1
- *Saponaria officinalis* Z3–9 H9–1
- *Viola odorata* Z6–8 H8–6

Perennials with hot flowers

Red can dominate everything around it but it can also inspire a planting and bring it to life. Some shades, however, are difficult to place close to some other colors. Yellow and gold are the brightest colors in the garden and can overwhelm paler shades if used to excess. Both seem brightest when viewed against a green backdrop.

Monarda 'Gardenview Scarlet'
GARDENVIEW SCARLET BERGAMOT
☼ ◊◆ Z4–9 H9–1
↕24–36in (60–90cm) ↔24in (60cm)
Stiff upright plant that seldom needs staking. Flowers appear from mid- to late summer.

Hibiscus coccineus
SCARLET HIBISCUS
Ⓝ ☼ ◆ Z6–15 H12–1 ↕10ft (3m) ↔4ft (1.2m)
An uncommon perennial with lobed leaves. Flowers are on the tops of the stems in summer and early fall. The base of the plant becomes woody.

Canna indica 'Phaison'
PHAISON CANNA
☼ ◊ Z7–11 H12–7 ↕7ft (2.1m) ↔4ft (1.2m)
Modern canna hybrids come in a wide range of colors: pink, red, yellow, orange, and bitone. Foliage may be bright green, shades of red, or variously striped.

MORE CHOICES

- *Achillea* 'Coronation Gold' *Z4–9 H9–2*
- *Cuphea micropetella Z11–12 H12–1*
- *Gaillardia grandiflora* 'Goblin' *Z3–8 H8–1*
- *Geum chiloense* 'Fire Opal' *Z5–9 H9–5*
- *Geum chiloense* 'Red Wings' *Z5–9 H9–5*
- *Heuchera* 'Mount St. Helens' *Z3–8 H8–1*
- *Kniphofia triangularis Z6–9 H9–1*
- *Lilium tigrinum Z2–7 H7–1*
- *Lychnis x arkwrightii* 'Vesuvius' *Z4–7 H7–1*
- *Phlox paniculata Z4–8 H8–1*

Phlomis russeliana
STICKY JERUSALEM SAGE
☼ ◆ Z4–9 H9–1 ↕to 36in (90cm) ↔30in (75cm)
Imposing plant with wrinkled leaves that are woolly beneath. Mid-summer flowers are carried in several whorls around the stem and make good cut-flowers.

Oenethera fruticosa
SUNDROPS
Ⓝ ☼ ◗ Z4–8 H8–1 ↕3ft (1m) ↔12in (30cm)
Flowers from late spring to late summer on erect, branching plants. Foliage turns dull red after fall frosts. Prefers moderately fertile to fertile soil.

Salvia elegans
PINEAPPLE SCENTED SAGE
☀ ◊◗ Z8–11 H12–1 ↕4ft (1.2m) ↔3ft (1m)
Open-branched, woody perennial with foliage that smells of fresh pineapples when crushed. May be evergreen in the south and flowers in late summer.

Crocosmia x 'Lucifer'
LUCIFER MONTBRETIA
☼ ◊ Z6–9 H9–6 ↕to 3ft (1m) ↔10in (25cm)
This robust hybrid that blooms in midsummer prefers moderately fertile, organic soil. Can be dug up and stored like gladiolus where not hardy.

Asclepias tuberosa
BUTTERFLY WEED
Ⓝ ☼ ◊ Z4–9 H9–2 ↕30in (75cm) ↔18in (45cm)
Blooms in midsummer. Prefers fertile, well-drained, loamy soil. Susceptible to aphids, mealybugs, rust, and bacterial and fungal leaf spots.

Lychnis chalcedonica
JERUSALEM CROSS, MALTESE CROSS
☼ ☀ ◊ Z4–8 H8–1 ↕32in (80cm) ↔18in (45cm)
Summer flowers on stiff upright stems that have pairs of toothed leaves, which may brown and fall early in prolonged dry spells. Site behind lower plants.

Penstemon 'Prairie Fire'
PRAIRIE FIRE BEARDTONGUE
☼ ◊ Z3–8 H8–1 ↕24in (60cm) ↔12in (30cm)
Complex hybrid that has been grown for many years. Stiff stems carry branched heads of bloom in early summer and again in early fall if deadheaded.

Perennials with cool flowers

Blue gives the impression of space and distance and blends well with all other colors, toning down the hot shades. Pale pinks and lilacs shades are also harmonious and blend well with most bright colors; while white and cream are the most relaxing of all and create a sense of harmony when grown close to brighter blooms.

Ruellia brittoniana 'Chi Chi'
MEXICAN PETUNIA
☼ ◐ ◊ ◆ Z7–12 H12–10
↕ 4ft (1.2m) ↔12–18in (30–45cm)
Tall, robust upright plant with constant scattering of petunia-shaped flowers. Forms a solid backdrop.

MORE CHOICES

- *Boltonia* 'Pink Beauty' Z4–8 H9–2
- *Campanula persicifolia* 'Telham Beauty' Z3–9 H9–1
- *Ceratostigma plumbaginoides* Z6–9 H9–6
- *Liriope muscari* 'Monroe White' Z6–10 H12–1
- *Monarda* 'Croftway Pink' Z4–9 H9–2
- *Platycodon grandiflorus* 'Double Blue' Z7–9 H9–1
- *Plumbago auriculata* 'Royal Cape' Z6–9 H9–1
- *Salvia guaranitica* Z7–10 H12–8
- *Salvia uliginosa* Z8–11 H12–7
- *Tradescantia virginiana* 'Zwanenburg Blue' Z5–8 H8–2

Nepeta 'Six Hills Giant'
SIX HILLS GIANT CATMINT
☼ ◐ ◊ Z4–8 H8–1 ↕to 36in (90cm) ↔24in (60cm)
Upright, clump-forming plant with masses of flowers in summer and attractive, gray aromatic leaves. Cut back after flowering to encourage re-bloom.

Sisyrinchium angustifolium
NARROWLEAF BLUE-EYED GRASS
☼ ◊ Z5–8 H8–5 ↕12in (30cm) ↔3in (8cm)
Short-lived individual flowers are borne in succession during summer on a self-seeding, semi-evergreen, delicate-looking perennial.

Baptisia australis
FALSE INDIGO
Ⓝ ☼ ◊ Z3–9 H9–1
↕30in (75cm) ↔24in (60cm)
Blooms in early summer. Seedpods are ornamental. Best used in the back of a border or as a specimen plant. It attracts birds.

Caryopteris x *clandonensis* 'Longwood Blue'
LONGWOOD BLUE MIST SHRUB
☼ ◊ Z6–9 H9–1 ↕3ft (1m) ↔5ft (1.5m)
A woody-based perennial that can become a small shrub if not pruned in spring. Cut back almost to the ground to promote new flower growth in late summer.

Agapanthus 'Loch Hope'
LOCH HOPE BLUE AFRICAN LILY
☼ ◊ ♦ Z8–11 H12–1
↕3–4ft (1–1.2m) ↔20in (50cm)
Equally good in containers. Long-lasting flowers appear in late summer and keep color until they die.

Amsonia hubrectii
NARROW-LEAF BLUESTAR
Ⓝ ☼ ☀ ♦ Z6–8 H8–5 ↕3ft (1m) ↔4ft (1.2m)
Flowers in late spring. Willowlike midgreen leaves turn bright yellow in fall. Tolerant of most soil types. Equally at home in a wildflower garden or border.

Tradescantia x *andersoniana* 'Iris Pritchard'
J. C. WEGULIN SPIDERWORT
☼ ☀ ♦ Z5–9 H9–5
↕16–24in (40–60cm) ↔18–24in (45–60cm)
Spiderworts need dividing every 2-3 years. Flowers only last a day but the plant flowers for 2 months.

HERBACEOUS PLANTS

Perennials for cut flowers

One of the joys of having a flower garden is being able to cut fresh blooms for the home. Even two or three spikes placed in a slender vase add a touch of class to the dining table. Most of the plants shown here benefit from regular cutting and will continue to send up new flowers over a long period. Some can also be dried for use in winter arrangements.

Achillea 'Coronation Gold'
CORONATION GOLD YARROW
☼ 💧 Z3–9 H9–1 ↕3ft (1m) ↔18in (45cm)
A stiff, well-branched, upright hybrid. Flowering begins in early summer and continues for many weeks. Dries well, keeping its color.

Platycodon grandiflorus
BALLOON FLOWER
☼ 💧 Z4–9 H9–1 ↕24in (60cm) ↔12in (30cm)
Late to start growing in spring so do not damage when cultivating. Does best in light shade in the south. There is also a white-flowered variety and a dwarf one.

Rudbeckia fulgida var. *sullivantii* 'Goldsturm'
GOLDSTURM BLACK EYED SUSAN
Ⓝ ☼ ◑ 💧 Z4–9 H9–1 ↕2ft (60cm) ↔18in (45cm)
A very popular front-of-the-border plant that flowers very freely on much-branched stems in late summer. More drought-tolerant than some of this genus.

Crocosmia masoniorum
GIANT MONTBRETIA
☼ 💧 Z6–9 H9–2 ↕4ft (1.2m) ↔12–18in (30–45cm)
The arching spikes of flowers appear in midsummer above the sword-shaped foliage. Protect with a mulch instead of lifting at the limits of hardiness. It resents disturbance.

MORE CHOICES

- *Alstromeria pulchella* Z8–11 H12–7
- *Artemisia ludoviciana* 'Silver King' Z5–9 H12–8
- *Campanula barbata* Z5–8 H8–5
- *Chrysanthemum* 'Clara Curtis' Z5–9 H9–1
- *Delphinium cheilanthum* Z3–8 H7–3
- *Digitalis purpurea* Z4–8 H9–1
- *Equisetum hyemale* Z3–11 H12–1
- *Gaillardia x grandiflora* 'Kobold' Z3–8 H8–1
- *Helleborus orientalis* Z4–8 H8–3
- *Iris germanica* cvs. Z4–9 H9–2
- *Liatris spicata* 'Alba' Z4–9 H9–1
- *Paeonia officinalis* 'Festiva Maxima' Z3–8 H8–1
- *Physostegia virginiana* 'Vivid' Z4–8 H8–1
- *Salvia greggi* Z7–9 H9–4
- *Solidago* 'Cloth of Gold' Z5–9 H9–5
- *Spigelia marilandica* Z5–9 H9–2
- *Stokesia laevis* Z5–9 H9–5
- *Veronica spicata* 'Sunny Border Blue' Z3–8 H8–1

Echinacea purpurea 'Bright Star'
BRIGHT STAR PURPLE CONEFLOWER
Ⓝ ☼ ◊◆ Z3–9 H9–1 ↕to 32in (80cm) ↔18in (45cm)
Flowers from midsummer to early fall and prefers a deep humus-rich soil. Named forms, such as this, are not as invasive in the garden as the species.

Gypsophila paniculata
BABY'S BREATH
☼ ◊ Z5–9 H9–1 ↕8–12in (20–30cm) ↔6in (15cm)
Much used by florists as a summer filler, this should have a place in every garden. It needs an alkaline soil. 'Bristol Fairy' is the commonly grown double form.

Phlox paniculata 'David'
DAVID GARDEN PHLOX
☼ ◐ ◆ Z4–8 H8–1 ↕↔42in (1.2m)
This robust variety blooms from midsummer to early autumn and is mildew resistant, which is unusual for this species. Grows best in fertile soil.

Eupatorium coelestinum
MISTFLOWER
Ⓝ ☼ ◐ ◆ Z5–11 H9–1
↕3ft (1m) ↔24–36in (60–90cm)
Upright plant with soft blooms in late summer to fall. Good plant for a wildflower garden and also does well in a wet location. Sometimes called hardy ageratum.

Evergreen Perennials

Although the majority of perennials are classed as herbaceous since their foliage dies back to the ground each fall, there are some that remain evergreen and help provide color to the garden in winter. Many of these also have showy flowers during the summer months, while others are grown mainly for their foliage effect.

Santolina chamaecyparissus
LAVENDER COTTON
☼ ◊ Z6–9 H9–4 ↕20in (50cm) ↔3ft (1m)
A woody perennial grown mainly for its aromatic gray foliage. It makes an excellent edging plant that can be trimmed to keep it to size. The flowers are a bonus.

Thymus x *citriodorus* 'Doone Valley'
DOONE VALLEY THYME
☼ ◊ Z6–9 H9–6 ↕5in (13cm) ↔14in (35cm)
Low spreading plant with attractive aromatic foliage even when not in flower. The early summer blooms are a magnet for bees. Shear lightly after flowering.

Heuchera sanguinea 'Splendens'
SPLENDENS CORAL BELLS
Ⓝ ☼ ◐ ◑ Z3–8 H8–1 ↕28in (70cm)
Clump-forming perennial with flowers carried in summer well above the kidney-shaped leaves. Prefers fertile organic soil. Can be grown as a groundcover.

Iberis sempervirens
CANDYTUFT
☼ ◊ Z5–9 H9–3 ↕12in (30cm) ↔24in (60cm)
Flowers appear from late spring to early summer on this spreading evergreen perennial. Prefers marginally to moderately fertile soil; does well in a rock garden.

Galium odoratum
SWEET WOODRUFF
☼ ◑ ◊ ◆ Z5–8 H8–5 ↕18in (45cm) ↔indefinite
A charming creeper that spreads by rhizomes, but easy to remove. Flowers open in late spring. Foliage is scented when dried. This was used as a "strewing herb."

Epimedium x *rubrum*
RED BARRENWORT
◑ ◊ Z4–8 H8–1 ↕12in (30cm) ↔8in (20cm)
Evergreen leaves are red when young and also turn red with the arrival of cool fall weather. Prefers fertile, organic, well-drained soil.

Lamium maculatum 'Beacon Silver'
BEACON SILVER DEADNETLE
☼ ◑ ◊ Z4–8 H8–1 ↕8in (20cm) ↔3ft (1m)
Sprawling groundcover that forms a dense mat. Small spikes of red-purple to pink flowers in summer. Roots readily and can become invasive if neglected.

MORE CHOICES

- *Bergenia* cvs. Z4–9 H9–2
- *Dianthus gratianopolitanus* 'Bath's Pink' Z3–9 H9–1
- *Rosmarinus officinalis* Z8–11 H12–8
- *Satureja montana* Z5–8 H12–1
- *Sedum acre* Z3–8 H8–1
- *Viola odorata* Z6–8 H8–6

Artemisia 'Powis Castle'
POWIS CASTLE WORMWOOD
☼ ◊ Z7–9 H12–8 ↕2ft (60cm) ↔3ft (1m)
Low, mound-forming, evergreen shrub with aromatic foliage. Bears sparse clusters of yellow-tinged silver flowers in summer.

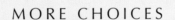

Lavandula angustifolia
ENGLISH LAVENDER
☼ ◊ Z5–8 H8–5 ↕3ft (1m) ↔4ft (1.2m)
Slow-growing, evergreen shrub with fragrant foliage. Summer flowers are white to blue-purple. Leaves and flowers can be dried for sachets.

Perennials with coarse, bold foliage

Although most perennials are grown for their flowers, there are some whose foliage is equally important, if not more so. For example, only a few hostas have showy flowers, but they all have attractive foliage. Use these large leaves to give contrast and to add a different texture to a mixed planting, even when the flowers are absent.

Hibiscus moscheutos
ROSE MALLOW, SWAMP HIBISCUS
Ⓝ ☼ ♦ Z5–10 H12–1
↕8ft (2.5m) ↔3ft (1m)
Blooms during summer. Prefers well-drained, organic soil, in which it will grow rapidly to shrub size. Watch out for Japanese beetle infestations in summer.

Ligularia przewalskii
SHAVALSKI'S LIGULARIA
☼ ◑ Z5–8 H8–1 ↕to 6ft (3m) ↔3ft (1m)
Makes a bold statement when in flower in summer. Similar to the better known 'Rocket' but taller, its leaves are divided into narrow fingers.

Salvia officinalis
COMMON SAGE
☼ ◊◑ Z5–8 H8–5 ↕to 32in (80cm) ↔3ft (1m)
Culinary herb that makes a good edging plant. Varieties with purple-tinged or variegated leaves are available. Spikes of pale lilac flowers in early summer.

MORE CHOICES

- *Acanthus mollis* Z7–11 H12–7
- *Canna* x *generalis* Z7–11 H12–1
- *Dicentra spectabilis* Z3–9 H9–1
- *Helleborus foetidus* Z6–9 H9–6
- *Hemerocallis hybrids* Z3–10 H12–2
- *Lamium maculatum* Z4–8 H8–1
- *Ligularia dentata* Z4–8 H8–1
- *Salvia sclarea* Z5–9 H9–3
- *Stachys byzantina* Z4–8 H8–1
- *Tetrapanax papyriferus* Z6–11 H12–6
- *Verbascum olympicum* Z5–9 H9–5
- *Yucca filamentosa* Z4–11 H12–5

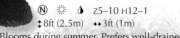

Bergenia cordifolia
HEARTLEAF BERGENIA
☼ ◊◑ Z3–8 H8–1
↕24in (60cm) ↔30in (75cm)
A parent of many newer named varieties. The 10in (25cm) leaves turn a burgundy red in the cold but remain over winter. It flowers in early spring.

Filipendula rubra
QUEEN OF THE PRAIRIE
Ⓝ ☼ ♦ Z3–9 H9–1 ↕6–8ft (2–2.5m) ↔4ft (1.2m)
Fragrant flowers in midsummer. A spreading plant, it forms large clumps of irregularly cut, pinnate leaves. Prefers moderately fertile, leafy soil.

Lupinus hybrids
HYBRID LUPINES
☼ ◐ ◊ pH Z4–8 H8–1
↕16–36in (40–90cm)
↔12–16in (30–40cm)
Often short-lived in the hot conditions of parts of this region, lupines can be treated as annuals which, planted in late fall, will bloom the following spring. If they survive to flower again it is a bonus.

Alchemilla mollis
LADY'S MANTLE
◐ ◊ Z4–7 H7–1 ↕↔20in (50cm)
Tiny flowers produced from early summer to early fall can be used in fresh and dried arrangements. This sturdy groundcover prefers organic soil.

Hosta sieboldiana
SIEBOLD'S HOSTA
◐ ♦ Z3–9 H9–1 ↕3ft (1m) ↔4ft (1.2m)
Possibly the very first hosta exported from Japan, this is the parent of many hybrids. The puckered leaves and elegant flower spikes are loved by flower arrangers.

Alcea rosea
HOLLYHOCK
☼ ◊ Z3–9 H10–3 ↕6ft (2m) ↔24in (60cm)
Upright, short-lived, summer-blooming perennial usually grown as a biennial. Many colorful single and double cultivars are available. Grow in moderately fertile soil.

Polygonatum odoratum
FRAGRANT SOLOMON'S SEAL
◐ ● ♦ Z3–8 H9–1
↕34in (85cm) ↔12in (30cm)
Spreading by creeping rhizomes, this forms a large clump with flowers that perfume the garden on a spring evening. 'Variegatum' has white-edged leaves.

Perennials with fine, textured foliage

While the shape of the foliage on perennials differs greatly, most have lance-shaped to broad leaves, which may be entire, somewhat dissected, or divided into individual leaflets. The plants shown here have narrow to lacy leaves that contrast with surrounding plants, especially when they are not in bloom. The difference in textures adds interest to the garden all summer long.

Achillea millefolium
YARROW
Ⓝ ☼ 💧 Z3–9 H9–1 ↕↔24in (60cm)
Blooms from early to late summer. Tolerates a wide range of soil conditions. Self-sows, so deadhead after blooming if you don't want volunteers popping up.

Dicentra eximia
TURKEY CORN, FRINGED BLEEDING HEART
Ⓝ ☀ 💧 Z3–8 H10–1 ↕24in (60cm) ↔18in (45cm)
A mound-shaped plant that flowers in early spring. Grow this in a woodland location. Several named forms have white or darker pink flowers.

Paeonia tenuifolia
FERNLEAF PEONY
☼ ☀ 💧 Z3–8 H8–1 ↕↔28in (70cm)
This is among the first peonies to flower. The flowers are short-lived, but the foliage makes this an attractive plant all summer. There is also a double-flowered form.

MORE CHOICES

- *Aconitum napellus* Z3–8 H8–3
- *Adiantum capillus-veneris* Z7–11 H9–3
- *Adonis vernalis* Z4–7 H7–1
- *Allium schoenoprasum* Z5–11 H9–1
- *Artemisia schmidtiana* Z5–8 H8–5
- *Centaurea cineraria* Z7–11 H12–1
- *Festuca glauca* Z4–8 H8–1
- *Heuchera sanguinea* Z3–8 H8–1
- *Liatris spicata* Z4–9 H9–5
- *Linum perenne* Z5–8 H8–5
- *Pulsatilla vulgaris* Z5–7 H7–5
- *Verbena* 'Sissinghurst' Z7–11 H12–1

Tanacetum parthenium
FEVERFEW
☼ 💧 Z4–9 H9–1
↕18–24in (45–60cm) ↔12in (30cm)
An aromatic plant often used for herbal tea. Short-lived, with a woody base, it makes a good edging.

Aquilegia canadensis
CANADIAN COLUMBINE
Ⓝ ☼ ☀ 💧 Z3–8 H8–1 ↕3ft (1m) ↔12in (30cm)
A delicate-looking perennial with dark green leaves divided into leaflets. Prefers fertile soil, but too much fertility causes lanky growth. Often self-sows.

Boltonia asteroides
BOLTONIA
Ⓝ ☼ ☀ 💧 Z4–8 H9–1 ↕6ft (2m) ↔3ft (1m)
A strong-stemmed plant with blue-green leaves and flowers from late summer into early fall in white, lilac, or pinkish purple. Divide every few years.

Perovskia atriplicifolia
RUSSIAN SAGE
☼ ◊ Z6–9 H9–6 ↕4ft (1.2m) ↔3ft (1m)
Flowers from summer to early autumn. Bloom period can be extended by deadheading older flowers. Grows well in minimally to moderately fertile soil.

Nepeta x faassenii
FAASSEN'S CATMINT
☼ ◊ Z4–8 H8–1 ↕↔18in (45cm)
Flowers from early summer to early autumn. Cut back scented foliage after flowering to keep plants tight and encourage repeat flowering. Also known as *N. mussinii.*

Coreopsis verticillata 'Moonbeam'
MOONBEAM TICKSEED
Ⓝ ☼ ◐ ◊ Z3–8 H9–1 ↕↔18in (45cm)
Flowers freely from early summer to autumn. Deaheading helps extend the bloom period. This cultivar has an upright habit and is drought resistant.

Rosmarinus officinalis
ROSEMARY
☼ ◊ Z8–11 H12–8
↕↔5ft (1.5m)
Evergreen aromatic leaves. Rosemary is a popular culinary herb and an attractive garden plant. Flowers are produced mostly at or near shoot tips.

Santolina chamaecyparissus
LAVENDER COTTON
☼ ◊ Z6–9 H9–4 ↕20in (50cm) ↔3ft (1m)
Spreading, evergreen mound bears summer flowers, best removed after they fade. Use in a mass planting, in rock gardens, or as a low hedge. Salt-tolerant.

Geranium sanguineum 'Striatum'
STRIPED BLOODY CRANESBILL
☼ ◊ Z3–8 H8–1 ↕4–6in (10–15cm) ↔12in (30cm)
This more compact form of the species prefers the same conditions and is prone to the same problems as the species.

Perennials with purple or burgundy foliage

Dark foliage tends to be gloomy, so its use should be kept to a minimum; use it in individual plants or in small groups. This color shows off pale-colored flowers well, and some red shades go with plants with reddish purple foliage, but not with the blue-purples. This is a color for planting in bright light, because it disappears in a shaded location.

Euphorbia dulcis 'Chameleon'
CHAMELEON SPURGE
Z3–8 H10–1 ↕↔12in (30cm)
Greenish yellow flowers with purple-tinged bracts appear in early summer. Foliage changes from purple in spring to burgundy, then finally red. Self-sows.

Heuchera micrantha 'Palace Purple'
PALACE PURPLE HEUCHERA
Z4–8 H8–1 ↕↔18in (45cm)
The original selection has deep purple foliage that fades to a bronzy purple in time. Plants are now often grown from seed and may lack that color intensity.

Canna 'Australia'
AUSTRALIA CANNA
Z7–11 H12–7 ↕5ft (1.5m) ↔20in (50cm)
Frost-tender, these need to be started indoors in the North but can be planted directly into the garden where the growing season is longer. Lift in fall before hard frost.

Foeniculum vulgare 'Purpureum'
PURPLE FENNEL
Z6–9 H9–6 ↕6ft (1.8m) ↔18in (45cm)
Young foliage is a dull purple, becoming a blue-green as it matures This perennial can be used in cooking, like the regular green fennel. It may seed freely.

Tulbaghia violacea
SOCIETY GARLIC
Z7–10 H10–7
↕18–24in (45–60cm) ↔10in (25cm)
Gray-green leaves have burgundy tinge, especially in bright sun. Starry lilac flowers appear in late spring.

Ajuga reptans 'Caitlin's Giant'
CATLIN'S GIANT BUGLEWEED
Z3–9 H9–1 ↕6in (15cm) ↔3ft (1m)
This large-leafed and large-flowered form blooms from late spring to early summer. Grows well in most soil types. Prone to fungal leaf spot and crown rot.

Cimicifuga ramosa 'Brunette'
BRUNETTE AUTUMN SNAKEROOT
◑ 💧 Z3–9 H9–1 ↕4ft (1.2m) ↔3ft (1m)
A clump-forming plant that prefers an organic soil. The foliage is attractive all summer, and the flowers appear in fall. Variety *atropurpurea* is similar, but taller.

MORE CHOICES

- *Ajuga reptans* 'Purpurea' Z3–9 H9–1
- *Rodgersia podophylla* Z5–8 H8–5
- *Salvia officinalis* 'Purpurescens' Z4–10 H10–1
- *Setcreasea pallida* 'Purple Heart' Z11–11 H12–10
- *Sedum telphinum* 'Matrona' Z4–9 H9–4

Penstemon digitalis 'Husker Red'
HUSKER RED PENSTEMON
Ⓝ ☼ ◑ 💧 Z3–8 H8–1
↕30in (75cm) ↔12in (30cm)
Flowers from early to late summer. Tolerant of high humidity and grows in moderately to marginally fertile soil. Prone to foliage diseases, slugs, and snails.

Ophiopogon planiscapus 'Nigrescens'
BLACK MONDO GRASS
☼ ◑ 💧 pH Z6–11 H12–1
↕8in (20cm) ↔12in (30cm)
Grow this under white-barked trees like Himalayan white birch, or with light green hostas such as 'Lemon Lime'. Bell-shaped purplish white flowers appear in summer.

Sedum 'Sunset Cloud'
SUNSET CLOUD SEDUM
☼ 💧 Z6–9 H9–6 ↕6in (15cm) ↔12in (30cm)
A useful plant for edging, rock walls, or dry-stone paving. Late summer flowers last for several weeks and new foliage is red-tinged, darkening with age.

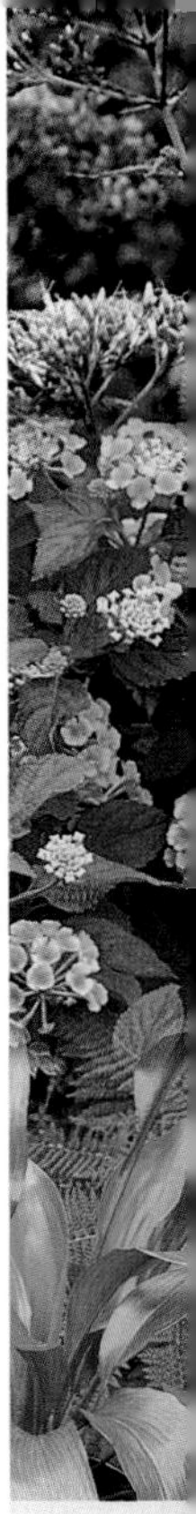

Perennials with golden foliage

Eye-catching from a distance, the plants described here tend to draw you into the garden to discover their identity. Most need to be grown in full sun to retain their brightness – they tend to turn green in shade – but shade-loving hostas and plants, such as bleeding heart and meadowsweet, will need protection from the hot midday sun.

Hosta 'Gold Standard'
PLANTAIN LILY
Z3–8 H9–2 ↕30in (75cm) ↔3ft (1m)
Funnel-shaped, lavender-blue flowers bloom high above the foliage. Can be used as an accent plant or groundcover under deciduous trees. Best in fertile soil.

Yucca filamentosa 'Golden Sword'
GOLDEN SWORD YUCCA
Z4–11 H12–5 ↕6ft (2m) ↔5ft (1.5m)
Yellow-centered leaves distinguish this cultivar. It flowers from late spring into summer. Prefers well-drained soil, and it tolerates drought.

Centaurea montana 'Gold Bullion'
GOLD BULLION MOUNTAIN BLUET
Z3–8 H8–1
↕18in (45cm) ↔24 (60cm)
The species can be a weed, taking over large areas with underground shoots, but this cultivar is more refined and spreads slowly. Flowers from spring into summer.

Tanacetum vulgare 'Isla Gold'
ISLA GOLD TANSY
Z4–8 H8–1 ↕24–36in (60–90cm) ↔indefinite
A vigorous, easy-to-grow plant that self-seeds freely, although its seedlings will most likely revert to green. Small, buttonlike yellow flowers appear in the summer.

Acorus gramineus 'Ogon'
JAPANESE SWEET FLAG
Z10–11 H12–2 ↕to 10in (25cm) ↔6in (15cm)
Gives the impression of tall, semi-evergreen iris leaves. Flowers are inconspicuous. Susceptible to wet and dry root rots, rust, and various fungal leaf spots.

Hakonechloa macra 'Aureola'
GOLDEN JAPANESE FOREST GRASS
Z5–9 H9–4 ↕14in (35cm) ↔16in (40cm)
Forms mounds of arching leaves that are bright yellow with narrow green stripes until they turn red in fall. Pale green spikelets open late summer to midautumn.

Dicentra spectabilis 'Gold Heart'
GOLD HEART BLEEDING HEART
Z3–9 H9–1 ↕2ft (60cm) ↔3ft (90cm)
The bright leaves are carried on peach-colored stems. The flowers appear in mid- to late spring. It tends to go dormant in summer unless grown in full shade and cooler climates.

Aquilegia 'Mellow Yellow'
MELLOW YELLOW COLUMBINE
Z4–7 H7–1 ↕30in (75cm) ↔24in (60cm)
A recent introduction that will mostly come true from seed, although there may be a few green seedlings. White or very pale blue flowers appear in late spring.

MORE CHOICES

- *Agastache foeniculum* 'Golden Jubilee' Z6–10 H10–6
- *Farfugium japonicum* 'Aureomaculatum' Z7–8 H8–6
- *Lamium maculatum* 'Connors Gold' Z4–8 H8–1
- *Miscanthus sinensis* 'Zebrinus' Z4–9 H9–1
- *Stachys byzantina* 'Primrose Heron' Z4-8 H8-1
- *Tradescantia x andersoniana* 'Blue and Gold' Z5-9 H9-5
- *Tricyrtis fomosana* 'Guilty Pleasure' Z6–9 H9–6
- *Veronica prostrata* 'Aurea' Z5–8 H8–3

Filipendula ulmaria 'Aurea'
GOLDEN MEADOWSWEET
Z3–9 H9–1 ↕36in (90cm) ↔24in (60cm)
Fragrant white flowers open in summer above the lacy foliage. Cut back after flowering for a second growth of brightly colored leaves. May burn badly in full sun.

Lysimachia nummularia 'Aurea'
GOLDEN CREEPING JENNY
Z4–8 H8–1 ↕2in (5cm) ↔indefinite
A very vigorous, stem-rooting evergreen that can cover a fairly large area in just one season. Bright yellow, cup-shaped flowers in summer add interest.

HERBACEOUS PLANTS

Perennials with silver, gray, or blue foliage

The cool foliage appearance of these plants makes them a perfect foil for brighter colors. Low-growing and spreading species are ideal at the front of the border and are especially effective in front of dark flowers or foliage. Taller plants can be utilized as a buffer between bold colors. Ornamental grasses with blue foliage are another good source of cool color.

Hosta 'Hadspen Blue'
HADSPEN BLUE HOSTA
☀ 💧 Z3–8 H8–1
↕8in (20cm) ↔14in (35cm)
A small clump-forming plant that spreads slowly, it needs protection from sun or its leaves will scorch badly. 16in (40cm) spikes of white, bell-shaped flowers in summer.

Lychnis coronaria
ROSE CAMPION
☼ ☀ 💧 Z4–8 H8–1 ↕32in (80cm) ↔18in (45cm)
Branching plant with gray woolly stems and leaves, flowers in summer. It is fairly short-lived, but leaves behind seedlings that are easy to remove while small.

Stachys byzantina 'Silver Carpet'
SILVER CARPET LAMB'S EARS
☼ 💧 Z4–8 H8–1
↕18in (45cm) ↔24in (60cm)
This non-flowering variety is preferable to the species which has floppy stems of small pink flowers. It makes an excellent edging or contrast plant at the front of a border.

Verbascum olympicum
OLYMPIC MULLEIN
☼ 💧 Z5–9 H9–5 ↕6ft (2m) ↔3ft (1m)
The basal rosette of silver woolly leaves are attractive before the flower spike grows in summer. Flowers last for 6–8 weeks and plants may rebloom in fall if the old spike is cut.

Festuca glauca 'Blue Glow'
BLUE GLOW BLUE FESCUE
☼ 💧 Z4–8 H8–1
↕12in (30cm) ↔10in (25cm)
Good in mass plantings and as container plants, they grow better in northern areas. Can differ in degrees of blueness.

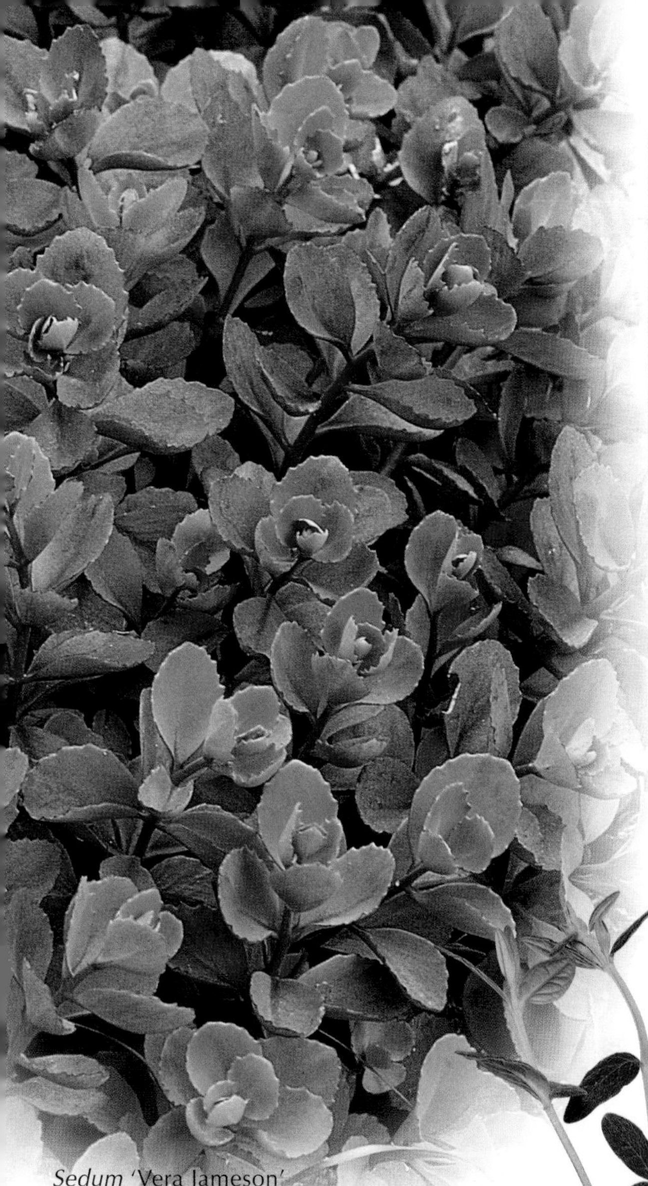

MORE CHOICES

- *Aquilegia alpina* Z4–7 H7–1
- *Artemisia schmidtiana* 'Silver Mound' Z5–8 H8–5
- *Athyrium nipponicum* 'Pictum' Z5–8 H8–1
- *Marrubium vulgare* Z4–9 H10–2
- *Hosta glauca* Z3–9 H9–1
- *Rosmarinus officinalis* 'Huntington Carpet' Z8–10 H10–12
- *Santolina incana* Z6–9 H9–4

Lamium maculatum 'Beacon Silver'
BEACON SILVER DEADNETTLE
Z4–8 H8–1
↕8in (20cm) ↔24in (60cm)
A creeping plant with stems that root easily and form a dense mat that will take light foot traffic. Pink flowers from early to midsummer.

Sedum 'Vera Jameson'
VERA JAMESON STONECROP
Z4–9 H9–1 ↕12in (30cm) ↔18in (45cm)
This hybrid blooms on purple stems from late summer to early autumn. Like most sedums, it prefers moderately fertile soil but is tolerant of poorer ones.

Teucrium fruticans
SHRUBBY GERMANDER
Z8–9 H9–8 ↕24–36in (60–90cm) ↔12ft (4m)
A woody-based, evergreen plant with arching stems, often grown in the perennial border. Whorls of pale blue flowers with prominent stamens open in summer on the ends of the shoots.

Artemisia ludoviciana 'Silver King'
CUDWEED, WHITE SAGE
Ⓝ Z5–9 H12–8
↕4ft (1.2m) ↔24in (60m)
A clump-forming perennial with foliage that turns red in fall. Flower heads are borne from midsummer to autumn. Best in well-drained, low-fertility soil.

Perovskia atriplicifolia 'Blue Spire'
RUSSIAN SAGE
Z6–9 H9–6 ↕4ft (1.2m) ↔3ft (1m)
The aromatic foliage and flowers make this attractive all summer. Cut back to 6in (15cm) in early spring. The stems are woody and break out from the lower par.

Perennial groundcovers

Most of these are best suited for a perennial or mixed border, where they form spreading clumps that smother weeds. Use the different foliage colors and textures to add interest beneath shrubs or in a woodland garden. Sun-lovers can be used around a tree base to eliminate the need for close mowing. The bugleweed and deadnettle can be used as a lawn replacement.

Saxifraga stolonifera
MOTHER OF THOUSANDS
Z7–9 H9–5 ↕↔to 12 in (30cm)
Forms a slow-growing mat with interesting mottled leaves. New plantlets form on the ends of thin runners. Does well in baskets and planters where it trails nicely.

Hosta 'Hadspen Blue'
HADSPEN BLUE PLANTAIN LILY
Z3–9 H9–1 ↕10in (25cm) ↔24in (60cm)
One of many forms of blue-leaved hosta with foliage that varies in shape, from plate-like to slender and pointed. Those with blue foliage need more shade than the yellow-leaved varieties.

Ajuga reptans
CARPET BUGLEWEED
Z3–9 H9–1
↕6in (15cm) ↔36in (90cm)
A tough plant that will survive under heavy foot traffic. It is equally at home in sun or shade and can invade a lawn. Variegated varieties are brighter.

Hosta 'Lemon Lime'
LEMON LIME PLANTAIN LILY
Z3–9 H9–1
↕6in (15cm) ↔18in (45cm)
Good border-front edging plant, if it gets shade during the heat of the day. Spreads quickly, but is not invasive. Attractive when grown under dark-leaved shrubs.

Lamium maculatum 'Beacon Silver'
BEACON SILVER DEADNETTLE
Z4–8 H8–1
↕8in (20cm) ↔24in (60cm)
A creeping plant with stems that root easily and form a dense mat that will take light foot traffic. Pink flowers from early to midsummer. Can be invasive.

Lysimachia nummularia
MONEYWORT
☼ ◐ ◇ ◑ ● Z3–8 H8–1
↕2–4in 5–10cmx) ↔12in (30cm)
A spreading plant that will grow quickly in most soils, even in a bog garden, and can become invasive. A form with yellow leaves is available and almost as rampant-growing.

MORE CHOICES

- *Ajuga reptans* 'Atropurpurea' Z3–9 H9–1
- *Ajuga reptans* 'Burgundy Glow' Z3–9 H8–2
- *Asarum shuttleworthii* 'Callaway' Z5–9 H9–1
- *Ceratostigma plumbaginoides* Z6–9 H9–6
- *Hosta* 'Blue Bush' Z3–9 H9–1
- *Hosta* 'Gold Standard' Z3–8 H9–2
- *Hosta* 'Midas Touch' Z3–9 H9–2
- *Hosta* 'Sum and Substance' Z3–8 H9–2
- *Lippia nodifolia* Z8–11 H12–1
- *Liriope muscari* Z6–10 H12–1
- *Liriope muscari* 'Big Blue' Z6–10 H12–1
- *Liriope muscari* 'Monroe White' Z6–10 H12–1
- *Liriope muscari* 'White' Z6–11 H12–1

Viola cornuta
HORNED VIOLET
☼ ◐ ◇ Z6–9 H9–1 ↕8in (12–20cm) ↔8in (20cm) or more
Forms a dense, spreading evergreen mat with slightly fragrant flowers in spring and early summer. Cut back fairly hard after flowering to keep the plants compact.

Asarum europaeum
EUROPEAN WILD GINGER
◐ ● ◑ Z4–8 H8–1 ↕3in (8cm) ↔12in (30cm)
Easy to tell from the native species by leaves that are shiny, rather than dull, and evergreen. It creeps slowly and forms compact carpets. This flowers in late spring.

Epimedium x *warleyensis*
WARLEY BARRENWORT
◐ ◑ Z5–9 H9–5 ↕20in (50cm) ↔3ft (1m)
A slow-spreading, evergreen plant with leaves that are hairy beneath and tinted red in spring and fall. The flowers are produced in late spring.

Mazus reptans
CREEPING MAZUS
Z5–8 H8–5 ↕2in (5cm) ↔12in (30cm)
A prostrate plant that forms a green carpet. Two-lipped flowers appear in late spring and persist for several weeks. Needs good drainage.

Ardisia japonica
MARLBERRY
Z6–9 H9–1 ↕18in (45cm) ↔indefinite
A woody-based plant that spreads by underground runners and forms a dense carpet. Nodding heads of star-shaped, white to pale pink flowers in summer give these persistent fruits.

Stachys byzantina
LAMB'S EARS, WOOLLY BETONY
Z4–8 H8–1
↕18in (45cm) ↔24in (60cm)
An excellent edging plant that makes a good foil for brighter flowers. The flowers detract from the foliage; the flowerless variety 'Silver carpet' may be preferable.

Vinca major
GREATER PERIWINKLE
Z7–9 H9–7
↕18in (45cm) ↔indefinite
Prostrate trailing plant with woody crown and arching stems. Flowers from spring to early fall. Useful as trailing plant in containers.

Vinca minor
LESSER PERIWINKLE
Z4–9 H9–1 ↕4–8in (10–20cm) ↔indefinite
Similar to the greater periwinkle but with smaller leaves and flowers, and more mat-forming. Varieties with white, pink, or double flowers, or with white-edged leaves, are slower growing.

Liriope muscari 'Silvery Sunproof'
SILVERY SUNPROOF LILYTURF
Z6–10 H12–1 ↕↔12–18in (30–45cm)
Although the spikes of flowers are freely produced in late summer to fall, grow this for the foliage effect. It will withstand considerable sunlight, but benefits from mid-day shade.

Liriope muscari 'Lilac Beauty'
LILAC BEAUTY LILYTURF
Z6–10 H12–1 ↕↔2ft (60cm)
Unlike 'Silver Sunproof', this variety is grown mainly for its fall flowers, although it makes a good groundcover for the rest of the year. Both varieties are evergreen.

Phlox subulata 'Marjorie'
MOSS PHLOX
Z3–8 H8–1
↕6in (15cm) ↔20in (50cm)
One of many forms of moss phlox that form low groundcovering mats. If left untrimmed after flowering, it will self-seed with abandon.

Pachysandra terminalis
JAPANESE SPURGE
Z4–8 H8–1
↕8in (20cm) ↔indefinite
Spreading evergreen, excellent groundcover under shrubs or in a woodland garden. Has white summer flowers, but glossy foliage is the main attraction.

Tulbaghia violacea
SOCIETY GARLIC
Z7–10 H10–7 ↕18–24in (45–60cm) ↔10in (25cm)
Clump-forming, with narrow, strap-like, onion-scented leaves 12in (30cm) long. Flower heads rise above the foliage from summer to early fall. Good container plant.

MORE CHOICES

- *Liriope spicata* Z6–11 H12–1
- *Ophipogon japonicus* 'Nana' Z6–10 H12–1
- *Ophiopogon planiscapus* 'Nigrescens' Z6–11 H12–1
- *Pilea microphylla* Z11 H12–1
- *Plectranthus microphylla* Z10–11 H12–1
- *Selaginella uncinata* Z6–9 H9–5
- *Viola odorata* Z6–8 H8–6
- *Wedelia trilobata* Z11 H12–10
- *Zebrina pendula* Z11 H12–10

Southern heirloom perennials

These are the plants that were grown by the early settlers who often brought them as seeds or cuttings. Some are native plants that earned their place in the early gardens because of their beauty or fragrance, or because some part of the plant was edible. Many have been since used to produce modern hybrids and superior varieties.

Hemerocallis fulva
COMMON DAYLILY, TIGER LILY
Z3–9 H12–1 ↕3ft (1m) ↔4ft (1.2m)
This is the common daylily that has naturalized itself. Almost impossible to kill, it is still widely grown and thrives under many soil and moisture conditions.

Convallaria majalis
LILY-OF-THE-VALLEY
Z2–7 H7–1 ↕6in (15cm) ↔indefinite
Bears sweetly scented spring flowers. A handful of cultivars show varying flower color and leaf variegation. Prefers moist organic soil and leaf mold mulch.

Sempervivum tectorum
HENS AND CHICKS
Z4–8 H8–1 ↕6in (15cm) ↔20in (50cm)
Each rosette gives rise to others that root to slowly form a weed-resistant carpet. Old rosettes die after flowering. Botanical name means "lives forever."

MORE CHOICES

- *Achillea* spp. Z4–9 H9–2
- *Arundo donax* Z6–11 H12–1
- *Aspidistra elatior* 'Variegata' Z13–15 H12–1
- *Crinum* spp. Z7–10 H10–7
- *Hemerocallis* cvs. Z3–10 H12–2
- *Iris* cvs. Z4–8 H8–1
- *Lycoris* spp. Z8–10 H10–8
- *Mirabilis jalapa* Z11–15 H12–9
- *Physostegia* spp. Z2–8 H8–2
- *Saxifraga stolonifera* Z7–9 H9–5
- *Tradescantia* spp. Z3–10 H12–1

Oenothera fruticosa
SUNDROPS
Z4–8 H8–1 ↕3ft (1m) ↔12in (30cm)
Bears sweetly scented spring flowers. A handful of cultivars show varying flower color and leaf variegation. Prefers moist organic soil and leaf mold mulch.

Chrysanthemum 'Clara Curtis'

CLARA CURTIS CHRYSANTHEMUM

☼ 💧 Z5–9 H9–1 ↕30in (75cm) ↔24in (60cm)

A showy border plant that is very free-flowering in late summer, before the fall 'mums. Thrives in most soils. Fragrant flowers are good for cutting.

Leucanthemum vulgare

OX-EYE DAISY

☼ ◑ 💧 Z3–8 H8–1

↕12–36in (30–90cm) ↔24in (60cm)

A slow-spreading clump that flowers freely in late spring and early summer. Deadhead to prevent seeding. This European native is now naturalized.

Hedychium coronarium

WHITE GINGER LILY

☼ ◑ 💧 Z7–11 H12–7

↕to 10ft (3m) ↔3ft (1m)

Lance-shaped leaves are downy underneath. Highly fragrant, late-summer flowers open from a narrow spike and are 4in (10cm) across. Native to India.

Hibiscus trionum

FLOWER-OF-AN-HOUR

☼ 💧 Z10–11 H12–8

↕30in (75cm) ↔20in (50cm)

A short-lived perennial that is often grown as an annual. Blooms from summer to early fall and flowers give inflated, bladder-like seed pods.

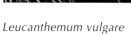

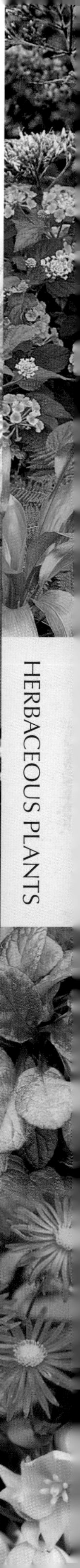

Perennial herbs

Plant these close to the house where it is easy to pop out and pick a few leaves or stems for use in the kitchen. Some, like the *Santolina*, make a good edging or front-of-the-border plant, while others, such as *Mentha*, can be invasive and are best kept contained in a large sunken planter. These species form the backbone of an herb garden.

Satureja montana
WINTER SAVORY
☼ ◯ Z5–8 H12–1
↕16in (40CM)
↔8in (20cm)
Leaves used fresh or dried to flavor soups, stews, and many dishes. Makes a small woody-based plant that grows well in poor soils and in light shade.

Rumex acetosa
GARDEN SORREL
☼ ◯◐ Z4–8 H12–2 ↕↔1–2ft (30–60cm)
Used as pot herb to add a slightly vinegary taste to salads and cooked dishes. Easy to grow in any soil except very wet. May self-seed unless deadheaded.

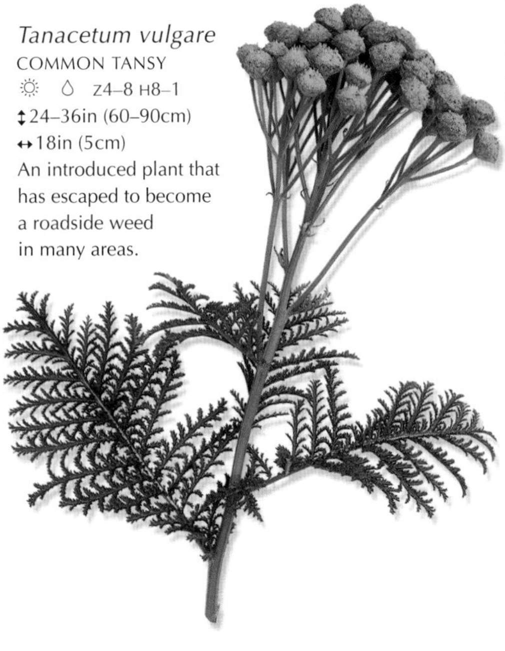

Tanacetum vulgare
COMMON TANSY
☼ ◯ Z4–8 H8–1
↕24–36in (60–90cm)
↔18in (5cm)
An introduced plant that has escaped to become a roadside weed in many areas.

Rosmarinus officinalis
ROSEMARY
☼ ◯ Z8–11 H12–8 ↕↔5ft (1.5m)
Evergreen aromatic leaves. Rosemary is a popular culinary herb and an attractive garden plant. Flowers are produced mostly at or near shoot tips .

Hyssopus officinalis
HYSSOP
☼ ◯◐● Z6–9 H9–6 ↕24in (60cm) ↔3ft (1m)
Bushy perennial that may be evergreen in the south. Grows best in stony, dry, slightly acid soils. Used to flavor sauces, soups, pickles, and meat.

Santolina chamaecyparissus
LAVENDER COTTON
☼ ○ Z6–9 H9–4 ↕20in (50cm) ↔3ft (1m)
Spreading evergreen mound bears summer flowers, best removed after they fade. Use in a mass planting, in rock gardens, or as a low hedge. Salt-tolerant.

Mentha spicata
SPEARMINT
☼ ● Z3–7 H7–1 ↕3ft (1m) ↔indefinite
Grow this vigorously spreading perennial where it can be contained. Flowers in pink or white appear during summer. Valued for its sweet-smelling (sometimes pungent) leaves.

Thymus vulgaris
COMMON THYME
☼ ○ Z4–9 H9–1 ↕12in (30cm) ↔16in (40cm)
This bushy, cushion-forming subshrub produces purple or white flowers in spring and early summer. The most commonly grown thyme for culinary use.

Calamintha nepeta
LESSER CALAMINT
☼ ☀ ○ ● Z5–9 H9–5
↕8in (45cm) ↔20–30in (50–75cm)
European mint-relative that grows best on akaline soils and has become naturalized in the eastern US.

MORE CHOICES

- *Allium tuberosum* Z4–8 H8–1
- *Armoracia rusticana* Z3–10 H12–1
- *Artemisia* spp. Z5–11 H12–1
- *Foeniculum vulgare* Z4–9 H9–1
- *Mentha pulegium* Z7–9 H12–2
- *Mentha suaveolens* 'Variegata' Z6–9 H9–5
- *Monarda* spp. Z4–9 H9–1
- *Origanum* 'Aureum' Z5–9 H9–5
- *Origanum vulgare* Z4–9 H10–2
- *Ruta graveolens* Z5–9 H9–5
- *Salvia officinalis* Z5–8 H8–5
- *Salvia officinalis* 'Tricolor' Z7–8 H8–1
- *Saponaria* spp. Z2–8 H8–1
- *Symphytum officinale* Z3–9 H9–1
- *Tanacetum parthenium* Z4–9 H9–1
- *Teucrium chamaedrys* Z4–9 H12–4
- *Thymus* x *citriodorus* 'Argenteus' Z6–9 H9–6
- *Thymus* x *citriodorus* 'Aureus' Z6–9 H9–6

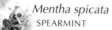

Melissa officinalis 'Aurea'
GOLD LEMON BALM
☼ ○ Z3–7 H7–1 ↕3ft (1m) ↔18in (45cm)
May become invasive if grown in too-rich soil. Moist soil and light shade may improve flavor. The green-leaved form is used for teas and drinks.

Wildflowers

These species are all native to North America but not always to this region. Combine to create meadows, integrate with other perennials in mixed borders, or use small groups of one species to provide food for wildlife. Most spread slowly by runners or seeding. Named forms exist for some, but may not come true from seed.

Monarda didyma
BEE BALM, BERGAMOT
Ⓝ ☼ ◐ ○ Z4–11 H12–1
↕18in (45cm) ↔2ft (60cm)
A slowly suckering plant that blooms from mid- to late summer. Very attractive to bees and hummingbirds but subject to powdery mildew. The leaves are used to flavor Earl Grey tea.

Mertensia pulmonarioides
VIRGINIA BLUEBELLS
Ⓝ ◐ ○ Z3–7 H7–1
↕24in (60cm) ↔18in (45cm)
Flowers open from pink-tinted buds in mid- to late spring. Grow in well-drained, organic soil. Prone to problems but usually outgrows them.

Boltonia asteroides
BOLTONIA
Ⓝ ☼ ◐ ● Z4–8 H9–1 ↕6ft (2m) ↔3ft (1m)
A strong-stemmed plant with blue-green leaves and flowers from late summer into early fall in white, lilac, or pinkish purple. Divide every few years.

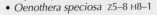

Sisyrinchium angustifolium
NARROWLEAF BLUE-EYED GRASS
Ⓝ ☼ ○ Z5–8 H8–5 ↕12in (30cm) ↔3in (8cm)
Short-lived individual flowers are borne in succession during summer on a self-seeding, semievergreen, delicate-looking perennial.

MORE CHOICES

- *Aquilegia canadensis* Z3–8 H8–1
- *Aster novae-angliae* Z4–8 H8–1
- *Chelone lyonii* Z3–9 H9–3
- *Coreopsis auriculata* Z4–9 H9–1
- *Coreopsis verticillata* Z4–9 H9–1
- *Eupatorium coelistinum* Z5–11 H9–1
- *Gaillardia pulcherrima* Z10–11 H12–1
- *Geranium maculatum* Z4–8 H8–1
- *Helianthus angustifolia* Z6–9 H9–4
- *Lobelia cardinalis* Z2–8 H8–1
- *Lupinus perennis* Z4–8 H9–1
- *Oenothera speciosa* Z5–8 H8–1

Tiarella cordifolia
FOAMFLOWER
Ⓝ ◐ ◊ Z3–8 H7–1
↕8in (20cm) ↔12in (30cm) or more
Free-spreading plant that makes a good groundcover, flowering a long time in summer. Foliage often takes on bronze fall tints.

Chrysogonum virginianum
GOLDENSTAR
Ⓝ ☼ ◐ ◊ Z5–9 H9–2
↕10in (25cm) ↔24in (60cm)
Spreading low groundcover with creeping rhizomes and leafy runners. Excellent for woodland garden.

Tradescantia virginiana
SPIDERWORT
Ⓝ ☼ ◐ ♦ Z5–9 H9–5
↕24in (60cm) ↔24in (60cm)
Tufted branching plant with pale blue to purple flowers from early summer to fall. One parent of the hybrid common in gardens. Self-seeds freely.

MORE CHOICES

- *Phlox carolina* Z5–8 H8–5
- *Phlox paniculata* Z4–8 H8–1
- *Phlox subulata* Z3–8 H8–1
- *Rudbeckia fulgida* Z4–9 H9–1
- *Salvia coccinea* Z9–10 H12–1
- *Silene virginica* Z4–8 H9–3
- *Solidago altissisma* Z3–10 H10–3
- *Stokesia laevis* Z5–9 H9–5
- *Verbena rigida* Z8–15 H12–1
- *Verbena tenuisecta* Z8–11 H12–8
- *Vernonia gigantea* Z5–9 H9–5

Iris cristata
DWARF CRESTED IRIS
Ⓝ ◐ ♦ Z4–10 H10–1
↕4in (10cm) ↔indefinite
Grows from a shallow rhizome that creeps on the surface and spreads fairly rapidly. Blooms in spring. There is a white-flowered form, plus other color variants.

Echinacea purpurea
PURPLE CONEFLOWER
Ⓝ ☼ ◊ Z3–9 H9–1 ↕to 5ft (1.5m) ↔18in (45cm)
Flowers from midsummer to early autumn and prefers deep organic soil. The cultivars bred from this native plant are often more suitable for the garden border.

Daylilies: the genus *Hemerocal*

There are probably more varieties of daylily than any other plant, and those shown here are a small representation of the genus. Divided into dormant, semi-evergreen, and evergreen, all can be grown in this region but the semi-evergreen may die down in the northern parts. Flowers on many modern varieties last more than a single day, especially on tetraploid varieties.

Hemerocallis 'Gentle Shepherd'
GENTLE SHEPHERD DAYLILY
☼ ♦ Z3–10 H12–2 ↕18in (45cm)
There is no pure white daylily, but this cultivar comes very close. This semi-evergreen variety blooms in early summer on a branched flower scape.

Hemerocallis 'Red Rum'
RED RUM DAYLILY
☼ ◊♦ Z4–11 H12–1 ↕16in (40cm)
A semi-evergreen, mid-season variety with an extended bloom time, the flowers are 4in (10cm) in diameter and carried on branched scapes.

Hemerocallis 'Siloam Virginia Henson'
SILOAM VIRGINIA HENSON DAYLILY
☼ ◊♦ Z3–10 H12–1 ↕↔16in (40cm)
This early to mid-season evergreen is one of many from the same breeder with the word "Siloam" in the name. The dark ring in the center is called an eyezone.

Hemerocallis 'Stella de Oro'
STELLA DE ORO DAYLILY
☼ ♦ Z3–9 H12–1 ↕12in (30cm) ↔18in (45cm)
This plant is vigorous and free flowering and blooms early, repeating throughout the season. It prefers fertile soil. Arguably it is the finest of all daylilies.

Hemerocallis 'Lady Fingers'
LADY FINGERS DAYLILY
Z3–10 H12–2 ↕34in (85cm)
Daylilies with narrow petals like this are known as "spiders." The foliage is arching and the flower scapes are branched with 6in (15cm) blooms in mid-season. A dormant variety.

Hemerocallis 'Cat's Cradle'
CAT'S CRADLE DAYLILY
Z3–10 H12–2 ↕30in (75cm)
Another spider but without the green throat of 'Lady Fingers'. An early to mid-season, evergreen type, it does best when protected from hard freezes.

Hemerocallis 'Joan Senior'
JOAN SENIOR DAYLILY
Z3–9 H12–1 ↕↔24in (60cm)
Flowers from early to midseason and then repeats. Introduced in 1977. Semi-evergreen foliage. Selected offspring of *H.* 'Loving Memory' and 'Little Infant'.

Hemerocallis 'Pardon Me'
PARDON ME DAYLILY
Z5–11 H12–1 ↕↔18in (45cm)
Free-flowering, bearing fragrant flowers in midseason and repeating reliably. Foliage is deciduous. Introduced in 1982. Selected descendant of *H.* 'Little Grapette'.

Hemerocallis 'Hyperion'
HYPERION DAYLILY
Z3–10 H12–2
↕↔3ft (90cm)
Fragrant flowers appear from early to midseason. The narrow leaves are deciduous. Introduced in 1925 and still grown widely.

MORE CHOICES

- *Hemerocallis* 'Chicago Queen' Z3–11 H12–2
- *Hemerocallis* 'Little Greenie' Z3–11 H12–1
- *Hemerocallis* 'Midnight Magic' Z3–11 H12–1
- *Hemerocallis* 'Tetrina's Daughter' Z3–10 H12–1

Hemerocallis fulva
COMMON DAYLILY, TIGER LILY
Z3–9 H12–1 ↕3ft (1m) ↔4ft (1.2m)
The common daylily that has naturalized widely. Almost impossible to kill, it is still widely grown and thrives under many soil and moisture conditions.

Lilies: the genus *Lilium*

At least one member of this large family of bulbs can find a home in every garden. There are lilies for sun and shade, for wet and dry locations, and for heavy and light soils. The most common groups are the Asiatic, trumpet, and Oriental hybrids, which all have many named varieties, some of which are shown here.

Lilium candidum
MADONNA LILY
Z6–9 H9–6 ↕↔3–6ft (1–2m)
A shiny, bright green basal leaf rosette gives rise to a tall flower stalk in summer. The flowers are sweetly fragrant. Susceptible to *Botrytis* (gray mold).

Lilium 'Enchantment'
ENCHANTMENT LILY
Z2–8 H8–1 ↕3ft (1m)
An old Asiatic lily much grown as a potted plant or for cut flowers. One of the easiest lilies to grow, it multiplies readily and survives under poor soil conditions.

Lilium 'Black Beauty'
BLACK BEAUTY LILY
Z3–8 H8–1 ↕6ft (18.m)
Plant this trumpet lily in spring or fall, spacing the bulbs at least 18in (45cm) apart to give them room to multiply for several years without becoming crowded.

Lilium martagon
MARTAGON LILY
☼ ◊ Z3–8 H8–1 ↕6ft (18.m)
A vigorous clump-forming lily in cultivation for centuries, it is the parent of many modern hybrids. Shade-tolerant, it should be planted in large groups.

Lilium 'Connecticut King'
CONNECTICUT KING LILY
☼ ◊ Z3–8 H8–1 ↕3ft (1m)
After 'Enchantment', this is probably the most widely grown Asiatic lily. The up-facing flowers are carried on stout stems and defy bad weather. An excellent cut flower.

Lilium regale
REGAL LILY
☼ ◊ Z3–8 H8–1 ↕6ft (18.m)
One of the easiest of the trumpet lilies, although early spring growth is liable to damage from late frosts. Plant with only 1in (2.5cm) of soil over the tip of the bulb.

MORE CHOICES

- *Lilium* 'African Queen' Z3–8 H8–1
- *Lilium auratum* Z3–8 H8–1
- *Lilium* 'Black Dragon' Z3–8 H8–1
- *Lilium* 'Casa Blanca' Z3–8 H8–1
- *Lilium formosanum* Z5–8 H8–4
- *Lilium michauxii* Z3–8 H8–1
- *Lilium* 'Mont Blanc' Z3–8 H8–1
- *Lilium* 'Stargazer' Z3–8 H8–1
- *Lilium superbum* Z4–8 H8–1

Lilium longiflorum
EASTER LILY
◑ ◊ Z7–9 H9–1 ↕16–39in (40–100cm)
Widely grown as a commercial pot plant forced into bloom for Easter, in the garden it blooms in early summer. A good container plant and highly fragrant.

Lilium
'Mont Blanc'
MONT BLANC LILY
☼ ◊ Z3–8 H8–1
↕28in (70cm)
A sturdy lily with scattered brown spots in the center of the petals. Introduced in 1978, it is a reliable plant that multiplies readily in good soil.

Irises: the genus *Iris*

The most popular irises in this genus are the bearded or German types. Varieties range from a few inches (10cm) to three feet (1m) in height and bloom from early spring; many are sweetly scented. Many other groups – such as Siberian, Japanese, and Louisiana – and a wide range of species, are also commonly grown. Most bulbous irises flower in early spring.

Iris foetidissima
GLADWIN, STINKING IRIS
☼ ☀ ◑ Z4–9 H9–2 ↕3ft (1m)
This summer-blooming beardless iris gets its name from the foliage, which smells rank when bruised. Prefers moderately fertile, well-drained soil.

Iris fulva
COPPER IRIS
Ⓝ ☀ ◑ Z4–9 H9–3 ↕4ft (120cm)
Spreading slowly by creeping stems, this parent of many hybrids known as Louisiana irises, grows in the wild in river bottoms, wet in spring but dry in summer.

Iris sibirica 'Caesar's Brother'
CAESAR'S BROTHER SIBERIAN IRIS
☼ ☀ ○ Z4–9 H9–1 ↕30in (75cm)
Flowering after the more widely grown bearded iris, this is an older variety that has been much used to produce modern hybrids. Foliage turns yellow in fall.

Iris innominata
WOODLAND IRIS
Ⓝ ☼ ☀ ◑ Z7–9 H9–7 ↕6–20in (6–25cm)
Flowers can also be cream to pale lavender and purple. Prefers fertile, well-drained, loamy soil. Susceptible to aphids and mealybugs, especially when in bloom.

Iris cristata
DWARF CRESTED IRIS
Ⓝ ☀ ● Z4–10 H10–1 ↕4in (10cm)
This spring bloomer grows from a shallow rhizome that creeps on the surface and spreads gradually. It performs best in part or dappled shade.

MORE CHOICES

- *Iris bucharica* Z5–9 H9–5
- *Iris graminea* Z6–9 H9–5
- *Iris kaempferi* Z3–9 H9–1
- *Iris laevigata* Z4–9 H9–1
- *Iris unguicularis* Z7–9 H9–7
- *Iris versicolor* Z3–9 H9–1

Iris 'Beverley Sills'
BEVERLEY SILLS IRIS
☼ ◐ ◊ Z3–9 H9–1 ↕36in (90cm)
This iris won the top award from the American Iris Society in 1985. As with all bearded irises, rhizomes should be planted with tops slightly above soil level.

Iris 'Ming Dynasty'
MING DYNASTY IRIS
☼ ◐ ◊ Z3–9 H9–1 ↕3ft (1m)
In bearded irises, this coloring, where there are streaks or stipples of a second color, is known as "plicata." This generally occurs on white or yellow varieties.

Iris 'Silver Years'
SILVER YEARS IRIS
☼ ◐ ◊ Z3–9 H9–1 ↕3ft (1m)
This is one of many bearded irises with white flowers, although they also come in many other colors. There are also white selections of smaller bearded irises.

Iris ensata
JAPANESE IRIS
☼ ♦ Z3–9 H9–1 ↕2–3ft(60–90cm)
Blooming in summer, these are great for a shallow pool or bog garden. There are many named varieties with flowers up to 6in (15cm) across, in a wide range of colors and often with ruffled petals.

Iris reticulata
NETTED IRIS
☼ ◊ Z4–9 H8–4 ↕4–6in (10–15cm)
A bulbous iris that flowers in early spring and goes dormant the rest of the year. Named varieties come in shades of blue and violet and are easy to grow.

Sage: the genus *Salvia*

Salvias can be annuals, perennials, or small shrubs, and are mostly found growing in sunny, fairly dry locations, like rocky slopes, meadows, and woodland borders. Many are aromatic; others have dense woolly or silver foliage. Flowers are mainly shades of blue, but are red or purple in some warm-climate species. Most flower for a long time and attract wildlife.

Salvia guaranitica
ANISE SAGE
Z7–10 H12–8 ↕5ft (1.5m) ↔24in (60cm)
A shrubby perennial with thin upright stems and rough, toothed oval leaves. It flowers from late summer to fall. Named forms have brighter flowers.

Salvia greggii
AUTUMN SAGE
Ⓝ Z7–9 H9–4 ↕↔12–20in (30–50cm)
Somewhat woody sub-shrub with small gray-green leaves. The flowers, which can be pink or white, are in short spikes from late summer to fall. Native to Texas.

Salvia uliginosa
BOG SAGE
Z8–11 H12–7 ↕to 6ft (2m) ↔36in (90cm)
A clump-forming, rhizomatous perennial with deeply toothed, very aromatic leaves. Flowers from late summer to midautumn. Flowers can also be white.

Salvia leucantha
MEXICAN BUSH SAGE
Z9–11 H12–4
↕24–39in (60–100cm) ↔16–36in (40–90cm)
Large clumps of white-woolly branches carry small white flowers with purple bracts in late spring to fall.

Salvia coccinea 'Coral Nymph'
CORAL NYMPH TEXAS SAGE
☼ ◑ ◊ Z10–12 H12–1 ↕16in (40cm) ↔12in (30cm)
Erect bushy plant grown as annual in cooler climes. Flowers appear from midsummer onwards. Other varieties have red or white flowers and may be taller.

Salvia elegans
PINEAPPLE SCENTED SAGE
◑ ◊♦ Z8–11 H12–1 ↕4ft (1.2m) ↔3ft (1m)
An open-branched, woody perennial with foliage that smells of fresh pineapples when crushed. It flowers in late summer and may be evergreen in the South.

Salvia 'Indigo Spires'
INDIGO SPIRES SAGE
☼ ◑ ◊♦ Z8–11 H12–7 ↕3ft (1m) ↔12in (30cm)
A bushy plant with spikes of flowers from mid- to late summer. Flowers start to open when the spikes are small; as the spikes lengthen, they twist in a spiral.

Salvia officinalis 'Tricolor'
TRICOLOR COMMON SAGE
☼ ◑ ◊ Z5–8 H8–1 ↕30in (90cm) ↔3ft (1m)
A form of the common culinary sage that is not quite as hardy, and has a slightly less herbal scent. Makes a good edging. Cut back fairly hard in early spring to encourage new growth with the brightest possible foliage.

Salvia patens 'Cambridge Blue'
CAMBRIDGE BLUE GENTIAN SAGE
☼ ◑ ◊ Z8–9 H9–8 ↕18–24in (45–60cm) ↔18in (45cm)
An erect perennial that is covered in glandular hairs. Loose small spikes of paired flowers are produced from summer to fall. There is also a white-flowered form. May be grown as an annual.

Salvia praetensis 'Haematodes'
GREECIAN MEADOW CLARY
☼ ◊ Z3–9 H9–1 ↕2–3ft (60–90cm) ↔18in (45cm)
A group of similar plants that differ from the common meadow clary by having branched stems that are a blood-red color, and darker flowers produced from late spring to late summer.

MORE CHOICES

- *Salvia argentea* Z5–8 H8–5
- *Salvia azurea* Z9–10 H10–9
- *Salvia elegans* 'Honey Melon' Z8–11 H12–1
- *Salvia farinacea* Z8–10 H12–1
- *Salvia guaranitica* Z7–10 H12–8
- *Salvia guaranitica* 'Black and Blue' Z8–11 H12–8
- *Salvia guaranitica* 'Blue Enigma' Z5–8 H8–5
- *Salvia leucantha* 'Midnight' Z9–11 H12–4
- *Salvia madrensis* Z6–9 H9–5
- *Salvia microphylla* Z12–15 H12–10
- *Salvia officinalis* 'Icterina' Z5–8 H8–5
- *Salvia regla* Z7–9 H9–6
- *Salvia sclarea var. turkestanica* Z5–9 H9–3
- *Salvia splendens* 'Van Houttei' Z9–11 H12–1

Ferns for shaded gardens

Many ferns are woodland plants so it is not surprising that they are able to tolerate shade. Some need moist conditions; others do better in soils that become dry in summer. Some are evergreen, others die down in fall, while a few are evergreen only in the Deep South. There are many named forms of some of these, available from specialist nurseries.

Osmunda regalis
ROYAL FERN
Ⓝ ☼ 💧 Z2–10 H9–1 ↕6ft (2m) ↔3ft (1m)
An impressive deciduous fern that produces its ornamental fertile fronds in summer. Grow in fertile organic soil. It is prone to rust. Rootstock is source of osmunda fiber.

Dryopteris marginalis
MARGINAL WOOD FERN
Ⓝ ☀ ◑ Z3–8 H8–1 ↕24in (60cm) ↔12 (30cm)
An evergreen fern with blue-green summer foliage. It prefers an organic soil and is drought tolerant once established. Excellent groundcover for a shady hillside.

Cyrtomium falcatum
JAPANESE HOLLY FERN
☼ ☀ ○ ◑ Z6–15 H12–10 ↕24in (60cm) ↔3ft (1m)
Grows well in acid and alkaline soils and will spread slowly to form a colony. Makes a good container or houseplant. Cultivars have toothed fronds.

Woodwardia areolata
NETTED CHAIN FERN
Ⓝ ☼ 💧 pH Z2–8 H8–1 ↕↔18in (45cm)
Grows best in an acid soil that is never allowed to dry out. Forms a spreading clump with underground rhizomes. New fronds covered with light brown scales.

Athyrium filix-femina
LADY FERN
Ⓝ ☀ 💧 Z4–9 H9–1 ↕4ft (1.2m) ↔3ft (1m)
The deciduous foliage radiates out from the center of the rhizome. Adaptable to many soil conditions, but it prefers fertile, highly organic soil.

MORE CHOICES

- *Asplenium trichomanes* Z5–8 H8–3
- *Botrychium virginianum* Z7–9 H9–7
- *Cystopteris fragilis* Z4–8 H8–1
- *Dennstaedtia punctilobula* Z3–8 H8–1
- *Dicksonia punctilobula* Z9–10 H12–10
- *Dryopteris filix-mas* Z4–8 H8–1
- *Gymnocarpium dryopteris* Z4–8 H8–1
- *Osmunda cinnamomea* Z3–9 H9–1
- *Phegopteris hexagonptera* Z3–8 H8–1
- *Polystichum acrostichoides* Z3–8 H8–1
- *Thelypteris kunthii* Z6–9 H9–5

Athyrium niponicum 'Pictum'
JAPANESE PAINTED FERN
☀ 💧 Z5–8 H8–1
↕12in (30cm) ↔indefinite
Showy, arching fronds increase slowly from spreading clumps on this deciduous fern. They color up best when the plants are grown in light shade.

Dryopteris erythrosora
JAPANESE SHIELD FERN
☀ 💧 Z5–9 H9–1
↕18in (45cm) ↔12in (30cm)
Copper-colored, evergreen new foliage, which may be red in cool climates, appears in early fall. Establishes slowly and does well in containers.

Thelypteris kunthii
SOUTHERN MAIDEN FERN
Ⓝ ☼☀ 💧💧 Z6–9 H9–5 ↕↔4ft (1.2m)
Growing from long creeping rhizomes, the deciduous foliage is a good summer accompaniment to shrubs or large perennials. Fast-growing, it does best in a slightly acid soil. Divide in spring or fall.

Polystichum acrostichoides
CHRISTMAS FERN
Ⓝ ☀ 💧 Z3–8 H8–1 ↕24in (60cm) ↔18in (45cm)
Shuttlecock-like, evergreen foliage emerges from clumping rhizomes as silvery fiddleheads. Clumps enlarge over time but do not spread aggressively.

Adiantum pedatum
MAIDENHAIR FERN
Ⓝ ☀ 💧 Z3–8 H8–1 ↕↔12–16in (30–40cm)
A popular, easy-to-grow, deciduous fern that is worth a place in every shady garden. Spreads slowly by underground stems. Native to eastern North America.

Evergreen ferns

Ferns are an indispensable part of a shaded garden, and grow easily in moist locations. Surprisingly tough, their rich texture compliments broad-leaved plants. Many die to the ground in fall, but those showen here grace the garden year-round. Where not hardy, many of these make very good houseplants, especially if given a light misting two to three times a week.

Asplenium nidus
BIRD'S-NEST FERN
Ⓝ ☼ 💧 Z13–15 H12–3 ↕4ft (1.2m) ↔2ft (60cm)
Widely grown fern that makes a good pot or container plant. In the garden, grow between rocks, which it will colonize. Other forms have pleated or lobed fronds.

Cyrtomium falcatum
JAPANESE HOLLY FERN
☼ ☀ 💧💧 Z6–15 H12–10 ↕24in (60cm) ↔3.5ft (1.1m)
Widely grown for its shiny, long-lasting fronds, this fern grows equally well in acid or alkaline soils and will form large colonies. It is often sold as a houseplant.

Nephrolepis exaltata 'Bostoniensis'
BOSTON FERN
Ⓝ ☀ 💧 Z13–15 H12–1 ↕↔36in (90cm) or more
The species itself is hardly ever grown but this variety is probably the most popular of all ferns. Has given rise to many different forms since introduced in 1870.

Dryopteris marginalis
MARGINAL WOOD FERN
Ⓝ ☀ 💧 Z3–8 H8–1 ↕24in (60cm) ↔12 (30cm)
An evergreen fern with blue-green summer foliage. It prefers an organic soil and is drought tolerant once established. Excellent groundcover for a shady hillside.

Asplenium scolopendrium 'Crispum'
HART'S-TONGUE FERN
☼ 💧 Z6–8 H8–6 ↕28in (70cm) ↔24in (60cm)
Unusual fern grows best on alkaline soils and can even seed itself into brick walls. Species has smooth leaves, other varieties may be lobed. May be sold as *Phyllitis*.

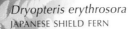

Dryopteris erythrosora
JAPANESE SHIELD FERN
☀ 💧 Z5–9 H9–1 ↕18in (45cm) ↔12in (30cm)
Copper-colored, evergreen new foliage, which may be red in cool climates. Appears in early fall, establishes slowly, and does well in containers.

Blechnum spicant
DEER FERN
Ⓝ Z10–11 H12–10 ↕30in (75cm) ↔18in (45cm)
The older sterile fronds lay out horizontally on this tufted evergreen fern that grows from short creeping rhizomes. Contrasts attractively with finer foliage.

Polystichum munitum
SWORD FERN
Ⓝ Z3–8 H8–1
↕4ft (1.2m) ↔12in (30cm)
Similar in appearance but much larger than the related *P. acrostichoides* and with more leathery leaves. The large fronds may live for several years.

Polypodium polypodioides
RESURRECTION FERN
Ⓝ Z8–11 H12–8 ↕to 12in (36cm)
An interesting fern that is capable of withstanding considerable periods of drought; the fronds curl up to reduce water loss. When moisture returns, the fronds uncurl – hence resurrection.

MORE CHOICES

- *Arachniodes simplicior* Z12–15 H12–10
- *Asplenium platyneuron* Z3–9 H9–1
- *Asplenium trichomanes* Z5–8 H8–3
- *Athyrium niponicum* 'Pictum' Z5–8 H8–1
- *Cyathea cooperi* Z11–12 H12–10
- *Cyrtomium falcatum* Z6–15 H12–10
- *Cyrtomium fortunei* Z7–10 H10–7
- *Dicksonia antartica* Z12–15 H12–10
- *Dryopteris filix-mas* Z4–8 H8–1
- *Dryopteris seiboldii* Z6–8 H8–6
- *Polypodium virginianum* Z5–8 H8–5
- *Polystichum andersonii* Z6–9 H9–6
- *Polystichum polyblepharum* Z6–8 H8–5
- *Polystichum setiferum* 'Plumosum Densum' Z6–9 H9–6
- *Woodwardia fimbriata* Z8–9 H9–8

Rumohra adiantiformis
LEATHERLEAF FERN
Z8–11 H12–8 ↕20–60in (50cm–1.5m)
Young fronds covered in silvery white scales that remain on the stem but darken with age. Leaves are long lasting and remain turgid when cut.

Polystichum acrostichoides
CHRISTMAS FERN
Ⓝ Z3–8 H8–1 ↕24in (60cm) ↔18in (45cm)
Shuttlecock-like, evergreen foliage emerges from clumping rhizomes as silvery fiddleheads . Clumps enlarge over time but do not spread aggressively.

Ornamental grasses

Many ornamental grasses have showy seed heads that add interest to the garden once the main flowering season is over. Some have leaves striped in white or yellow; others have a steel-blue color. Their narrow upright foliage is a good contrast to broad-leaved plants. Most are clump-forming but some spread by underground runners and are ideal for stabilizing banks.

Carex elata 'Aurea'
BOWLES' GOLDEN SEDGE
Z5–9 H9–3 ↕28in (70cm) ↔18in (45cm)
Narrow yellow leaves have a thin green stripe. Color is best in the new spring foliage but remains good for summer. Foliage burns badly if soil is too dry.

Carex siderosticha 'Variegata'
VARIEGATED CREEPING BROADLEAF SEDGE
Z6–9 H9–3 ↕12in (30cm) ↔16cm (40cm)
Slowly spreading, this tough and adaptable perennial has pale brown flower spikes in late spring. Prone to rust, smuts, leaf spots, and aphids.

Calamagrostis x *acutiflora* 'Overdam'
OVERDAM FEATHER REED GRASS
Z5–9 H9–1 ↕4ft (1.2m) ↔4ft (1.2m)
A very effective plant for the border, starting into growth early in spring and continuing to be decorative into winter. The plumes stand up to wind and rain.

Chasmanthium latifolium
RIVER OATS
(N) Z5–9 H9–5 ↕3ft (1m) ↔24in (60cm)
Upright clumps of foliage have feathery flower spikes in summer that produce pendulous, oatlike seed heads. They hang on into winter, surviving fall rains.

Cortaderia selloana
PAMPAS GRASS
Z7–11 H12–7 ↕8ft (2.5m) ↔4ft (1.2m)
Blooms in late summer; the plumes persist into winter. Tolerant of most watering regimes. Prefers fertile, well-drained soil. Susceptible to *Helminthosporium* leaf spot.

MORE CHOICES

- *Andropogon gerardii* Z2–7 H7–1
- *Andropogon virginicus* Z2–7 H7–1
- *Cortaderia selloana* 'Rendatleri' Z7–11 H12–7
- *Eragrostis spectabilis* Z9–10 H10–9
- *Miscanthus floridus* Z6–9 H9–3
- *Miscanthus sinensis* 'Autumn Light' Z5–9 H9–1
- *Miscanthus sinensis* 'Cabaret' Z5–9 H9–1
- *Miscanthus sinensis* 'Cosmopolitan' Z4–9 H9–1
- *Miscanthus sinensis* 'Kaskade' Z5–9 H9–5

Muhlenbergia capillaris
PINK HAIR GRASS
Ⓝ ☼ ◑ ◊ ◆ Z7–9 H9–6 ↕↔30 in (75cm)
Flowers appear in fall and, after turning pale brown, remain attractive into winter. Most effective in large plantings. Native from Massachusetts to Florida.

Cymbopogon citratus
LEMON GRASS
☼ ◆ Z10–11 H12–1 ↕5ft (1.5m) ↔3ft (1m)
A favored ingredient in Asian cuisine, it can be planted out for the summer, in the garden or a container, and survive the winter on a sunny window ledge inside.

Miscanthus sinensis 'Gracillimus'
EULALIA, MAIDENGRASS
☼ ◊ Z5–9 H9–1 ↕4ft (1.2m) ↔30in (45cm)
Leaves of this cultivar are more narrow and curved than the species and have white midribs. Flowers appear in fall; seedheads persist throughout winter.

Miscanthus sinensis 'Strictus'
PORCUPINE GRASS
☼ ◊ ◆ Z5–9 H9–1 ↕8ft (2.5m) ↔4–10ft (1.2–3m)
This is similar to zebra grass with pale bands on the foliage, but more upright and less likely to be damaged by high winds. Pink flowers in late summer give the seed-heads shown here.

Pennisetum alopecuroides 'Moudry'
BLACK FLOWERING MOUNTAIN GRASS
☼ ◊ Z6–9 H9–3 ↕↔3ft (1m)
Bears flower spikes from summer to fall. Seeds of this cultivar are black, giving the spikes a dark cast. Prefers moderately fertile soil.

Setaria palmifolia 'Rubra'
RED PALM GRASS
☼ ◐ ◊ Z9–10 H10–9 ↕↔3–6ft (1–2m)
This will not survive temperatures below 40°F (4°C) and should be moved inside before any chance of frost. Excellent container plant, grown for its foliage.

Pennisetum villosum
FEATHERTOP
☼ ◊ Z9–15 H12–1 ↕↔24in (60cm)
This marginally hardy grass is easy to grow from seed. It is a very showy species that also does well in containers and is used by florists as a cut flower.

Deschampsia caespitosa
TUFTED HAIR GRASS
☼ ◐ ◊◈◆ Z4–8 H8–1
↕6ft (2m) ↔5ft (1.5m)
An excellent evergreen grass that prefers cool locations with adequate moisture but does well in parts of this region. Airy heads of tiny flowers appear in summer.

Phyllostachys aurea
GOLDEN BAMBOO
☼ ◐ ◈ Z7–11 H12–7 ↕6–30ft (2–10m) ↔indefinite
A vigorous spreading bamboo that is excellent for holding steep slopes or as a hedge or screen. It also makes a good container plant. The decorative golden stems can be used as walking sticks.

Schizachyrium scoparium
LITTLE BLUESTEM
Ⓝ ☼ ◊ Z2–7 H7–1 ↕3ft (1m) ↔12in (30cm)
One of the characteristic grasses of tallgrass prairie. Very tolerant of moisture and soil. Foliage color is variable, ranging from bluish to bright green.

Panicum virgatum 'Cloud Nine'
CLOUD NINE SWITCH GRASS
Ⓝ ☼ ◊ Z3–9 H9–1 ↕5–7ft (1.5–2.1m) ↔3ft (1m)
The new foliage, in late spring, is a good blue-green, turning as fall approaches. The flower spikes weather well and will last all winter, surviving wind and rain.

Arundo donax 'Versicolor'
GIANT REED
☼ ♦ Z7–15 H12–1
↕8–10ft (2.5–3m) ↔2ft (60cm)
Terminal clusters of light green to purple spikelets are produced from mid- to late fall. The habit is suggestive of corn plants. Also called *A. donax* 'Variegata'.

Pleioblastus auricomus
GOLDEN-STRIPED BAMBOO
☼ ♦ Z7–15 H12–1 ↕↔5ft (1.5m)
A fast-growing, rhizomatous bamboo that makes a good container plant where its aggressive growth can be controlled. Drought-tolerant when established.

Panicum virgatum 'Hänse Herms'
HÄNSE HERMS SWITCH GRASS
Ⓝ ☼ ◊ Z3–9 H9–1 ↕3ft (1m) ↔30in (75cm)
Foliage starts to turn red in late summer, burgundy by fall. Pink summer flowers last well and seed heads are wind and rain resistant, adding winter color.

Stipa gigantea
GIANT FEATHER GRASS
☼ ◊ Z8–15 H12–1 ↕8ft (2.5m) ↔4ft (1.2m)
This grass needs a dry soil in winter, it will not survive wet conditions. The flowers, which come out in summer, dry well for winter arrangements.

MORE CHOICES

- *Miscanthus sinensis* 'Kliene Fountain' Z4–9 H9–1
- *Miscanthus sinensis* 'Morning Light' Z5–9 H9–1
- *Miscanthus sinensis* 'Zebrinus' Z4–9 H9–1
- *Panicum virgatum* 'Heavy Metal' Z5–9 H9–4
- *Phalaris arundinacea var. picta* Z4–9 H9–1
- *Sorghastrum nutans* Z4–9 H9–1

Low-growing grasses

Dwarf ornamental grasses serve several purposes in the garden. They can act as a low edging, give a contrast in foliage to more common perennials, or be a source for dried flowers. They are very popular in commercial landscapes because of their toughness and lack of problems. They come in a range of foliage colors that blend well with other plants.

Pennisetum alopecuroides 'Little Bunny'
LITTLE BUNNY DWARF FOUNTAIN GRASS
☼ ◊ Z5–9 H9–1 ↕10in (25cm) ↔12in (30cm)
Bears flower spikes from summer to fall. Use to soften the foreground of a bed or in a mass planting. Prefers poor to moderately fertile soil.

Imperata cylindrica 'Rubra'
JAPANESE BLOOD GRASS
☼ ◑ Z5–9 H9–3 ↕20in (50cm) ↔indefinite
Leaves start green but quickly transform to deep blood red. This perennial grass is a slow spreader. Also known as *I. cylindrica* 'Red Baron'.

Deschampsia caespitosa
TUFTED HAIR GRASS
☼ ◐ ◊ ◑ ● Z4–8 H8–1 ↕6ft (2m) ↔5ft (1.5m)
An excellent evergreen grass that prefers cool locations with adequate moisture but does well in most of this region. Airy heads of tiny flowers appear in summer.

Briza media
COMMON QUAKING GRASS, TREMBLING GRASS
☼ ◐ ◊ Z4–11 H12–1 ↕3ft (1m) ↔12in (30cm)
This grows on both acidic and alkaline soils. Flowers appear in late spring and turn from purple-tinted green to straw brown as they age. They dry well.

Hakonechloa macra 'Aureola'
GOLDEN JAPANESE FOREST GRASS
☼ ◐ ◑ Z5–9 H9–4
↕14in (35cm) ↔16in (40cm)
Forms mounds of arching leaves that are bright yellow with narrow green stripes until they turn red in fall. Pale green spikelets open late summer to midautumn.

MORE CHOICES

- *Arrhenatherium elatus* subsp. *bulbosum* Z5–8 H8–5
- *Bouteloua gracilis* Z5–9 H9–5
- *Bromus inermis* 'Skinner's Gold' Z6–8 H12–1
- *Chasmanthium latifolium* Z5–9 H9–5
- *Festuca glauca* Z4–8 H8–1
- *Helictotrichon sempervirens* Z4–9 H9–1
- *Koeleria glauca* Z6–9 H9–6
- *Leymus secalinus* Z5–8 H10–1
- *Millium effusum* 'Aureum' Z6–9 H9–6
- *Molinia caerulea* 'Variegata' Z4–8 H8–1
- *Muhlenbergia capillaris* Z7–9 H9–6
- *Nassella tenuissima* Z7–9 H9–6
- *Pennisetum orientale* Z6–10 H10–4
- *Pennisetum villosum* Z9–15 H12–1
- *Schizachyrium scoparium* Z2–7 H7–1
- *Sporobolus heterolepsis* Z3–8 H10–2
- *Stenotaphrum secundatum* 'Variegatum' Z9–11 H12–9

Grasslike plants

Plants such as sedges, rushes, and bamboos are not technically members of the grass family, but are often considered grasses horticulturally because they have similar foliage and form. Like grasses, some are suited to wet garden sites and others require dry spots. Use them in the same way as grasses, to add foliage contrast in form or color.

Equisetum hyemale
COMMON HORSETAIL
Ⓝ ☼ 💧 Z3–11 H12–1 ↕to 4ft (1.2m) ↔indefinite
Invasive species that should be planted in a container to restrict its growth. Extremely adaptable. Ancient species, little changed since the time of the dinosaurs.

MORE CHOICES

- *Acorus calamus* 'Variegatus' Z10–11 H12–2
- *Arundinaria viridistrata* Z7–15 H12–1
- *Bambusa oldhamii* Z8–11 H12–8
- *Butomus umbellatus* Z3–11 H8–5
- *Carex comans* 'Frosted Curl' Z7–9 H9–7
- *Carex elata* 'Aurea' Z5–9 H9–3
- *Carex pendula* Z5–9 H9–5
- *Cyperus alternifolia* Z13–15 H12–10
- *Cyperus papyrus* Z13–15 H12–6
- *Hypoxis hirsuta* Z5–8 H8–4
- *Juncus effusus* 'Spiralis' Z6–9 H9–6
- *Liriope muscari* Z6–10 H10–6
- *Luzula nivea* Z4–9 H9–1
- *Ophiopogon japonicus* Z7–10 H12–1
- *Phormium tenax* Z9–11 H12–6
- *Phyllostachys aureosulcata* Z5–11 H12–3
- *Phyllostachys nigra* Z7–11 H12–4
- *Pleioblastus pygmaeus* Z5–10 H10–5
- *Sasa veitchii* Z6–15 H12–1
- *Schoenoplectus lacustris* subsp. *tabernaemontani* 'Zebrinus' Z6–9 H9–6
- *Sisyrinchium angustifolium* Z5–8 H8–5
- *Typha latifolia* Z2–11 H12–1
- *Typha minima* Z3–11 H12–1
- *Yucca filamentosa* Z5–10 H12–1

Acorus gramineus 'Variegatus'
STRIPED JAPANESE SWEET FLAG
☼ 💧💧 Z10–11 H12–2
↕3–14in (8–35cm) ↔4in (15cm)
Do not allow to dry out or leaves may burn. Makes a good indoor plant. Evergreen in the South.

Phormium tenax
NEW ZEALAND FLAX
☼ 💧 Z9–11 H12–6 ↕10ft (3m) ↔3–6ft (1–2m)
Clump-forming perennial, good focal point, grows well in coastal locations. Striped, purple, and variegated forms available. Mulch in winter where borderline.

Arundo donax var. *versicolor*
STRIPED GIANT REED
☼ 💧 Z7–15 H12–1 ↕8–10ft (2.5–3m) ↔2ft (60cm)
Grow at the back of a border with protection from strong winds. Cut back hard in spring but beware of sharp, serrated leaf edges. May be sold as 'Variegata'.

Tropical plants

Where summers are hot and the danger of frost in winter is slight, adventurous gardeners use the plants shown here as permanent plantings. Some can survive low temperatures while dormant, but most need some protection should frost threaten. Grow these in containers where they are marginally hardy, and move inside for winter or give temporary shelter.

Allamanda cathartica 'Hendersonii'
HENDERSON'S GOLDEN TRUMPET
Z14–15 H12–10 ↕↔25–50ft (7.5–15m)
A vigorous climber with whorls of 3 or 4 lance-shaped leaves. From summer to fall, bronze-tinged buds open to give these bright blooms. Good conservatory plant.

Strelitzia reginae
BIRD OF PARADISE
Z13–15 H12–1 ↕to 6ft (2m) ↔3ft (1m)
Three-petaled flowers open from boatshaped bracts from winter to spring. An excellent container plant, it forms large clumps over time.

MORE CHOICES

- *Acalypha wilkesiana* Z14–15 H12–1
- *Acalypha hispida* Z11 H12–6
- *Aloe vera* Z10–11 H12–3
- *Alpinia zerumbet* 'Variegata' Z14–15 H12–10
- *Asparagus densiflorus* 'Sprengeri' Z13–15 H12–1
- *Breynia disticha* 'Roseopicta' Z14–15 H12–10
- *Brugmansia versicolor* Z11–12 H12–10
- *Clerodendrum speciosissimum* Z13–15 H12–10

Plumeria alba
WHITE FRANGIPANI
Z11–12 H12–10 ↕20ft (6m) ↔12ft (3.5m)
A spreading deciduous shrub with spirally arranged leaves that are hairy beneath. The very fragrant flowers are borne in terminal clusters from summer to fall.

Bougainvillea 'Miss Manila'
MISS MANILA BOUGAINVILLEA
☼ ◊ Z13–15 H12–1 ↕25–40ft (8–12m)
One of many named forms of bougainvillea that come in a range of red, pink, mauve, salmon, yellow, and white shades. They are all weak spiny climbers.

Schefflera arboricola 'Trinette'
VARIEGATED SCHEFFLERA
☼ ● ◑ ● Z11–12 H12–1 ↕to 20ft (6m) ↔8ft (2.5m)
Upright shrub commonly grown as a houseplant. Outdoors, when it receives a cool dormant period, upright sprays of red flowers produce in summer.

Codiaeum variegatum
CROTON
☼ ☀ ◊ ◑ Z13–15 H12–10
↕3–8ft (1–2.5m) ↔3–6ft (1–2m)
Grown for its multicolored foliage, this needs a high potassium fertilizer during the growing season. Leaf coloration is best in full sun. The variety pictum has narrow leaves.

Alpinia zerumbet
PINK PORCELAIN LILY
☀ ◑ Z14–15 H12–10 ↕10ft (3m) ↔3–4ft (1–1.2m)
Makes a good container plant where its arching stems can be seen to best advantage. The variegated form is attractive when not in flower. May be sold as *A. speciosa* or *A. nutans*.

Alpinia purpurata
RED GINGER
☀ ◑ Z11 H12–10 ↕10–12ft (3–4m) ↔24–36in (60–90cm)
A perennial that needs soil rich in organic matter. The upright red bracts carry small white flowers and persist long after the flowers have faded.

Aechmea fasciata
URN PLANT
☼ ◊◊ Z14–15 H12–1 ↕16in (40cm) ↔20in (50cm)
Grow this in a soil mix formulated for bromeliads. In summer, keep the central cup filled with water but do not fertilize. The rosette dies after flowering.

Clerodendrum thomsoniae
GLORY BOWER
☼ ◊◊ Z14–15 H12–1 ↕to 12ft (4m)
A climbing, summer-flowering vine. After the red flowers drop, the white bracts gradually turn pink, extending the display.

Ixora coccinea
FLAME OF THE WOODS
☼ ◊◊ Z14–15 H12–10 ↕8ft (2.5m) ↔6ft (2m)
A bushy shrub that flowers from spring to late fall with flower heads up to 4in (20cm) across. Modern hybrids come in shades from pink to orange and yellow.

MORE CHOICES

- *Clivia miniata* Z12–15 H12–10
- *Cordyline terminalis* 'Tricolor' Z0 H12–1
- *Costus barbatus* Z11 H12–1
- *Cyathea australis* Z10–11 H12–7
- *Ensete ventricosum* Z10–11 H12–1
- *Euphorbia cotinifolia* Z7–11 H12–7
- *Heliconia bihai* Z0 H12–10
- *Heliconia carabica* Z0 H12–10
- *Tecomaria capensis* Z12–15 H12–10

Pachystachys lutea
LOLLIPOP PLANT
☼ ◊♦ Z11–12 H12–10
↕to 3ft (1m) ↔18–30in (45–75cm)
A small upright shrub with flowers in late spring and early summer. The yellow bracts remain decorative long after the white flowers have fallen. A good border plant.

Thunbergia grandiflora
BLUE TRUMPET VINE
☼ ◊♦ Z14–15 H12–10
↕15–30ft (5–10m)
A vigorous vine with dark green, heart-shaped leaves. The flowers open in summer on short pendulous sprays growing from the leaf axils. There is also a white-flowered variety.

Passiflora coccinea
RED GRANADILLA
☼ ☀ ♦ Z14–15 H12–10 ↕12ft (4m)
A vigorous climber with slender red stems and lobed leaves covered in red hairs. Flowers, produced from summer to fall, may produce edible fruit.

Anthurium andraeanum
FLAMINGO LILY
☼ ☀ ♦ Z14–15 H12–10 ↕24in (60cm) ↔12in (30cm)
Grows best in a coarse soil enriched with organic matter. A parent of many named hybrids, it needs a cool resting period to flower well.

Justicia carnea
BRAZILIAN PLUME
☀ ◊♦ Z14–15 H12–10 ↕to 6ft (2m) ↔to 3ft (1m)
An erect evergreen shrub closely related to the lollipop plant (above). The 6in (15cm) spikes of flowers open in several flushes during the summer and fall.

Spring-flowering bulbs

Often the first to bloom after winter, plant some in a sun-trap to enjoy an early spring. Readily available and economical, plant in drifts across a perennial or shrub border, not just along the front. They make a superb display and after flowering will be hidden by emerging leaves. Many multiply rapidly and can be naturalized in lawns.

Crocus biflorus
SCOTCH CROCUS
Z3–8 H8–1
↕2½in (6cm) ↔2in (5cm)
Like all crocuses, this needs extremely good drainage, so coarse sand or fine gravel should be added to heavy soils before planting. Good in a rock garden.

Hyacinthoides hispanica 'La Grandesse'
LA GRANDESSE SPANISH BLUEBELL
Z4–9 H9–1
↕16in (40cm) ↔4in (10cm)
Flower spikes bloom in late spring above strap-shaped leaves. Hardier than the English bluebell. Other named forms in blue and pink are also easy to find.

Narcissus 'Grand Soleil d'Or'
GRAND SOLEIL D'OR DAFFODIL
Z7–9 H9–7 ↕18in (45cm)
↔indefinite
Showy daffodil that can also be used for forcing indoors. Needs very little cold treatment to initiate flowering. Sweetly scented flowers.

Allium giganteum
GIANT ORNAMENTAL ONION
Z3–9 H9–5 ↕6ft (2m) ↔12–14in (30–35cm)
Amazingly dense flowerheads bloom in summer. Strap-shaped leaves wither before the plant blooms. Grows best in fertile soil. Excellent cut flower.

Fritillaria imperialis
CROWN IMPERIAL
☼ 💧 z4–9 H8–2 ↕3ft (1m) ↔12in (30cm)
A heavy feeder, it needs a mulch of a rich compost or an application of phosphorus and potassium in early spring to bloom well the following year.

Muscari armeniacum
ARMENIAN GRAPE HYACINTH
☼ 💧 Z4–8 H8–1 ↕8in (20cm) ↔2in (°5cm)
A vigorous species that increases rapidly. Plant in fall, or in summer following division. There are many other readily available *Muscari* species and cultivars.

Trillium erectum
PURPLE TRILLIUM
Ⓝ ☼ 💧 Z4–9 H7–3 ↕20in (50cm) ↔12in (30cm)
Outward-facing flowers appear in spring. Prefers acidic to neutral soil rich in organic matter. Mulch in fall with leaf mold.

MORE CHOICES

- *Allium karativiense* Z3–9 H9–5
- *Bulbocodium vernum* Z4–9 H9–4
- *Eranthis hyemalis* Z4–9 H9–1
- *Erythronium americanum* Z3–9 H9–2
- *Tulipa* cvs. Z3–8 H8–1
- *Zephyranthes atamasco* Z7–10 H12–10

Hippeastrum 'Red Lion'
RED LION AMARYLLIS
☼ ☼ 💧 Z11–15 H9–1 ↕20in (50cm) ↔12in (30cm)
A large-flowered hybrid that blooms in different colors. Commonly grown as houseplants where not hardy, they flower in winter then.

Agapanthus 'Loch Hope'
LOCH HOPE BLUE AFRICAN LILY
☼ 💧💧 Z8–11 H12–1
↕3–4ft (1–1.2m) ↔20in (50cm)
A good border or container plant, this vigorous perennial forms bold clumps of large arching leaves.

Allium moly
GOLDEN GARLIC
☼ 💧 Z3–9 H9–1 ↕10in (25cm) ↔2in (5cm)
An easy-to-grow onion that is not invasive. The stems curl over, making this a good choice for edging a path. The foliage has a slight garlic scent when crushed.

Leucojum vernum
SPRING SNOWFLAKE
☼ 💧 Z4–8 H9–3 ↕12in (30cm)
A choice species for the front of a woodland bed, but it must not be allowed to become dry in summer, even when the foliage has died down, or flowering will be greatly reduced.

Summer-flowering bulbs

Often stately, frequently eye-catching, and always interesting, summer-flowering bulbs deserve a place in every garden. Easy to grow, most are readily available at larger garden centers. Some may need to be lifted in fall and be stored indoors over-winter in the northern part of this region, but all are hardy in the South.

Galtonia canadicans
SUMMER HYACINTH
☼ ◆ Z7–10 H10–7 ↕3–4ft (1–1.2m) ↔4in (10cm)
Fragrant flowers appear in late summer. Grow in fertile soil from fall-planted bulbs. Provide heavy winter mulch in colder areas, and protection from slugs.

Lycoris radiata
RED SPIDER LILY
☼ ◊ Z7–10 H10–7 ↕16in (40cm) ↔6in (15cm)
Flowers in late summer and early autumn, held above strap-shaped, dark green leaves. Plant bulbs in fall in fertile soil, with the neck of the bulb at the surface.

Allium tuberosum
GARLIC CHIVES
☼ ◊ Z4–8 H8–1 ↕10–20in (25–50cm)
Free-flowering onion that blooms in late summer and early fall, the flat leaves can be used like regular chives. Deadhead to prevent seeding. Can be invasive.

Zephyranthes candida
RAIN LILY
☼ ◊ Z7–9 H9–6 ↕10in (25cm) ↔3in (8cm)
Blooms late summer to early fall. Plant this bulbous perennial 4in deep in a soil-based potting mix. Keep soil evenly moist during the overwintering period.

Eucomis bicolor
PINEAPPLE FLOWER
z8–10 H10–8 ↕↔12–24in (30–60cm)
This bulbous perennial should be planted just below the soil surface in very well-drained, moderately fertile soil. Restrict water during winter dormancy.

Camassia cusickii
BLUE CAMASS
Ⓝ z3–11 H12–1
↕32in (80cm) ↔4in (10cm)
Grows best in a good soil with added organic matter. Dig and divide in late summer as foliage dies down.

Gloriosa superba 'Rothschildiana'
GLORY LILY
z11–12 H12–7
↕to 6ft (2m) ↔1–1½ ft (30–45cm)
Tuberous perennial that climbs by twining leaf tendrils. Flowers from mid-summer and good container plant.

Crinum x *powellii*
POWELL'S SPIDER LILY
z7–11 H12–8 ↕5ft (1.5m) ↔12in (30cm)
Grow in fertile, fairly moist soil in the garden or use in containers. In most of this region, bring indoors before danger of hard frost and store over winter like a dahlia.

MORE CHOICES

- *Crinum bulbispermum* 'Ellen Bosanquet' z7–11 H12–8
- *Crinum bulbispermum* 'Milk and Wine' z7–11 H12–8
- *Curcuma petiolaris* z13–15 H12–10
- *Lilium longifolium* z7–9 H9–1
- *Lycoris squamigera* z6–11 H12–6
- *Polianthes tuberosa* z7–11 H11–7
- *Sprekelia* spp. z13–15 H12–6
- *Zephyranthes citrina* z7–10 H10–7

Bulbs for naturalizing

These are bulbs you can plant and forget and they will bloom every year. Some are best suited to a woodland garden, receiving shade during the heat of summer; others can be planted in a mixed border where the foliage of the spring-flowering species will be hidden by other plants as it dies down. A few can be planted in a lawn but don't mow until their leaves turn yellow.

Scilla siberica
SIBERIAN SQUILL
☼ ◐ ◇ Z3–8 H8–1
↕4–8in (10–20cm) ↔2in (5cm)
Flowers appear in spring. Plant bulbs in fall in moderately fertile, organic soil. Naturalizes well under trees and shrubs.

Lycoris radiata
RED SPIDER LILY
☼ ◇ Z7–10 H10–7 ↕16in (40cm) ↔6in (15cm)
Flowers in late summer and early autumn, held above strap-shaped, dark green leaves. Plant bulbs in fall in fertile soil, with the neck of the bulb at the surface.

Hyacinthoides hispanica 'La Grandesse'
LA GRANDESSE SPANISH BLUEBELL
● ◐ ◇ Z4–9 H9–1 ↕↔16in (40cm)
An excellent woodland plant that also comes in blue and pink. Flowers in late spring and bulbs multiply slowly and make large clumps.

Galanthus nivalis
COMMON SNOWDROP
◐ ◆ Z3–8 H8–1 ↕4–6in (10–15cm) ↔2–3in (5–8cm)
A bulbous perennial native from the Pyrenees to the Ukraine. Suitable for naturalizing in grass or in woodland but also at home in borders and rock gardens.

Anemone blanda 'Violet Star'
GRECIAN WINDFLOWER
☼ ◇ Z4–8 H8–1 ↕↔6in (5cm)
This grows best in a woodland location. The flowers close at night or on cloudy days. Soak new bulbs overnight before planting to improve survival.

MORE CHOICES

- *Allium moly* Z3–9 H9–1
- *Crocosmia* 'Lucifer' Z5–9 H9–5
- *Eranthis cilicica* Z4–9 H9–1
- *Fritillaria meleagris* Z4–9 H8–2
- *Muscari armeniacum* 'Blue Spike' Z4–8 H8–1
- *Muscari armeniacum* 'Heavenly Blue' Z4–8 H8–1

Leucojum aestivum 'Gravetye Giant'
GRAVETYE GIANT SNOWFLAKE
☼ ◆ Z4–9 H9–1 ↕3ft (1m) ↔3in (8cm)
This cultivar is much more robust than the species. Faintly chocolate-scented flowers appear in spring. Prefers organic soil. Susceptible to narcissus bulb fly.

Leucojum autumnale
AUTUMN SNOWFLAKE
☼ ◆ Z5–9 H9–1 ↕6in (15cm)
Grows best in soil that is allowed to become dry during summer but needs moisture during the growing season from mid- to late fall. Native to Spain and North Africa.

Muscari armeniacum
ARMENIAN GRAPE HYACINTH
☼ ◆ Z4–8 H8–1
↕8in (20cm) ↔2in (5cm)
A vigorous species, this increases rapidly. Plant in fall, or in summer following division. Many other species and cultivars are available.

Narcissus jonquilla 'Baby Moon'
BABY MOON NARCISSUS
☼ ◇ Z3–9 H9–1 ↕8in (20cm)
Flowering in late spring, this has several sweetly scented blooms on each stem. Easy to grow and increases readily in good soil. Plant in early autumn.

Narcissus jonquilla 'Pipit'
PIPIT NARCISSUS
☼ ◇ Z3–9 H9–1 ↕↔10in (25cm)
Fragrant with up to 4 flowers on each stem that turn to an ivory-white as they age. Plant in early fall so they have time to root before winter.

Erythronium americanum
YELLOW TROUT LILY
Ⓝ z3–9 H9–2 ↕2–10in (5–25cm) ↔2–3in (5–8cm)
Prefers organic soil that is not too rich. Sometimes large colonies fail to bloom in a given year. Prone to rust, smuts, fungal spots, and slugs. Native to the eastern US.

Trillium erectum
PURPLE TRILLIUM
Ⓝ z4–9 H7–3
↕20in (50cm) ↔12in (30cm)
Outward-facing flowers appear in spring. Prefers acidic to neutral soil rich in organic matter. Mulch in fall with leaf mold.

Ornithogalum umbellatum
STAR OF BETHLEHEM
z7–11 H12–7
↕12in (30cm) ↔4in (10cm)
Midspring flowering, this can become a real weed on light soils, but is not as invasive in heavier ones. Multiplies rapidly by seed and division; every small bulblet left in soil will grow.

Cyclamen hederifolium
BABY CYCLAMEN
z5–7 H9–7
↕4in (10cm) ↔4–6in (10–15cm)
Scented flowers in shades of pink to white are produced from mid- to late autumn. Leaves vary from triangular to heart-shaped. Also called *C. neapolitanum*.

MORE CHOICES

- *Narcissus* 'Galilee' z3–9 H9–1
- *Narcissus* 'Jerusalem' z3–9 H9–1
- *Narcissus jonquilla* z3–9 H9–1
- *Narcissus tazetta* z7–9 H9–1
- *Narcissus* 'Ziva' z3–9 H9–1
- *Oxalis crassipes* z8–10 H10–8
- *Trillium cuneatum* z6–9 H9–6
- *Zephyranthes atamasco* z7–10 H12–10

Ipheion uniflorum 'Froyle Mill'
FROYLE MILL SPRING STARFLOWER
z6–9 H9–6 ↕6–8in (15–20cm)
Foliage emerges in late fall and need a protective mulch where temperatures fall below 14°F (-10°C). The spring flowers are long-lasting. Good for naturalizing in lawns or borders.

Colchicum autumnale
MEADOW SAFFRON, NAKED BOYS
☼ ◊ Z4–9 H9–1 ↕6in (15cm) ↔3in (8cm)
Large flat leaves appear in spring and die down by midsummer. Flowers emerge in late summer or early fall. There are normally several flowers per bulb.

Zephyranthes candida
RAIN LILY
☼ ◊ Z7–9 H9–6 ↕10in (25cm) ↔3in (8cm)
Blooms late summer to early fall. Plant this deciduous bulbous perennial 4in (10cm) deep in a soil-based potting mix. Keep soil moist during the overwintering period.

Aquatic perennials

Garden pools are becoming very popular and even small garden centers now carry a choice of suitable plants. By selecting carefully, you can have flowers from early spring until frost. But keep in mind the plant's foliage: its different colors and textures will add interest to your garden when none of the plants are in flower.

Typha minima
DWARF CATTAIL
☼ 💧 Z3–11 H12–1 ↕18–24in (45–60cm) ↔12in (30cm)
Flowers are distinctive cylindrical spikes that appear from mid- to late summer and can be used in dried arrangements. Can become invasive in unlined ponds.

Orontium aquaticum
GOLDEN CLUB
Ⓝ ☼ 💧 Z6–10 H10–4 ↔24in (60cm)
A strange plant, related to calla lilies and jack-in-the-pulpit, that puts on an unusual but colorful display in spring. Leaves are waterproof and appear dry if pushed below the surface.

Pontederia cordata
PICKEREL WEED
Ⓝ ☼ 💧 Z3–11 H12–1 ↕30in (75cm) ↔18in (45cm)
Flowers are borne from late spring to fall. When grown in an aquatic container, the soil should be loamy and fertile. Can also be grown in water-filled barrels.

Sagittaria latifolia
WAPATO, DUCK POTATO
Ⓝ ☼ 💧 Z5–11 H12–5 ↕5ft (1.2m) ↔2ft (60cm)
Racemes of white flowers appear during summer. Flowers over a long period. Prefers a gravelly soil and will self-seed and spread. Tubers are wildlife food.

Nymphoides peltata
WATER FRINGE, YELLOW FLOATING HEART
☼ 💧 Z6–11 H12–6 ↕4in (10cm) ↔indefinite
Grow in water less that 2ft (60cm) deep. Spreads by runners. Plant in container in small pools. Flowers in summer. Native to Eurasia, now naturalized in South.

Acorus calamus
Ⓝ ☼ 💧 Z10–11 H12–2 ↕30in (75cm) ↔24in
Insignificant flowers appear from late spring to early summer. Does not produce fertile seeds, but it can spread widely by rhizomes.

MORE CHOICES

- *Aponogeton distachyos* Z9–10 H12–10
- *Butomus umbellatus* Z3–11 H8–5
- *Cyperus alternifolia* Z13–15 H12–10
- *Cyperus papyrus* Z13–15 H12–6
- *Lemma minor* Z9–15 H12–1
- *Ludwigia repens* Z5–11 H12–4
- *Marsilea mutica* Z6–11 H12–6
- *Myriophyllum aquaticum* Z6–11 H12–6
- *Nelumbo lutea* Z4–11 H12–1
- *Sagittaria platyphyllum* Z5–15 H12–1
- *Stratiotes aloides* Z5–11 H12–5

Iris versicolor
BLUE FLAG
Ⓝ ☼ 💧 Z3–9 H9–1
↕32in (80cm) ↔12in (30cm)
Easy-to-grow water iris, will take shallow water or bog conditions. Flowers on branched stems in late spring or early summer. Named forms have pink or white flowers.

Houttuynia cordatum 'Chameleon'
CHAMELEON PLANT
◐ 💧 Z5–11 H12–1 ↕4in (10cm) ↔indefinite
The multicolored foliage is the reason to grow this; flowers are insignificant. This spreading plant will also grow in dry soil. The green-leaved species is invasive.

Aquatic marginal plants

These are the plants to grow in areas beside the garden pool that are kept permanently moist by the overflow, or along the banks of a stream. Some will also grow in shallow water. They mostly resent being allowed to dry out for long periods, although some are equally happy in regular soil.

Zantedeschia aethopica
CALLA LILY
☼ 💧 z8–10 H10–4 ↕30in (75cm) ↔24in (60cm)
Rhizomatous perennial, evergreen in the South. Will grow in boggy conditions or water up to 12in (30cm) deep. Flowers produced from late spring to midsummer.

Iris fulva
COPPER IRIS
Ⓝ ◑ 💧 Z5–9 H9–3 ↕4ft (1.2m) ↔24in (60cm)
Spreads slowly by creeping stems, the Louisiana iris is parent to many hybrids. In the wild it grows in river bottoms, wet in spring but often dry in summer.

Iris pseudacorus
YELLOW FLAG
☼ 💧 Z5–8 H8–3 ↕6ft (2m) ↔indefinite
A vigorous iris that blooms from mid- to late spring. Ripe seeds fall from the capsule and then float away and spread to new locations.

Iris siberica 'White Swirl'
WHITE SWIRL SIBERIAN IRIS

Z4–9 H9–1 ↕3ft (1m)

These do not have the "beard" of the more common irises and flower a little later. They are more clump-forming, without the stout rhizomes. Many named forms in blue, mauve, and pink.

Eupatorium purpureum
PURPLE JOE PYE WEED

Ⓝ Z3–9 H9–1 ↕7ft (2.2m) ↔3ft (1m)

Blooms from midsummer to early autumn. Leaves smell like vanilla when bruised. Very attractive to butterflies, especially monarchs, and make a good cut flower. Prone to disease.

Lobelia cardinalis
CARDINAL FLOWER

Ⓝ Z2–8 H8–1

↕3ft (1m) ↔9in (23cm)

Flowers from summer to early autumn. Foliage is lance-shaped, bright green, and tinged with bronze. Best if grown in fertile organic soil, but short-lived.

Saururus cernuus
LIZARD'S TAIL

Ⓝ Z5–11 H12–5

↕9in (23cm) ↔12in (30cm)

Flowers appear in early summer. The group of nutlets that forms along the stem resembles a lizard's tail, giving the plant its common name. Spreads by runners.

Lysimachia nummularia
GOLDEN CREEPING JENNY

Z4–8 H8–1 ↕2in (5cm) ↔indefinite

A very vigorous, stem-rooting evergreen that can cover a fairly large area in just one season. Bright yellow, cup-shaped flowers in summer add interest.

MORE CHOICES

- *Aclepius incarnates* Z3–8 H8–1
- *Acorus gramineus* 'Ogon' Z10–11 H12–2
- *Canna* spp. Z8–11 H12–1
- *Cyperus alternifolia* Z13–15 H12–10
- *Cyperus haspans* Z7–11 H12–7
- *Houttuynia cordatum* 'Chameleon' Z5–11 H12–1
- *Hydrocotyle verticillata* Z5–11 H12–5
- *Hymenocallis liriosme* Z8–11 H12–8
- *Lysichiton americanus* Z7–9 H9–7
- *Miscanthus sinensis* 'Zebrinus' Z4–9 H9–1
- *Myriophyllum aquaticum* Z6–11 H12–6
- *Osmunda regalis* Z2–10 H9–1
- *Pontederia cordata* Z3–11 H12–1
- *Thalia dealbata* Z6–11 H12–6
- *Typha minima* Z3–11 H12–1

Equisetum hyemale
COMMON HORSETAIL

Ⓝ Z3–11 H12–1 ↕to 4ft (1.2m) ↔indefinite

Invasive and should be planted in a container to restrict growth. This extremely adaptable, ancient species has changed little since the time of the dinosaurs.

Waterlilies

There are two types of waterlilies: hardy and tropical. Hardy ones can be grown in the whole Southeast region. They may be white, pink, red, or yellow. Tropicals are only reliably hardy in zone 10 or warmer, where water temperatures remain above 70°F (21°C), and must be wintered indoors in cooler zones. They add blue to the color range.

Nymphaea 'Gladstoneana'
GLADSTONEANA WATERLILY
☼ 💧 Z10–11 H12–1 ↔10ft (3m)
Day-blooming flowers measure to 7in (18cm). Tropical with 12in (30cm), light bronze leaves with overlapping lobes, one raised.

Nymphaea 'Moorei'
MOORE'S WATERLILY
☼ 💧 Z3–11 H12–1
↕5in (13cm) ↔3–4ft (1–1.2m)
The 4–5in (10–13cm) flowers are barely fragrant and bloom during the day. This hardy waterlily has large green leaves with purple specks.

Nymphaea 'Mrs. Martin E. Randig'
MRS. RANDIG WATERLILY
Ⓝ ☼ 💧 Z10–11 H12–1 ↔4–6ft (1.2–2m)
An adaptable day-blooming tropical lily that can be used in pools as small as 2ft (60cm), or in very large ones. It frequently grows new plantlets on the upper leaf surface.

Nymphaea 'Attraction'
ATTRACTION WATERLILY
☼ 💧 Z3–11 H12–1 ↔to 5ft (1.5m)
Slightly fragrant, day-blooming flowers measure up to 7in (18cm) across. Hardy waterlily with 10in (25cm), dark green leaves that are bronzy red when young.

Nymphaea 'Escarboucle'
ESCARBOUCLE WATERLILY
☼ 💧 Z3–11 H12–1 ↔to 10ft (3m)
Day-blooming flowers measure 7in (18cm) wide. Hardy waterlily with 10in (25cm), midgreen leaves that are brown-tinged when young.

Nymphaea 'Director George T. Moore'

DIRECTOR MOORE WATERLILY

☼ 💧 Z10–11 H12–1 ↔10ft (3m)

Day-blooming tropical with unusual purple stamens and wide-opening flowers up to 8in (20cm) across. Leaves are marked with brownish flecks.

Nymphaea 'Blue Beauty'

BLUE BEAUTY WATERLILY

☼ 💧 Z10–11 H12–1 ↔6ft (2m)

A fragrant, day-blooming tropical lily that is very free-flowering and popular. It needs a medium to large pool to grow well and holds the flowers well above the water.

Nymphaea 'Firecrest'

FIRECREST WATERLILY

☼ 💧 Z3–11 H12–1 ↔to 4ft (1.2m)

Day-blooming flowers measure 6in across. Hardy with 9in (15cm), mid-green leaves that are dark purple when young.

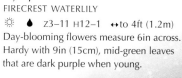

Nymphaea 'Virginalis'

VIRGINALIS WATERLILY

☼ 💧 Z3–11 H12–1 ↔4ft (1.2m)

A hardy waterlily with rounded leaves that are purple to bronze when they open. The fragrant flowers are up to 5in (14cm) across. Grow in water to 20in (50cm) deep.

MORE CHOICES

- *Nymphaea* 'Albida' Z3–11 H12–1
- *Nymphaea* 'Charlene Strawn' Z3–11 H12–1
- *Nymphaea* 'Chromatella' Z3–11 H12–1
- *Nymphaea* 'Comanche' Z4–11 H12–1
- *Nymphaea* 'Laydekeri' Z3–11 H12–1
- *Nymphaea* 'Tetragona' Z3–11 H12–1
- *Nymphaea* 'Wood's White Knight' Z10–11 H12–7
- *Victoria amazonica* Z3–11 H12–6

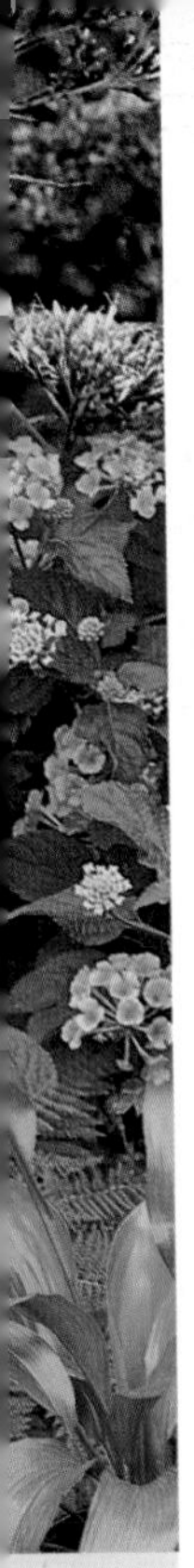

Pentas lanceolata 'Kermesina'
KERMESINA STAR CLUSTER
☼ ◐ ◊ Z10–11 H12–1 ↕6ft (2m) ↔3ft (1m)
Free-flowering, shrubby perennial with hairy leaves normally used as an annual. Good in borders or containers. Prune in late winter if required.

MORE CHOICES

- *Asclepias curassavica* Z9–11 H12–6
- *Callistephus chinensis* H9–1
- *Clarkia amoena* H7–1
- *Coreopsis tinctoria* Z4–9 H12–1
- *Dahlia* hybrids Z8–11 H12–1
- *Gaillardia* spp. Z3–8 H8–1
- *Gazania* x *splendens* Z8–11 H12–3
- *Lobularia maritime* Z11–12 H12–1
- *Phlox drummondii* H12–1
- *Zinnia elegans* H12–1

HERBACEOUS PLANTS

Annuals for butterflies

Many annual or tender perennial plants provide the nectar that butterflies feed on. These are not always the same plants that attract hummingbirds since butterflies can exist on much smaller quantities of nectar. Many flowers in the daisy family, which have multiple small flowers on a compact head, are an excellent attractant for butterflies.

Verbena hybrida 'Peaches and Cream'
PEACHES AND CREAM VERBENA
☼ ◊ Z9–11 H12–1 ↕12in (30cm) ↔18in (45cm)
May by upright, bushy, or spreading, depending on variety, which comes in a range of colors. Good container plants.

Ocimum basilicum 'Dark Opal'
SWEET BASIL
☼ ◊ Z9–11 H11–1
↕12–24in (30–60cm) ↔12in (30cm)
Easily raised from seed, forms with colored or puckered leaves are good in gardens.

Tithonia rotundifolia 'Torch'
TORCH MEXICAN SUNFLOWER
☼ ◊ Z10–11 H12–1 ↕to 6ft (2m) ↔12in (30cm)
Good back-of-the-border plant that self-seeds in warmer climates. Fast-growing and easy, makes a good cut flower.

Salvia splendens
SCARLET SAGE
☼ ◊ ◑ Z11–12 H12–1
↕16in (40cm) ↔9–14in (25–35cm)
While red is the original color, modern varieties come in a wider range, in considerably different sizes.

Cleome hasslerana 'Rose Queen'
ROSE QUEEN SPIDER FLOWER
☼ ◊ Z11 H12–1 ↕4ft (1.2m) ↔18in (45cm)
Upright stems with tiny spines at base of leaf stalks. Fragrant flowers also come in white and pale pink. Good accent plant and self-seeds but not invasive.

Catharanthus roseus
POLKA-DOT
☼ ◊ Z12–15 H12–1 ↕↔12–24in (30–60cm)
Excellent plants for hot dry locations. Also come in red, pink, and rose shades, often with a contrasting center. May be listed as *Vinca* in some catalogs.

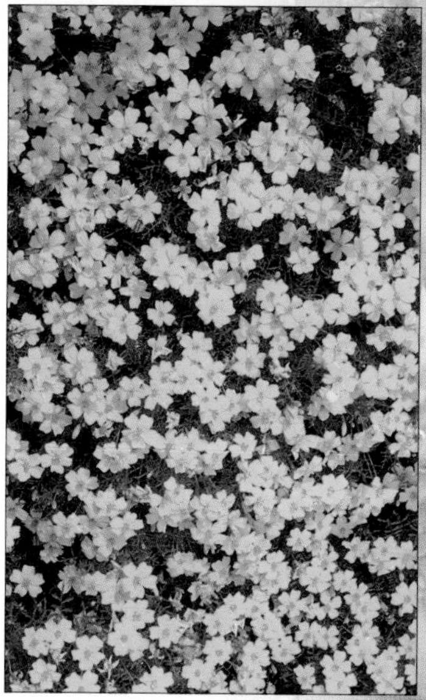

Tagetes tenuifolia 'Lemon Gem'
LEMON GEM MARIGOLD
☼ ◊ H12–1 ↕9in (23cm)
Upright bushy plants with masses of small single flowers from spring to late summer. The petals are edible and make a colorful addition to salads. 'Orange Gem' is similar. Other marigolds are often taller.

Gomphrena globosa
GLOBE AMARANTH
☼ ◊ Z11–12 H12–1
↕12in (30cm) ↔8in (20cm)
Flowerheads in shades of red, pink, lavender, purple, orange, or white appear from summer to early autumn. Grows best in well-drained soils.

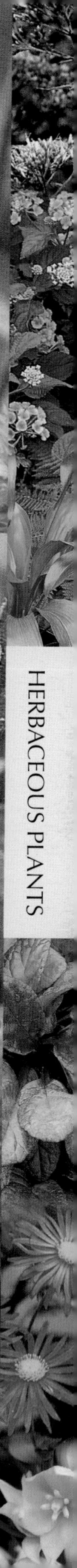

Annuals for sandy soils

Sandy soils are notorious for drying quickly after rain and being low in nutrients. Despite these drawbacks, there are plants other than cacti and succulents that can survive in such harsh conditions. While the ones shown here will grow in poor, sandy soils, the addition of some moisture-holding humus will improve their growth dramatically.

Torenia fournieri
WISHBONE FLOWER
Z12–13 H6–1 ↕12in (30cm) ↔9in (23cm)
A slow-growing annual. Very fine seed that needs to be sown about 10 weeks before planting time. Should not be allowed to dry out once planted.

Sanvitalia procumbens
CREEPING ZINNIA
H12–1 ↕to 8in (20cm) ↔18in (45cm)
Spreading groundcover that flowers freely and makes a dense mat. Also used in planters to trial. Easy to grow from seed started indoors.

Rudbeckia hirta
BLACK-EYED SUSAN
Ⓝ Z3–7 H7–1 ↕3ft (1m) ↔18in (45cm)
Flowers freely throughout much of summer. Strains are available in a variety of heights and doubleness. Easy from seed; often short-lived. Tolerates heavy clay.

Melampodium paludosum
AFRICAN ZINNIA
Z11–12 H12–1 ↕6in (15cm) ↔8in (20cm)
A mound-shaped plant that tolerates heat, humidity, and drought. Easy to grow from seed sown 6 weeks before the last frost date. Makes a good container plant.

MORE CHOICES

- *Centaurea cyanus* H7–1
- *Clarkia amoena* H7–1
- *Helenium* spp. Z4–8 H8–1
- *Ipomoea quamoclit* Z12–13 H12–6
- *Portulaca grandiflora* H12–1
- *Ricinus communis* Z11–14 H12–1

Gazania rigens 'Talent Yellow'
TREASURE FLOWER
☼ ◊ Z8–11 H12–1
↕6–16in (15–40cm) ↔12in (30cm)
Perennials in the south, these are most often grown as annuals. Take considerable frost in fall and keep blooming. Good cut flowers.

Catharanthus roseus 'Polka Dot'
MADAGASCAR PERIWINKLE
☼ ◊ Z12–15 H12–1
↕↔12–24in (30–60cm)
Rarely grown a few years ago, there are now many named forms that also come in red, pink, and rose shades, often with a constrasting center. Does well in heat.

Gaillardia pulchella 'Red Plume'
BLANKET FLOWER
Ⓝ ☼ ◊ Z10–11 H12–1
↕18in (45cm) ↔12in (30cm)
Bushy plant with lance-shaped, green-gray leaves. Many single-flowered varieties with yellow or red and yellow petals.

Limonium sinuatum
STATICE
☼ ◊ H9–3
↕8in (45cm) ↔12in (30cm)
A perennial grown as an annual except in USDA Zones 8 and 9, this flowers from summer to fall in shades of pink, white, yellow, and blue. Prefers sandy soil.

Coreopsis tinctoria
CALLIOPSIS
Ⓝ ☼ ◐ ◊ Z4–9 H12–1
↕4ft (1.2m) ↔12–18in (30–45cm)
Stiff-stemmed plant often included in wild-flower mizes. Easy to grow from seed and will self-seed.

Sun-loving annuals

Fast-growing annuals, or tender perennials, give you the ability to realize gardening expectations very quickly. Because they are short lived, they also allow you to change the look of a garden area from one year (or even one season) to the next. They are extremely useful for filling gaps in your sunny beds as you wait for perennials and shrubs to grow.

MORE CHOICES

- *Abutilon* spp. Z9–11 H12–1
- *Ageratum houstonianum* Z10–13 H12–1
- *Alternanthera ficoidea* Z11–12 H12–1
- *Brassica oleracea* Z8–9 H9–1
- *Capsicum annuum* 'Tabasco' H12–1
- *Celosia argentea* 'Fairy Fountains' Z11 H12–3
- *Centaura cyanus* H7–1
- *Cleome hassleriana* Z3–8 H9–1
- *Daucus carota* Z3–9 H9–1
- *Delphinium* spp. Z3–7 H7–1
- *Gladiolus* spp. Z8–10 H9–1
- *Ipomoea batatas* 'Blackie' Z11–12 H12–1
- *Melampodium* 'Medallion' Z11–12 H12–1
- *Papaver orientalis 'Helen Elisabeth'* Z4–9 H9–1
- *Perilla frutescens* H12–1

Catharanthus roseus 'Raspberry Red'
MADAGASCAR PERIWINKLE
Z12–15 H12–1 ↕↔12–24in (30–60cm)
One of the bright new hybrid periwinkle. Also commonly known as vinca, and also come in white, pink, and rose.

Calendula officinalis
POT MARIGOLD
H6–1 ↕30in (75cm) ↔18in (45cm)
A good children's plant that is very easy to grow. An old plant that is used as a pot herb. The edible petals can be added to salads. Will probably self-seed.

Zinnia elegans 'Dreamland'
DREAMLAND GARDEN ZINNIA
H12–1 ↕8–12in (20–30cm) ↔1ft (30cm)
One of a very large selection of zinnias that vary greatly in height and flower size. Tall, large-flowered varieties make good cut flowers and attract butterflies.

Celosia argentea 'Olympia Scarlet'
OLYMPIA SCARLET COCKSCOMB
☼ ◊◐ H9–2 ↕8in (20cm)
Also come in pink, orange, and yellow. The closely related feather celosia has plume-like spikes of flowers and likes similar conditions.

Petunia x *hybrida* 'Pink Wave'
PINK WAVE PETUNIA
☼ ◊ Z9–11 H12–1 ↕8in (45cm) ↔3–5ft (1–1.5m)
Make excellent groundcovers for a sunny bank. Also used in planters and trail over the edge. Other petunias are more upright.

MORE CHOICES

- *Sanvitalia procumbens* H12–1
- *Tithonia rotundifolia* Z10–11 H12–1
- *Verbena hybrida* 'Showtime' Z9–11 H12–1
- *Viola wittrockiana* 'Jolly Joker' Z8–11 H9–1

Scaevola aemula
FAIRY FAN FLOWER
☼ ☀ ◊◐ Z11–12 H12–1 ↕↔20in (50cm)
Austrialian native is widely used in planters and hanging baskets where its flowers can be seen best.

Zinnia angustifolia 'Mexicana'
MEXICAN ZINNIA
☼ ◊ H12–1 ↕24in (60cm) ↔12in (30cm)
An erect, bushy, small-flowered annual, usually with simpler flowers on much branched plants. May be *Z. angustifolia* in catalogs.

Helianthus annuus 'Sunspot'
SUNSPOT SUNFLOWER
Ⓝ ☼ ◊◐ H12–1 ↕↔24in (60cm)
10in (25cm) heads of flowers on a compact plant. Other varieties reach 10ft (3m) in height. Birds enjoy the central disk of seeds when ripe.

Salvia splendens 'Sizzler'
SIZZLER SCARLET SAGE
☼ ◊ Z11–12 H12–1
↕10–12in (25–30cm) ↔9–14in (23–35cm)
Modern varieties of Salvia come in a wide range of colors, but red bloom best. Also differ in height.

Annuals for shade

Every garden has some shade – even if only that cast by a house – and finding plants suited to such sites can be challenging. Other gardens with structures, such as solid fences or many trees, can accomodate an entire bed of shade-loving plants. Shown here are some outstanding annuals and tender perennials that will survive in and add color to shady spots.

Caladium bicolor 'Rosebud'
ROSEBUD ANGEL WINGS
◐ ● 💧 pH Z15–15 H12–4 ↕↔24in (60cm)
There are many forms of angel wings, in a variety of color combinations. Use several plants of the same variety, rather than a jumble of different forms.

Nicotiana alata
FLOWERING TOBACCO
◐ ● 💧 Z10–11 H12–1 ↕5ft (1.5m) ↔3ft (1m)
These come in a wide range of sizes and colors. Modern hybrids have a slight fragrance and flower freely. May be perennial in the South.

Caladium bicolor 'Pink Beauty'
PINK BEAUTY ANGEL WINGS
◐ ● 💧 pH Z15–15 H12–4
↕↔24in (60cm)
This is one of several hybrids with leaves mottled with maroon, red, pink, or white. Grow in a woodland soil and store at 55°F (13°C) overwinter.

Solenostemon scutellarioides 'Midway Red'
MIDWAY RED COLEUS
☼ ◐ 💧 Z11–12 H12–1 ↕↔3ft (1m)
An interesting plant with a new botanical name. Leaves may be almost one color or splashed with a variety of shades. Small blue flowers should be pinched off when they appear.

Lobularia maritima
SWEET ALYSSUM
☼ ◐ 💧 Z10–11 H12–1
↕2–12in (5–30cm) ↔8–12in (20–30cm)
An old favorite grown for its sweetly scented flowers, which can also be rose, pink, or mauve. It is short-lived but often self-seeds. Best as a winter annual.

MORE CHOICES

- *Begonia semperflorens-cultorum* Z11–15 H12–1
- *Begonia tuberhybrida* Z13–15 H12–1
- *Browallia speciosa* 'Blue Bells' Z10–11 H8–1
- *Catharanthus roseus* Z12–15 H12–1
- *Cleome hassleriana* Z11 H12–1
- *Cuphea ignea* Z10–11 H12–6
- *Impatiens hawkeri* Z9–15 H7–1
- *Impatiens walleriana* 'Super Elfin' Z10–15 H12–1
- *Salvia splendens* Z11–12 H12–1
- *Tolmiea menziesii* Z6–9 H9–6
- *Viola tricolor* Z3–9 H12–1

Impatiens balsamina
GARDEN BALSAM
H12–1 ↕30in (75cm) ↔18in (45cm)
Colors range from white, pink, red, and lilac as well as bicolors and doubled forms with only a light scent. Prefers organic, well-drained soils.

Impatiens 'Tango'
TANGO IMPATIENS
H12–1
↕14in (35cm) ↔12in (30cm)
One of the New Guinea types of impatiens, it can be grown from seed, while most others must be grown from cuttings. Large flowers and often-colored foliage.

Salvia elegans
PINEAPPLE SCENTED SAGE
Z8–11 H12–1
↕4ft (1.2m) ↔3ft (1m)
Open-branched, woody plant with foliage that, when crushed, smells of fresh pineapples. Flowers in late summer and may be evergreen and perennial in the South.

Ageratum houstonianum
AGERATUM, FLOSS FLOWER
Z10–13 H12–1 ↕↔8in (20cm)
Fast-growing, mounding annual. Flowers appear in summer and autumn and vary from bright or gray-blue to pink or white. Good butterfly plant.

Annual vines

These fast-growing plants can provide a temporary screen or can be used to cover a trellis while permanent climbers become established. They can also be planted at the top of a retaining wall to trail downward or be used to cover chain-link fencing and turn it into an attractive feature. With the exception of sweet peas (*Lathyrus odoratus*), these climbers need to be planted after danger of frost has passed.

Passiflora coccinea
RED GRANADILLA
Z14–15 H12–10 ↕12ft (4m)
A vigorous climber with slender red stems and lobed leaves covered in red hairs. Flowers, produced from summer to fall, may produce edible fruit.

Lagenaria leucantha 'Maxima'
MAXIMA WHITE FLOWERED GOURD
Z12–15 H12–10 ↕15ft (4.5m)
Bottle gourds come in several different shapes and can be hollowed out and used as containers, bird boxes, or polished for indoor decoration.

MORE CHOICES

- *Allamanda cathartica* Z14–15 H12–10
- *Bougainvillea spectabilis* cvs. Z9–11 H12–1
- *Clerodendrum thomsoniae* Z14–15 H12–1
- *Cobaea scandens* Z11–13 H12–10
- *Cocculus carolina* Z5–9 H9–5
- *Cucurbita* spp. H12–1
- *Ipomoea multifida* H12–1
- *Ipomoea nil* 'Scarlett O'Hara' H12–1
- *Ipomoea quamoclit* Z12–13 H12–6
- *Lathyrus odorata* Z9–10 H8–1
- *Luffa aegyptiaca* H9–1
- *Lycopersicon lycopersicum* 'Sweet 100' Z9–15 H12–9
- *Manettia cordifolia* Z12–15 H12–10
- *Passiflora incarnata* Z6–8 H10–7
- *Rhodochiton* spp. Z11–11 H7–1
- *Senecio confusus* Z13–15 H12–10
- *Solanum jasminoides* Z9–11 H12–3
- *Stigmaphyllon ciliatum* Z14–15 H12–10
- *Thunbergia alata* Z11–15 H12–10

Ipomoea (Mina) lobata
SPANISH FLAG
☼ ○ Z13–15 H12–10 ↕6–15ft (2–5m)
A perennial climber usually grown as an annual for its summer flowers. Stems and leaf-stalks are crimson and flowers fade to yellow, then white, as they age.

Lablab purpurea
HYACINTH BEAN
☼ ○ Z10–11 H12–1 ↕6–20ft (2–6m)
A vigorous twining perennial climber grown as an annual. Fragrant purple flowers from midsummer onward produce pods (edible after careful cooking).

Phaseolus coccineus
SCARLET RUNNER BEAN
Ⓝ ☼ ○◑ H12–1 ↕4–6ft (1.2–2m) ↔6–9in (15–22cm)
Although generally grown for its flowers, the fresh pods have a better flavor than most bush beans. Old beans can be dried for use in stews and Mexican dishes.

Ipomoea alba
MOONFLOWER
Ⓝ ☼ ◑ Z12–15 H12–10
↕15ft (5m)
Twining plant with 3-lobed leaves up to 8in (20cm) long. Flowers are in small clusters and open at dusk from early summer onwards.

Thunbergia grandiflora
BLUE TRUMPET VINE
☼ ○◑ Z14–15 H12–10
↕15–30ft (5–10m)
Vigorous, woody tropical climber, with dark green leaves, native to India, that is grown as an annual. Fertilize monthly during summer to ensure continual flowering.

Mandevilla splendens
RED RIDING HOOD
◐ ○ Z13–15 H12–10 ↕10–20ft (3–6m)
Branched tropical climber with hairy stems and pointed leaves. Flowers appear from mid-summer in clusters of 3-5 and are up to 4in (10cm) across.

Cardiospermum halicacabum
BALLOON VINE
Ⓝ ☼ ○◑ Z10–15 H12–1 ↕12ft (4m)
Narrow, woody-based climber with small greenish flowers from summer to fall that give the balloon-like fruits turning brown at maturity. Also know as Love-in-a-puff.

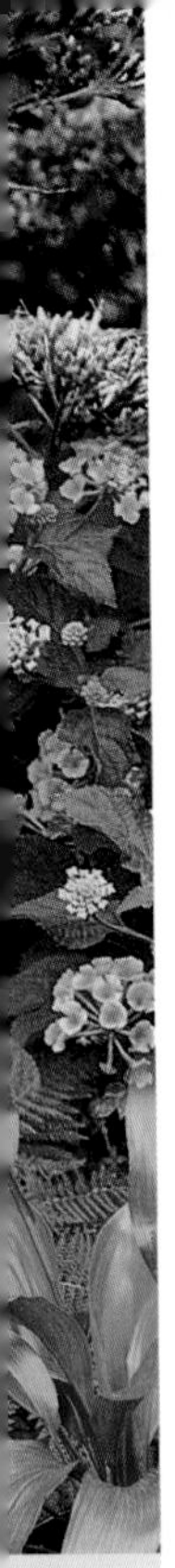

Cool-weather annuals

Many annuals will not grow during the hottest months of summer; even when given adequate water, they do not survive high temperatures. The plants shown here are better adapted to cool seasons, ranging from early and late summer in the north of this region, to late fall and winter in the extreme South.

Papaver nudicaule
ICELAND POPPY
☼ ◊ Z2–7 H9–2
↕12in (30cm) ↔6in (15cm)
A short-lived but very free-flowering annual that will probably self-seed. It makes a good cut flower when you sear the stem with a flame to make it last longer.

Centaurea cyanus
BACHELOR'S BUTTONS
☼ ◊ H7–1 ↕1–3ft (30cm–1m) ↔1ft (30cm)
Flower colors also include purple, red, pink, and white. Easy to grow from seed. The flowers last well when cut and may be dried.

Consolida ajacis 'Blue Cloud'
BLUE CLOUD LARKSPUR
☼ ◊ H9–1
↕1–4ft (30–120cm) ↔12–20in (23–30cm)
Can be sown in situ and then self-sow. Allow to shed seed before pulling out old plants. Blooms for a long time during the cool months.

Antirrhinum majus 'Sonnet'
SONNET SNAPDRAGON
☼ ◊ Z8–11 H12–1
↕8–12in (20–30cm) ↔to 12in (30cm)
Deadhead to prevent seed formation and to continue flowering. Available as a mix or as separate colors.

Viola x *wittrockiana* 'Jolly Joker'
JOLLY JOKER PANSY
☼ ◐ ◊ ◆ Z8–11 H9–1
↕6–9in (16–23cm)
↔9–12in (23–30cm)
Excellent winter annuals in a wide range of colors, often two-toned. Not easy to grow from seed.

Senecia cineraria 'Cirrus'
CIRRUS DUSTY MILLER
☼ ◊ Z8–10 H12–8 ↕↔12in (30cm)
Evergreen small shrubs that are used as annuals, grown from seed each year. They make good edging plants or can be used in blocks as dividers between brighter annuals.

Delphinium grandiflorum
'Blue Butterfly'
BLUE BUTTERFLY DELPHINIUM
Z3–8 H8–1
↕8–20in (20–50cm)
↔9–12in (23–30cm)
Short-lived perennial that is grown as an annual in this region. Sow in late summer for flowers the following spring. Pale blue and white varieties available.

MORE CHOICES

- *Alcea rosea* 'Zabrinus' Z3–9 H10–3
- *Centaurea cineraria* 'Silver Feather' Z7–11 H12–1
- *Cheiranthus* spp. Z7–8 H9–2
- *Consolida ambigua* 'Super Imperial' Z7–9 H9–1
- *Digitalis* spp. Z4–8 H9–1
- *Hesperis matronalis* Z3–8 H9–3
- *Lathyrus odoratus* Z9–10 H8–1
- *Lavandula* spp. H12–1
- *Myosotis sylvatica* 'Royal Blue Improved' Z5–8 H8–1
- *Primula* 'Polyantha' Z4–8 H8–1
- *Schizanthus* spp. H4–1
- *Viola tricolor* Z3–9 H12–1

Brassica oleracea
FLOWERING KALE
Z8–9 H9–1 ↕↔18in (45cm)
This ornamental relative of cabbage and kale is grown for its colorful fall foliage. Biennials, they flower the following year if allowed to stand.

Bellis perennis
ENGLISH DAISY
Z4–8 H8–1 ↕↔2–8in (5–20cm)
This single-flowered form can become a serious weed if allowed to seed. Double forms, easy from seed, are more showy and do not cause this problem.

Dianthus barbatus
SWEET WILLIAM
Z5–9 H8–1
↕28in (70cm) ↔12in (30cm)
Really a biennial or short-lived perennial. Sown in fall to flower the following spring and early summer.

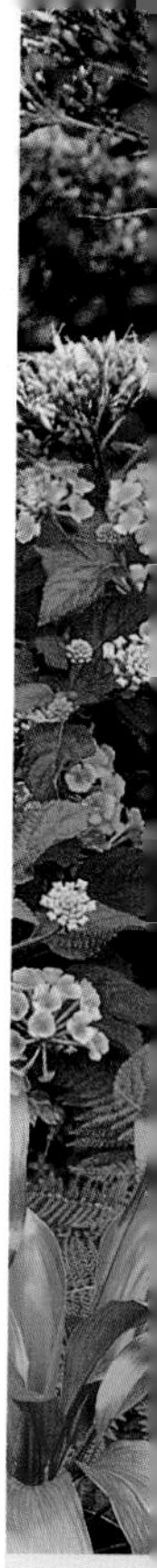

Iberis umbellata Fairy Series
FAIRY GLOBE CANDYTUFT
☼ ◊ H8–1 ↕6–12in (15–30cm) ↔9in (23cm)
Long-lasting, scented heads of blooms in a range of white to rose shades on a bushy plant. They are easy to grow from seed and can be sown directly into the garden.

Petunia x hybrida 'Blue Vein'
BLUE VEIN PETUNIA
☼ ◑ ◊ Z9–11 H12–1 ↕10–15in (25–38cm) ↔12–36in (30–90cm)
This is one of many named varieties of multiflora petunias that have numerous small blooms over a long period. They are good bedding plants and can also be used in planters.

Rudbeckia hirta
BLACK-EYED SUSAN
☼ ◑ ◊ Z3–7 H7–1
↕12–36in (30–90cm) ↔12–18in (30–45cm)
Branching, somewhat hairy perennials, mostly grown from seed as annuals. Named varieties may have petals tipped or streaked with red or bronze, or may have double flowers.

Digitalis purpurea
FOXGLOVE
☼ ◊ Z4–8 H9–1 ↕6ft (200m) ↔24in (60cm)
Annuals or biennials with named forms in varying heights. A basal rosette of hairy leaves with upright spikes of flowers. 'Foxy' is a dwarf annual variety.

Calendula officinalis
POT MARIGOLD, SCOTCH MARIGOLD
☼ ◑ ◊ H6–1 ↕30in (75cm) ↔18in (45cm)
Fast-growing annuals that will often re-seed themselves. Named forms come in shades of yellow and orange and may be double. Petals are edible.

Tropaeolum majus
Gleam Series
GLEAM NASTURTIUM
☼ ◊ Z11–12 H12–1
↕16in (40cm) ↔24in (60cm)
Easy annuals that flower best in poor soil. Flowers may also be red, orange, or pastel.

Hesperis matronalis
DAME'S VIOLET
☼ ◑ ◊ Z4–9 H9–1
↕36in (90cm)
↔18in (45cm)
Biennial or short-lived perennial, grown as an annual in this region, it will probably self-seed. Scented flowers may be pink, rose, or white.

Coreopsis grandiflora 'Badengold'
BADENGOLD TICKSEED
☼ ◊ Z4–9 H9–1 ↕36in (90cm) ↔18in (45cm)
Short-lived perennial often grown as an annual from seed. Flowers are in individual stems but are freely produced. A good cut flower. Other varieties have double flowers.

Lobelia erinus
SAPPHIRE LOBELIA
☼ ◑ ◊ Z2–8 H8–1 ↕6in (15) ↔4–6in (10–15cm)
Trailing form good for planters and windowboxes; will not thrive in high temperatures. Varieties are bushy and make good edging plants. Also in pink and white.

Linum grandiflorum 'Rubrum'
SCARLET FLAX
☼ ◊ H8–1 ↕18in (45) ↔6in (15cm)
Upright, well-branched, and free-flowering; often included in wildflower mixes although it is native to North Africa. Also white and blue-purple varieties.

Annuals for backgrounds and screens

Use these to fill bare places at the back of a border, to create a temporary screen, or give privacy to a summer patio. Most are fast growing and will quickly provide their lush foliage to hide unwanted views. Some can be used as specimen plants, dotted through smaller annuals where they add height to an otherwise flat planting. Others grow well in containers.

Senna alata
EMPRESS CANDLE PLANT
☼ ◊ Z11–12 H12–10
↕6–30ft (2–10m) ↔6–15ft (2–5m)
Tropical erect to spreading shrub or small tree grown as annual in the South. Blooms from summer to fall.

Pennisetum setaceum 'Rubrum'
PURPLE FOUNTAIN GRASS
☼ ◊ Z9–10 H12–1
↕3ft (1m) ↔18in (45cm)
A showy grass, commonly grown as an annual. The attractive seed heads can be more than 12in (30cm) in length and last from late summer to frost. All parts of the plant are tinged purple.

Ricinus communis
CASTOR BEAN
☼ ◊ Z11–14 H12–1
↕6ft (1.8m) ↔3ft (1m)
Easy to grow from seed, makes an imposing statement and can grow into a large shrub in a single season if given enough heat and moisture. Seeds are poisonous.

Acalypha hispida
RED-HOT CAT'S TAIL
☼ ◑ ◊ Z11–15 H12–6 ↕6–10ft (2–3m) ↔3–6ft (1–2m)
A tropical shrub that is used as an annual for its broad, deep-green foliage and long tassels of showy flowers. It can be cut back in fall and overwintered as a houseplant if not too large.

Abelmoschus esculentus 'Burgundy'
BURGUNDY OKRA
☼ ◊ H12–6 ↕3–6ft (1–2m) ↔to 3ft (1m)
A decorative variety of this southern vegetable with 6in (15cm) pods that turn red when ripe, and stems of deep burgundy. Good for dried arrangements. An All-America Selection winner.

Tithonia rotundifolia
MEXICAN SUNFLOWER
☼ 💧 H12–1 ↕6ft (2m) ↔12in (30cm)
Strong-growing, free-flowering annual with toothed leaves, hairy beneath. Individual flowers up to 3in (8cm) across. 'Goldfinger' is more compact, to 30in (75cm).

Helianthus debilis subsp. *cucumerifolius* 'Italian White'
ITALIAN WHITE SUNFLOWER
☼ 💧 H12–1 ↕to 7ft (2.2m) ↔4ft (1.2m)
One of many colored forms of sunflower. Good cut flowers that are a few inches to over a foot (30cm).

Cleome hassleriana 'Rose Queen'
SPIDER FLOWER
☼ 💧 H12–1 ↕to 5ft (1.5m) ↔18in (45cm)
Strong stems with small spines at the leaf bases carry scented flowers all summer. Grows best in a fertile, light sandy soil. Water freely during dry periods. Good cut flowers.

Celosia spicata 'Argentea'
WHEAT CELOSIA
☼ 💧 H9–2 ↕3ft (1m) ↔18in (45cm)
Closely related to the more common feather celosias, this is taller with narrow spikes of blooms. They make good cut flowers and can be dried for use in winter arrangements.

MORE CHOICES

- *Cleome hassleriana* 'Helen Campbell' H12–1
- *Cosmos bipinnatus* 'Sea Shells Mixture' H12–1
- *Hibiscus moscheutos* Z5–10 H12–1
- *Tagetes erecta* 'Doubloon' H12–1
- *Tibouchina grandiflora* Z13–15 H12–10

Annuals with hot flowers

These bright colors add a sense of urgency, but be careful not to overdo them. Red can dominate the landscape if overused, but tones down when placed close to pale yellow or cream. Bright gold tints can also draw the eye to the exclusion of everything else if used to excess. Separate these hot colors with pale shades, light pinks, soft blues, creams, and of course white.

Amaranthus caudatus
AMARANTHUS, LOVE-LIES-BLEEDING
☼ 💧 Z10–15 H12–1 ↕5ft (1.5m) ↔30in (75cm)
Flowers range from crimson to purple or blood red (hence the common name) or green, as in 'Viridis'. Tolerates poor soil; best in moderately fertile soil.

Calendula officinalis
POT MARIGOLD
☼ ◐ 💧 H6–1 ↕30in (75cm) ↔18in (45cm)
Single or double flowers all summer long. Quite cold tolerant, will self-seed in mild regions and flower during winter. Edible petals give color to salads.

Cuphea ignea
CIGAR FLOWER
☼ 💧 Z10–11 H12–6 ↕30in (75cm) ↔36in (90cm)
Small tropical shrub, easy to grow from seed as an annual. Single flowers open in leaf axils from spring to fall. Makes a good conservatory plant in bright light.

Gerbera jamesonii
BARBERTON DAISY
☼ 💧 Z11 H12–6 ↕18in (45cm) ↔24in (60cm)
Clump-forming perennial, increasingly popular as an annual. Mixed-color strains grown from seed used as bedding or pot-plants.

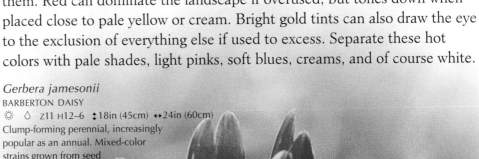

Sanvitalia procumbens
CREEPING ZINNIA
☼ ◊ H12–1 ↕8in (20cm) ↔18in (45cm)
Prostrate annual with small flowers freely produced all summer. Good in containers or hanging baskets. Named varieties more prostrate and may have orange flowers.

Gaillardia pulchella Plume Series
PLUME BLANKET FLOWER
Ⓝ ☼ ◊ Z10–11 H12–1
↕18in (45cm) ↔12in (30cm)
Upright bushy annual with spoon-shaped leaves. Very free-flowering, all summer long.

Tropaeolum majus
NASTURTIUM
☼ ◊ ◐ Z11–12 H12–1 ↕3–10ft (1–3m) ↔5–15ft (1.5–5m)
Tough plant, grows easily from seed sown *in situ*. Does well in poor dry soils, over-rich soils give foliage and few flowers. Good for planters. Edible flowers and leaves have peppery taste.

Zinnia elegans cultivar
COMMON ZINNIA
☼ ◊ H12–1 ↕24–30in (60–75cm) ↔12in (30cm)
This is one of a large number of zinnia cultivars that flower in a wide range of colors and heights. Flowers can be single or double. They are subject to several diseases and pests.

Tithonia rotundifolia 'Torch'
TORCH MEXICAN SUNFLOWER
☼ ◊ H12–1
↕6ft (2m) ↔12in (30cm)
An upright, robust branching annual with strong stems and hairy leaves that deer avoid. Free-flowering over a long period, this plant makes a good cut flower. 'Fiesta del Sol' is a dwarf form, growing to 30in (75cm).

MORE CHOICES

- *Asclepius curassavica* Z9–11 H12–6
- *Begonia semperflorens-cultorum* Z11–15 H12–1
- *Celosia cristata* H9–2
- *Coreopsis tinctoria* Z4–9 H12–1
- *Cosmos sulphureus* 'Bright Lights' H12–1
- *Gazania rigens* Z8–11 H12–1
- *Gomphrena globosa* 'Strawberry Fields' Z11–12 H12–1
- *Helianthus annuus* H12–1
- *Helichrysum bracteatum* Z10–11 H12–1
- *Impatiens* 'New Guinea' Z9–15 H7–1
- *Impatiens wallerana* Z10–15 H12–1
- *Melampodium paludosum* Z11–12 H12–1
- *Portulaca grandiflora* Z9–11 H12–1
- *Rudbeckia hirta* Z3–7 H7–1
- *Salvia splendens* Z11–12 H12–1
- *Tagetes erecta* H12–1
- *Tagetes lucida* Z8–13 H12–1
- *Tagetes patula* 'Queen Sophia' H12–1
- *Thunbergia alata* Z11–15 H12–10
- *Verbena* x *hybrida* Z11–15 H12–1
- *Zinnia angustifolia* H12–1

Tagetes tenuifolia 'Lemon Gem'
LEMON GEM MARIGOLD
☼ ◊ H12–1 ↕to 9in (23cm) ↔to 16in (40cm)
Upright bushy plant with masses of small single flowers from spring to late summer. Other marigolds have larger, often double flowers on taller plants, in a range of yellow to bronze colors.

Annuals with cool flowers

Cool blues, pinks, mauves, and creams set off the more flamboyant colors and can prevent them from becoming dominant. In general, these colors blend well, although some pinks and mauves can clash. Pale colors seem almost luminous and stand out in shade, where brighter hues would disappear. They are also more visible at dusk.

Borago officinalis
BORAGE
☼ ◊ H12–1 ↕3ft (1m) ↔1ft (30cm)
Flowers appear from late spring to late summer and are attractive to bees. Used for its cucumber-like taste and its medicinal properties. Annual or biennial.

Catharanthus roseus 'Polka Dot'
POLKA DOT PERIWINKLE
☼ ◊ Z12–15 H12–1 ↕↔12–24in (30–60cm)
Excellent and increasingly available plants for hot dry locations. Also come in red, pink, and rose shades, often with a contrasting center. May be listed as *Vinca*.

Lathyrus odoratus 'Aqua'
AQUA SWEET PEA
☼ ◊ Z9–10 H8–1 ↕to 6ft (2m) ↔2ft (60cm)
Sweetly scented climbing annual needs cool soil to germinate and cool weather in early stages of growth. Hundreds of named forms in a wide range of colors, not all "cool."

Exacum affine
PERSIAN VIOLET

☼ ○ H7–1 ↕ ↔8–12in (20–30cm)

Bushy evergreen perennial normally grown as an
annual or pot-plant. Needs frequent watering during
dry periods but roots may rot if kept too wet.

Consolida ajacis
LARKSPUR

☼ ◑ H9–1

↕1–4ft (30–120cm) ↔12in (30cm)

Species has fine foliage and forms a blue cloud
in summer. Modern hybrids' flowers are dense spikes.

Gilia capitata
QUEEN ANNE'S THIMBLES

Ⓝ ☼ ○ H12–1

↕18–24in (45–60cm) ↔9in (23cm)

Summer-flowering annual from grasslands in western
North America. Sow where they are to flower.

MORE CHOICES

- *Ageratum houstonianum* z10–13 H12–1
- *Brachycome iberdifolia* z5–8 H9–3
- *Browallia speciosa* z14–15 H12–1
- *Centaurea cyanus* H7–1
- *Cleome hassleriana* z11 H12–1
- *Cosmos bipinnatus* 'Sea Shells' H12–1
- *Dianthus barbatus* z5–9 H8–1
- *Digitalis purpurea* z4–8 H9–1
- *Eustoma grandiflora* z8–11 H12–1
- *Gomphrena globosa* z11–12 H12–1
- *Heliotropum arborescens* z12–15 H12–9
- *Impatiens hawkeri* 'New Guinea'
 z9–15 H7–1
- *Impatiens walleriana* z10–15 H12–1
- *Lavatera trimestris* H12–1
- *Linaria maroccana* H9–1
- *Lobelia* spp. z3–9 H9–2
- *Myosotis sylvatica* z5–8 H7–1
- *Nierembergia hippomanica* var. *violacea*
 z7–11 H12–7
- *Nigela damascena* H12–1
- *Petunia* x *hybrida* z12–13 H7–1
- *Salvia farinacea* 'Victoria' z8–11 H12–1
- *Salvia viridis* H9–1
- *Torenia fournieri* z12–13 H6–1

Tweedia caerulea
BLUE TWEEDIA

☼ ○ z12–15 H12–10 ↕to 3ft (1m)

A small scrambling sub-shrub commonly grown as an
annual from seed. Flower buds are pink and older
flowers fade to purple. May be sold as *Oxypetalum*.

Annuals for foliage

Although most annuals are grown for the display of flowers they produce, there are a few that are grown purely for their foliage. Flowers, if they appear at all, are usually small and do not add to the plants' attractiveness. If allowed to develop, they may even cause the plant to die. The plants listed here are not all technically annuals, but can be treated as such.

Ocimum basilicum 'Purple Ruffles'
PURPLE RUFFLES BASIL
☼ ◊ Z9–10 H10–1 ↕24in (60cm) ↔12in (30cm)
Ornamental basil lacks the pungency of culinary ones, and are not suitable as herbs. Makes good edging.

Senecio cineraria 'Silver Dust'
SILVER DUST DUSTY MILLER
☼ ☀ ◊ Z8–11 H12–8 ↕↔12in (30cm)
One of several silver-leaved plants commonly called Dusty Miller. Sprays of yellow flowers may appear the second summer in the South, where the plant survives winter.

Ipomoea batatas 'Blackie'
BLACKIE SWEET POTATO
☼ ◊ Z11–12 H12–1 ↕20ft (6m)
A tender climber that is often used as a trailing plant for containers and hanging baskets. Purple flowers may be produced in warmer parts of the Northeast.

Petroselinum crispum 'Champion Moss Curled'
MOSS CURLED PARSLEY
☼ ◊ Z5–8 H9–1 ↕12in (30cm) ↔18in (45cm)
Equally useful as a garnish or an edging, this is one of several forms of parsley with frilled, crinkled leaves.

Solenostemon scutellarioides 'Plum Parfait'
PLUM PARFAIT COLEUS
☼ ☀ ♦ Z11–12 H12–1 ↕↔3ft (1m)
This is the new botanical name for the plant gardeners have long known as *Coleus blumei*. Easy to grow. Many forms have leaves colored in a myriad of ways.

Acalypha wilkesiana
MATCH-ME-IF-YOU-CAN
☼ ◐ ◊ Z14–15 H12–1 ↕↔to 6ft (2m)
Tropical shrub grown from cuttings. The common name comes from the variety of patterns on the leaves, with no two alike. Also makes a good houseplant.

Hibiscus acetosella 'Coppertone'
COPPERTONE MALLOW
☼ ◊ Z10–11 H12–1 ↕2–5ft (.6–1.5m) ↔3ft (1m)
Upright, fast-growing plant with yellow or reddish flowers in late summer. Use as an accent plant dotted through smaller annuals. May be sold as 'Red Shield.'

Foeniculum vulgare 'Purpureum'
FENNEL
☼ ◑ Z6–9 H9–6 ↕6ft (1.8m) ↔18in (45cm)
Young foliage is a dull purple, becoming a blue-green as it matures This perennial can be used in cooking, like the regular green fennel. It may seed freely.

Colocasia esculenta 'Black Magic'
COMMON NAME
◐ ◑● pH Z8–11 H12–8 ↕5ft (1.5m) ↔24in (60cm)
Grown as a staple food in tropical countries, the two varieties shown here are more decorative with colored stems and veins.

MORE CHOICES

- *Amaranthus ficoidea* 'Golden Threads' H12–5
- *Amaranthus ficoidea* 'Rosea Nana' H12–5
- *Brassica* sp. 'Red Boar' Z14–15 H12–10
- *Caladium bicolor* Z15 H12–4
- *Helichrysum petiolarum* Z11–15 H12–10
- *Hibiscus acetosella* 'Red Shield' Z10–11 H12–1
- *Ipomoea batatas* 'Margarita' Z11–12 H12–1
- *Perilla* 'Magilla Gorilla' H9–1
- *Salvia argentea* Z5–8 H8–5

Annuals for cut flowers

If space permits, plant a cutting garden in an inconspicuous place, where you can grow plants in straight rows solely for cutting. These can include annuals and perennials, such as peonies and obedient plants, with flowers that last well in water. Spread your cut-flower plants across your average garden so that collecting blooms for the house will not leave a big hole in the display.

Consolida ajacis
LARKSPUR
☼ H9–1
↕1–4ft (30–120cm) ↔12in (30cm)
Species has fine foliage and forms a blue cloud in summer. Can be direct-sown and will then self-seed.

Molucella laevis
BELLS OF IRELAND
☼ Z9–11 H11–1 ↕3ft (1m) ↔9in (23cm)
Interesting green calyces surround the small white to pale, purplish pink, fragrant flowers The flower stalks appear in late summer and can be dried.

Cosmos bipinnatus
COSMOS
☼ H12–1 ↕to 5ft (1.5m) ↔18in (45cm)
Free-flowering with blooms up to 4in (10cm) across, an excellent addition to any border. Tolerates poor dry soil, but not wet. Deadhead to prolong blooming.

Matthiola incana 'Cinderella'
CINDERELLA BROMPTON STOCK
☼ Z7–8 H8–1 ↕↔10in (25cm)
Available with single or double, sweetly scented flowers, these bloom within 10 weeks of seeding. Other varieties can be up to 30in (75cm) tall.

Lathyrus odoratus cvs.
SWEET PEA
☼ Z9–10 H8–1 ↕6ft (2m) ↔2ft (60cm)
Sweetly scented climbing annual, needs cool soil to germinate and cool weather in early stages of growth. Hundreds of named varieties in a wide range of colors.

Centaurea cyanus
BACHELOR'S BUTTONS
☼ H7–1
↕1–3ft (30cm–1m) ↔1ft (30cm)
Flower colors also include purple, red, pink, and white. Easy to grow from seed. Flowers last well.

Rudbeckia hirta 'Becky Mixed'
BECKY BLACK-EYED SUSAN
☼ ◐ ◊ Z3–7 H7–1 ↕3ft (1m) ↔18in (45cm)
Flowers freely throughout much of summer. Strains are available in a variety of heights and doubleness. Easy from seed but short lived. Tolerates heavy clay.

Tithonia rotundifolia 'Torch'
TORCH MEXICAN SUNFLOWER
☼ ◊ Z10–11 H12–1
↕6ft (2m) ↔12in (30cm)
Upright annual with strong stems and hairy leaves that deer avoid. Free-flowering over a long period. 'Fiesta del Sol' is a dwarf form, to 30in (75cm).

MORE CHOICES

- *Antirrhinum majus* 'Topper' Z7–9 H9–1
- *Calendula officinalis* H6–1
- *Callistephus chinensis* H9–1
- *Celosia cristata* H9–2
- *Cleome hassleriana* Z11 H12–1
- *Eustoma grandiflora* Z8–11 H12–1
- *Gilia capitata* H12–1
- *Gomphrena globosa* Z11–12 H12–1
- *Gypsophila elegans* Z5–9 H9–1
- *Helianthus annuus* H12–1
- *Iberis umbellata* H12–1
- *Limonium sinuatum* H9–3
- *Lunaria annua* Z3–9 H9–1
- *Nigella damascena* H12–1
- *Papaver nudicaule* Z2–7 H9–2
- *Physalis alkekengi* Z3–9 H8–1
- *Salvia farinacea* Z8–11 H12–1
- *Salvia leucantha* Z9–11 H12–4
- *Scabiosa atropurpurea* Z4–11 H8–3
- *Tagetes erecta* H12–1
- *Tropaeolum majus* Z11–12 H12–1
- *Tweedia caerulea* Z12–15 H12–10
- *Zinnia elegans* H12–1

Digitalis purpurea
FOXGLOVE
◐ ◆ Z4–8 H9–1 ↕3–5ft (1–1.5m) ↔2ft (60cm)
Blooms appear in early summer. Can be biennial or perennial. Prefers well-drained soil and tolerates poor, dry soils. Prone to crown and root rot as well as rust.

Coreopsis tinctoria
CALLIOPSIS
Ⓝ ☼ ◐ ◊ Z4–9 H12–1 ↕4ft (1.2m) ↔18in (45cm)
Species is a good addition to a wildflower garden. Named varieties have petals of red to mahogany and may be a solid color or banded with yellow.

Ornamental vegetables and herbs

While they can be combined to make a colorful potager or kitchen garden in the French style, these vegetables and herbs can also be integrated into existing perennial or annual plantings, as in the old English cottage gardens. With care, leaves or stems can be cut from most of the plants shown here without spoiling their decorative effect.

Petroselinum crispum
PARSLEY
Z5–9 H9–1 ↕32in (80cm) ↔24in (60cm)
An excellent edging plant, this grows quickly to form a green carpet of stems that can be used in the kitchen. More decorative than the flat-leaved Italian parsley.

Beta vulgaris 'Bright Lights'
BRIGHT LIGHTS SWISS CHARD
H12–1 ↕24in (60cm) ↔12in (30cm)
Bright variety with stems of red, orange, yellow, pink, purple, and white. Pick the outer leaves regularly to ensure new stems. Small leaves are good in salads.

Beta vulgaris
SWISS CHARD
H12–1
↕↔12–18in (30–45cm)
Various single-color varieties can be used as food or to give contrast to the border. 'Ruby Red' has dark red stems and veins, 'Bright Yellow' has yellow, and 'Fordhook Giant' has white.

Phaseolus coccineus
SCARLET RUNNER BEAN
Z8–9 H9–1
↕10ft (3m) ↔1ft (30cm)
An annual climber with edible beans that become tough if allowed to grow too large. Makes a good temporary screen that blooms all summer providing the beans are kept picked.

Brassica oleracea 'Rebor'
FLOWERING KALE
Z8–9 H9–1 ↕↔18in (45cm)
This ornamental relative of cabbage and kale is grown for its rounded colorful foliage, suitable for fall or winter bedding or for containers. These biennials flower the following year if allowed to stand. Leaves may have a white or pink coloration.

Tetragonia tetragonoides
NEW ZEALAND SPINACH

☼ ○ ◐ z10–11 H12–1 ‡↔3ft (1m)

Bushy perennial usually grown as an annual; heat and drought tolerant; provides a spinach substitute during hot weather. Soak seeds for 24 hours, sow in place.

Capsicum annuum cultivars
PEPPER

☼ ○ ◐ z9–11 H12–1 ‡↔2ft (60cm)

Peppers come in a variety of sizes and shapes. White flowers are followed by green fruit that turn shades of red, yelow, orange, purple, and ivory. Annual.

Anethum graveolens
DILL

☼ ○ H12–1 ‡24in (60cm) ↔12in (30cm)

The lacy foliage is a good contrast to most perennials and can be used in cooking, as can the seeds. The flower heads are a magnet for butterflies. Self-seeds.

MORE CHOICES

- *Beta vulgaris* 'Oxblood' H12–1
- *Brassica oleacea* 'Redbor' z7–11 H6–1
- *Capsicum annuum* 'Habanero' z9–15 H12–1
- *Cichorium endiva* 'Green Curled' H8–3
- *Cichorium intybus* 'Ceriolo' z3–11 H12–2
- *Curcurbita pepo* 'Goldrush' H12–2
- *Cynara cardunculus* 'Gigante' z7–9 H9–7
- *Fragaria x ananassa* 'Pink Panda' z5–9 H9–5
- *Lactuca sativa* 'Lollo Rossa' z8–11 H12–1
- *Lageneria siceraria* H9–1
- *Luffa aegyptica* 'Jade' H9–1
- *Phaseolus vulgaris* 'Royal Burgundy' H12–1
- *Physalis ixocarpa* z11–12 H12–7
- *Solanum melongena* 'Casper' H12–5
- *Zea mays* 'Strawberry Corn' H12–1

Solanum melongena
EGGPLANT

☼ ○ ◐ z11 H12–1 ‡↔2–3ft (60–90cm)

Highly attractive vegetables with large lilac flowers shaped like tomato blooms. Fruits come in white, purple, white speckled purple, and green. Annual.

PART III

GARDENING TECHNIQUES

including Selecting Plants, Planting, Pruning, and Propagation

Once you've planned your SMARTGARDEN™ and have determined what you'd like to grow, it's time to put on the gardening gloves. Here are pointers on selecting healthy plants and detecting potentially unhealthy ones; planting them correctly; pruning trees, shrubs, and other woody plants; and propagating new plants by various methods.

SELECTING PLANTS

Choosing plants at the nursery or garden center does not need to be a long, complicated process: basically, look for plants that appear healthy and that avoid extremes, such as too much top-growth compared to the root ball, or too little foliage on stems that barely support the leaves. Spend more time on choosing longer-lived and more expensive trees and shrubs than on herbaceous plants.

CHOOSING A TREE

Container-grown tree

Before buying one of these, remove it from its container to examine the roots. Do not buy a potbound tree (with a mass of congested roots) or one with thick roots protruding from the holes.

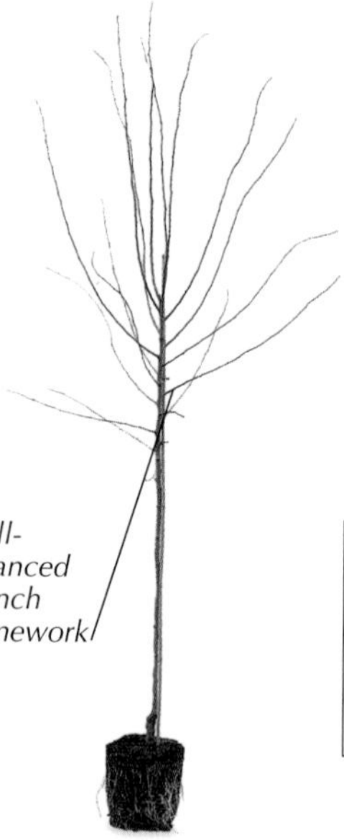

GOOD EXAMPLE

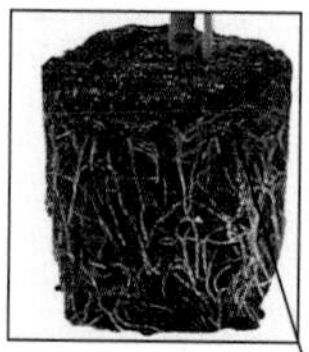

POOR EXAMPLE

Bare-root tree

These have virtually no soil around the roots. Examine the roots to check that they are not damaged or diseased and that there is no sign of dryness that may have been caused by exposure to air or sunlight.

GOOD EXAMPLE

POOR EXAMPLES

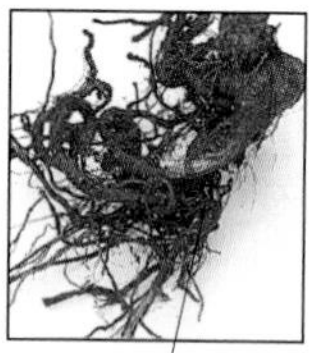

Balled-and-burlapped tree

Buy and plant a balled-and-burlapped tree when dormant in fall or early spring, following the same basic examination criteria as for both container-grown and bare-root trees.

GOOD EXAMPLE

x CUPRESSOCYPARIS LEYLANDII

SELECTING A CONTAINER-GROWN SHRUB

Look through the drainage holes (or carefully slide the shrub out of its container) to check for a well-developed root system. If present, the shrub is probably container-grown and is not containerized (meaning it was recently removed from the open ground and put into a container). The roots should have healthy, white tips. Reject plants with poorly developed root systems, with coiled roots or root balls, or with roots protruding from the container, since these rarely establish or grow well.

GOOD EXAMPLE

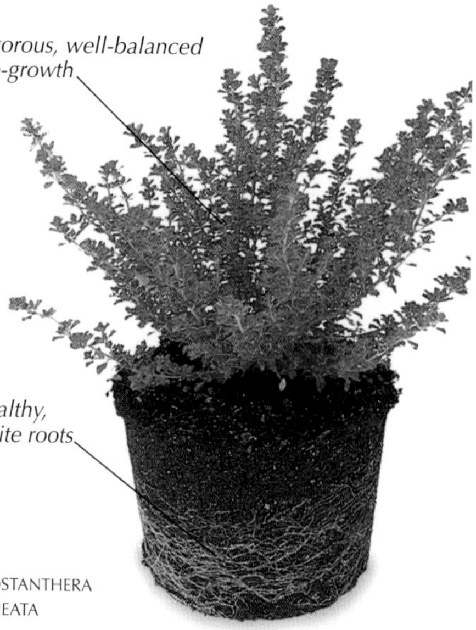

PROSTANTHERA CUNEATA

POOR EXAMPLE

Pruning congested roots

Tease out potbound roots, and cut back any that are very long and damaged.

SELECTING CLIMBERS

Climbing plants are usually sold container-grown, although a few may be sold bare-root. Choose a healthy-looking plant with a well-balanced framework of strong shoots, and reject any that show signs of pest infestation or disease. For potgrown plants, turn the pot over and check that the tips of the young roots are just showing. If so, the plant is well-rooted. Reject potbound plants – those that have tightly coiled roots or a mass of roots protruding through the drainage holes. Bare-root plants should have plenty of healthy, well-developed fibrous roots that are in proportion to the amount of top-growth.

GOOD EXAMPLE

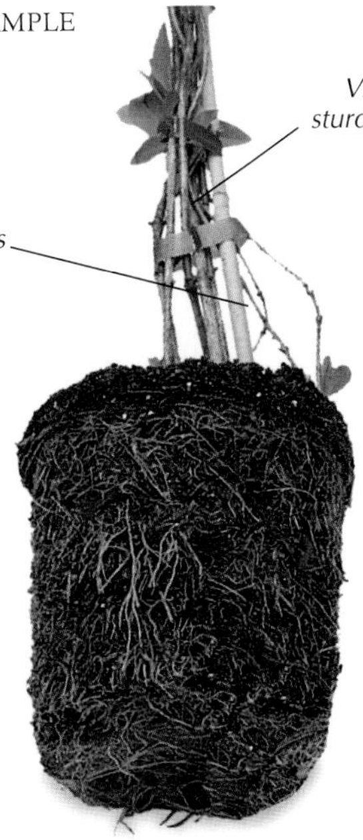

LONICERA

POOR EXAMPLES

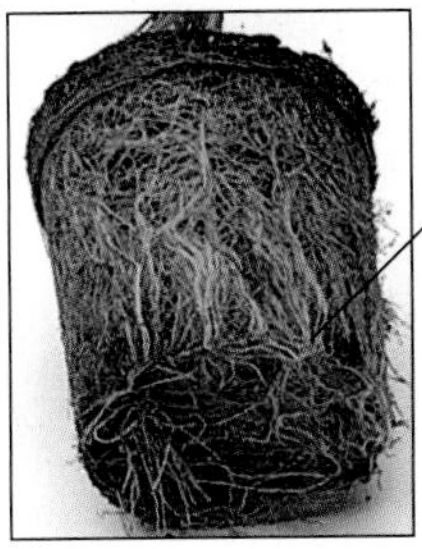

SELECTING HEALTHY ROSES

Bare-root bush rose

Examine the plant carefully: if the stems appear dried out (the bark will be shriveled), or buds have started growing prematurely (producing blanched, thin shoots), do not buy it.

GOOD EXAMPLE

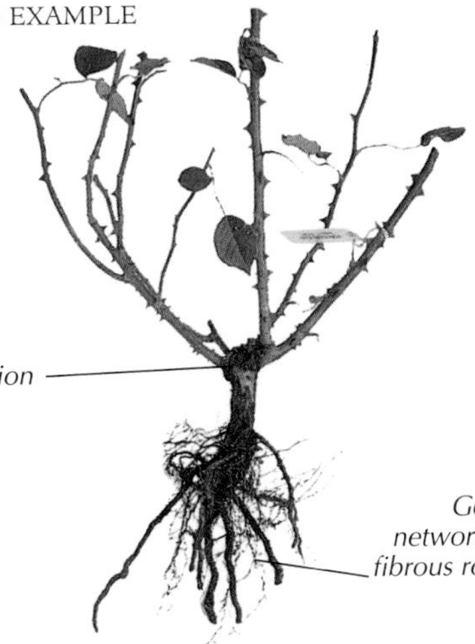

POOR EXAMPLE

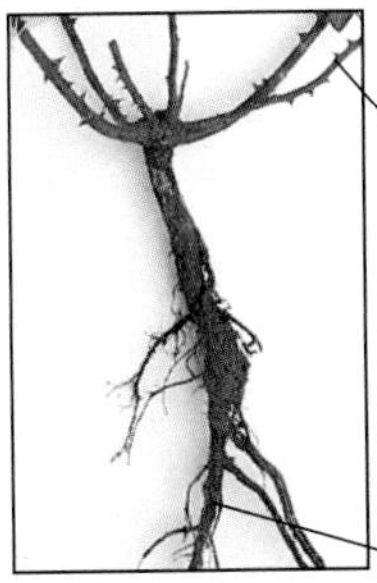

Container-grown rose

Check that the plant has not been recently potted up: hold the plant by its main shoot and gently shake it. If it does not move around in the soil mix, it is well-established and a good buy.

GOOD EXAMPLE

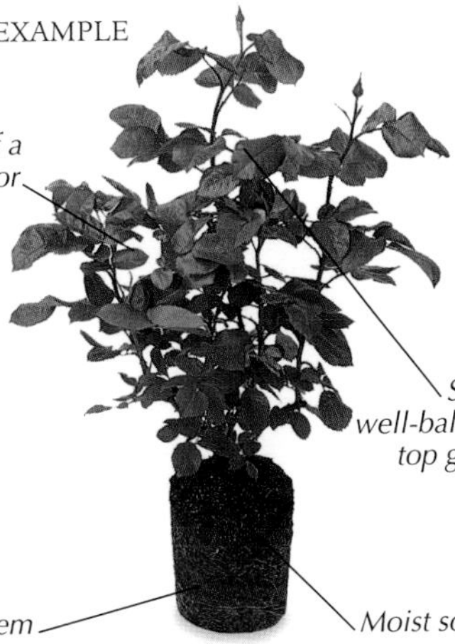

POOR EXAMPLE

Standard rose

Choose a standard rose with a balanced head of shoots, since it is likely to be viewed from all sides. A straight main stem is best, although a slightly crooked stem is acceptable.

GOOD EXAMPLE

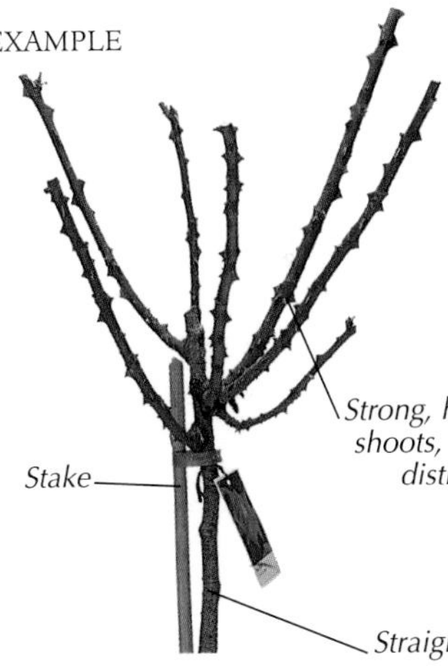

POOR EXAMPLE

CHOOSING HERBACEOUS PLANTS

Most herbaceous plants are sold container-grown, but bare-root plants are also sometimes available from fall to early spring, when they are dormant. If buying herbaceous plants at the beginning of the growing season, check that there are strong, emerging shoots. Plants that have a few fat, healthy-looking buds are better than those that have a large number of weaker ones.

GOOD EXAMPLE

IMPATIENS CULTIVAR

GOOD EXAMPLE

LUPINE

POOR EXAMPLES

SELECTING BULBS, CORMS, TUBERS, AND SIMILAR PLANTS

Most bulbs are sold in a dry state during their dormant period. Buy these as early as possible before they start into growth; most daffodils, for example, normally start producing roots in late summer, and most other spring-flowering bulbs will begin to grow by early fall. Fall-flowering crocuses and *Colchicum* species and hybrids especially benefit from early planting; specialized nurseries sell them in midsummer. All fall-flowering bulbs are best bought and planted by late summer. Summer-flowering bulbs (such as *Gladiolus*, *Dahlia*, and *Canna*) are available for purchase in spring.

Bulbs tend to deteriorate if kept dry too long; they will have a shorter growing period and take some time to recover and flower satisfactorily, so buy and plant them as soon as they are available. Do not buy or plant any bulbs that are mushy or slimy, or any that feel much lighter than a bulb of similar size of the same kind (they are probably dried up and dead).

GOOD EXAMPLES

DAFFODIL (SINGLE-NOSED)

DAFFODIL (TWIN-NOSED)

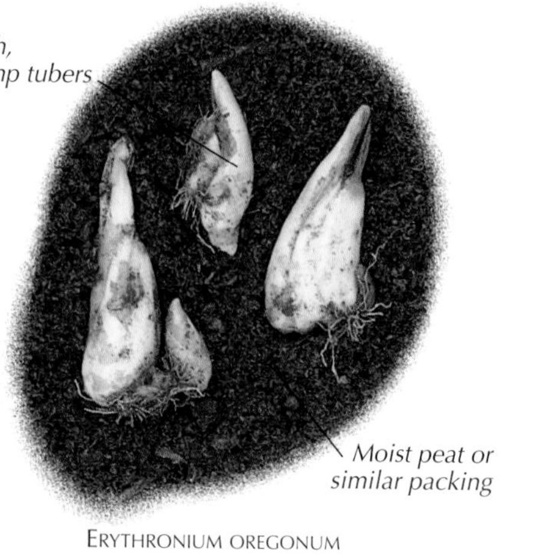

ERYTHRONIUM OREGONUM

POOR EXAMPLES

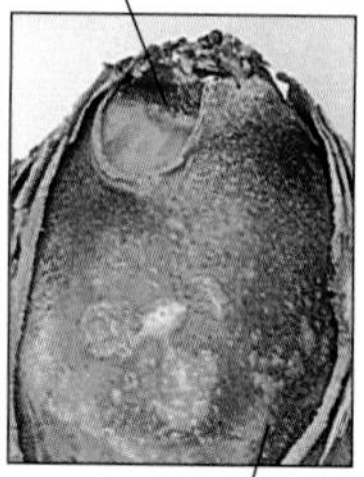

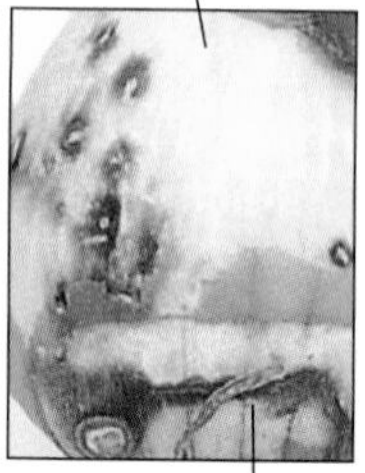

CORYDALIS SOLIDA

SELECTING PLANTS FOR THE WATER GARDEN

When selecting aquatic plants at the nursery or garden center, look for clean, fresh-looking, and vigorous specimens, growing in tanks that are free from algae and duckweed (*Wolffia*). Check that the undersides of the leaves are free from jellylike deposits of snail eggs and that there are no strands of blanketweed in the foliage. Mail-order plants should appear plump and green; if they look weak and limp, they are unlikely to grow well. If buying plants by mail order, use a specialized supplier.

Marginal plant

GOOD EXAMPLE

CALTHA PALUSTRIS

POOR EXAMPLE

Surface floater

GOOD EXAMPLE

STRATIOTES ALOIDES

POOR EXAMPLE

SELECTING CACTI AND OTHER SUCCULENTS

When buying cacti and other succulents, choose healthy, pest- and disease-free, unblemished plants that show strong new growth (unless you are buying the plants when they are dormant) or have flower buds forming. Do not buy damaged or even slightly shriveled specimens, or any with dull, dry, or limp segments. Also reject plants that have outgrown their pots.

GOOD EXAMPLE

REBUTIA SPECIES

POOR EXAMPLE

GOOD EXAMPLE

CRASSULA OVATA

POOR EXAMPLE

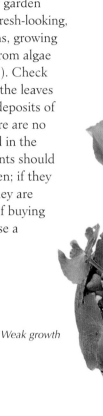

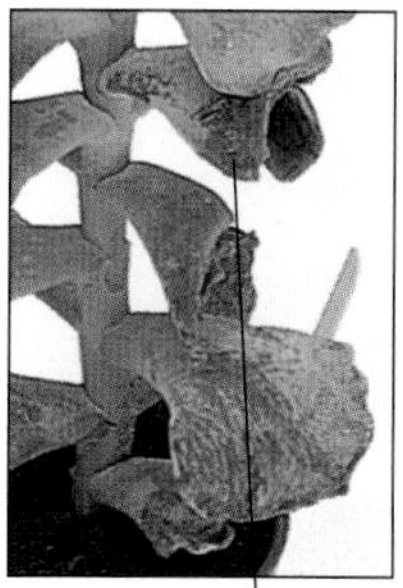

PLANTING

When selecting and planting trees, shrubs, and woody climbers, it is vital to take account of the general weather pattern of your area as well as your garden's individual microclimate, because these factors will determine whether a given plant is hardy and has a reasonable chance of surviving in your garden. Proper planting and aftercare will increase the likelihood of survival.

PLANTING A CONTAINER-GROWN TREE

First, thoroughly moisten the soil mix in the container – if it is very dry, stand the container in water for half an hour or until the soil mix is moist throughout (the bubbles will stop rising). Then remove the container, cutting it away if necessary, taking care not to damage the roots excessively. Gently tease out the roots with your fingers or a hand fork (or with pruners, if the roots are thickly congested) to encourage them to grow into the surrounding soil; this is essential with a potbound plant. If there are any broken or damaged roots, trim them back with pruners. It is important to check that the planting depth is correct. If a tree is planted too deeply, its roots may not receive enough oxygen and the tree may grow more slowly or even die; if planted too shallowly, the roots may dry out.

1 Mark out the area of the hole to be dug – about 3 or 4 times the diameter of the tree's root ball. Lift any grass or weeds, then dig out the hole to about 1½ times the depth of the root ball.

2 Scarify the sides and bottom of the hole with a fork. There is no need to improve the soil unless the quality is very poor, such as dense heavy clay or very infertile sand.

3 Drive the stake into the hole, just off center and on the windward side. Lay the tree on its side and slide it out of the pot. Gently tease out the roots without breaking up the root ball.

4 Hold the tree next to the stake and spread out the roots. Lay a stake across the hole to check the planting depth. Adjust this by adding or removing some soil.

5 Backfill around the tree with more topsoil, working it down the root ball, and then gently firm the soil. Build up soil around the hole to form a watering ring.

6 Cut back damaged stems, long sideshoots, and weaker, lower branches (see inset). Apply a mulch 2–3in (5–7cm) deep around the area.

PLANTING A CONTAINER-GROWN SHRUB

Fall and spring are the optimum times for planting container-grown and containerized shrubs. Planting in fall allows the roots to establish while the ground is still warm, so the shrub should be growing vigorously before hot dry weather the next summer. In some areas, planting can be carried out during mild weather in winter, but not when the ground is very cold or frozen. Roots will not begin growth in very cold soil, and there is a risk that they may freeze. A possible disadvantage to spring planting is that top-growth is likely to develop before the roots establish adequately and, if there is a long spell of hot dry weather, watering may be required to help the plants survive.

Placing one hand on top of the soil mix and around the shrub to support it, carefully ease the plant out of its container. Place the shrub in the prepared hole.

Lay a stake alongside to check that the soil level is the same as before. If necessary, adjust the planting depth by adding or removing topsoil beneath the shrub.

Backfill around the shrub with the removed soil, firming in stages to prevent air pockets from forming. Once the hole has been filled with soil, carefully firm around the shrub with your heel or hands.

Prune any diseased, damaged, or weak wood, and cut back any inward-growing or crossing stems to an outward-growing shoot or bud.

Using a watering ring

To help retain water, create a shallow depression and a low wall of soil around the shrub. Cover the area with mulch, then allow the ring to settle on its own.

TRANSPLANTING A SHRUB

Careful selection and siting of a shrub should make transplanting unnecessary, although sometimes it may be desirable or unavoidable. In general, the younger the shrub, the more likely it is to reestablish after being moved. Most young shrubs may be lifted bare-root when dormant. Established shrubs that have large root systems should be lifted with a ball of soil around the roots before being moved. Spring (before bud break) and mid- to late fall are the best times to do this.

Using a spade, mark out a circle around the extent of the shrub's branches (here *Ilex aquifolium* 'Golden Milkboy'). Tie in (or prune off) any trailing stems, or wrap the shrub in burlap, to prevent the stems from being damaged. Dig a circular trench around the plant.

Use a fork to loosen the soil around the root ball. Continue to carefully fork away soil from around the shrub's root ball to reduce its size and weight.

Undercut the root ball with a spade, cutting through woody roots if necessary to separate them from the surrounding soil.

Pull some burlap up around the root ball and tie it securely. Remove the shrub from its hole, then transport it to its new position.

Remove or untie the burlap when replanting. Plant with the soil mark at the same level as before. Firm, water well, and mulch.

PLANTING A CLIMBER AGAINST A WALL

Before removing the plant from its pot, make sure that the soil mix is moist. Water the plant well, so that the root ball is thoroughly wet, and then allow it to drain for at least an hour. Remove the surface layer of soil mix to eliminate weeds, and then invert the pot, taking care to support the plant as it slides out.

If the roots have begun to curl around inside the pot, gently tease them out. Any dead, damaged, or protruding roots should be cut back to the perimeter of the root ball. Position the plant so that the top of the root ball is just level with the surrounding soil. It is advisable to plant clematis more deeply, however. Climbers that have been grafted (as is the case with most wisterias) should be planted with the graft union 2½in (6cm) below soil level to encourage rooting of the cultivar.

1 Attach a support 12in (30cm) above the soil and 2in (5cm) from the wall. Dig a hole 18in (45cm) from the wall. Loosen the soil at the base and add compost.

2 Soak the climber's root ball well. Position it in the hole at a 45° angle, placing a stake across to check the planting level. Spread the roots away from the wall.

3 Fill in around the plant and firm and level the soil, ensuring that no air pockets remain between the roots and that the plant is fully supported.

4 Untie the stems from the central stake and select 4 or 5 strong shoots. Insert a stake for each shoot and attach it to the lowest wire. Tie in the shoots.

5 Using pruners, trim back any weak, damaged, or wayward shoots to the central stem. This establishes the initial framework for the climber.

6 Water the plant thoroughly (here *Jasminum mesnyi*). Cover the surrounding soil with a deep mulch to retain moisture and discourage weeds.

PLANTING A BARE-ROOT ROSE

Bare-root roses are best planted just before or at the beginning of their dormant period (in fall or early winter) to lessen the shock of transplanting. Early spring is better in areas that have bad winters. Plant roses as soon as possible after purchase. If there is any delay, perhaps because of unsuitable weather, it is best to heel them into a spare piece of ground, with the roots buried in a shallow trench. Alternatively, store the roses in a cool and frost-free place, and keep the roots moist. If the roots of a bare-root rose look dry before planting, soak the roots in a bucket of water for an hour or two until they are thoroughly moist.

Remove diseased, damaged , or crossing shoots and straggly stems; trim thick roots by one-third. Dig a hole and fork in compost mixed with bone meal or fertilizer.

2 Center the rose in the hole and spread out the roots evenly. Lay a stake across the hole to check that the bud union will be at the correct depth for the type of rose and your climate zone (above ground in warmer areas, below in colder).

3 In 2 or 3 stages, water the hole and backfill with soil after the water has drained out. Do not walk on the backfilled soil to avoid compacting the soil and breaking the roots.

PLANTING A CLIMBING ROSE

Train climbers grown against a wall or fence along horizontal wires that are about 18in (45cm) apart and held in place by vine eyes or strong nails. If the brickwork or masonry is very hard, drill holes for the vine eyes with a $\frac{3}{16}$in (4.7mm) bit. Keep the wires 3in (7cm) away from the wall to allow air circulation and discourage diseases. The ground next to a wall is likely to be dry, since it is in a rain shadow and the masonry absorbs moisture from the soil. Plant about 18in (45cm) from the wall where the soil is less dry and water from eaves will not drip on the rose. Prepare the soil and planting hole, and trim the rose, as for bush roses. Fan out its roots. Train the shoots along stakes, but keep each stake far enough from the roots to avoid damaging them.

Place the rose in the planting hole, leaning it toward the wall at an angle of about 45° so that the shoots reach the lowest support wire. Place a stake across the hole to check the planting depth.

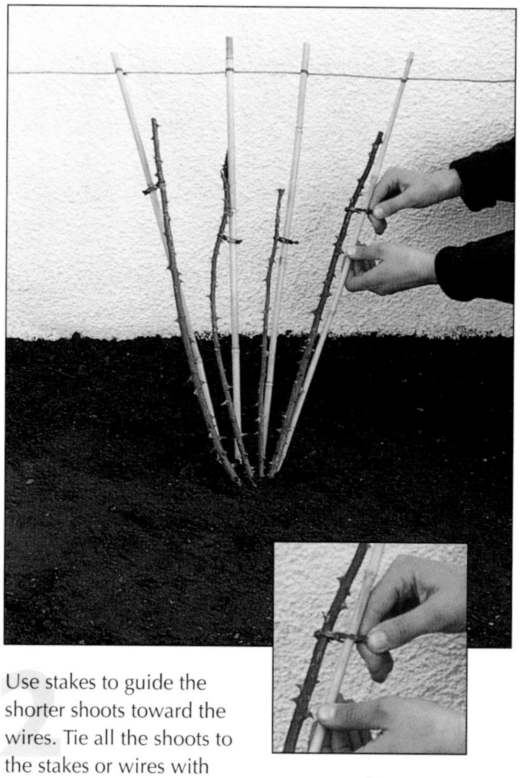

Use stakes to guide the shorter shoots toward the wires. Tie all the shoots to the stakes or wires with plastic straps (see insert).

PLANTING A STANDARD ROSE

A standard rose needs a stake, placed on the side of the prevailing wind, to support it. Paint the entire stake with a preservative that is not toxic to plants, then allow it to dry. Insert the stake very firmly near the center of the planting hole before positioning the rose to avoid damaging the roots and, as a result, encouraging suckers from below the graft union. Position the rose next to the stake, and check that it just reaches the base of the lowest branches; if necessary, adjust the height of the stake. Use a stake or rake handle to make sure that the bud union is at the correct level.

Position the stake in the hole so that the rose stem will be in the center. Drive the stake into the ground and check that the top is just below the head of the rose.

Place a stake across the hole to check the planting depth. Use the old soil mark on the stem as a guide and plant at the correct depth. Fill in the hole, then water.

Use a tie just below the head of the rose, and another halfway up the stem, to attach the rose to the stake. Cut out weak or crossing shoots.

PLANTING A CONTAINER-GROWN PERENNIAL

Perennials grown in containers may be planted out at any time of year when the soil is workable, but the best seasons are spring and fall. Planting in fall helps the plants establish quickly before the onset of winter, because the soil is still warm enough to promote root growth, yet it is unlikely to dry out. In cold areas, however, spring planting is better for perennials that are not entirely hardy or that dislike wet conditions.

1 In a prepared bed, dig a hole 1½ times wider and deeper than the plant's root ball.

2 Gently scrape off the top 1¼in (3cm) of soil to remove weeds and weed seeds. Carefully tease out the roots around the sides and base of the root ball.

3 Check that the plant crown is at the correct depth when planted and fill in around the root ball. Firm gently around the plant, then water it in thoroughly.

PLANTING ANNUALS INTO OPEN GROUND

Before you plant out annuals, first prepare the bed, water the young plants thoroughly, and then allow them to drain for an hour or so. To remove a plant from its pot, invert it, supporting the stem with a finger on either side. Then tap the rim against a hard surface. If plants are in trays without divisions, hold the tray firmly with both hands, then tap one side sharply on the ground to loosen the medium.

1 Break the pack apart and carefully remove each seedling (here *Tagetes*) with its root ball intact.

2 Place each plant in a hole large enough to take its root ball, making sure the plant is slightly lower in the soil than it was in its container.

3 Gently firm the soil in the well around the plant so that there are no air pockets. Water the area.

PLANTING DEPTHS

While most perennials are best planted out at the same soil level as they were in their pots, a number grow better if planted higher or deeper, depending on their individual requirements. Some prefer a raised, well-drained site, while others thrive in deeper, moist conditions.

ASTER

GROUND-LEVEL PLANTING
The majority of perennials should be planted so that the crown of the plant is level with the surrounding soil.

SISYRINCHIUM STRIATUM 'AUNT MAY'

RAISED PLANTING
Set plants that are prone to rot at the base, and variegated plants that tend to revert, with their crowns slightly above the ground.

HOSTA

SHALLOW PLANTING
Plant perennials that require a moist environment with their crowns about 1in (2.5cm) below ground level.

POLYGONATUM

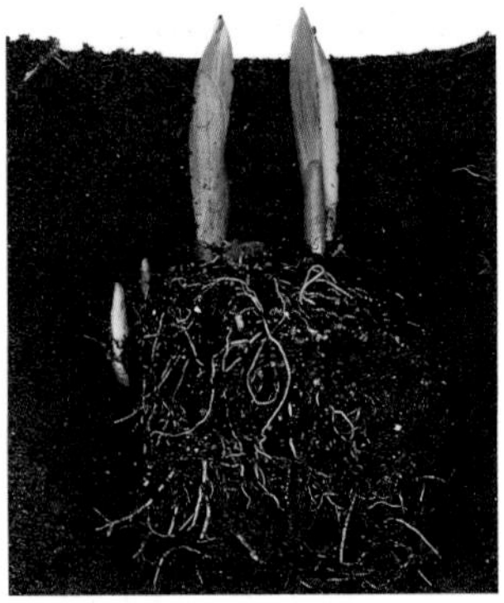

DEEP PLANTING
Plant perennials with tuberous root systems so that their crowns are about 4in (10cm) below the soil surface.

PLANTING LARGE BULBS IN GRASS

When planting bulbs that are to be naturalized in grass, first cut the grass as short as possible. Random rather than regimented planting achieves a more natural effect; scatter the bulbs gently by hand over the area and plant them where they have fallen, making sure that they are at least one bulb's width apart. Dig holes with a trowel or use a bulb planter, which cuts out plugs of sod and soil to a depth of about 4–6in (10–15cm); dig deeper if necessary for larger bulbs. Check that all the holes are at the correct depth and that the bulbs are the right way up before inserting them and replacing the sod, then give them a good watering.

1 Clean the bulbs (here daffodils), removing any loose outer coatings and old roots. Scatter the bulbs randomly over the planting area, then make sure that they are at least their own width apart.

2 Make an individual hole for each bulb, using a bulb planter to remove a circle of sod and a core of soil to a depth of about 4–6in (10–15cm).

3 Place a pinch of bone meal, mixed with a little of the soil from the core, into each hole and put in a bulb with the growing point uppermost.

4 Break up the underside of the core over the bulb so that it is completely covered with loose soil. Then replace the remains of the core on top of it.

5 Replace the lid of sod and firm it in gently, taking care not to damage the growing point of the bulb. Fill in any gaps in the grass with more soil.

PLANTING BULBS IN THE OPEN

Dry, loose bulbs should be planted as soon as possible after purchase, usually in late summer or early fall (plant summer-flowering bulbs in early to midspring); otherwise, keep them cool and dry until you can plant them. Bulbs are usually best planted several to a large hole dug out with a spade, but they may also be planted singly. Do not make the outline of the planting area or the spacing of the bulbs symmetrical: this looks unnatural, and if one or two bulbs fail, they will leave unsightly gaps.

Planting bulbs

SINGLY
Plant each bulb in a separate hole at the appropriate depth. Draw back the prepared soil with a trowel, and firm it down gently afterward.

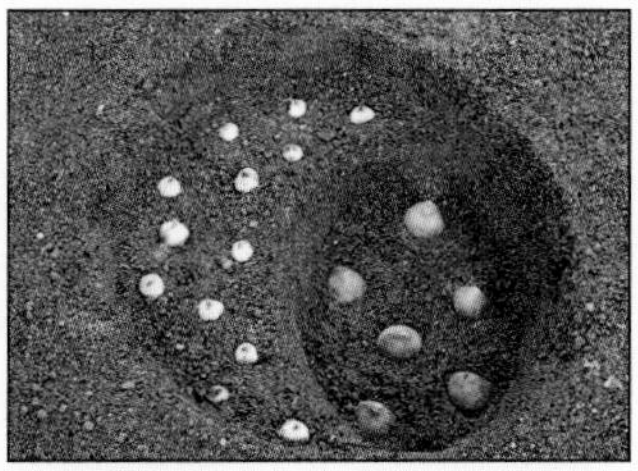

IN LAYERS
Two or more kinds of bulb may be planted in the same space. Plant each kind at its correct depth, carefully covering each layer before planting the next type of bulb.

1 Dig out a large hole in well-prepared ground. Plant the bulbs (here tulips), at least 3 times their own depth, and 2–3 widths apart.

2 For a natural effect, space the bulbs randomly. Once they are in position, gently draw the soil over them with your hand to avoid displacing or damaging them.

3 Tamp down the soil over the planted area with the back of a rake. Avoid walking heavily on the soil surface, because this might damage the growing points.

PLANTING DEEP-WATER AND MARGINAL PLANTS

Whether planting in beds or free-standing containers, settle the plants firmly in the soil, because they are very buoyant and may become dislodged. Always plant in moist soil, and soak containers well before immersing them in the pond. A top-dressing of grit, coarse sand, or pea gravel to a depth of 1in (2.5cm) prevents soil from floating out and clouding the water and discourages hungry or curious fish from disturbing the plants. When submerging the containers in deep water, thread string through the sides to form handles; this makes it much easier to position the basket, which can then be gradually lowered onto the bottom.

1 Choose a planting basket to accommodate the plant roots, and line it with burlap or closely woven polypropylene.

2 Fill the basket with heavy, moist soil to a depth of at least 2in (5cm). Center the plant (here *Aponogeton distachyos*).

3 Fill with more soil to within ½in (1cm) of the rim of the basket, firming the plant in well to give it good anchorage.

4 Top-dress the container with washed grit or pea gravel to a depth of 1in (2.5cm).

5 Trim away any surplus liner with scissors. Tie string handles to the rim of the basket on opposite sides.

6 Hold the basket by the string handles, then gently lower it onto blocks or the marginal shelf. Release the handles.

Surface floaters

With a new planting, include some surface-floating plants to discourage the growth of algae. When the ornamental plants become more established, some of the floaters should be removed. In a large pond, a line may be drawn across the pond from both ends to bring plants within reach. Duckweed in particular is very persistent, so choose less vigorous species.

Surface-floating plants have no anchorage because their roots obtain nutrients directly from the water. Their initial positioning is unimportant, since the groups are moved around on the surface by wind.

Surface-floating plants (here *Stratiotes aloides*) may be placed on the water's surface; in warm weather they multiply rapidly, giving valuable surface shade.

PLANTING IN A HANGING BASKET

A wide range of plants can be grown in a hanging basket, including annuals, tender perennials, succulents (as shown here), and even weak-stemmed shrubs, such as fuchsias. Make sure that the basket is completely clean. Wire baskets should be lined with a commercial liner or a layer of sphagnum moss. Do not line the basket with plastic, since this restricts drainage. If using a plastic basket that has an attached drainage tray, be sure to place a piece of screening over the drainage hole(s) to prevent the soil mix from washing out.

1 Line a wire hanging basket with a layer of moist sphagnum moss. The layer should be 1¼in (3cm) thick when compressed.

2 Fill the basket almost to the brim with a mix of 1 part sharp sand to 3 parts soil-based potting mix. Prepare a hole for the plant in the center of the basket.

3 Insert the plant (here a *Schlumbergera*), spreading out the roots. Fill in gently but firmly with soil mix so that there are no air pockets around the roots.

4 If planting succulents, as here, wait 2–3 days after planting before watering the finished basket. Otherwise, water immediately and then allow the basket to drain before hanging it.

REPOTTING AN INDOOR PLANT

Indoor plants need periodic repotting to accommodate their growth and to replenish the soil mix. A potbound plant has retarded growth, and water runs straight through the soil mix. Repot before this, so that the plant develops well. A few plants, such as amaryllis (*Hippeastrum*), enjoy confined roots, so repot them less often, and top-dress occasionally. The best time to repot is at the start of the growing season, although fast-growing plants may need repotting a few times in one season. The process may delay flowering, because the plant initially concentrates its energy on new root growth. Avoid repotting a dormant plant; it will not respond to the moisture and fertility, and it may rot.

1 Before potting a plant (here *Dracaena deremensis* 'Souvenir de Schriever'), make sure that its root ball is moist by watering it thoroughly about an hour beforehand. Select a pot that is one or two sizes larger than the old one. Make sure the pot is clean (whether washed, disinfected, or new) to avoid spreading diseases. The fresh potting mix should be of the same type as that in the old pot.

2 Remove the plant by inverting the pot and sharply tapping the rim on a hard surface to loosen the root ball. Support the plant as it slides out of the pot.

3 Gently tease out the root ball with a small fork or your fingers. Put some moist potting mix in the base of the new pot.

4 Insert the plant so that its soil mark is level with the rim base. Fill in with soil mix to within ½in (1.5cm) of the rim, firm, water, and place in position (right).

PRUNING

Pruning and training both aim to make sure that plants are as vigorous and healthy as possible, are at the least risk of infection from disease, and are free of structural weakness at maturity. They can also create striking features by enhancing ornamental qualities, such as bark, flowers, foliage, and fruit. However, pruning always causes some stress, so learn when and how to prune.

PRUNING AND TRAINING YOUNG TREES

Young trees benefit from formative pruning to make sure that they develop a strong, well-balanced framework of evenly spaced branches. This involves the removal of dead, damaged, and diseased wood, as well as any weak or crossing branches. Formative pruning may also be used to determine the tree's shape as it grows: for example, a young feathered tree may be pruned over several years to form a standard, or perhaps trained against a wall as an espalier.

Feathered tree

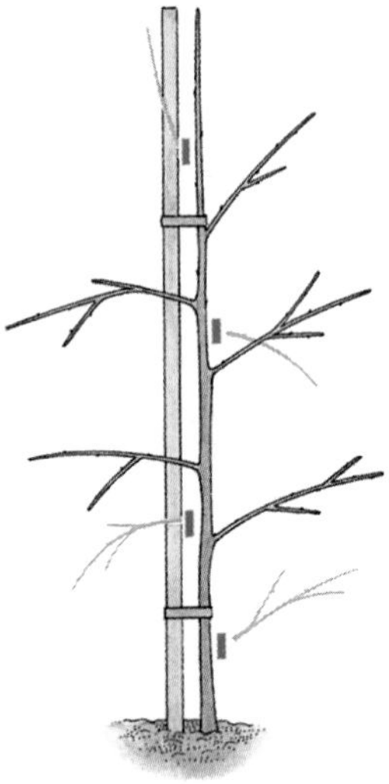

Feathered tree
Remove congested and crossing shoots, then cut out any laterals that are small, spindly, or badly positioned, to achieve a well-balanced framework of branches.

Central-leader standard

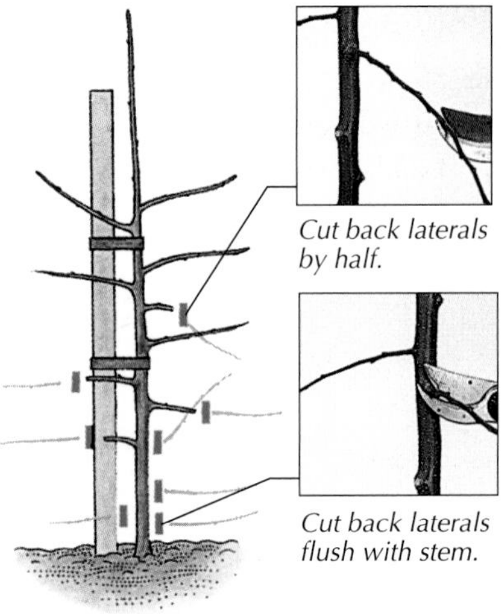
Cut back laterals by half.
Cut back laterals flush with stem.

Year 1
On the lowest third of the tree, cut back laterals to the main stem; on the middle third, cut back laterals by half. Remove any weak or competing leaders.

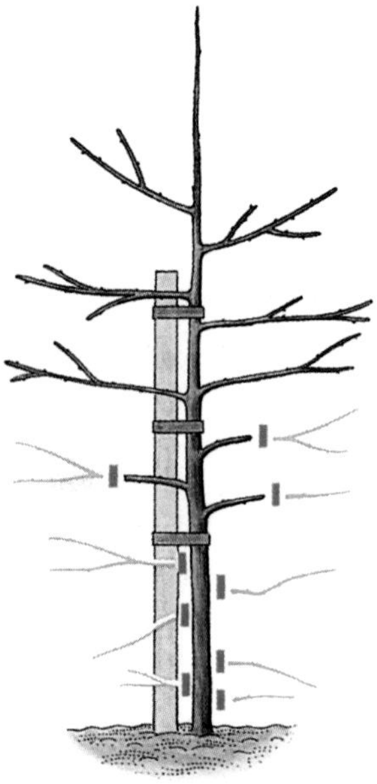

Years 2 and 3
Continue the process, removing the lowest laterals completely and cutting back by about half those laterals that are on the middle third of the tree.

Branched-head standard

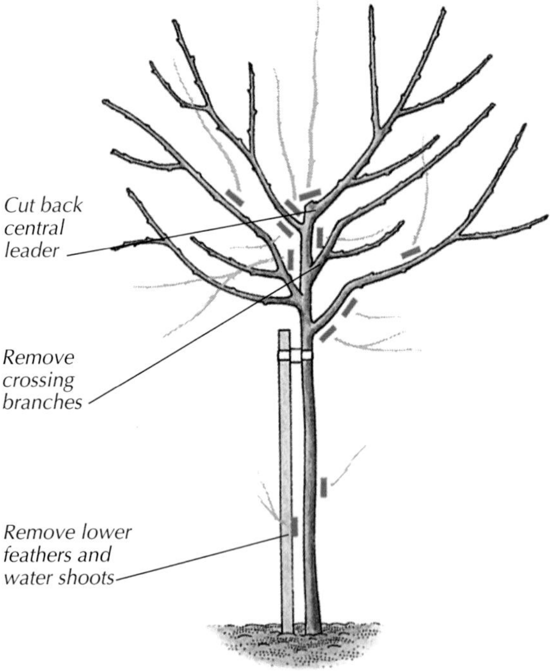
Cut back central leader
Remove crossing branches
Remove lower feathers and water shoots

Remove crossing laterals and any growths on the lower third of the tree. Cut back the leader to a healthy bud or shoot.

Weeping tree

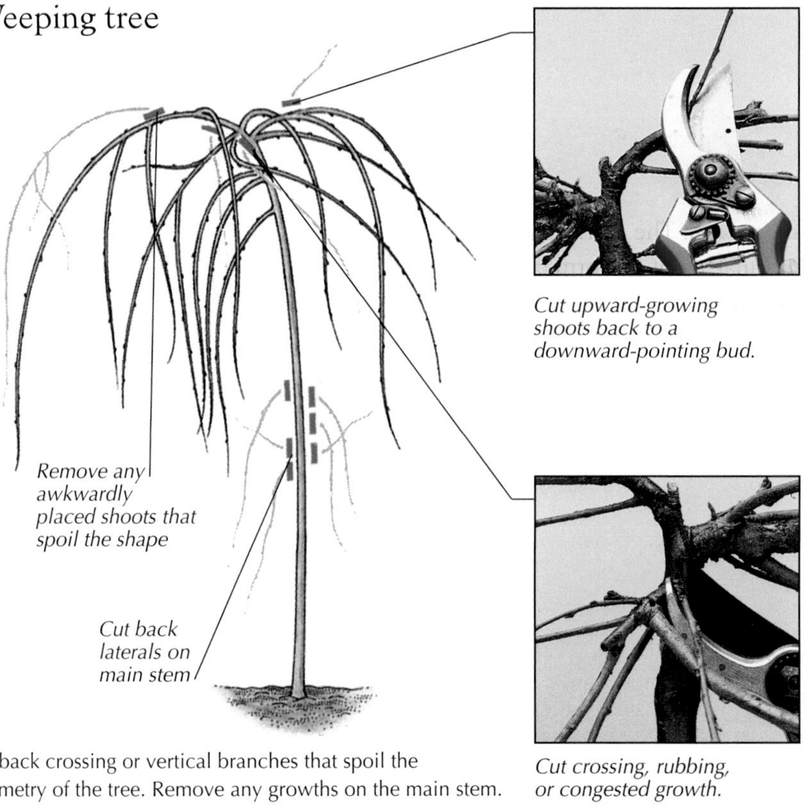
Remove any awkwardly placed shoots that spoil the shape
Cut back laterals on main stem
Cut upward-growing shoots back to a downward-pointing bud.
Cut crossing, rubbing, or congested growth.

Cut back crossing or vertical branches that spoil the symmetry of the tree. Remove any growths on the main stem.

FORMATIVE PRUNING AND TRAINING

The aim of formative pruning is to make sure that a shrub has a framework of well-spaced branches. The amount of formative pruning required depends very much on the type of shrub and on the quality of the plants available. (It is usually best to start with a quality plant from a good source.) Evergreen shrubs generally need little formative pruning. Excessive growth resulting in an unbalanced shape should be lightly pruned in midspring, after the shrub has been planted. Deciduous shrubs are much more likely to require formative pruning than evergreen shrubs. This should be carried out in the dormant season, between midfall and midspring, at or after planting.

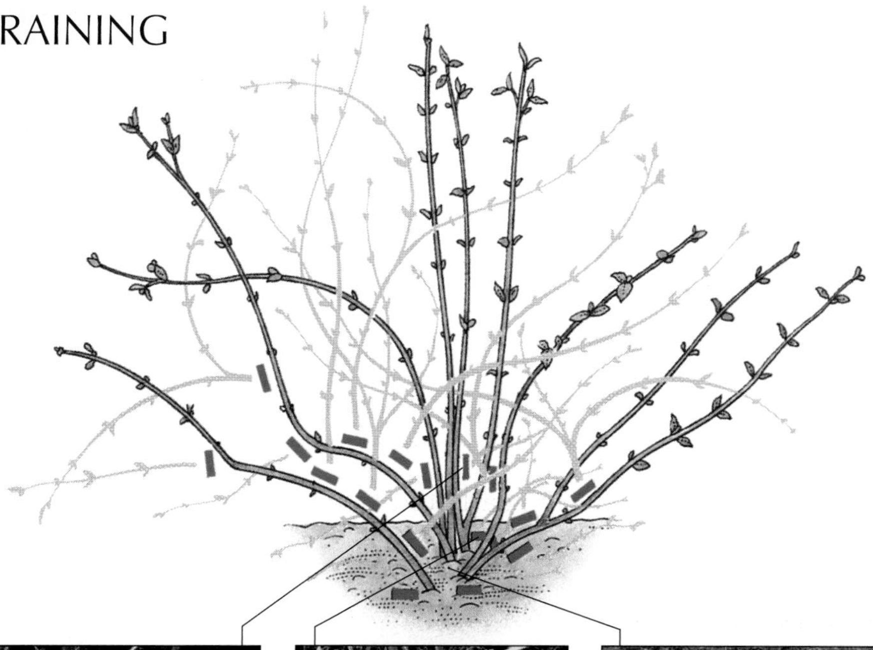

Coppicing a shrub for winter stem color

Coppicing stimulates the growth of colorful, vigorous stems. Cut back all stems to about 2–3in (5–8cm) from the base before growth begins in spring, and then fertilize and mulch well.

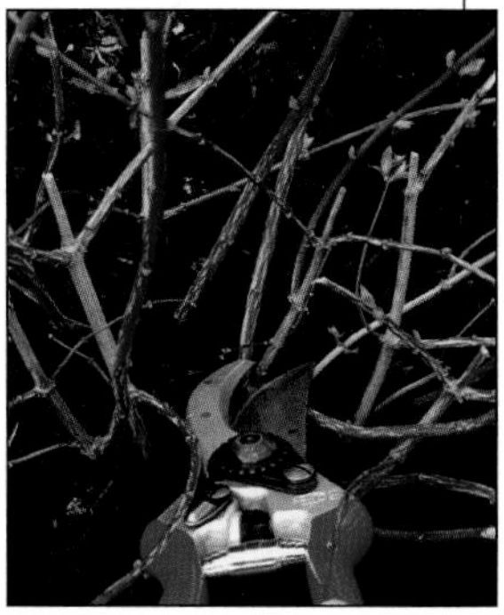

Prune back crossing or congested shoots to an outward-facing bud or cut right back to the base.

Prune out any very weak and spindly, or long and straggly, stems, cutting them right back to the base.

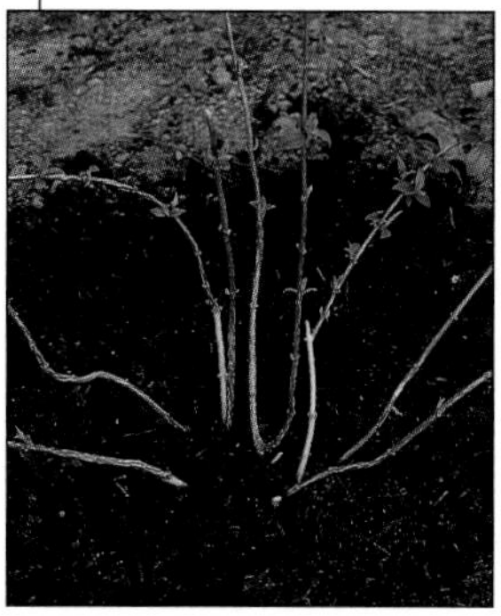

Also remove any very awkward stems that spoil the shape of the shrub, to leave an evenly balanced framework.

WHY, HOW, AND WHERE TO CUT

Pruning normally stimulates growth. The actively growing terminal shoot or dormant growth bud of a stem is often dominant, inhibiting by chemical means the growth of buds or shoots below it. Pruning to remove the ends of stems affects the control mechanism, resulting in more vigorous development of lower shoots or growth buds. Hard pruning promotes more vigorous growth than light pruning. This needs to be kept in mind when correcting the shape of an unbalanced shrub. Prune weak growth hard, but strong growth only lightly.

Opposite shoots
Prune stems with opposite buds to just above a strong pair of buds or shoots, using a clean straight cut.

Alternate shoots
For plants with alternate buds, prune to just above a bud or shoot, using a clean angled cut.

Making an angled cut
Angle the cut so that its lowest point is opposite the base of the bud and the top just clears the bud.

PRUNING ROSES

The purpose of pruning roses is to promote new, vigorous, disease-free shoots developing to replace the old weakened ones, and so produce a reasonably attractive shape and the optimum display of blooms. Training a plant stimulates the production of flowering sideshoots and directs new growth. A pair of sharp, high-quality pruners is essential, and always wear thornproof gloves.

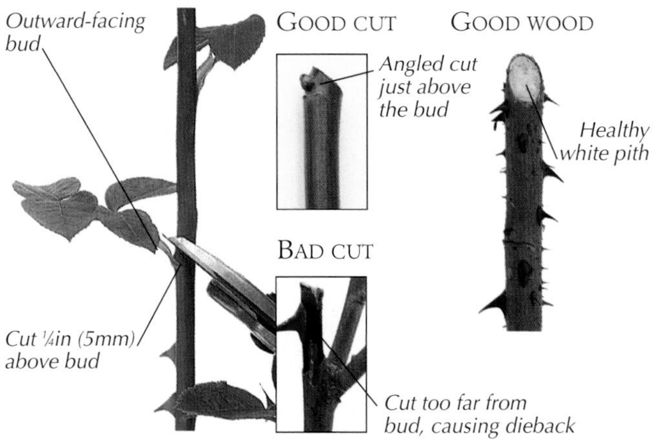

Pruning a newly planted bush rose

Prune a newly planted bush rose to about 3in (8cm) above ground level. Cut back to outward-facing buds, and remove any cold-damaged growth.

PRUNING HYBRID TEA AND GRANDIFLORA ROSES

Depending on the extent of winter kill and on the differences among cultivars, in colder areas the main shoots should be pruned back to between 8–10in (20–25cm). In milder areas, the shoots may be cut down less severely, to about 18–24in (45–60cm). For exhibition-quality blooms, cut the main shoots back hard to leave only two or three buds.

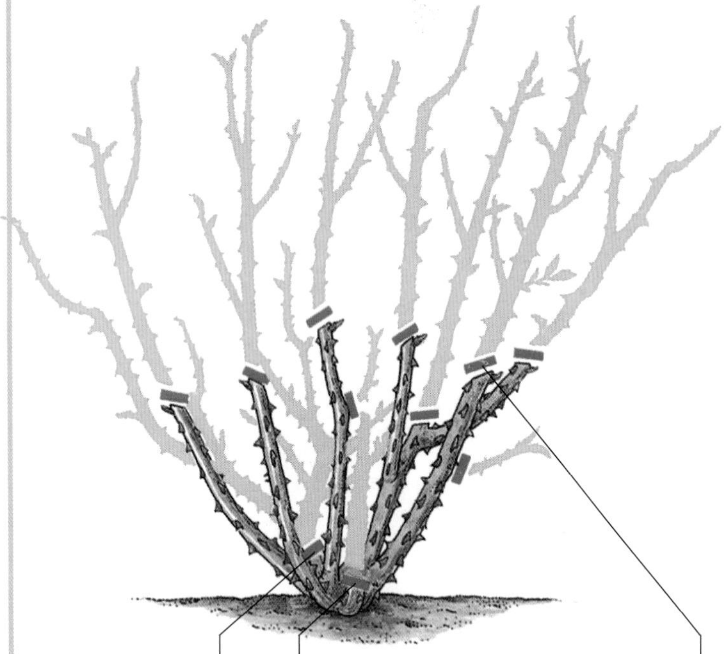

Cut out crossing, congested, and twiggy or spindly growth.

Remove dead wood and any that shows signs of damage or disease.

Prune main shoots to within about 8–10in (20–25cm) of ground level.

PRUNING FLORIBUNDA ROSES

When pruning Floribundas, cut out any unproductive wood as for Hybrid Teas. Reduce sideshoots by about one-third on smaller cultivars, and by two-thirds on taller-growing ones. Cut back the main shoots to 12–15in (30–38cm), but reduce the shoots of taller cultivars by about one-third. Do not prune them any harder, (unless growing for exhibition) because this will significantly reduce the number of blooms.

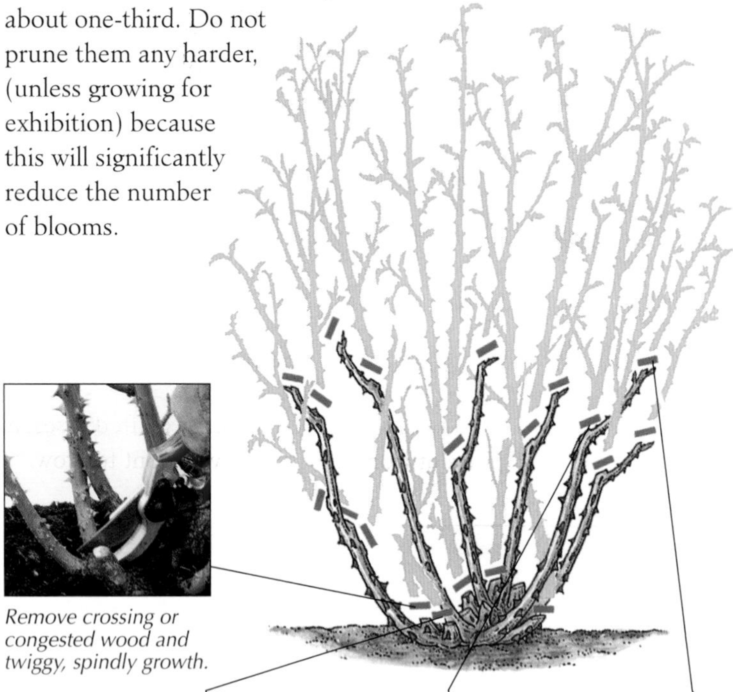

Remove crossing or congested wood and twiggy, spindly growth.

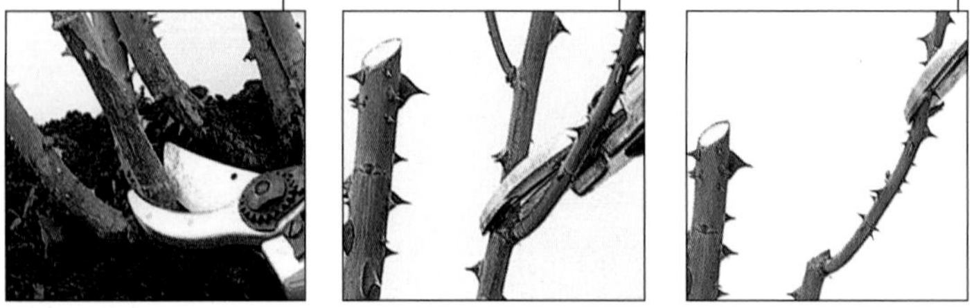

Prune out all dead, damaged, or diseased wood to a healthy bud.

Prune main shoots to 12–15in (30–38cm) from ground level.

Reduce sideshoots by one- to two-thirds, cutting to a bud.

PRUNING STANDARD AND MINIATURE ROSES

Most standards are formed from Hybrid Teas or Floribundas budded onto a straight unbranched stem. Prune as for their bush relatives, but cut back the main shoots so that they are all roughly equal in length. If the head is unbalanced, prune the shoots on the denser side less hard so that they do not produce as much new growth as those on the thinner side.

Standard rose

Before
In the spring, prune a standard rose to prevent the plant from becoming too top-heavy and to produce an evenly shaped, floriferous head.

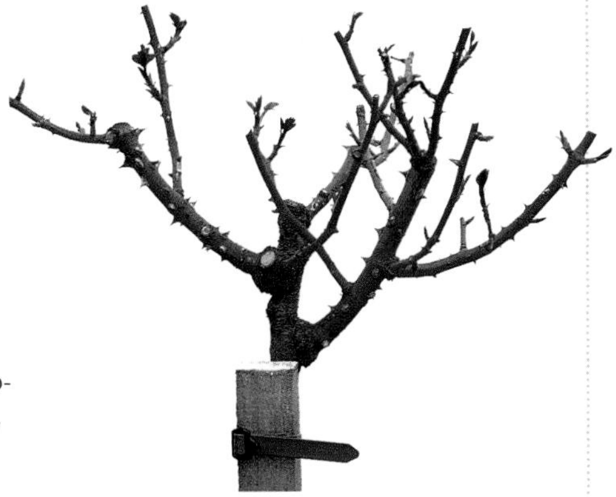

After
All dead and damaged wood and any crossing stems have been removed to leave healthy shoots. The main shoots have been reduced to 8–10in (20–25cm), and the side-shoots by about one-third.

There are two methods: either give them the minimum of attention (remove dead growth, thin out tangles, and shorten overly long shoots) or treat them like small Hybrid Teas or Floribundas (remove all growth except the strongest shoots, and then cut them back by one-third or more).

Miniature rose

Before (Method Two)
Miniature roses often produce a mass of twiggy growth. The shape of this plant is unbalanced by overly vigorous shoots growing from the base.

After (Method Two)
Excessively twiggy and spindly growth, crossing shoots, and damaged wood have been removed, and vigorous shoots have been cut back by half.

DEALING WITH SUCKERS

Suckers usually look quite different from the rest of the plant, often with leaves of a different shape or color, and they often grow more strongly. Remove any suckers as soon as they appear. This prevents the rootstock from wasting energy on the sucker's growth. Damage to the roots, caused by severe cold or any accidental nicks from hoes, other implements, or a stake, may stimulate the production of suckers. Shoots on the stem of a standard rose are also suckers, since the stem is actually part of the understock. As with other grafted roses, any suckers will look different from the cultivar you want to grow.

REMOVING A SUCKER FROM A STANDARD ROSE
Pull away any suckers growing from the rose stem (see inset), taking care not to rip the bark.

With a trowel, carefully scrape away the soil to expose the top of the rootstock. Check that the suspect shoot arises from below the bud union.

Using gloves to protect your hands, pull the sucker down and away from the rootstock. Trim the wound, refill the hole, and gently firm the soil.

How a sucker grows

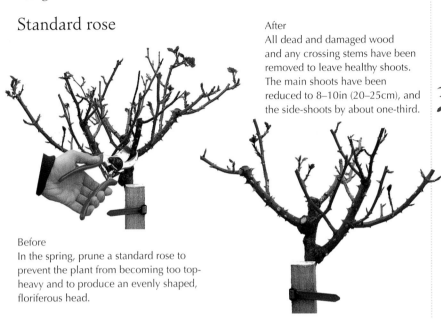

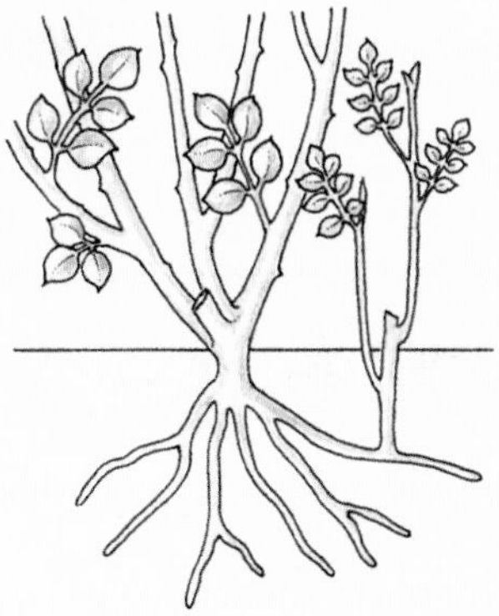

The sucker (right) grows directly from the rootstock. If cut back only at ground level it will regrow and divert further energy from the main part of the plant.

PEGGING DOWN ROSES

This technique is an effective (although time-consuming) way of increasing flower production on roses that tend to send up long, ungainly shoots with flowers only at the tips. In late summer or fall, bend the shoots over gently, taking great care not to snap them, then peg the shoots firmly into the ground. This has much the same result as horizontally training the shoots of climbing and rambler roses.

Select long, noflowering shoots, and prune the soft tips. Gently bend each shoot over, then peg it to the soil with sturdy wire pins (see inset).

PRUNING GALLICA ROSES

Many of these old-fashioned roses produce a twiggy tangle of shoots that should be regularly thinned out to improve air circulation and bloom quality and to make the plant more attractive. After flowering, shorten the sideshoots only, and remove any dead or diseased wood. Gently clip Gallica roses used for hedging to maintain a neat shape. Follow their natural outline: do not attempt to shape them into a formal hedge, since this would remove many of the sideshoots on which flowers are produced in the following year.

Thin out twiggy growth regularly, and remove spent blooms by cutting back to the main shoot.

On mature plants, cut out up to one-quarter of old main shoots at the base.

Shorten side shoots, but not the main shoots, by about two-thirds. Cut out any dead, diseased, or weak wood.

PRUNING ALBA, CENTIFOLIA, DAMASK, AND MOSS ROSES

After flowering, reduce both main shoots and sideshoots. At the end of summer, cut back any overly long shoots that might whip about in the wind and cause wind-rock damage to the roots.

A general note on pruning the old-fashioned roses: some of these roses have a very individual growth habit and do not conform neatly to a specific pruning program. For these, it is best to observe the way the plant grows for the first few years, and then adapt a specific program (such as one of those given here) to how the rose reacts to the program. Some old-fashioned roses resent pruning and will respond by turning into very unattractive plants.

Cut back any overly long, whippy shoots by about one-third.

Prune sideshoots to about two-thirds of their length.

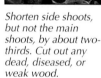

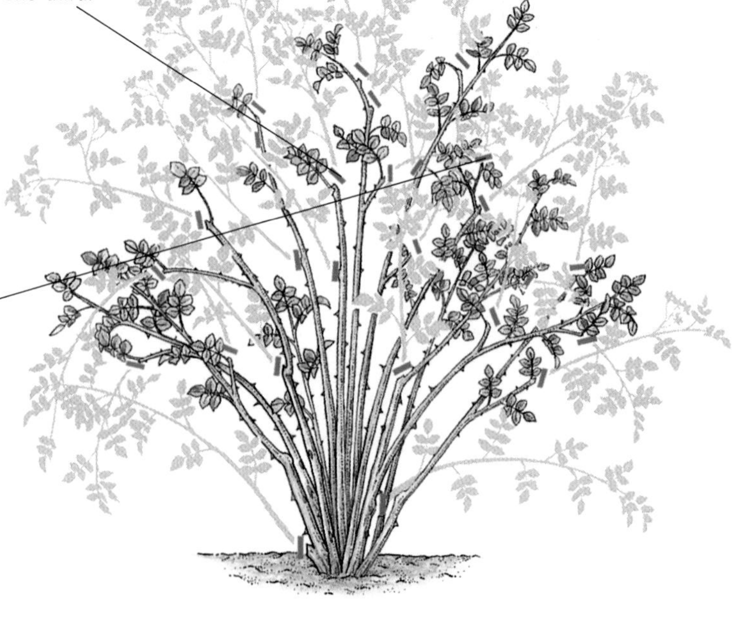

Reduce main shoots by one-quarter to one–third.

PRUNING AND TRAINING CLIMBING ROSES

These roses require minor pruning but regular annual training. In their first year (and in their second unless they have made exceptional growth), do not prune climbers, except to remove any dead, diseased, or weak growth. Never hard prune climbing sports of bush roses (roses with the word "climbing" in their name; for example 'Climbing Peace') in the first two years, since they may revert to the bush form. Begin training as soon as the new shoots are long enough to reach the supports; train them sideways along horizontal supports to encourage flowering. Where this is not possible, choose a cultivar that is halfway between a tall shrub and a climbing rose. Many of these flower well from the plant base without special training.

Reduce the sideshoots by about two-thirds or about 6in (15cm), cutting above an outward-facing bud.

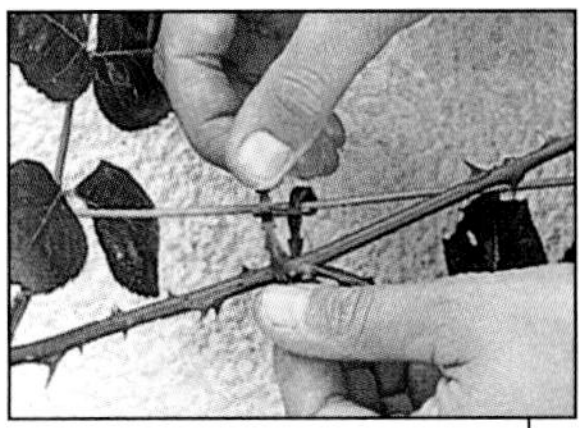

Tie all new shoots into horizontal wires 6–8in (15–20cm) apart. The shoots should not cross each other.

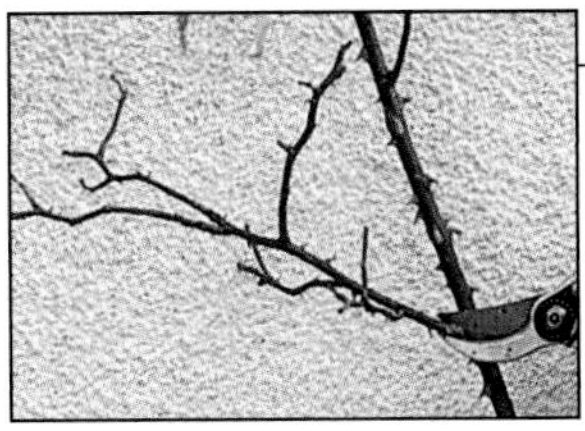

Remove any diseased, dead, or twiggy growth, cutting back to healthy wood or the main shoot.

PRUNING AND TRAINING MATURE RAMBLER ROSES

Ramblers produce much more growth from the base than most climbers and, if not carefully managed, grow into a vicious tangle of unmanageable shoots. Prune ramblers in summer, after they flower. In the first two years, restrict pruning to cutting back all the sideshoots by about 3in (7.5cm) to a vigorous shoot; also, remove dead or diseased wood. In later years, prune and train more heavily to maintain the framework: remove the oldest shoots to the ground, and train in new shoots that spring up from the base.

Cut sideshoots back to leave between 2 to 4 healthy buds or shoots.

Cut back any old spent shoots ground level, using loppers.

Tie all shoots into the wires as close to the horizontal as possible. Secure any loose wires.

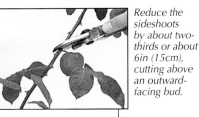

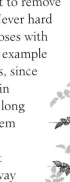

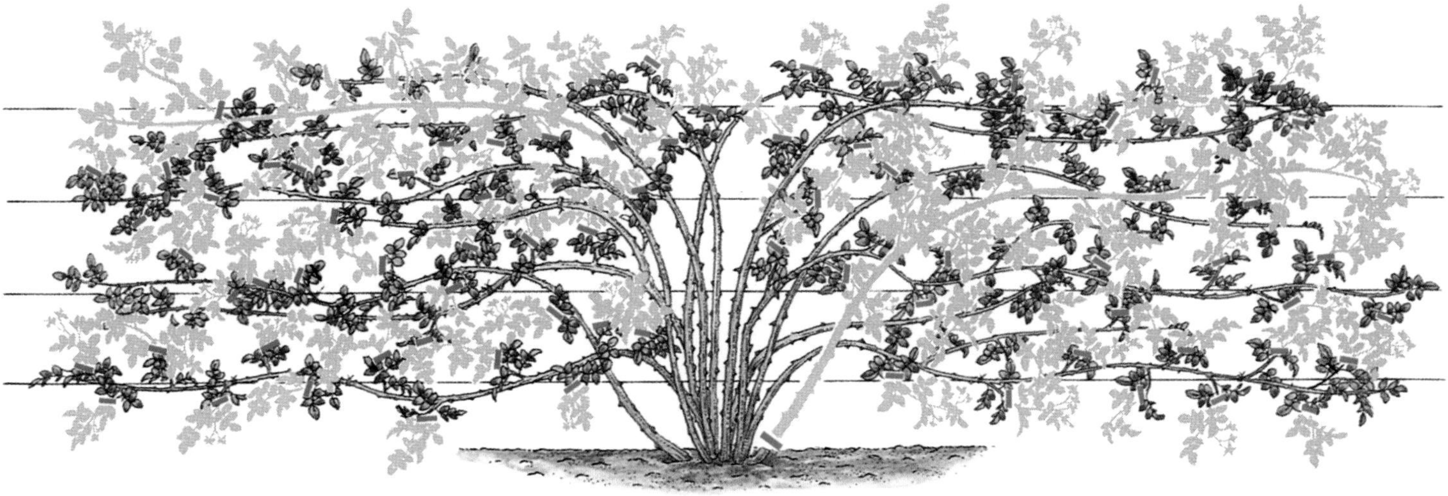

PROPAGATION

Producing new plants from existing ones is one of the most satisfying of all horticultural pursuits. From a simpler technique (sowing seeds) to the more elaborate (such as layering), growing your own allows you to raise a number of plants at minimum expense, such as for a hedge, and greatly increases your selections, especially if you grow annuals and vegetables from seed.

HARDWOOD CUTTINGS

Many deciduous trees and shrubs (as well as some evergreens) may be rooted from hardwood cuttings outdoors in fall and winter. If your winters are long and harsh or excessively wet, the cuttings usually die if left outside, but they can be rooted in deep boxes in a frost-free basement or root cellar instead. Select cuttings just after a hard frost. Choose strong, vigorous shoots of the current season's growth. For species that do not root easily, tie cuttings into small bundles, then plunge them into a sand bed.

For deciduous plants: trim off tips and cut stems into 8in (20cm) lengths. Make a horizontal cut just below a node, and a sloping cut to mark the top. Dip the base in hormone rooting compound. Insert them 2in (5cm) apart, 6in (5cm) deep, in soil-based rooting medium in pots, either in a cold place or outdoors.

Strip leaves and sideshoots from bottom half of cutting

For evergreens: cut shoots into sections 8–10in (20–25cm) long. Trim just above a leaf at the tip and below another at the base. Strip leaves from bottom half of cutting. Insert 5–8 cuttings in a 6in (15cm) pot. Place in a closed case with slight bottom heat, or in a clear plastic bag. Rooting occurs in 6–10 weeks.

SEMIRIPE CUTTINGS

Many conifers, as well as certain broadleaved evergreens such as hollies (*Ilex*) and *Magnolia grandiflora*, may be propagated readily from semiripe cuttings. After insertion, check the cuttings periodically, watering them only to keep them from drying out. Remove any fallen leaves as soon as they appear, since these may rot and spread disease to the cuttings. During cold spells, cold frames should be insulated with burlap or a similar covering.

The ideal semiripe cutting is taken from current season's growth that has begun to firm up; the base is quite firm, while the tip is soft and still actively growing. Such stems will offer some resistance when bent.

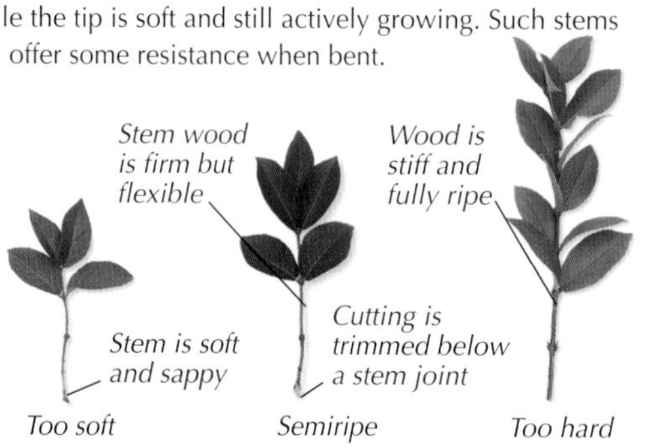
Stem wood is firm but flexible
Wood is stiff and fully ripe
Stem is soft and sappy
Cutting is trimmed below a stem joint
Too soft
Semiripe
Too hard

DISTINGUSHING SEMIRIPE WOOD

1 In mid- to late summer, select a healthy semiripe shoot of the current season's growth (here *Aucuba*), then sever the cutting just above a stem joint with clean sharp pruners.

2 Remove sideshoots from the stem with a sharp knife. Trim the stem to 4–6in (10–15cm), cutting just below a stem joint. Remove the soft tip and the lowest pair of leaves.

3 To stimulate rooting, cut a shallow sliver of bark, ½–1in (1–2.5cm) long, from the base of the stem; do not expose the pith. This process is known as wounding.

4 Dip the base of the cutting in hormone rooting compound. Make sure that the entire wound receives the thinnest possible (but uniform) coating, then shake off the excess.

5 Place cuttings 2–3in (5–8cm) apart in standard rooting medium in a nursery bed outdoors (or in pots in a closed case). Label with name and date. Water and cover.

SOFTWOOD AND GREENWOOD CUTTINGS

This method of propagation is suitable for some tree species, although it is more commonly used for shrubs. Softwood cuttings are taken from the fast-growing tips of new shoots and usually root very easily. They wilt rapidly, however, so it is vital to prepare and insert them as quickly as possible after removing them from the parent plant.

SOFTWOOD CUTTINGS
Take softwood cuttings in spring and early summer from the new season's growth before it has begun to firm up. Choose vigorous nonflowering shoots with 2 or 3 pairs of leaves, cutting just below a stem joint.

GREENWOOD CUTTINGS
Take greenwood cuttings in late spring to midsummer, just as new stems begin to firm up. They are less prone to wilt and easier to handle than softwood and root as readily. Treat them exactly as for softwood cuttings.

Remove the soft tip, because it is vulnerable to rot and scorch

1. Remove the soft tip just above a leaf joint, as well as the lowest pair of leaves. Cut large leaves in half to reduce moisture loss. Trim the base just below a leaf joint; the stem should be 1½–2in (4–5cm) long.

2. Fill a 5in (13cm) pot with rooting medium. Make 2 or 3 holes around the edge, then insert the cuttings so that the lowest leaves lie just above the surface and are not touching each other.

Vent of closed case will be opened gradually to harden off rooted cuttings

3. After watering thoroughly with a commercial fungicidal solution, label and place pots in a closed case heated, if possible, at the base to 59°F (15°C). Keep in a shaded place, out of direct sun.

4. Once cuttings have rooted, admit more air to harden them off. Knock out of the pot, tease apart, and pot up singly into 3½in (9cm) pots of soil mix. Pinch out growing tips to encourage bushy growth.

SIMPLE LAYERING

The long, trailing shoots of climbers may often be propagated by simple layering if they do not root naturally. A shoot is wounded and pegged down into the surrounding soil. This induces it to root at a node to provide a young plant that is later separated from the parent. Layers of many climbers that have been pegged down in spring will develop strong root systems by fall, at which time they can be separated from the parent plant. Layering also works for many shrubs and a few trees.

1. Dig a hole, about 3in (8cm) deep in prepared soil, with a shallowly sloping side next to the parent plant and a nearly vertical slope on the far side. Mix a little sand and organic matter into the bottom of the hole if soil is heavy.

2. Trim off sideshoots and leaves. At the point where the underside of the stem touches the soil, make a slanting cut through to the middle of the stem to make a "tongue" of bark, or remove a 1in (2.5cm) sliver of bark.

3. Dust the wound with some hormone rooting compound. Peg the stem down securely into the bottom of the hole using several U-shaped, galvanized wire pins, placing them on either side of the wound.

4. Bend the stem tip up against the vertical side of the hole and secure with a stake. Backfill, firm, and water in. Keep weed-free and moist. A layer should be well-rooted within a year, then sever it.

5. Plant the layer in a 5in (13cm) pot of standard soil mix, then water and label it. You could plant it into its permanent position in the garden if it has produced enough roots. Watch its watering needs carefully.

PROPAGATING PERENNIALS BY DIVISION

This method is suitable for propagating many perennials that have a spreading rootstock and produce plenty of shoots from the base. As well as being a way of increasing stocks, in many cases division rejuvenates the plants and keeps them vigorous, since old or unproductive parts are discarded. Most plants should be divided when they are dormant (or are about to go dormant, or are just emerging from dormancy) from late fall to early spring, but not in extremely cold, wet, or dry weather, because these conditions may make it difficult for the divided plants to reestablish successfully. Try to do this on an overcast calm day.

1 Lift the plant to be divided, taking care to insert the fork far enough away from the plant so that the roots are not damaged. Shake off surplus soil.

2 Separate plants with a woody center by chopping through the crown with a spade. Use a trowel for smaller, less dense clumps.

Alternative method

Divide densely rooted herbaceous plants (here *Hemerocallis*) using 2 forks inserted back to back in the center. Larger tougher clumps will require the help of an assistant.

3 Divide the plant into smaller pieces by hand, retaining only healthy vigorous sections, each with several new shoots.

4 Cut back the old top-growth, then replant the divided sections to the same depth as before. Firm in and water thoroughly.

DIVIDING HOSTAS

Large hostas with tough rootstocks should be divided using a spade or back-to-back forks. Hostas that have looser fleshy rootstocks may be separated by hand; this technique may be necessary to avoid damaging smaller-growing cultivars. For quick reestablishment of a clump, include several buds on an individual division, but if making many plants is your goal and you can wait longer for mature clumps, separate the clump into single or double buds, as long as each division has enough roots to sustain it. Trim any damaged parts with a knife, then replant as soon as possible. If there is a delay, store the plants under cover and keep moist.

Tough fibrous roots
Divide the crown with a spade. Each section should include several developing buds.

Loose fleshy roots
Divide small plants and those with a loose rootstock by pulling the clump apart by hand.

DIVIDING RHIZOMATOUS PLANTS

Divide plants with thick rhizomes, such as *Bergenia* and rhizomatous irises, by splitting the clump into pieces by hand, then cutting the rhizomes into sections, each with one or more growth points. Bamboos have tough rootstocks that either form dense clumps with short rhizomes or have long, spreading rhizomes. Divide dense clumps with a spade or two back-to-back forks; cut spreading rhizomes into sections (each of which should have three nodes or joints) with pruners. In all cases, trim excessively long roots before replanting.

Lift the plant to be divided (here an iris), inserting the fork well away from the rhizomes to avoid damaging them.

Shake the clump to remove any loose soil. Using your hands or a hand fork, split the clump into manageable pieces.

Discard any old rhizomes, then detach the new, young rhizomes from the clump and neatly trim off their ends.

Dust the cut areas with fungicide. Trim long roots by one-third. For irises, cut the leaves into a "fan" about 6in (15cm) tall to prevent wind-rock.

Plant the rhizomes at least 6in (15cm) apart. The rhizomes should be half buried, with their leaves and buds upright. Firm in well, then water.

PROPAGATING PERENNIALS BY ROOT CUTTINGS

This is a useful method of propagating perennials that have fairly thick, fleshy roots, such as *Papaver orientale*; it also works very well for horseradish (*Armoracia*). Take care to minimize damage to the parent plant when cutting its roots, and replant it immediately. Root cuttings are most successful when they are taken during the plant's dormant period, usually just before winter. Note: plants with thinner roots, such as *Anemone*, are done slightly differently. Lay the cuttings flat on the medium, then cover and treat as for thicker root cuttings.

Lift the plant (here *Acanthus*) when dormant and wash the roots. Cut roots of pencil thickness close to the crown.

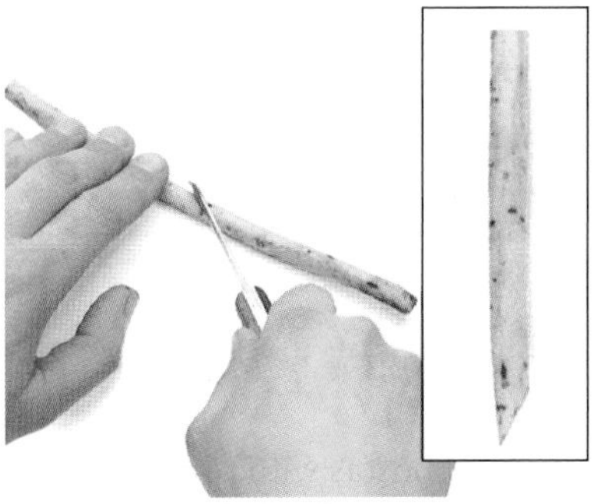

Cut each into lengths of 2–4in (5–10cm). Make a straight cut at the upper end and an angled cut at the lower (inset).

Insert the cuttings into holes made in pots of moist rooting medium, then firm. The top end of each cutting should be flush with the surface.

Top-dress the pots of cuttings with coarse grit, label them, and place them in a cold frame until the cuttings root.

When the cuttings have developed young shoots, pot them up into individual pots filled with soil-based potting mix. Water and label the pots (see inset).

SOWING IN DRILLS

Seeds sown in drills produce seedlings growing in straight rows at regular intervals, so they are readily distinguished from weed seedlings, which are randomly distributed. Using either a trowel tip or the corner of a hoe, mark out shallow drills at a width depending on the ultimate size of the plants. Sow seeds thinly and evenly by sprinkling or placing them in each drill at the appropriate depth for the plants being sown, then carefully draw back the displaced soil. Label each row, then water gently but thoroughly with a fine spray. This technique is traditionally used for sowing vegetables, but it works equally well for annuals and biennials, especially in cutting gardens.

Using a line of string as a guide, make a furrow about 1in (2.5cm) deep with a hoe.

Alternative Step

If the seeds are pelleted, place them individually in the base of the drill.

Dribble the seeds from your hand to make sure they are scattered evenly.

Carefully rake the soil back over the drill without dislodging the seeds.

BROADCAST SOWING

Before sowing, mark the outline of the area for different plants with sand to keep track the balance of colors, heights, and habits of each of the plants to be used, especially annuals. After sowing, label the area, then water the area gently but thoroughly with a fine spray. This method is particularly suitable for taprooted annuals, such as *Clarkia*, *Gypsophila*, and poppies (*Papaver*), which are best sown where they are to flower, since they do not transplant readily.

Prepare the soil by raking to produce a fine tilth. Scatter the seeds thinly over the prepared area from your hand or from the packet.

Rake over the area lightly at right angles to cover the seeds so that they are disturbed as little as possible. Water gently but thoroughly.

THINNING SEEDLINGS

To prevent overcrowding, seedlings usually need to be thinned. Do this when the soil is moist and the weather mild, taking care to retain the sturdier seedlings where possible and to achieve even spacing. To minimize disturbance to a seedling being retained, press the soil around it with your fingers as the surplus seedlings are extracted. Thinnings may be used to fill sparse areas caused by uneven sowing or irregular germination, or they may be planted elsewhere in the garden.

To thin small seedlings, nip them out at ground level so that the roots of the remaining seedlings are not disturbed.

Lift seedlings gently, keeping as much soil around them as possible. If moving them, place them in a clear plastic bag to retain moisture.

SOWING IN A TRAY

Many annuals, biennials, perennials, herbs, and vegetables are usually sown in containers so that they can germinate and develop under cover and then be planted out as young plants when conditions are favorable. Pots, seed pans (shallow pots), seed trays, and packs are all suitable containers, depending on the number of seeds to be sown and the space they require. Most seedlings will need to be pricked out before they are large enough to be planted out (see below). Peat pots are useful for seedlings that do not transplant well, since the whole pot may be planted out without disturbing the roots.

1 Fill the seed tray with a standard sowing medium, then level with a presser board to ½in (1cm) below the rim.

2 Sprinkle the seeds thinly over the surface of the medium to achieve an even distribution.

3 Cover the seeds with a layer of sieved, moist soil mix to about the same thickness as the seeds themselves. Water the seeds in lightly.

4 Place a piece of glass or clear plastic sheeting over the tray to maintain even humidity.

5 Shade the tray with netting if the tray is in direct sunlight. Remove both glass and netting as soon as germination starts.

PRICKING OUT OF A PACK

Seedlings raised in trays or pans need to be transplanted into larger containers before they become overcrowded, because they may quickly become weak and spindly if deprived of sufficient space or light, and damping off (a disease) may develop. This process is known as pricking out. It enables the seedlings to continue to develop properly until they are ready for planting out in the open garden. Fill the new containers with a soil-based mix, then firm gently to eliminate any air pockets. Small pots, no more than 3in (6cm) in diameter, or compartmentalized plastic packs are ideal for individual seedlings; larger pots, pans, or trays can be used for several plants.

1 Carefully separate the seedlings, handling them by their seed leaves, not their more delicate stems. Try to keep plenty of medium around the roots.

2 Transplant each seedling into a separate section of a pack. Firm the soil mix around each one with your fingers or a dibber, then water.

APPENDICES

GOVERNMENT RESOURCES: COOPERATIVE EXTENSION SERVICE

AL
Auburn University
Department of Horticulture
101 Funchess Hall
Auburn, AL 36849
(334) 844-4444
http://www.aces.edu/

AR
University of Arkansas
Division of Agriculture
Cooperative Extension Service
2301 South University Avenue
Little Rock, AR 72204
(501) 671-2000
http://www.uaex.edu/

DE
University of Delaware
College of Agriculture and Natural Resources
113 Townsend Hall
Newark, DE 19717
(302) 831-2501
http://ag.udel.edu/extension/

FL
University of Florida
Institute of Food and Agricultural Sciences
1008 McCarty Hall
Gainesville, FL 32611-0180
(352) 392-1761
http://extension.ifas.ufl.edu/

GA
University of Georgia
College of Agricultural and
Environmental Sciences
109 Conner Hall
Athens, GA 30602-7505
(706) 542-3824
http://www.ces.uga.edu/

KY
Department of Horticulture
N-318 Agricultural Sciences North
University of Kentucky
Lexington, KY 40546-0091
(859) 257-4302
http://ces.ca.uky.edu/ces/

LA
Department of Horticulture
Louisana State University
137 Julian Miller Hall
Baton Rouge , LA 70803
(225) 578-2222
http://www.lsuagcenter.com/nav/extension/extension.asp

MD
University of Maryland
College of Agriculture and Natural Resources
1210 Symons Hall
College Park, MD 20742-5551
http://www.agnr.umd.edu/MCE/
(800) 342-2507

MS
Mississippi State University
Department of Plant and Soil Sciences
117 Dorman Hall
Mississippi State, MS 39762
(662) 325-2311
http://msucares.com/

NC
Department of Horticultural Science
North Carolina State University
Box 7609
Raleigh, NC 27695-7609
(919) 515-3131
http://www.ces.ncsu.edu/

SC
Clemson University
Cooperative Extension
103 Barre Hall
Clemson, SC 29634-0101
(864) 656-3382
http://www.clemson.edu/extension/

TN
Tennessee State University
Cooperative Extension Program
3500 John A. Merritt Blvd.
Nashville, TN 37209-1561
(615) 963-1351
http://www.tnstate.edu/cep/

VA
Virginia Polytechnic Institute
and State University
Department of Horticulture
Blacksburg, VA 24061-0327
(540) 231-5451
http://www.ext.vt.edu/

WV
West Virginia University
Agriculture & Natural Resources Program
2078 Agricultural Sciences Building
Morgantown, WV 26506-6108
(304) 293-6131
http://www.wvu.edu/~exten/

GARDENING WEB SITES

The Internet provides a rich source of information on every facet of the horticultural world. In addition to the web sites maintained by many botanical gardens and research facilities, many gardening centers offer their plants and horticultural products on the internet. The following sites may be particularly helpful or enlightening.

USDA Plant Database
http://plants.usda.gov/

NeoFlora
http://www.neoflora.com/

Internet Directory for Botany
http://www.botany.net/IDB/

RHS Horticultural Database
http://www.rhs.org.uk/databases/summary.asp

Directory of Horticulture Web Sites
http://depts.washington.edu/hortlib/resources/dir_hort_websites.shtml

GardenNet
http://www.gardennet.com/

GardenWeb
http://www.gardenweb.com/

Hortiplex Database
http://hortiplex.gardenweb.com/plants/

Plant Facts
http://plantfacts.ohio-state.edu/

HortNet Plant Image Gallery
http://www.hort.net/gallery/

Tropicos Image Index
http://mobot.mobot.org/W3T/Search/vast.html

Lady Bird Johnson Wildflower Center
http://www.wildflower.org/

Betrock's Hortworld
http://www.hortworld.com/

OTHER USEFUL HORTICULTURAL ORGANIZATIONS

A good source of information about specific plants and many have local chapters where you can meet fellow enthusiasts. Most do not have a settled office. Use their web sites to find the closest chapter.

American Horticultural Society
http://www.ahs.org

All-America Selections
A non-profit organization devoted to promoting the best annuals. They have display gardens across the country.
http://www.all-americaselections.org/

All-America Rose Selections
A similar organization devoted to the rose.
http://www.rose.org/

American Camellia Society
http://www.camellias-acs.com/

American Hemerocallis Society
http://www.daylilies.org/

American Hosta Society
http://www.hosta.org/

American Iris Society
Local shows and meetings.
http://www.irises.org/

American Orchid Society
http://www.orchidweb.org

American Peony Society
http://www.americanpeonysociety.org/

American Rhododendron Society
http://www.rhododendron.org/

American Rose Society
http://www.ars.org/

The International Lilac Society
http://lilacs.freeservers.com/

North American Lily Society
Local shows and meetings.
http://www.lilies.org/

North American Rock Garden Society
A good source of rare plants.
http://www.nargs.org/

BOTANIC GARDENS AND ARBORETA

Most have good, labeled collections of trees, shrubs, perennials, and often annual display beds. Many run classes and demonstrations. They are good places to see mature plants you may be considering for your own garden.

Alabama

Bellingrath Gardens and Home
12401 Bellingrath Gardens Road
Theodore, AL 36582
(251) 973-2217
http://www.bellingrath.org/

Birmingham Botanical Gardens
2612 Lane Park Road
Birmingham, AL 35223
(205) 414-3900
http://www.bbgardens.org/

Donald E. Davis Arboretum
Biological Sciences
101 Life Sciences Building
Auburn University, AL 36849-5407
(205) 844-5770

Dothan Area Botanical Gardens
5130 Headland Avenue
Dothan, AL 36303
(334) 793-3224
http://www.dabg.com/

Huntsville Botanical Garden
4747 Bob Wallace Avenue
Huntsville, AL 35805
(256) 830-4447
http://www.hsvbg.org/

Mobile Botanical Gardens
South Alabama Botanical and Horticultural Society
P.O. Box 8382
Mobile, AL 36608
(334) 342-0555

Arkansas

Botanical Garden of the Ozarks
P.O. Box 3079
Fayetteville, AR 72702-1072
(501) 443-6638
http://www.bgso.org/

Garvan Woodland Gardens
P.O.Box 22240
Hot Springs, AR 71903-2240
(501) 262-9300
http://www.garvangardens.org/

Delaware
University of Delaware Botanic Gardens
Department of Plant & Soil Sciences
University of Delaware
Newark, DE 19717
(302)-831-2531
http://ag.udel.edu/udbg/

Florida
American Orchid Society Botanical Garden
16700 AOS Lane
Delray Beach, FL 33446-4351
(561) 404-2000
http://www.orchidweb.org/

Fairchild Tropical Garden
10901 Old Cutler Road
Coral Gables, FL 33156-4299
(305) 667-1651
http://www.fairchildgarden.org/

Flamingo Gardens
3750 S. Flamingo Road
Fort Lauderdale, FL 33330
(954) 473-2955
http://www.flamingogardens.org/

Florida Botanical Gardens
12175 125th Street North
Largo, FL 33774
(727) 582-2100
http://www.flbg.org/

Harry P. Leu Gardens
1920 North Forest Avenue
Orlando, FL 32803-1537
(407) 246-2620
http://www.leugardens.org/

Key West Botanical Garden
P.O. Box 2436
Key West, FL 33045
(305) 296-1504
http://prometheus.cc.emory.edu/kwbs/

Miami Beach Botanical Garden
2000 Convention Center Drive
Miami Beach, FL 33139
(305) 673-7256
http://www.miamibeachbotanicalgarden.org/

Montgomery Botanical Center
11901 Old Cutler Road
Miami, FL 33156
(305) 667-3800
http://www.montgomerybotanical.org/

Mounts Botanical Garden
559 North Military Trail
West Palm Beach, FL 33415-1395
(561) 233-1751
http://www.mounts.org/

Sunken Gardens
1825 4th Street North
St. Petersburg, FL 33704
(727)551-3100

Georgia
Atlanta Botanical Garden
1345 Piedmont Avenue Northeast
Atlanta, GA 30309-3366
(404) 876-5859
http://www.atlantabotanicalgarden.org/

Callaway Gardens
P. O. Box 2000
Pine Mountain, GA 31822-2000
(800) 225-5292
http://www.callawaygardens.com/

Chatham County Botanical Garden
1388 Eisenhower Drive
Savannah, GA 31406
(912) 356-3591

Columbus Botanical Garden
P.O. Box 1313
Columbus, GA 31902
(706) 565-9624

Ferrell Gardens at Hills and Dales
P. O. Box 790
LaGrange, GA 30241
(706) 882-3242

Georgia Southern Botanical Garden
P. O. Box 8039
Statesboro, GA 30460-8039
(912) 871-1114
http://www2.gasou.edu/garden/

Lockerly Arboretum
1534 Irwinton Road
Milledgeville, GA 31061
(478) 452-2112
http://www.lockerlyarboretum.org/

State Botanical Garden of Georgia
2450 South Milledge Avenue
Athens, GA, 30605
(706) 542-1244
http://www.uga.edu/~botgarden/

Waddell Barnes Botanical Gardens
100 College Station Drive
Macon, GA 31206
(478) 471-2780
http://www.maconstate.edu/

Kentucky
Bernheim Arboretum and Research Forest
P. O. Box 130
Clermont, KY 40110
(502) 955-8512
http://www.bernheim.org/

University of Kentucky Arboretum
500 Alumni Drive
Lexington, KY 40503
(859) 257-6955
http://www.uky.edu/arboretum/

Yew Del Gardens
P. O. Box 1334
Crestwood, KY 40014
(502) 241-4788
http://www.yewdellgardens.org/

Louisiana
Hilltop Arboretum
P. O. Box 82608
Baton Rouge, LA 70884-2608
(225) 767-6916
http://www.lsu.edu/hilltop/

Hodges Gardens
P. O. Box 340
Florien, LA 71429
(318) 586-3523

Jungle Gardens
P. O. Box 126
Avery Island, LA 70513
(318) 365-8173

Longue Vue House and Gardens
7 Bamboo Road
New Orleans, LA 70124-1065
(504) 488-5488
http://www.longuevue.com/

Maryland

Adkins Arboretum
12610 Eveland Road
P. O. Box 100
Ridgely, MD 21660
(443) 634-2847
http://www.adkinsarboretum.org/

Annmarie Garden
175 Main Street
Prince Frederick, MD 20678
(410) 326-4640
http://www.annmariegarden.org/

Brookside Gardens
1800 Glenallan Avenue
Wheaton, MD 20902
(301) 962-1400

Salisbury University Arboretum
1101 Camden Avenue
Salisbury, MD 21801
(410) 543-6200
http://www.salisbury.edu/

Mississippi

Mynelle Gardens
City of Jackson
4736 Clinton Boulevard
Jackson, MS 39209
(601) 960-1894

North Carolina

Botanical Gardens at Asheville
151 W.T. Weaver Boulevard
Asheville, NC 28804
(828) 252-5190
http://www.ashevillebotanicalgardens.org/

Cape Fear Botanical Garden
P. O. Box 53485
Fayetteville, NC 28305
(910) 486-0221
http://www.capefearbg.org/

Daniel Stowe Botanical Garden
6500 South New Hope Road
Belmont, NC 28012
(704) 825-4490
http://www.dsbg.org/

J. C. Raulston Arboretum
North Carolina State University
Raleigh, NC 27695-7609
(919) 515-3132
http://www.ncsu.edu/jcraulstonarboretum/

North Carolina Arboretum
100 Frederick Law Olmsted Way
Asheville, NC 28806-9315
(828) 665-2492

North Carolina Botanical Garden
University of North Carolina at Chapel Hill
CB 3375, Totten Center
Chapel Hill, NC 27599-3375
(919) 962-0522
http://www.unc.edu/depts/ncbg/

UNC Charlotte Botanical Gardens
University of North Carolina, Charlotte
Charlotte, NC, 28223
(704) 687-4055
http://www.gardens.uncc.edu/

South Carolina

Kalmia Gardens of Coker College
1624 West Carolina Avenue
Hartsville, SC 29550-4906
(843) 383-8145
http://www.coker.edu/kalmia/

Mepkin Abbey Botanical Garden
1098 Mepkin Abbey Road
Moncks Corner, SC 29461
(843) 761-8528

South Carolina Botanical Garden
Clemson University
130 Lehotsky Hall
Clemson, SC 29634-0101
(864) 656-3015
http://virtual.clemson.edu/groups/scbg/

Tennessee

Cheekwood Botanical Gardens
1200 Forest Park Drive
Nashville, TN, 37205
(615) 353-2148
http://www.cheekwood.org/

East Tennessee State University Arboretum
Box 70703, Dept. of Biological Sciences,
Johnson City, TN 37614
(423) 439-8635
http://www.etsu.edu/arboretum/

Memphis Botanic Garden
750 Cherry Road
Memphis, TN 38117-4699
(901) 685-1566
http://www.memphisbotanicgarden.com/

University of Tennessee Arboretum
901 South Illinois Avenue
Oak Ridge, TN 37830
865-483-3571
http://www.taes.utk.edu/stations/utforest/

University of Tennessee Botanical Gardens
105 Moody Avenue
Martin, TN, 38238
(901) 587-7650

Virginia

Boxerwood Gardens
963 Ross Road
Lexington, VA 24450
(540) 463-2697
http://www.boxerwood.org/

Edith J. Carrier Arboretum and
Botanical Gardens
James Madison University, MSC 7015
Harrisonburg, VA 22807
(540) 568-3194
http://www.jmu.edu/arboretum/

Meadowlark Botanical Gardens
9750 Meadowlark Gardens Court
Vienna, VA 22182
(703) 255-3631
http://www.nvrpa.org/meadowlark.html

Norfolk Botanical Garden
6700 Azalea Garden Road
Norfolk, VA 23518-5337
(757) 441-5830
http://www.norfolkbotanicalgarden.org/

Orland E. White Arboretum
Blandy Experimental Farm
400 Blandy Farm Lane
Boyce, VA, 22620, USA
http://www.virginia.edu/~blandy/

Virginia Tech Horticulture Garden
Department of Horticulture, Saunders Hall
Blacksburg, VA 24061-0327
(540) 231-5970
http://www.hort.vt.edu/VTHG/

West Virginia

Core Arboretum
P.O. Box 6057
Morgantown, WV 26506-6057
(304) 293-5201
http://www.as.wvu.edu/biology/facility/
arboretum.html

INDEX

Page numbers given in italics refer to catalog pages on which the plants are illustrated. In plant entries, topics that relate to the main entries appear first; subentries for species and cultivars always follow the general subentries.

D

E

F

M

N

O

ACKNOWLEDGMENTS

DK Publishing Inc. and the American Horticultural Society (AHS) would like to express special thanks to Dr. H. Marc Cathey for his vision of a SmartGarden™ and for promoting these important principles to the American gardener; to Katy Moss Warner for her keen eye and superb leadership; to Arabella Dane for the use of her Showtime database and her countless hours of support; to Mary Ann Patterson for believing in and coordinating this project from its conception; to Mark Miller for hours of research; to David Ellis for his editor's savvy.

William E. Barrick is Executive Director of Bellingrath Gardens and Home in Theodore, Alabama. He is also Past President of the American Association of Botanical Gardens and Arboreta, Past Chairman of the AHS, and a recipient of the Arthur Hoyt Scott Medal.

Horticultural editor Trevor Cole, is the author of three books and many articles. He has received awards for his writing from the Garden Writers Association of America, the International Lilac Society, and the North American Rock Garden Society. He is horticultural consultant for DK Publishing in the US and Canada, *Reader's Digest,* and Mitchel Beazley.

Rita Pelczar, author of the core text for each of the SmartGarden™ Regional Guides, has written articles for numerous American gardening magazines and has contributed to several books. As an associate editor for *The American Gardener,* she wrote a four-year series of articles highlighting principles of the SmartGarden™ program.

PHOTO CREDITS

Abbreviations Key
T = Top B= Bottom C=Center L= Left R = Right

Courtesy of the American Camellia Society: 210 BL

***The American Gardener* Magazine:** Mary Yee 18L, 19CR

Antique Rose Emporium: Mike Shoup 214 TC, 215 TL, 215 TR, 215 C, 215 B, 216 BR, 217 TL, 218 TL, 218 BL, 218 BC, 219 B

Ball Horticultural Company: 77 R

Paul Bromfield Aquatics: 272 BL, 296 CR

Courtesy of W. Atlee Burpee www.burpee.com: 265 TL

Courtesy of the gardens at Calloway www.callawayonline.com: 54 TL

Trevor Cole: 43 BR, 76 BR, 86 TC, 87 TR, 88 TL, 94 BL, 96 TC, 98 R, 99 TR, 100 TC, 100 TR, 100 L, 101 TL, 101 BL, 103 TR, 106 BL, 109 CL, 109 BC, 109 BR, 113 CR, 116 CL, 116 TR, 116 B, 117 BL, 117 BR,139 TL, 144 TL, 155 TL, 176 TC, 176 C, 176 TR, 177 TL, 178 TR, 178 BC, 179 TR, 179 C, 179 BC, 183 TR, 190 TL, 191 BL, 194 BL, 194 BC, 194 BR, 196 TC, 208 TL, 208 TR, 208 B, 209 TC, 209 BR, 216 TL, 216 BL, 217 TC, 228 BL, 228 BR, 244 BR, 251 C, 256 BL, 261 C, 268 BC, 270 TL, 271 BC, 271 BR, 282 CR, 298 B, 303 TR, 303 CR, 303 TL, 305 C, 305 BR, 308 BR, 310 TL, 312 TR, 313 TR, 320 BR, 321 BL, 334 BR, 336 TC, 340 TR, 341 TL, 344 BC, 348 TR, 348 BR, 349 TR, 349 BL, 349 BR, 355 TL

Corbis: Peter Reynolds 41, Tom Brakefield 42TL, Richard Hamilton 51 TL, Marc Muench 54 TR, Ric Ergenbright 54 BL

Emerald Coast Growers: 312 BC, 314 TC

FLPA: S. Maslowski 61

Gardenphotos.com: Graham Rice 114 TR, 221 TR; Judy White 89 TR, 113 TL, 118 TL, 120 TR, 123 TL, 129 CL, 144 BL, 182 BC, 185 BL, 142 BR, 143 BR, 145 BR, 155 TC, 167 BC, 174 BL, 180 C, 196 BL, 201 TL, 257 TR, 275 TL, 285 TL, 286 BR, 292 TL, 292 TR, 306 TR, 313 CL, 330 TL, 338 TR, 340 TL, 347 TL, 352 R, 356 BC

Garden & Wildlife Matters Picture Library: Sheila Apps 46 T; M. Collins 60 BR; John Feltwell 168 BL, 172 BL, 343 C, 344 BR; Garden & Wildlife Matters Photo Library 7 BR, 14 TL, 26 BL, 26 TR, 32 BL, 36 BL, 37 BL, 38 BR, 39 TR, 45 TR, 50 BR, 60 BL, 62 BL, 65 TR, 67 R, 68 BR, 72 TR, 72 TL, 73 B, 102 CR, 123 BL, 124 TC, 125 BR, 133 TR, 135 TL, 139 BR, 144 CL, 149 TL, 149 BR, 153 BR, 196 TL, 197 L, 202 BL, 202 R, 233 R,235 TC, 237 BR, , 242 BR, 276 L, 314 TR, 314 CR, 315 BL,332 CR, 333 TL, 339 TL, 342 L; Martin P. Land 323 BL; Colin Milkins 51 BL; John and Irene Palmer 172 TL, 332 TR; Debi Wager 47 BL

Garden Picture Library: Mark Bolton 346 TR; Philippe Bonduel 339 BL; Brian Carter 89 TL, 119 TR, 127 BL, 151 TR, 189 BL, 227 TR, 339 TR, 346 TC; Bob Challinor 333 BR; Densey Clyne 302 TC, 330 BL; Elizabeth Crowe 332 TL, 332 B; Francois de Heel 123 TR; Jack Elliot 297 BL, 302 BR; David England 155 TR; Christopher Fairweather 171 TC, 348 TL; John Feltwell 139 C; Suzie Gibbons 59 BR, John Glover 25 TL, 94 TL, 108 TL, 137 TL, 148 TC, 165 TC, 198 TL, 204 TL, 227 CL, 256 TR, 287 BL, 309 TC, 333 TR; Sunniva Harte 24 B, 164 BL, 306 B, 308 C; Neil Holmes 253 TR, 259 CL; Michael Howes 153 TL; Jacqui Hurst 213 TL; Lynn Keddie 166 TR; Lamontagne 221 TL, 346 TL; Jane Legate 29 TR; Mayer/LeScanff 313 BR; Clive Nichols 211 TC; Marie O'Hara 70 BL; Howard Rice 30 BL, 219 C, 312 BR, 335 R, 349 TL; Ellen Rooney 23 TR; John Ferro Sims 299 BL; JS Sira 165 BL, 206 TL, 280 TC; Janet Sorrell 244 BC, 260 B; Friedrich Strauss 336 BL; Ron Sutherland 7 TL, 75; Juliette Wade 166 B, 294 TL; Mel Watson 334 TR; Jo Whitworth 343 TL

Lewis Advertising of Birmingham Alabama: 76 BL

Monrovia: 7 BL, 21 TR, 35 BL, 84 TR, 88 BL, 96 TL, 96 BL, 96 BR, 97 BR, 99 BC, 103 BR, 105 R, 107 TL, 111 C, 115 TC, 115 TR, 119 CL, 128 BL, 130 TL, 133 C, 134 TL, 134 TC, 134 BL, 135 TR, 136 CR, 136 BR, 137 CL, 140 CR, 142 TL, 143 CL, 143 TC, 144 TR, 148 TL, 148 BL, 148 BR, 151 TL, 152 TR, 152 BL, 152 BR, 153 TC, 153 TR, 154 BL, 155 BL, 157 TL, 158 TL, 159 TC, 159 TR, 159 BC, 159 BR, 160 TC, 160 TR, 161 TR, 161 BR, 162 TL, 163 TR, 163 BR, 164 TL, 164 BR, 167 TL, 167 BL, 168 BR, 169 BC, 170 BL, 172 CR, 173 TL, 174 BC176 BR, 178 TL, 179 TL, 182 TR, 183 TL, 183 BL, 184 TL, 186 TL, 188 TL, 191 TR, 193 TL, 193 TC, 195 TC, 195 TL, 195 BL, 197 TR, 197 CR, 197 C, 199 TL, 199 TR, 200 TL, 200 BL, 201 BL, 201 BR, 203 C, 203 BR, 204 TR, 204 BL, 205 TL, 205 TC, 205 TR, 205 BL, 205 BR, 206 TC 206 TR, 206 BR, 207 TR, 207 CL, 207 BR, 210 TL, 210 TC, 210 TR, 210 BR, 211 TL, 211 TR, 211 BR, 213 TC, 213 TR, 213 CL, 213 B, 226 BL, 227 B, 228 TL, 229 BR, 240 BL, 243 TR, 244 TR, 251 TR, 252 BL, 253 BR, 254 TC, 254 TR, 255 BR, 258 TC, 259 TC, 260 TR, 263 CR, 264 TR, 268 TL, 274 TL, 281 TL, 283 TL, 284 TL, 290 TL, 291 TL, 291 TR, 291 C, 292 BL, 299 TC, 299 CL, 302 BL, 307 TR, 308 BL, 311 TL, 311 BL, 312 TL, 314 TL, 315 TL, 316 TR, 331 BL, 347 TR

Netherland Flower Bulb Center: 325 BL

Steven Nikkila: 146 TL, 157 BL, 199 BL, 288 TR, 146 TR, 170 TL, 187 BR, 190 BL, 138 TC, 138 TR, 138 BC, 138 BR, 139 BL, 147 TL, 164 TR, 172 TR, 196 C, 198 TR, 198 CR, 225 TR, 225 BR, 243 TL, 261 TR, 297 TL, 338 TL

Carole Ottesen: 132 TR

Plant Delights Nursery: Tony Avent 21 BL, 145 TC, 160 BR, 226 BR, 237 C, 238 BR, 241 TL, 242 BL, 245 TL, 245 TR, 255 TL, 255 TR, 261 TL, 264 TL, 265 BR, 269 TL, 269 C, 270 BL, 270 BC, 272 TL, 273 BR, 275 BL, 282 TC, 293 TL, 293 C, 297 BR, 304 BR, 307 TL, 307 BC, 308 TC, 310 TR, 311 TR, 313 TL, 355 BC

Felder Rushing: 79

Courtesy of the Online Virginia Tech Weed ID Guide, http://www.ppws.vt.edu/weedindex.htm: 73 TC

Patricia Welsh: 19 TR, 19 BR, 44 BR, 69 B

The Publisher would also like to thank the following DK Photographers who have contributed to this book:

Peter Anderson, Sue Atkinson, Blooms of Bressingham, Michael Booher, Booker Seeds, Clive Boursnell, Deni Brown, Jonathan Buckley, Andrew Butler, Cambridge Botanic Garden, Beth Chatto, Eric Crichton, Geoff Dann, Andrew de Lory, Christine M. Douglas, Alistair Duncan, Andreas Einsiedel, John Fielding, Neil Fletcher, Roger Foley, John Glover, Derek Hall, David W. Hardon, Jerry Harpur, Stephan Hayward, Dr. Alan Hemsley, C. Andrew Henley, Ian Howes, Jacqui Hurst, Anne Hyde, International Coffee Organization, Dave King, Jane Miller, RHS Garden Wisley, Howard Rice, Tim Ridley, Barbara Rothenberger, Royal Botanical Garden, Edinburgh, Bob Rundle, Les Saucier, Savill Garden, Windsor, Mike Severns, Steven Still, Joseph Strach, Richard Surman, R. Tidman, Juliette Wade, Colin Walton, Matthew Ward, Alex Watson, Steven Wooster, Francesca York